T0305216

Credit Risk Analytics

Wiley & SAS Business Series

The Wiley & SAS Business Series presents books that help senior-level managers with their critical management decisions.

Heuristics in Analytics: A Practical Perspective of What Influences Our Analytical World by Carlos Andre, Reis Pinheiro, and Fiona McNeill

Hotel Pricing in a Social World: Driving Value in the Digital Economy by Kelly McGuire

Implement, Improve and Expand Your Statewide Longitudinal Data System: Creating a Culture of Data in Education by Jamie McQuiggan and Armistead Sapp

Killer Analytics: Top 20 Metrics Missing from Your Balance Sheet by Mark Brown

Mobile Learning: A Handbook for Developers, Educators, and Learners by Scott McQuiggan, Lucy Kosturko, Jamie McQuiggan, and Jennifer Sabourin

The Patient Revolution: How Big Data and Analytics Are Transforming the Healthcare Experience by Krisa Tailor

Predictive Analytics for Human Resources by Jac Fitz-enz and John Mattox II

Predictive Business Analytics: Forward-Looking Capabilities to Improve Business Performance by Lawrence Maisel and Gary Cokins

Statistical Thinking: Improving Business Performance, Second Edition by Roger W. Hoerl and Ronald D. Snee

Too Big to Ignore: The Business Case for Big Data by Phil Simon

Trade-Based Money Laundering: The Next Frontier in International Money Laundering Enforcement by John Cassara

Understanding the Predictive Analytics Lifecycle by Al Cordoba

Unleashing Your Inner Leader: An Executive Coach Tells All by Vickie Bevenour

Using Big Data Analytics: Turning Big Data into Big Money by Jared Dean

The Visual Organization: Data Visualization, Big Data, and the Quest for Better Decisions by Phil Simon

Visual Six Sigma, Second Edition by Ian Cox, Marie Gaudard, Philip Ramsey, Mia Stephens, and Leo Wright

For more information on any of the above titles, please visit www.wiley.com.

Credit Risk Analytics

Measurement Techniques, Applications, and Examples in SAS

Bart Baesens
Daniel Rösch
Harald Scheule

WILEY

Library of Congress Cataloging-in-Publication Data:

Names: Baesens, Bart, author. | Rösch, Daniel, 1968– author. | Scheule, Harald, author.
Title: Credit risk analytics : measurement techniques, applications, and examples in SAS / Bart Baesens, Daniel Rösch, Harald Scheule.
Description: Hoboken, New Jersey : John Wiley & Sons, Inc., [2016] | Series: Wiley & SAS business series | Includes index.
Identifiers: LCCN 2016024803 (print) | LCCN 2016035372 (ebook) | ISBN 9781119143987 (cloth) | ISBN 9781119278344 (pdf) | ISBN 9781119278283 (epub)
Subjects: LCSH: Credit–Management–Data processing. | Risk management–Data processing. | Bank loans–Data processing. | SAS (Computer file).
Classification: LCC HG3751 .B34 2016 (print) | LCC HG3751 (ebook) | DDC 332.10285/555–dc23
LC record available at https://lccn.loc.gov/2016024803

Printed in the United States of America

Cover image: Wiley
Cover design: © styleTTT/iStockphoto

10 9 8 7 6 5 4 3 2 1

Contents

Acknowledgments

It is a great pleasure to acknowledge the contributions and assistance of various colleagues, friends, and fellow credit risk analytics lovers to the writing of this book. This text is the result of many years of research and teaching in credit risk modeling and analytics. We first would like to thank our publisher, John Wiley & Sons, for accepting our book proposal less than one year ago, and Rebecca Croser for providing amazing editing work for our chapters.

We are grateful to the active and lively scientific and industry communities for providing various publications, user forums, blogs, online lectures, and tutorials, which have proven to be very helpful.

We would also like to acknowledge the direct and indirect contributions of the many colleagues, fellow professors, students, researchers, and friends with whom we have collaborated over the years.

Last but not least, we are grateful to our partners, kids, parents, and families for their love, support, and encouragement.

We have tried to make this book as complete, accurate, and enjoyable as possible. Of course, what really matters is what you, the reader, think of it. The authors welcome all feedback and comments, so please feel free to let us know your thoughts!

Bart Baesens
Daniel Rösch
Harald Scheule
September 2016

About the Authors

Bart Baesens

Bart Baesens is a professor at KU Leuven (Belgium) and a lecturer at the University of Southampton (United Kingdom). He has done extensive research on big data and analytics, credit risk modeling, customer relationship management, and fraud detection. His findings have been published in well-known international journals and presented at top-level international conferences. He is the author of various books, including *Analytics in a Big Data World* (see http://goo.gl/kggtJp) and *Fraud Analytics Using Descriptive, Predictive, and Social Network Techniques* (see http://goo.gl/P1cYqe). He also offers e-learning courses on credit risk modeling (see http://goo.gl/cmC2So) and advanced analytics in a big data world (see https://goo.gl/2xA19U). His research is summarized at www.dataminingapps.com. He regularly tutors, advises, and provides consulting support to international firms with respect to their big data, analytics, and credit risk management strategy.

Daniel Rösch

Daniel Rösch is a Professor of Business and Management and holds the chair in Statistics and Risk Management at the University of Regensburg (Germany). Prior to joining the University of Regensburg in 2013, he was Professor of Finance and Director of the Institute of Banking and Finance at Leibniz University of Hannover from 2007 to 2013. He earned a PhD (Dr. rer. pol.) in 1998 for work on empirical asset pricing. From 2006 to 2011 he was visiting researcher at the University of Melbourne. Since 2011 he has been visiting professor at the University of Technology in Sydney. His research interests cover banking, quantitative financial risk management, credit risk, asset pricing, and empirical statistical and econometric methods and models. He has published numerous papers in leading international journals, earned several awards and honors, and regularly presents at major international conferences.

Rösch's service in the profession has included his roles as president of the German Finance Association, co-founder and member of the board of directors of the Hannover Center of Finance, and deputy managing director of the work group Finance and Financial Institutions of the Operations Research Society. He currently serves on the editorial board of the *Journal of Risk Model Validation*. Professor Rösch has worked with financial institutions and supervisory bodies such as Deutsche Bundesbank in joint research projects. Among others, his work has been funded by Deutsche Forschungsgemeinschaft, the Thyssen Krupp Foundation, the Frankfurt Institute for Finance and Regulation, the Melbourne Centre for Financial Studies, and the Australian Centre for International Finance and Regulation. In 2014 the German Handelsblatt ranked him among the top 10 percent of German-speaking researchers in business and management.

Harald Scheule

Harald "Harry" Scheule is Associate Professor of Finance at the University of Technology, Sydney, and a regional director of the Global Association of Risk Professionals. His expertise is in the areas of asset pricing, banking, credit and liquidity risk, home equity release, house prices in distress, insurance, mortgages, prudential regulation, securities evaluation, and structured finance

Scheule's award-winning research has been widely cited and published in leading journals. He currently serves on the editorial board of the *Journal of Risk Model Validation*. He is author or editor of various books.

Harry has worked with prudential regulators of financial institutions and undertaken consulting work for a wide range of financial institutions and service providers in Asia, Australia, Europe, and North America. These institutions have applied his work to improve their risk management practices, comply with regulations, and transfer financial risks.

CHAPTER **1**

Introduction to Credit Risk Analytics

Welcome to the first edition of *Credit Risk Analytics: Measurement Techniques, Applications, and Examples in SAS*.

This comprehensive guide to practical credit risk analytics provides a targeted training guide for risk professionals looking to efficiently build or validate in-house models for credit risk management. Combining theory with practice, this book walks you through the fundamentals of credit risk management and shows you how to implement these concepts using the SAS software, with helpful code provided. Coverage includes data analysis and preprocessing, credit scoring, probability of default (PD) and loss given default (LGD) estimation and forecasting, low default portfolios, Bayesian methods, correlation modeling and estimation, validation, implementation of prudential regulation, stress testing of existing modeling concepts, and more, to provide a one-stop tutorial and reference for credit risk analytics.

This book shows you how to:

- Understand the general concepts of credit risk management
- Validate and stress test existing models
- Access working examples based on both real and simulated data
- Learn useful code for implementing and validating models in SAS
- Exploit the capabilities of this high-powered package to create clean and accurate credit risk management models

WHY THIS BOOK IS TIMELY

Despite the high demand for in-house models, there is little comprehensive training available. Practitioners are often left to comb through piecemeal resources, executive training courses, and consultancies to cobble together the information they need. This

1

book ends the search by providing a thorough, focused resource backed by expert guidance.

Current Challenges in Credit Risk Analytics

Commercial banks are typically large in size, and their fundamental business model continues to rely on financial intermediation by (1) raising finance through deposit taking, wholesale funding (e.g., corporate bonds and covered bonds), and shareholder capital, and (2) lending, which is a major source of credit risk.

Commercial bank loan portfolios consist to a large degree of mortgage loans, commercial real estate loans, and small and medium-sized enterprise (SME) company loans. SME loans are often backed by property collateral provided by the SME owners. The reliance of commercial bank loan portfolios on real estate is fundamental. Note that various types of mortgage loans exist. Examples are prime mortgages, subprime mortgages, reverse mortgages, home equity loans, home equity lines of credit (HELOCs), and interest-only loans, as well as variable, fixed-rate, and hybrid loans, to name a few.

Further loan categories include consumer loans (car loans, credit card loans, and student loans) and corporate loans. Loans to large companies also exist but compete with other funding solutions provided by capital markets (i.e., issuance of shares and corporate bonds).

Other sources of credit risk are fixed income securities (e.g., bank, corporate, and sovereign bonds), securitization investments, contingent credit exposures (loan commitments and guarantees), credit derivatives, and over-the-counter (OTC) derivatives.

Credit risk was at the heart of the global financial crisis (GFC) of 2007 to 2009 and is the focus of this book. Post GFC, prudential regulators have increased risk model requirements, and rigorous standards are being implemented globally, such as:

- Implementation of Basel III: The Basel rules concern capital increases in terms of quantity and quality, leverage ratios, liquidity ratios, and impact analysis. We will discuss the Basel rules in more detail later.

- Stress testing: Regulators require annual stress tests for all risk models.

- Consistency across financial institutions and instruments: Regulators are currently identifying areas where regulation is applied in inconsistent ways.

- Reinvigoration of financial markets (securitization): A number of markets, in particular the private (i.e., non-government-supported) securitization market, have declined in volume.

- Transparency: Central transaction repositories and collection of loan-level data mean more information is collected and made available to credit risk analysts.

- Increase of bank efficiency, competition, deregulation, and simplification: The precise measurement of credit risk is a central constituent in this process.

Risk model methodologies have advanced in many ways over recent years. Much of the original work was based in science where experiments typically abstracted from business cycles and were often applied within laboratory environments to ensure that the experiment was repetitive. Today, credit risk models are empirical and rely on historical data that includes severe economic downturns such as the GFC.

State-of-the-art credit risk models take into account the economic fundamentals of the data generating processes. For example, it is now common to include the life cycle of financial products from origination to payoff, default, or maturity while controlling for the current state of the economy. Another aspect is the efficient analysis of available information, which includes Bayesian modeling, nonparametric modeling, and frailty modeling. Risk models are extended to exploit observable and unobservable information in the most efficient ways.

Despite all these advancements, a word of caution is in order. All empirical risk models remain subject to model risk as we continue to rely on assumptions and the historical data that we observe. For example, it is quite common to obtain R-squared values of 20 percent for linear LGD and exposure at default (EAD) models. As the R-squared measures the fraction of the observed variation that is explained by the model, these numbers suggest that there is a considerable amount of variation that these models do not explain. Providing more precise models will keep us busy for years to come!

A Book on Credit Risk Analytics in SAS

In our academic research, we work with a number of software packages such as C++, EViews, Matlab, Python, SAS, and Stata. Similar to real languages (e.g., Dutch and German), being proficient in one package allows for quick proficiency in other packages.

In our dealings with credit risk analysts, their financial institutions, and their regulators, we realized that in the banking industry SAS is a statistical software package that has come to be the preferred software for credit risk modeling due to its functionality and ability to process large amounts of data. A key consideration in the industry for using SAS is its quality assurance, standardization, and scalability. We will discuss this point in the next chapter in more detail.

Most documentation available for statistical software packages has been developed for scientific use, and examples usually relate to repeatable experiments in medicine, physics, and mathematics. Credit risk analytics is multidisciplinary and incorporates finance, econometrics, and law. Training material in this area is very limited, as much of the empirical work has been triggered by the digitalization and emergence of big data combined with recent econometric advances. Credit risk analytics requires the consideration of interactions with the economy and regulatory settings, which are both dynamic and often nonrepeatable experiments. We learned a great deal from existing literature but continuously reached limits that we had to overcome. We have collected much of this research in this text to show you how to implement this into your own risk architecture.

Structure of the Book

This book contains 15 chapters. We deliberately focused on the challenges in the commercial banking industry and on the analysis of credit risk of loans and loan portfolios.

Following the introduction in the first chapter, the book features three chapters on the preparation stages for credit risk analytics. The second chapter introduces Base SAS, which allows you to explicitly program or code the various data steps and models, and SAS Enterprise Miner, which provides a graphical user interface (GUI) for users that aim to extract information from data without having to rely on programming. The third chapter introduces how basic statistics can be computed in SAS, and provides a rigorous statistical explanation about the necessary assumptions and interpretations. The fourth chapter describes how data can be preprocessed using SAS.

Next, we have included five chapters that look into the most modeled parameter of credit risk analytics: the probability of default (PD). The fifth chapter develops linear scores that approximate the default probabilities without the constraints of probability measures to be bounded between zero and one. Credit scores are often provided by external appraisers to measure default behavior. Examples are real estate indexes, bureau scores, collateral scores, and economic indicators. The sixth chapter discusses methodologies to convert scores and other pieces of information into default probabilities by using discrete-time hazard models. Discrete-time methods are relatively simple, and their estimation is robust and has become a standard in credit risk analytics. The seventh chapter builds further on this and estimates default probabilities using continuous-time hazard models. These models explicitly model the life cycle of a borrower and do not assume that observations for a given borrower are independent over time, which discrete-time hazard models often do. The eighth chapter discusses the estimation of default probabilities for low default portfolios, which is a particular concern for small portfolios in relation to large and/or specialized loans.

In the next section, we consider other important credit risk measures. In Chapter 9, we estimate default and asset correlations. We compute credit portfolio default rates and credit portfolio loss distributions using analytical and Monte Carlo simulation–based approaches, and show the reader how correlations can be estimated using internal data. The tenth chapter presents marginal loss given default (LGD) models and LGD models that condition on the selecting default event. The eleventh chapter discusses exposure at default (EAD) models, which are similar in structure to LGD models.

In the last part of the book, we discuss capstone modeling strategies that relate to the various models built in prior sections. Chapter 12 discusses Bayesian models, which allow the analyst to base the model estimation on the data set and prior information. The priors may stem from experts or information collected outside the analyzed system. We show how to implement Bayesian methods and where they might be most useful. Chapter 13 reviews concepts of model validation along with regulatory requirements, and Chapter 14 discusses stress testing of credit risk models by building credit risk measures conditional on stress tests of the macroeconomy, idiosyncratic information, or parameter uncertainty. Chapter 15 concludes the book.

The companion website (www.creditriskanalytics.net) offers examples of both real and simulated credit portfolio data to help you more easily implement the concepts discussed.

THE CURRENT REGULATORY REGIME: BASEL REGULATIONS

We take a closer look at the Basel I, Basel II, and Basel III Capital Accords. These are regulatory guidelines that were introduced in order for financial institutions to appropriately determine their provisions and capital buffers to protect against various risk exposures. One important type of risk is credit risk, and in this section we discuss the impact of these accords on the development of PD, LGD, and EAD credit risk models. The Basel regulations underly many aspects of credit risk analytics, and we will come back to the various issues in later chapters.

Regulatory versus Economic Capital

Banks receive cash inflow from various sources. The first important sources are bank deposits like savings accounts, term accounts, and so on. In return, the depositors receive a fixed or variable interest payment. Another source is the shareholders or investors who buy shares, which gives them an ownership in the bank. If the firm makes a profit, then a percentage can be paid to the shareholders as dividends. Both savings money and shareholder capital are essential elements of a bank's funding. On the asset side, a bank will use the money obtained to make various investments. A first investment, and part of a key banking activity, is lending. Banks will lend money to obligors so that they can finance the purchase of a house or a car, study, or go traveling. Other investments could be buying various market securities such as bonds or stocks.

Note that these investments always have a risk associated with them. Obligors could default and not pay back the loan, and markets could collapse and decrease the value of securities. Given the societal impact of banks in any economic system, they need to be well protected against the risks they are exposed to. Bank insolvency or failure should be avoided at all times, and the risks that banks take on their asset side should be compensated by appropriate liabilities to safeguard their depositors. These people should be guaranteed to always get their savings money back whenever they want it. Hence, a bank should have enough shareholder capital as a buffer against losses. In fact, we could include retained earnings and reserves and look at equity or capital instead. In other words, a well-capitalized bank has a sufficient amount of equity to protect itself against its various risks. Thus, there should be a direct relationship between risk and equity.

Usually, this relationship is quantified in two steps. First, the amount of risk on the asset side is quantified by a specific risk number. This number is then plugged into a formula that precisely calculates the corresponding equity and thus capital required. There are two views on defining both this risk number and the formula to be used.

The first view is a regulatory view whereby regulations such as Basel I, Basel II, and Basel III have been introduced to precisely define how to calculate the risk number and what formula to use. Regulatory capital is then the amount of capital a bank should have according to a regulation. However, if there were no regulations, banks would still be cognizant of the fact that they require equity capital for protection. In this case, they would use their own risk modeling methodologies to calculate a risk number and use their own formulas to calculate the buffer capital. This leads us to the concept of economic capital, which is the amount of capital a bank has based on its internal modeling strategy and policy. The actual capital is then the amount of capital a bank actually holds and is the higher of the economic capital and the regulatory capital. For example, Bank of America reports at the end of 2015 a ratio of total capital to risk-weighted assets using advanced approaches of 13.2 percent and a current regulatory minimum capital of 8 percent (this number will increase as Basel III is fully phased in). Therefore, the capital buffer is currently 5.2 percent.

Note that various types of capital exist, depending upon their loss-absorbing capacity. Tier 1 capital typically consists of common stock, preferred stock, and retained earnings. Tier 2 capital is of somewhat less quality and is made up of subordinated loans, revaluation reserves, undisclosed reserves, and general provisions. The Basel II Capital Accord also included Tier 3 capital, which consists of short-term subordinated debt, but, as we will discuss later, this has been abandoned in the more recent Basel III Capital Accord.

Basel I

The Basel Accords have been put forward by the Basel Committee on Banking Supervision. This committee was founded in 1974 by the G10 central banks. Nowadays, it counts 27 members. They meet regularly at the Bank for International Settlements (BIS) in Basel, Switzerland.

The first accord introduced was the Basel I Capital Accord, in 1988. As already mentioned, the aim was to set up regulatory minimum capital requirements in order to ensure that banks are able, at all times, to return depositors' funds. The Basel I Accord predominantly focused on credit risk and introduced the idea of the capital or Cooke ratio, which is the ratio of the available buffer capital and the risk-weighted assets. It put a lower limit on this ratio of 8 percent; in other words, the capital should be greater than 8 percent of the risk-weighted assets. We have been asked where this number comes from and speculate that it was an industry average at the time of implementation of the first Basel Accord. Changing the capital requirement by only a few percentage points is a challenging undertaking for large banks and takes many years. The capital could consist of both Tier 1 and Tier 2 capital, as discussed earlier.

In terms of credit risk, the Basel I Capital Accord introduced fixed risk weights dependent on the exposure class. For cash exposures, the risk weight was 0 percent, for mortgages 50 percent, and for other commercial exposures 100 percent. As an example, consider a mortgage of $100. Applying the risk weight of 50 percent, the risk-weighted assets (RWA) then become $50. This is the risk number we referred to earlier. We will now transform this into required capital using the formula that regulatory minimum capital is 8 percent of the risk-weighted assets. This gives us a required capital amount of $4. So, to summarize, our $100 mortgage should be financed by least $4 of equity to cover potential credit losses.

Although it was definitely a good step toward better risk management, the Basel I Accord faced some important drawbacks. First, the solvency of the debtor was not properly taken into account since the risk weights depended only on the exposure class and not on the obligor or product characteristics. There was insufficient recognition of collateral guarantees to mitigate credit risk. It also offered various opportunities for regulatory arbitrage by making optimal use of loopholes in the regulation to minimize capital. Finally, it considered only credit risk, not operational or market risk.

Basel II

To address the shortcomings of the Basel I Capital Accord, the Basel II Capital Accord was introduced. It consists of three key pillars: Pillar 1 covers the minimal capital requirement, Pillar 2 the supervisory review process, and Pillar 3 market discipline and disclosure. (See Exhibit 1.1.)

Under Pillar 1, three different types of risk are included. Credit risk is the risk faced when lending money to obligors. Operational risk is defined as the risk of direct or indirect loss resulting from inadequate or failed internal processes, people, and systems, or from external events. Popular examples here are fraud, damage to physical assets, and system failures. Market risk is the risk due to adverse market movements faced by a bank's market position via cash or derivative products. Popular examples here are equity risk, currency risk, commodity risk, and interest rate risk. In this

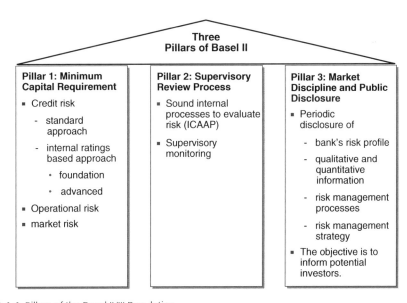

Exhibit 1.1 Pillars of the Basel II/III Regulation

book, we will closely look at credit risk. The Basel II Capital Accord foresees three ways to model credit risk: the standard approach, the foundation internal ratings based approach, and the advanced internal ratings based approach. All boil down to building quantitative models for measuring credit risk.

All quantitative models built under Pillar 1 need to be reviewed by overseeing supervisors. This is discussed in Pillar 2. Key activities to be undertaken are the introduction of sound processes to evaluate risk, such as the internal capital adequacy assessment process (ICAAP) and supervisory monitoring.

Finally, once all quantitative risk models have been approved, they can be disclosed to the market. This is covered by Pillar 3. Here, a bank will periodically disclose its risk profile, and provide qualitative and quantitative information about its risk management processes and strategies to the market. The objective is to inform the investors and convince them that the bank has a sound and solid risk management strategy, which it hopes will result in a favorable rating, in order for the bank to attract funds at lower rates.

Basel III

The Basel III Capital Accord was introduced as a direct result of the GFC. It builds upon the Basel II Accord, but aims to further strengthen global capital standards. Its key attention point is a closer focus on tangible equity capital since this is the component with the greatest loss-absorbing capacity. It reduces the reliance on models developed internally by the bank and ratings obtained from external rating agencies. It also places a greater emphasis on stress testing. (See Exhibit 1.2.)

For important banks, it stresses the need to have a loss-absorbing capacity beyond common standards. It puts a greater focus on Tier 1 capital consisting of shares and retained earnings by abolishing the Tier 3 capital introduced in Basel II, as it was deemed of insufficient quality to absorb losses. A key novelty is that it introduces a risk-insensitive leverage ratio as a backstop to address model risk. It also includes some facilities to deal with procyclicality, whereby due to a too cyclical nature of capital, economic downturns are further amplified. The Basel III Accord also introduces

	Basel II	Basel III
Common Tier 1 capital ratio (common equity = shareholders' equity + retained earnings)	2% * RWA	4.5% * RWA
Tier 1 capital ratio	4% * RWA	6% * RWA
Tier 2 capital ratio	4% * RWA	2% * RWA
Capital conservation buffer (common equity)	—	2.5% * RWA
Countercyclical buffer	—	0%–2.5% * RWA

Note: RWA = risk-weighted assets.

Exhibit 1.2 Basel III: Capital Requirements

a liquidity coverage and net stable funding ratio to satisfy liquidity requirements. We will not discuss those further, as our focus is largely on credit risk. The new Basel III standards took effect on January 1, 2013, and for the most part will become fully effective by January 2019. Compared to the Basel II guidelines, the Basel III Accord has no major impact on the credit risk models themselves. It does, however, introduce additional capital buffers, as we will discuss in what follows.

The Tier 1 capital ratio was 4 percent of the risk-weighted assets (RWA) in the Basel II Capital Accord. It was increased to 6 percent in Basel III. The common Tier 1 capital ratio whereby common Tier 1 capital consists of common equity, which is common stock and retained earnings, but no preferred stock, was 2 percent of the risk-weighted assets in Basel II and is 4.5 percent of the risk-weighted assets in Basel III. A new capital conservation buffer is introduced that is set to 2.5 percent of the risk-weighted assets to be covered by common equity. Also, a countercyclical capital buffer is added, ranging between 0 and 2.5 percent of the risk-weighted assets.

As already mentioned, a non-risk-based leverage ratio is introduced that should be at least 3 percent of the assets and covered by Tier 1 capital. Very important to note here is that we look at the assets and not risk-weighted assets, as with the previous ratios. The assets also include off-balance-sheet exposures and derivatives. The idea here is to add this ratio as a supplementary safety measure on top of the risk-based ratios.

Basel III includes (relative to Basel II) the capital conservation buffer, the countercyclical capital buffer, and, if relevant, an additional capital ratio for systemically important banks.

Basel Approaches to Credit Risk Modeling

In what follows, we will discuss how credit risk can be modeled according to the Basel II and III Capital Accords. Basically, there are three approaches available, as already discussed: the standardized approach, the foundation internal ratings based approach, and the advanced internal ratings based approach. The approaches differ in terms of their sophistication and level of flexibility related to using internally estimated risk numbers.

Standardized Approach

Let us first discuss the standardized approach. For nonretail exposures, this approach relies on external credit assessment institutions (ECAIs) to provide credit ratings. Popular examples of ECAIs are Moody's, Standard & Poor's, and Fitch. Given the crucial impact of these ECAIs, the Basel Accords have introduced eligibility criteria such as objectivity, independence, transparency, and disclosure that need to be fulfilled in order to be officially recognized as an ECAI. The ratings provided by the ECAIs will then be mapped to risk weights provided in the accords. Risk weights are provided for sovereigns, banks, corporates, and other exposures. The capital itself is then calculated as 8 percent of the risk-weighted assets.

For retail, the risk weight is 75 percent for nonmortgage exposures and 35 percent for mortgage exposures. Remember, in Basel I the risk weight for mortgages was higher at 50 percent. For corporates, the risk weights vary from 20 percent for AAA-rated exposures to 150 percent for exposures rated B or lower. For sovereigns, the risk weights vary from 0 percent for AAA-rated countries to 150 percent for countries rated B or lower. For loans already in default, the risk weight can go up to 150 percent. Note that the European Banking Authority (EBA) has introduced mapping schemes to transform an ECAI's credit ratings to credit quality steps, which can then be further mapped to risk weights using the European capital directive. Let us illustrate this with an example.

Assume we have a corporate exposure of $1 million. It is unsecured with a maturity of five years, and Standard & Poor's assigns an AA rating to it. Using the European directive, an AA rating corresponds to a credit quality step of 1, which, according to Article 122, will map to a risk weight of 20 percent. The risk-weighted assets thus become 20 percent out of $1 million, or $0.2 million. The regulatory minimum capital can then be calculated as 8 percent thereof or thus $0.016 million. The standardized approach also provides facilities for credit risk mitigation in case of collateralized loans.

Although the standardized approach looks simple and appealing at first sight, it suffers from inconsistencies between ratings of different ECAIs with the accompanying danger of banks' cherry-picking the ECAIs. It also has problems in terms of coverage of various types of exposures. For example, retail exposures are discriminated only in terms of mortgage or nonmortgage. A more detailed categorization is highly desirable. Ideally, every obligor should have his or her own risk profile, whereby not only default risk is considered, but also loss and exposure risk as measured by LGD and EAD.

Internal Ratings Based (IRB) Approach

The internal ratings based (IRB) approach is a more sophisticated approach for quantifying credit risk. It relies on four key risk parameters, which we will introduce first. The PD is the probability of default of an obligor over a one-year period. It is expressed as a decimal and when converted to percentage ranges between 0 and 100 percent. The EAD is the exposure at default and is the amount outstanding. It is measured in currency terms. The LGD is the loss given default or the ratio of the loss on an exposure due to default of an obligor on the amount outstanding (EAD). It is also expressed as a decimal and ranges between 0 and 100 percent.

The PD, LGD, and EAD parameters can now be used to calculate the expected loss (EL) which becomes PD * LGD * EAD. Suppose the EAD is $10,000 and the LGD equals 20 percent. This means that upon default 20 percent out of $10,000 will be lost (= $2,000). The probability of losing this amount equals the probability of default let's say 1 percent. The expected loss then becomes $20. These risk parameters are used in the IRB approach to quantify credit risk.

Basically, there are two subapproaches of the IRB approach, the foundation IRB approach and the advanced IRB approach. In the foundation IRB approach, the PD is estimated internally by the bank, while the LGD and EAD are either prescribed in

	PD	LGD	EAD	Asset Correlations
Foundation approach	Internal estimate	Regulator's estimate	Regulator's estimate	Regulator's estimate
Advanced approach	Internal estimate	Internal estimate	Internal estimate	Regulator's estimate

Exhibit 1.3 Basel Foundation and Advanced IRB Approach

the Basel Accord or provided by the local regulator. In the advanced IRB approach, all three risk parameters, PD, LGD, and EAD, can be estimated internally by the bank itself. Furthermore, regulators provide asset correlations, which measure the degree to which the asset values underlying the credit exposures are correlated. In this setting, the asset correlations are either constant or a monotone function that is declining with increasing PDs. (See Exhibit 1.3.)

A distinction is made between the following types of exposure classes: corporate, retail, central governments (sovereigns) and central banks, institutions, equity exposures, securitization positions, and other non-credit-obligation assets. The foundation IRB approach is typically not permitted for retail exposures. Hence, for retail exposures, you can choose either the standard or the advanced IRB approach. Once the PD, LGD, and EAD are known, risk weight functions provided in the Basel Accord or directive can be used to calculate the regulatory capital.

We will describe this process in more detail in Chapter 14 on stress testing, but, in essence, capital is set to equal unexpected losses (ULs). Unexpected losses are the difference between the credit value at risk (VaR) and the expected losses (ELs). The reason for this is embedded in the accounting regime for credit risk. Expected losses are provisioned for, and provisions are losses in the profit and loss (P&L) statement and hence already netted with the equity account. As a result, the capital of a bank should cover losses that exceed provisions, and these losses are called unexpected losses. The credit value at risk (VaR) is computed in a similar way as expected losses, with the distinction that PD, LGD, and EAD are stressed to reflect an economic downturn:

■ PD is stressed via the concept of a worst-case default rate given a virtual macroeconomic shock based on a confidence level of 99.9 percent and a sensitivity to the macroeconomy that is based on the asset correlation.

■ LGD is based on an economic downturn.

■ EAD is based on an economic downturn.

We will provide more specific details of the Basel regulations in the next chapters. These chapters include modeling default probabilities, loss given default, exposure at default, and validation as well as stress testing.

INTRODUCTION TO OUR DATA SETS

We have made four data sets available for student use via the book's companion website (www.creditriskanalytics.net). Exhibit 1.4 shows the four data sets and their applications.

Data Set HMEQ

The data set HMEQ reports characteristics and delinquency information for 5,960 home equity loans. A home equity loan is a loan where the obligor uses the equity of his or her home as the underlying collateral. The data set has the following characteristics:

- BAD: 1 = applicant defaulted on loan or seriously delinquent; 0 = applicant paid loan
- LOAN: Amount of the loan request
- MORTDUE: Amount due on existing mortgage
- VALUE: Value of current property
- REASON: DebtCon = debt consolidation; HomeImp = home improvement
- JOB: Occupational categories
- YOJ: Years at present job
- DEROG: Number of major derogatory reports

Data Set	Risk Segment	Chapter
HMEQ	Retail	5 Credit scoring
Mortgage	Retail	4 Exploratory data analysis
		6 Probabilities of default (PD): discrete time hazard models
		7 Probabilities of default: continuous time hazard models and practical implications
		8 Low default portfolios
		9 Default correlations and credit portfolio risk
		11 Exposure at default (EAD) and adverse selection
		12 Bayesian methods
		13 Model validation
		14 Stress testing
LGD	Corporate	10 Loss given default (LGD) and recovery rates
Ratings	Corporate	5 Credit scoring

Exhibit 1.4 Data Set Usage in This Book

- DELINQ: Number of delinquent credit lines
- CLAGE: Age of oldest credit line in months
- NINQ: Number of recent credit inquiries
- CLNO: Number of credit lines
- DEBTINC: Debt-to-income ratio

Data Set Mortgage

The data set mortgage is in panel form and reports origination and performance observations for 50,000 residential U.S. mortgage borrowers over 60 periods. The periods have been deidentified. As in the real world, loans may originate before the start of the observation period (this is an issue where loans are transferred between banks and investors as in securitization). The loan observations may thus be censored as the loans mature or borrowers refinance. The data set is a randomized selection of mortgage-loan-level data collected from the portfolios underlying U.S. residential mortgage-backed securities (RMBS) securitization portfolios and provided by International Financial Research (www.internationalfinancialresearch.org). Key variables include:

- id: Borrower ID
- time: Time stamp of observation
- orig_time: Time stamp for origination
- first_time: Time stamp for first observation
- mat_time: Time stamp for maturity
- balance_time: Outstanding balance at observation time
- LTV_time: Loan-to-value ratio at observation time, in %
- interest_rate_time: Interest rate at observation time, in %
- hpi_time: House price index at observation time, base year = 100
- gdp_time: Gross domestic product (GDP) growth at observation time, in %
- uer_time: Unemployment rate at observation time, in %
- REtype_CO_orig_time: Real estate type condominium = 1, otherwise = 0
- REtype_PU_orig_time: Real estate type planned urban development = 1, otherwise = 0
- REtype_SF_orig_time: Single-family home = 1, otherwise = 0
- investor_orig_time: Investor borrower = 1, otherwise = 0
- balance_orig_time: Outstanding balance at origination time
- FICO_orig_time: FICO score at origination time, in %
- LTV_orig_time: Loan-to-value ratio at origination time, in %
- Interest_Rate_orig_time: Interest rate at origination time, in %

- hpi_orig_time: House price index at origination time, base year = 100
- default_time: Default observation at observation time
- payoff_time: Payoff observation at observation time
- status_time: Default (1), payoff (2), and nondefault/nonpayoff (0) observation at observation time

Data Set LGD

The data set has been kindly provided by a European bank and has been slightly modified and anonymized. It includes 2,545 observations on loans and LGDs. Key variables are:

- LTV: Loan-to-value ratio, in %
- Recovery_rate: Recovery rate, in %
- lgd_time: Loss rate given default (LGD), in %
- y_logistic: Logistic transformation of the LGD
- lnrr: Natural logarithm of the recovery rate
- Y_probit: Probit transformation of the LGD
- purpose1: Indicator variable for the purpose of the loan; 1 = renting purpose, 0 = other
- event: Indicator variable for a default or cure event; 1 = event, 0 = no event

Data Set Ratings

The ratings data set is an anonymized data set with corporate ratings where the ratings have been numerically encoded (1 = AAA, and so on). It has the following variables:

- COMMEQTA: Common equity to total assets
- LLPLOANS: Loan loss provision to total loans
- COSTTOINCOME: Operating costs to operating income
- ROE: Return on equity
- LIQASSTA: Liquid assets to total assets
- SIZE: Natural logarithm of total assets

HOUSEKEEPING

We are planning to regularly update this book in the future and need your help. Please forward any feedback, errata, extensions, or topics that you would be interested in seeing covered in the next edition to us:

- Bart Baesens: bart.baesens@kuleuven.be
- Daniel Rösch: daniel.roesch@ur.de
- Harald Scheule: harald@scheule.com

Also check the book website for further details: www.creditriskanalytics.net.

Furthermore, we have generated a set of teaching slides that we are happy to share with university lecturers. Check the website or e-mail us if you are interested in obtaining the material.

We hope you have as much fun reading this book as we had writing it. Without further ado, let's get started and explore credit risk analytics.

Bart Baesens, Daniel Rösch, and Harry Scheule
September 2016

CHAPTER 2

Introduction to SAS Software

In this chapter, we will briefly overview the various types of SAS software that can be useful for credit risk modeling. It is not our aim to provide an exhaustive discussion on all functionality and options available, but rather to give a quick introduction on how to get started with each of the solutions. For more detailed information, we refer to the SAS website (http://www.sas.com), SAS training and books (http://support.sas.com/learn/), and SAS support (http://support.sas.com/).

SAS VERSUS OPEN SOURCE SOFTWARE

The popularity of open source analytical software such as R and Python has sparked the debate about the added value of SAS, which is a commercial tool. In fact, both commercial software as well as open source software have their merits, which should be thoroughly evaluated before any analytical software decision is made.

First of all, the key advantage of open source software is that it is obviously available for free, which significantly lowers the entry barrier to use it. However, this clearly poses a danger as well, since anyone can contribute to it without any quality assurance or extensive prior testing. In heavily regulated environments such as credit risk (e.g., Basel Accord), insurance (e.g., Solvency Accord, XXX and AXXX reserving) and pharmaceutics (e.g., Food and Drug Administration regulation), the analytical models are subject to external supervisory review because of their strategic impact to society, which is now bigger than ever before. Hence, in these settings many firms prefer to rely on mature commercial solutions that have been thoroughly engineered, extensively tested, validated, and documented. Many of these solutions also include automatic reporting facilities to generate compliance reports in each of the settings mentioned. Open source software solutions do not come with any kind of quality control or warranty, which increases the risk when using them in a regulated environment.

Another key advantage of commercial software like SAS is that the software offered is no longer centered on dedicated analytical workbenches such as data preprocessing and data mining, but on well-engineered business-focused solutions that automate the end-to-end activities. As an example, consider credit risk modeling, which starts from framing the business problem and continues to data preprocessing, analytical model development, backtesting and benchmarking, stress testing, and regulatory capital calculation. To automate this entire chain of activities using open source software would require various scripts, likely originating from heterogeneous sources, to be matched and connected together, resulting in a possible melting pot of software in which the overall functionality could become unstable and/or unclear.

Contrary to open source software, commercial software vendors also offer extensive help facilities such as FAQs, technical support hot lines, newsletters, and professional training courses. Another key advantage of commercial software vendors is business continuity—more specifically, the availability of centralized research and development (R&D) teams (as opposed to worldwide, loosely connected open source developers) who follow up on new analytical and regulatory developments. This provides a better guarantee that new software upgrades will provide the facilities required. In an open source environment, you would need to rely on the community to voluntarily contribute, which provides less of a guarantee.

A general disadvantage of commercial software is that it usually comes in prepackaged, black box routines (e.g., the PROCs in Base SAS), which, although extensively tested and documented, cannot be inspected by the more sophisticated data scientist. This is in contrast to open source solutions, which provide full access to the source code of each of the scripts contributed. To address this issue, SAS offers multiple programming environments within statistical procedures and the DATA step environment so that users can self-program applications, including estimation, simulation, and forecasting procedures.

Given this discussion, it is clear that both commercial software and open source software have their strengths and weaknesses. It is likely that they will continue to coexist, and interfaces should be provided for them to collaborate, as is the case for both SAS and R/Python.

BASE SAS

Base SAS is a fourth-generation programming language (4 GL) for data access, transformation, and reporting and is the foundation for all other SAS software. It includes the following features:

- A programming language
- A web-based programming interface
- A centralized metadata repository to store data definitions
- A macro facility
- Integration with big data solutions such as Hadoop and MapReduce

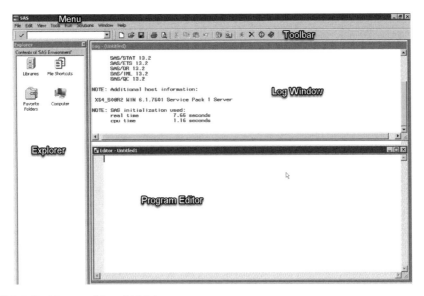

Exhibit 2.1 Start Screen of Base SAS 9.4

You can start SAS 9.4 by clicking Start (in Windows) ⇨ All Programs ⇨ SAS ⇨ SAS 9.4. You then encounter the windows shown in Exhibit 2.1.

The interface is divided into multiple components:

- **Menu:** Here you find all the functionality to edit, view, and run your SAS programs, together with some extra solutions and help functionality.
- **Toolbar:** This provides a selection of shortcut buttons to frequently used menu items.
- **Explorer:** Here you can explore the libraries that you have defined (or that have already been predefined) and browse folders on your computer.
- **Program Editor:** This is where you will write your SAS programs.
- **Log window:** Here you will see errors or warnings appear as you execute your SAS programs.
- **Result window** (hidden behind the Explorer): Summary with links to generated outputs.
- **Output** (hidden behind the Editor): Outputs from procedures.

Let's now enter the following program code in the Program Editor:

```
LIBNAME DATA "C:\Users";
RUN;
```

This first statement will create a SAS library DATA, which is a shortcut notation to a physical directory on disk (in our case C:\Users). Throughout the book, we capitalize

SAS commands and present user input in lowercase letters. Generally speaking, SAS commands end with a semicolon (;) and code sections with either the RUN; command for Base SAS, the QUIT command for PROC IML (see later discussion), or the %MEND command for macros (see later discussion).

SAS allows performing data manipulation using data steps:

```
DATA example;
SET data.mortgage;

/*Example for deletion of observations*/
IF FICO_orig_time< 500 THEN DELETE;

/*Example for generation of new variables*/
IF FICO_orig_time> 500 THEN FICO_cat=1;
IF FICO_orig_time> 700 THEN FICO_cat=2;

/*Example for data filtering*/
WHERE default_time=1;

/*Example for dropping of variables*/
DROP status_time;
RUN;
```

You can run it by clicking the running man icon on the toolbar or selecting Run, Submit from the menu above. Data steps start with the DATA command for the name of the new data set, followed by the SET command for the name of the original data set. The preceding code changes the original data set data.mortgage and generates a new data set mortgage by deleting observations, generating new variables, filtering the data, and dropping a variable.

Furthermore, SAS offers a set of built-in procedures (PROC ...). The following statement computes the mean, standard deviation, minimum, and maximum for the variables default_time, FICO_orig_time, ltv_orig_time, and gdp_time of the mortgage data set:

```
PROC MEANS DATA=data.mortgage;
VAR default_time FICO_orig_time ltv_orig_time gdp_time;
RUN;
```

The outcome will be as shown in Exhibit 2.2.

SAS/STAT

SAS offers a range of statistical procedures. These procedures generally estimate the parameters of parametric and semiparametric models. A first example is the linear regression model offered by PROC REG:

The MEANS Procedure

Variable	N	Mean	Std Dev	Minimum	Maximum
default_time	622489	0.0243506	0.1541354	0	1.0000000
FICO_orig_time	622489	673.6169217	71.7245579	400.0000000	840.0000000
LTV_orig_time	622489	78.9754596	10.1270521	50.1000000	218.5000000
gdp_time	622489	1.3810318	1.9646446	−4.1467109	5.1324642

Exhibit 2.2 Output PROC MEAN

The REG Procedure

Model: MODEL1

Dependent Variable: default_time

Parameter Estimates					
Variable	DF	Parameter Estimate	Standard Error	t Value	Pr > |t|
Intercept	1	0.07957	0.00259	30.71	<.0001
FICO_orig_time	1	−0.00011544	0.00000275	−42.02	<.0001
LTV_orig_time	1	0.00038077	0.00001944	19.59	<.0001
gdp_time	1	−0.00545	0.00009914	−55.02	<.0001

Exhibit 2.3 Output PROC REG

```
PROC REG DATA=data.mortgage;
MODEL default_time = FICO_orig_time ltv_orig_time gdp_time;
RUN;
```

The resulting parameter estimates in short form are shown in Exhibit 2.3.

MACROS IN BASE SAS

In SAS, you can define functions within the Macro language. Here you can see a macro that defines input arguments, which are passed to a regression model. Macros commence with the %MACRO command and conclude with the %MEND. The merit of the following macro is that you don't have to replicate PROC REG, as different covariate combinations are explored and you only need to change the variables included:

```
%MACRO example(datain, lhs, rhs);
PROC REG DATA=&datain;
MODEL &lhs = &rhs;
RUN;
%MEND example;
```

The REG Procedure

Model: MODEL1

Dependent Variable: default_time

Parameter Estimates					
Variable	DF	Parameter Estimate	Standard Error	t Value	Pr > |t|
Intercept	1	0.10289	0.00184	55.85	<.0001
FICO_orig_time	1	−0.00011660	0.00000272	−42.87	<.0001

Exhibit 2.4 Examples Macro 1

```
%example(datain=data.mortgage, lhs=default_time,
rhs=FICO_orig_time );
%example(datain=data.mortgage, lhs=default_time,
rhs=FICO_orig_time ltv_orig_time);
%example(datain=data.mortgage, lhs=default_time,
rhs=FICO_orig_time ltv_orig_time gdp_time);
```

The resulting output is shown in Exhibits 2.4, 2.5, and 2.6.

The REG Procedure

Model: MODEL1

Dependent Variable: default_time

Parameter Estimates					
Variable	DF	Parameter Estimate	Standard Error	t Value	Pr > |t|
Intercept	1	0.06835	0.00259	26.39	<.0001
FICO_orig_time	1	−0.00010867	0.00000275	−39.50	<.0001
LTV_orig__time	1	0.00036981	0.00001948	18.98	<.0001

Exhibit 2.5 Examples Macro 2

The REG Procedure

Model: MODEL1

Dependent Variable: default_time

Parameter Estimates					
Variable	DF	Parameter Estimate	Standard Error	t Value	Pr > |t|
Intercept	1	0.07957	0.00259	30.71	<.0001
FICO_orig_time	1	−0.00011544	0.00000275	−42.02	<.0001
LTV_orig_time	1	0.00038077	0.00001944	19.59	<.0001
gdp_time	1	−0.00545	0.00009914	−55.02	<.0001

Exhibit 2.6 Examples Macro 3

SAS OUTPUT DELIVERY SYSTEM (ODS)

SAS offers an output delivery system (ODS) that transforms outputs into SAS data sets that can then be transformed, fed into second-stage processes, or exported to a comma-separated values (CSV) file (and Excel). Here you can see an example for the preceding regression model where we generate a SAS data set named parameters that includes the parameter estimates of the model. PROC EXPORT exports these parameter estimates into a CSV file in the specified location path 'C:\Users\export.csv'.

```
ODS LISTING CLOSE;
ODS OUTPUT PARAMETERESTIMATES=parameters;
PROC REG DATA=DATA.mortgage;
MODEL default_time = FICO_orig_time ltv_orig_time gdp_time;
RUN;
ODS OUTPUT CLOSE;
ODS LISTING;


PROC EXPORT DATA=parameters REPLACE DBMS=CSV OUTFILE="C:\Users\export.csv";
RUN;
```

SAS/IML

SAS offers its own programming language, IML (Interactive Matrix Language), which is particularly powerful and flexible for matrix operations. The fundamental object of the language is a data matrix. You can use SAS/IML software interactively (at the statement level) to see results immediately, or you can submit blocks of statements or an entire program. It is also possible to encapsulate a series of statements by defining a module that can then be called later to execute all of its statements. Built-in operators and call routines are available to perform complex tasks in numerical linear algebra such as matrix inversion or the computation of eigenvalues. You can define your own functions and subroutines by using SAS/IML modules and perform operations on a single value, or take advantage of matrix operators to perform operations on an entire data matrix.

The SAS/IML language contains statements that enable data management. You can read, create, and update SAS data sets in SAS/IML software without using the DATA step.

You can program with the many features for arithmetic and character expressions in SAS/IML software. SAS/IML allows you to access a wide variety of built-in functions and subroutines designed to make your programming fast, easy, and efficient. Because SAS/IML software is part of the SAS system, you can access SAS data sets or external files with an extensive set of data processing commands for data input and output, and you can edit existing SAS data sets or create new ones.

SAS/IML software has a complete set of control statements, such as DO/END, START/FINISH, iterative DO, IF-THEN/ELSE, GOTO, LINK, PAUSE, and STOP, giving you all of the commands necessary for execution control and program modularization.

As a simple example, consider the following program taken from the SAS manual (SAS Institute Inc. 2015). It implements a numerical algorithm that estimates the square root of a number, accurate to three decimal places. The algorithm is implemented as the function MySqrt that performs the necessary calculations.

```
PROC IML;                      /* begin IML session */

START MySqrt(x);               /* begin module */
   y = 1;                      /* initialize y */
   DO UNTIL (w<1e-3);          /* begin DO loop */
      z = y;                   /* set z=y */
      y = 0.5#(z+x/z);         /* estimate square root */
      w = ABS(y-z);            /* compute change in estimate */
   END;                        /* end DO loop */
   RETURN(y);                  /* return approximation */
FINISH;
t = MySqrt({3,4,7,9});         /* call function MySqrt  */
s = SQRT({3,4,7,9});           /* compare with true values */
diff = t - s;                  /* compute differences */
PRINT t s diff;                /* print matrices */
QUIT;
```

As just illustrated, you can then call the MySqrt module to estimate the square root of several numbers given in a matrix literal (enclosed in braces) and print the results, as shown in Exhibit 2.7.

In this book, we will use IML primarily in the chapter on correlations, where we implement some numerical routines for estimating correlations and program Monte Carlo simulations for loss distributions, which can conveniently be coded and run via IML. The stress testing chapter also has PROC IML examples for modeling credit portfolio loss distributions.

t	s	diff
1.7320508	1.7320508	0
2	2	2.22E−15
2.6457513	2.6457513	4.678E−11
3	3	1.397E−9

Exhibit 2.7 Output PROC IML

SAS STUDIO

SAS Studio is a developmental web application for SAS that you access through your web browser. With SAS Studio, you can access your data files, libraries, and existing programs, and write new programs. It is also possible to use the predefined tasks in SAS Studio to generate SAS code. When you run a program or task, SAS Studio processes the SAS code on a SAS server. The SAS server can be a server in a cloud environment, a server in your local environment, or SAS installed on your local machine. After the code is processed, the results are returned to SAS Studio in your browser.

SAS ENTERPRISE MINER

SAS Enterprise Miner is the flagship data mining tool offered by SAS. It is characterized by an easy-to-use, drag-and-drop interface and works using a distributed client/server architecture. It allows for the building of analytical models using the SEMMA methodology: sampling, exploration, modification, modeling, and assessment. It also provides:

- Open source integration (e.g., with R)
- In-database and in-Hadoop scoring to deal with massive data sets
- Parallelized grid computing
- Support for XML and SAS macros

In what follows, we provide a brief overview of how to work with SAS Enterprise Miner.

Start Enterprise Miner by clicking Start (in Windows) ⇨ All Programs ⇨ SAS ⇨ SAS Enterprise Miner Client 14.1. Enter the user name and password as shown in Exhibit 2.8.

Click Log On to arrive at the screen shown in Exhibit 2.9.

We can choose to create a new project, open an existing or a recent project, inspect metadata that was defined earlier, or simply exit. Let's create a new project with the details shown in Exhibit 2.10.

Finish the wizard by clicking Next and Finish, which will give the result shown in Exhibit 2.11.

The interface is divided into multiple components:

- **General toolbar:** This toolbar provides a set of common utilities to assist in building your projects.
- **SEMMA toolbar:** This toolbar is a graphical set of node icons and tools for building process flow diagrams in the diagram workspace. To display the text name of any node or tool icon, position your mouse pointer over the icon. The nodes are grouped according to the SEMMA methodology (sampling, exploration, modification, modeling, and assessment).

Exhibit 2.8 Log on Screen of SAS Enterprise Miner

■ **Project panel:** This panel is used to manage and view data sources, diagrams, model packages, and list users.

■ **Properties panel:** This panel is used to view and edit the settings of any object that you select (including data sources, diagrams, nodes, results, and users).

■ **Diagram workspace:** This is used to build, edit, run, and save process flow diagrams. This is where you graphically build, order, and sequence the nodes that you use to analyze your data and generate reports.

■ **Help panel:** This panel displays a short description of the property that you select in the properties panel. Extended help can be found in the Help Topics selection from the Help main menu.

Exhibit 2.9 Welcome Screen of SAS Enterprise Miner

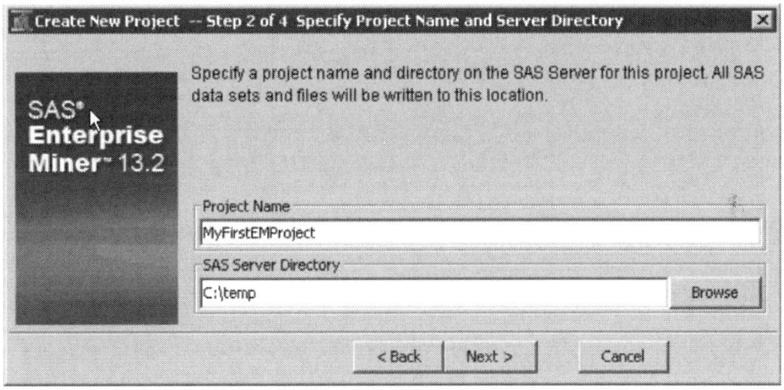

Exhibit 2.10 Creating a New Project in SAS Enterprise Miner

We will now first create a library to the physical directory on disk containing our data sets. In the properties panel, click on the button next to the Project Start Code property, and enter the information shown in Exhibit 2.12.

Click the Run Now button to run the statement. The mydata library has now been successfully created.

We can now right-click the Data Sources folder in the project panel (or select File ⇨ New ⇨ Data Source) to open the Data Source Wizard. In step 2 of this wizard, we select the HMEQ data set from the mydata library, as shown in Exhibit 2.13.

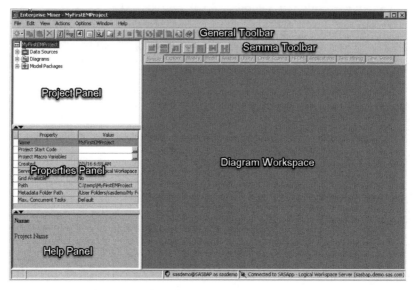

Exhibit 2.11 Start Screen of SAS Enterprise Miner

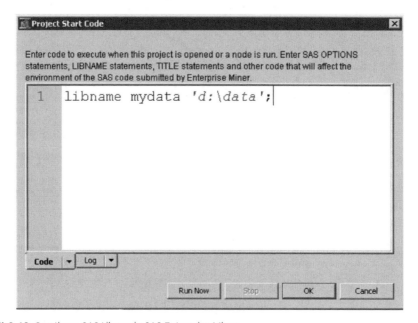

Exhibit 2.12 Creating a SAS Library in SAS Enterprise Miner

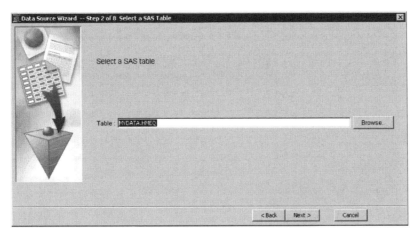

Exhibit 2.13 Selecting the HMEQ Data Set from the Mydata Library

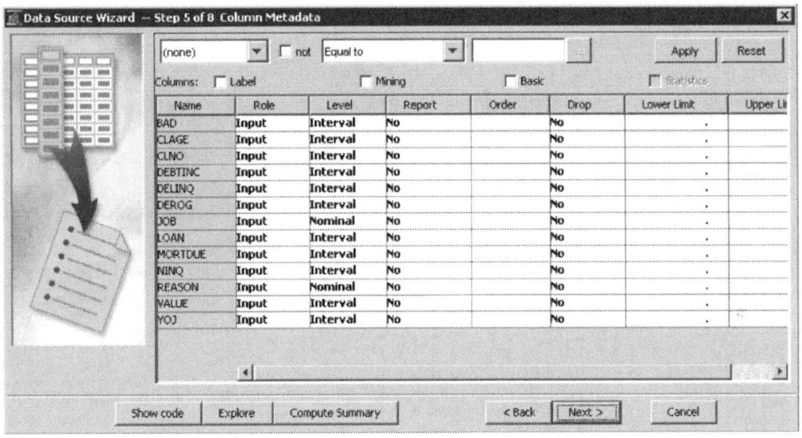

Exhibit 2.14 Specifying the Measurement Level and Measurement Role for the Variables

Click Next to proceed through steps 3 and 4. In step 5 of the wizard, you can set the measurement level and measurement role for each of the variables as shown in Exhibit 2.14.

Let's set the measurement role of the BAD variable to target, as this is our target default indicator. We can accept all other suggested settings for both the measurement role and level. We can now create our first SAS Enterprise Miner diagram by right-clicking Diagrams in the project panel and creating a new diagram MyFirstEM-Diagram, as shown in Exhibit 2.15.

The SEMMA toolbar has been activated. We can now drag and drop the HMEQ data set from the project panel to the diagram workspace as shown in Exhibit 2.16.

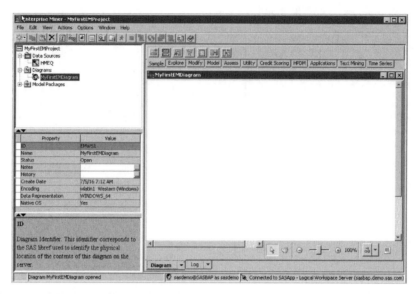

Exhibit 2.15 Creating a New Diagram

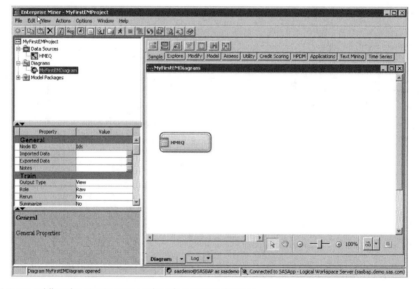

Exhibit 2.16 Adding the HMEQ Data to the Diagram Workspace

We are now ready to start analyzing this data set using nodes provided in the SEMMA toolbar. Go to the Explore tab, add a MultiPlot node to the diagram workspace, and connect it to the HMEQ data set as shown in Exhibit 2.17.

Right-click the MultiPlot node and click Run. After the run has finished, select Results. Inspect the graphs and output generated by this node.

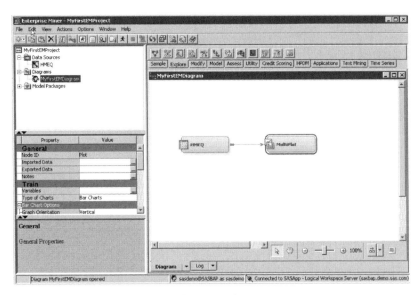

Exhibit 2.17 Adding a Multiplot Node to the Diagram Workspace

OTHER SAS SOLUTIONS FOR CREDIT RISK MANAGEMENT

SAS Credit Scoring for banking is a SAS solution to develop, validate, deploy, and track credit scorecards. Its primary focus is on probability of default (PD) risk. It is tightly integrated with Base SAS and SAS Enterprise Miner.

SAS Credit Risk Management for banking is an end-to-end solution to estimate PD, loss given default (LGD), and exposure at default (EAD) and combine them into regulatory capital. It features an extensive catalog of prebuilt regulatory reports about risk-weighted assets (RWA), expected losses, unexpected losses, capital charges, and more. It also provides facilities to build customized reports. Each report can be inspected with roll-up and drill-down facilities by using SAS online analytical processing (OLAP) capabilities. The solution also assists in defining and performing stress testing.

SAS Model manager is a tool that supports the backtesting, benchmarking, and life cycle management of credit risk models. It provides a centralized model repository storing models as they progress through their lifecycle, making the analytical process fully traceable, which is handy for audit and compliance checking in a Basel environment.

Going forward, we focus on providing examples in Base SAS and SAS Enterprise Miner which we believe are the most useful tools for credit analysts.

REFERENCE

SAS Institute Inc. (2015), *SAS/IML 14.1 User's Guide: Technical Report*. Cary, NC: SAS Institute.

CHAPTER 3

Exploratory Data Analysis

INTRODUCTION

Exploratory data analysis is a means for gaining first insights and getting familiar with your data. Data are usually structured in a matrix form where the columns are *variables* (or attributes, characteristics, covariates) and the rows are *objects* or observations (e.g., persons, loans, or years) for the variables. Many databases are very complex. Exploring all data at hand typically requires dealing with masses of data, or big data. Looking at observations of variables object by object is therefore usually too time consuming, too costly, or simply not possible. If we were to examine every one, out of the more than 600,000 entries in our mortgage database for every variable, it would be impossible to draw any meaningful conclusions from this. Therefore we aggregate the information behind each variable and compute some *summary or descriptive statistics* and provide summarizing charts. We can do this in a *one-dimensional (univariate)* or a *multidimensional (multivariate)* way. One-dimensional data analysis treats every variable one by one and explores key measures for each variable separately whereas multidimensional data analysis treats variables jointly and explores dependencies and relations between variables. We start this chapter with univariate analysis and continue then with multivariate (particularly bivariate) analysis.

ONE-DIMENSIONAL ANALYSIS

We begin with exploratory data analysis, looking at variables separately in a one-dimensional way. This means we are only interested in empirical univariate distributions or parameters thereof, variable by variable, and do not yet analyze variables jointly or multivariately. The latter is done in the subsection where we are interested in correlations and dependencies between variables.

Observed Frequencies and Empirical Distributions

First we compute how often a specific value of a variable is observed. This is meaningful only when a variable has a finite set of possible values, that is, in technical terms, when the variable is measured on a *discrete scale*. A simple example is the default of a mortgage loan, which usually has only two possible values (one for default and another for nondefault). Otherwise, if virtually any value of a variable is possible and each entry has a different value, the variable is measured on a *continuous scale*. An example is gross domestic product (GDP) growth, which can theoretically (if measured fine-grained) take any possible value between $-\infty$ and $+\infty$.

Now, consider we have as a starting point a sample with n observations for a variable X (e.g., thousands of observations for the variable FICO score in the mortgage database). For each observation we measure a specific value of the FICO score, denoted by $x_1, \ldots, x_n$, which is called the *raw data*. Let the variable be either discrete or continuous, but grouped into classes (e.g., FICO scores from 350 to 370, 370 to 390). Then we denote the values or class numbers by $a_1, \ldots, a_k$ and count the absolute numbers of occurrence of each value or class number by:

$$h_j = h(a_j)$$

and the relative frequencies by:

$$f_j = \frac{h_j}{n}$$

Obviously, it holds that $\sum_{j=1}^{k} h_j = n$ and $\sum_{j=1}^{k} f_j = 1$. Moreover, we define the absolute and relative cumulative frequency $H(x)$ and $F(x)$ for each value x as the number or relative frequency of values being at most equal to x (i.e., being equal to x or lower).

$$H(x) = \sum_{a_j \leq x} h(a_j)$$

$$F(x) = \frac{H(x)}{n}$$

Graphically, this is a (nondecreasing) "stairway" function. In SAS, frequencies can easily be computed using PROC FREQ and graphically plotted using PROC UNIVARIATE. First, we compute the observed frequencies for the defaults in the data set. A default is coded as 1, and a nondefault is coded as 0.

```
PROC FREQ DATA=data.mortgage;
TABLES default_time;
RUN;
```

The output table (Exhibit 3.1) shows that there are 607,331 nondefaults and 15,158 defaults, which give relative frequencies of 97.56% and 2.44%, respectively, where the total number of observations is 622,489. Cumulative absolute (relative)

The FREQ Procedure

default_time	Frequency	Percent	Cumulative Frequency	Cumulative Percent
0	607331	97.56	607331	97.56
1	15158	2.44	622489	100.00

Exhibit 3.1 Absolute and Relative Frequencies

frequencies are 607,331 (97.526%) for all values lower than or equal to 0 and 622,489 (100%) for all values lower than or equal to 1.

Next, we compute histograms, which plot the absolute (or relative) frequencies for values or classes of variables and the empirical cumulative distribution function (CDF) exemplarily for the variable's FICO score (FICO_orig_time) and LTV at origination (LTV_orig_time). The distribution of relative frequencies (called by the command HISTOGRAM in PROC UNIVARIATE) in Exhibit 3.2 shows increasing percentages for FICO up to a value of almost 700 and then decreasing percentages. The distribution is not symmetric as the tail on the left is longer (fatter) than on the right of the distribution. It is skewed to the left and steep to the right. For LTV we see that similar values have a rather high relative frequency compared to others, particular the value of 80. This is because LTV is the ratio of the outstanding loan amount to the collateral value, and banks traditionally extend loans in the region of 80 percent. The percentages in both histograms add up to 100 percent.

The CDFs for both variables start at 0 percent to the left and end at 100 percent to the right. It is nondecreasing and for FICO it looks almost continuous, because FICO seems to be an almost continuous variable. For LTV we see some "jump points" (or discontinuity points) at the values where we identified high relative frequencies.

```
ODS GRAPHICS ON;
PROC UNIVARIATE DATA=data.mortgage;
VAR FICO_orig_time LTV_orig_time;
CDFPLOT FICO_orig_time LTV_orig_time;
HISTOGRAM FICO_orig_time LTV_orig_time;
RUN;
ODS GRAPHICS OFF;
```

Location Measures

In addition, or as an alternative to the description of the entire distribution, we often report summarizing measures. These measures give numerical characterizations about the location of the distribution, its dispersion, and its shape, and are generally

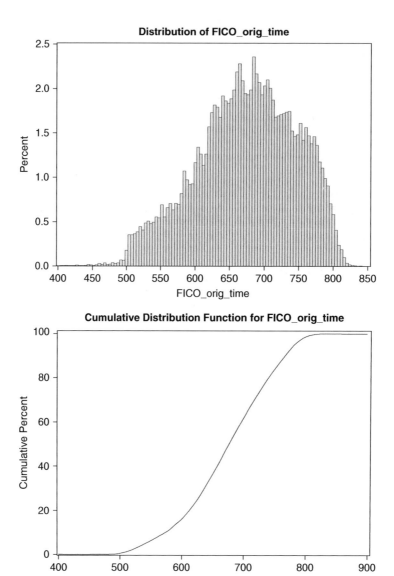

Exhibit 3.2 Histograms and CDF Plots

called "moments." Three measures for location are commonly used: the mean, the median, and the mode. The mean of a distribution, or arithmetic average, is an equally weighted sum of each value of a variable summed over all observations. Assume we have n values $x_1, \ldots, x_n$; then the mean is:

$$\bar{x} = \frac{1}{n} \sum_{i=1}^{n} x_i$$

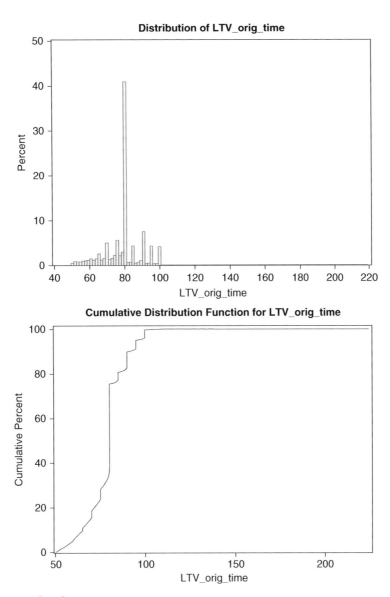

Exhibit 3.2 (*Continued*)

The mean requires a variable to be measured on a metric, continuous scale. Another measure for location is the median, which requires at least ordinally scaled (i.e., ranked values). Let the raw observations be ordered from lowest to highest; that is, create the ordered raw data as $x_{(1)} \leq x_{(2)} \leq \ldots \leq x_{(n)}$ where the values in the parentheses denote the rank number of the observation. Then, if the number n of observations is uneven, the median is defined as:

$$x_{Med} = x_{\left(\frac{n+1}{2}\right)}$$

That is, the variable value of the observation which is exactly in the middle of the ordered list. If n is even, the median is defined as the average of both observations in the middle of the ordered list;

$$x_{Med} = \frac{x_{\left(\frac{n}{2}\right)} + x_{\left(\frac{n}{2}+1\right)}}{2},$$

Finally, the mode is defined as the observation that is encountered most frequently in the data set; that is,

$$x_{Mod}: \text{Value with highest frequency}$$

Obviously, the mode is useful only when the variable is ordinal or categorical. Mean and median have important properties. The formula for the mean uses all data for its computation whereas the median processes only one (or two) data points. Thus, the mean is affected by extreme observations (outliers), whereas the median is robust with respect to outliers. If a distribution has one mode only and is symmetric, it holds that $\bar{x} = x_{Med} = x_{Mod}$. If it is skewed to the left (right) it holds that $\bar{x} \leq x_{Med} \leq x_{Mod}$ ($\bar{x} \geq x_{Med} \geq x_{Mod}$).

A more general expression for the median is a quantile. A p-quantile x_p with $0 < p < 1$, is defined as the value for which

- At least a proportion p of sample values is lower than or equal to x_p.
- At least a proportion $1 - p$ of sample values is higher than or equal to x_p.

That is,

$$\frac{number\,(x - values \leq x_p)}{n} \geq p \quad \text{and} \quad \frac{number\,(x - values \geq x_p)}{n} \geq 1 - p$$

Special quantiles are:

$x_{0.5}$:   median

$x_{0.25}, x_{0.75}$:   lower and upper quartiles

$x_{0.1}, x_{0.2}, \ldots, x_{0.9}$:   deciles

Measures of location can be computed via SAS PROC MEANS where the requested measures are specified after the PROC MEANS command; see SAS Institute Inc. (2015). In Exhibit 3.3 we show exemplarily the output for the default

The MEANS Procedure

Variable	N	Mean	Median	Mode	1st Pctl	99th Pctl
default_time	622489	0.0244	0.0000	0.0000	0.0000	1.0000
FICO_orig_time	622489	673.6169	678.0000	660.0000	506.0000	801.0000
LTV_orig_time	622489	78.9755	80.0000	80.0000	52.2000	100.0000

Exhibit 3.3 Location Measures

indicator, FICO and LTV. The binary default variable has a mean of 0.0244, which corresponds to the default rate of 2.44 percent. Mean and mode are zero, and as there are 2.44 percent defaults ("ones") in the data set, the 99 percent quantile is one. FICO and LTV have averages of 673.6169 and 78.9755, respectively, and the higher value for the median shows that both distributions are skewed to the left. The modes are 660 and 80, and 1 percent of all values are lower than or equal to 506 and 52.2, or higher than or equal to 801 and 100.

```
PROC MEANS DATA=data.mortgage
N MEAN MEDIAN MODE P1 P99 MAXDEC=4;
VAR default_time FICO_orig_time LTV_orig_time;
RUN;
```

Quantiles can be used for a graphical comparison with standard distributions, such as a normal distribution. The normal distribution is widely used in applications and is a symmetric distribution with a single mode. Using PROC UNIVARIATE, a quantile-quantile (Q-Q) plot can be created using the command QQPLOT, which compares for each value its quantile value with the theoretical value under a specific distribution. Here we use the normal distribution with the same mean and standard deviation as the empirical data. If the data were from a normal distribution, both the empirical and the theoretical quantiles should be roughly equal and lie on the diagonal line. In Exhibit 3.4, we see divergences for FICO and LTV, particularly for extreme observations, which signals that the empirical data have different tails than the theoretical normal distribution.

```
ODS GRAPHICS ON;
PROC UNIVARIATE DATA=data.mortgage NOPRINT;
QQPLOT FICO_orig_time LTV_orig_time
/NORMAL(MU=EST SIGMA=EST COLOR=LTGREY) ;
RUN;
ODS GRAPHICS OFF;
```

Dispersion Measures

Next, we discuss the most commonly used dispersion measures. The first is the span or range, which is simply the difference between the minimum and the maximum values. If we consider the ordered data set, then:

$$sp = x_{(n)} - x_{(1)}$$

The next two are mean squared error (MSE), sample variance, and standard deviation, which are defined as:

$$MSE = \frac{1}{n} \cdot \sum_{i=1}^{n} (x_i - \bar{x})^2$$

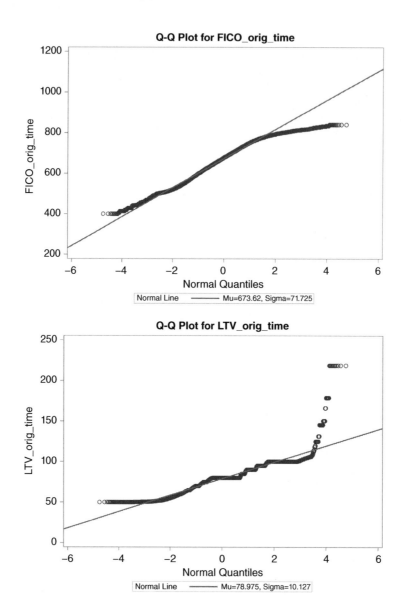

Exhibit 3.4 Q-Q Plot versus Normal Distribution

$$s^2 = \frac{1}{n-1} \cdot \sum_{i=1}^{n} (x_i - \overline{x})^2$$

$$s = +\sqrt{s^2}$$

All measures compute an average quadratic distance from the mean (or a square root of it). MSE and sample variance differ only in the factor $1/n$ or $1/(n-1)$,

The MEANS Procedure

Variable	N	Minimum	Maximum	Range	Quartile Range	Variance	Std Dev	Coeff of Variation
default_time	622489	0.0000	1.0000	1.0000	0.0000	0.0238	0.1541	632.9831
FICO_orig_time	622489	400.0000	840.0000	440.0000	103.0000	5144.4122	71.7246	10.6477
LTV_orig_time	622489	50.1000	218.5000	168.4000	5.0000	102.5572	10.1271	12.8230

Exhibit 3.5 Dispersion Measures

respectively, which has to do with some theoretical properties. For large n, the differences become negligible and both numbers almost coincide. Note that all three figures are computed using all variable values and thus are, like the mean, not robust with respect to outliers. Moreover, as the standard deviation is the square root of the variance (which is a squared distance), it is measured in the same unit as the original variable (and not in squared units). All three measures are scale dependent. In other words, a variable with higher values in general should exhibit a higher dispersion, all else being equal. To control for this, one can use a standardization and compute the coefficient of variation (CV), which is defined as:

$$v = \frac{s}{\bar{x}}$$

These measures can be computed using PROC MEANS with the relevant statistic options. Additionally, we compute the distance between the quartiles. (See Exhibit 3.5)

```
PROC MEANS DATA=data.mortgage
N MIN MAX RANGE QRANGE VAR STD CV MAXDEC=4;
VAR default_time FICO_orig_time LTV_orig_time;
RUN;
```

Skewness and Kurtosis Measures

Next we compute measures for the shape of the distribution: skewness and kurtosis. First, we define the standardized value for each variable as:

$$z_i = \frac{x_i - \bar{x}}{s}$$

Then the skewness is calculated in SAS as:

$$skew = \frac{1}{n} \sum_{i=1}^{n} z_i^3$$

which is the average of the deviations from the mean to the power of three. Similarly, the kurtosis is computed as:

$$kurt = \frac{1}{n} \sum_{i=1}^{n} z_i^4 - 3$$

The MEANS Procedure

Variable	N	Skewness	Kurtosis
default_time	622489	6.1719	36.0920
FICO_orig_time	622489	−0.3213	−0.4684
LTV_orig_time	622489	−0.1964	1.4364

Exhibit 3.6 Skewness and Kurtosis Measures

Note that mean and variance of the standardized values are 0 and 1, respectively. A negative value for the skewness shows that the distribution is skewed to the left; a positive value shows there is a skew to the right. Kurtosis measures the peakedness of the distribution. When you subtract the value of 3, as is the case in SAS, it is sometimes called excess kurtosis since the value is contrasted with the value of 3 for the normal distribution. Thus, a negative value signals a lower kurtosis and a positive value signals a higher kurtosis than the normal distribution. Both statistics can be computed in PROC MEANS using the respective commands. While the distribution for default is obviously strongly skewed to the right, FICO and LTV are left skewed, where FICO has a lower kurtosis than the normal distribution, and default and LTV a (strongly) higher kurtosis. (See Exhibit 3.6.)

```
PROC MEANS DATA=data.mortgage
N SKEW KURT MAXDEC=4;
VAR default_time FICO_orig_time LTV_orig_time;
RUN;
```

TWO-DIMENSIONAL ANALYSIS

Having explored the empirical data on a one-dimensional basis for each variable, we are usually also interested in interrelations between variables; for example, if and how variables have a tendency to comove together. Thus, variables can be analyzed jointly and the joint empirical distribution can be examined. Moreover, summarizing measures for dependencies and comovements can be computed.

Joint Empirical Distributions

The joint empirical distribution simultaneously computes the frequency distribution of two or more variables. Assume we have a sample size n and we have values $x_1,\ldots,x_n$ of attribute X (e.g., default) and values $y_1,\ldots,y_n$ of attribute Y (FICO) for each loan. Let

$$(x_1,y_1),\ldots,(x_n,y_n) \qquad \text{raw data}$$
$$n \qquad \text{sample size}$$

$a_1, \ldots, a_k$	attribute values / categories of variable X
$b_1, \ldots, b_l$	attribute values / categories of variable Y
$h_{ij} = h(a_i, b_j)$	joint absolute frequencies
$f_{ij} = f(a_i, b_j) = \frac{h_{ij}}{n}$	joint relative frequencies
$h_{i\cdot} = \sum_{j=1}^{l} h_{ij}$	absolute marginal frequencies of X
$f_{i\cdot} = \frac{h_{i\cdot}}{n} = f_1(a_i)$	relative marginal frequencies of X
$f_{\cdot j} = \frac{h_{\cdot j}}{n} = f_2(b_j)$	relative marginal frequencies of Y

Then the joint absolute (analogously relative) frequencies can be summarized in a two-way frequency table such that:

	b_1	$\cdots$	b_l	
a_1	h_{11}	$\cdots$	h_{1l}	$h_{1\cdot}$
$\vdots$	$\vdots$	$\ddots$	$\vdots$	$\vdots$
a_k	h_{k1}	$\cdots$	h_{kl}	$h_{k\cdot}$
	$h_{\cdot 1}$	$\cdots$	$h_{\cdot l}$	n

where the marginal frequencies of X in each row are the sums across the respective column, and the marginal frequencies of Y in each column are the sums across the respective row, and these are equal to the one-way (stand-alone) frequencies from the earlier subsection. As earlier, this table makes sense only if the variables are ordinal, categorical, or divided into groups if they are metric. In the following example, we compute the two-way frequency table for default versus FICO where FICO is divided into five groups, which is performed by PROC RANK. Then PROC FREQ is used to

The FREQ Procedure

Table of default_time by FICO_orig_time						
default_time	**FICO_orig_time(Values of FICO_orig_time Were Replaced by Ranks)**					
	0	**1**	**2**	**3**	**4**	**Total**
0	121213	119701	121069	121876	123472	607331
	19.47	19.23	19.45	19.58	19.84	97.56
	19.96	19.71	19.93	20.07	20.33	
	96.51	96.91	97.44	98.08	98.89	
1	4381	3820	3186	2385	1386	15158
	0.70	0.61	0.51	0.38	0.22	2.44
	28.90	25.20	21.02	15.73	9.14	
	3.49	3.09	2.56	1.92	1.11	
Total	125594	123521	124255	124261	124858	622489
	20.18	19.84	19.96	19.96	20.06	100.00

Exhibit 3.7 Two-Dimensional Contingency Table

compute the cross-tabulation of default versus FICO. The output table (Exhibit 3.7) shows the absolute and relative frequencies.

For example, 121,213 loans (or 19.47 percent of a total of $n = 622{,}489$ observations) had default status 0 and were in the lowest group (group 0) of the FICO scores. Altogether 607,331 loans were not in default, which is 97.56 percent of all loans (as stated earlier), and of those 607,331 nondefault loans a percentage of 19.96 percent were in FICO group 0. Altogether, 125,594 loans were in FICO group 0, and 121,213 of these (or 96.51 percent) did not default whereas 3.49 percent of all loans in FICO group 0 defaulted. An important result we can infer from the table is that the proportion of loans that defaulted decreases the higher the FICO group becomes (from 3.49 percent in group 0 to 1.11 percent in group 4). This leads to the conclusion that there should be some interrelation between FICO and default (i.e., the higher the FICO score, the lower the relative frequency of default).

```
DATA mortgage1;
SET data.mortgage;
RUN;


PROC SORT DATA = mortgage1;
BY id time;
RUN;


PROC RANK DATA = mortgage1
GROUPS=5
OUT=quint(KEEP=id time FICO_orig_time);
VAR FICO_orig_time;
RUN;


DATA new;
MERGE mortgage1 quint;
BY id time;
RUN;


PROC FREQ DATA=new   ;
TABLES default_time*FICO_ORIG_TIME;
RUN;
```

Another way of inferring the relation between both variables (without grouping FICO first) is to look at box plots, which can be requested in SAS using PROC BOX-PLOT; see SAS Institute Inc. (2015). The following program code plots FICO versus default where a separate box plot for each default category (0 and 1) is computed. A box plot consists of a box and whiskers. (See Exhibit 3.8.) In SAS the standard statistics represented by the box-and-whiskers plot are given as follows.

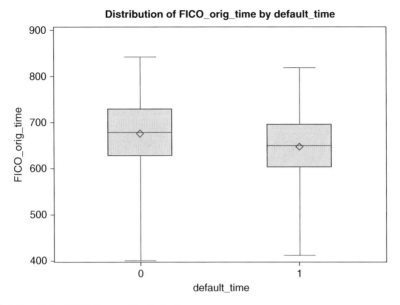

Exhibit 3.8 Box Plot of FICO Grouped by Default

Group summary statistic	Feature of box-and-whiskers plot
Maximum	End point of upper whisker
Third quartile (75th percentile)	Upper edge of box
Median (50th percentile)	Line inside box
Mean	Symbol marker
First quartile (25th percentile)	Lower edge of box
Minimum	End point of lower whisker

The following SAS codes then plot the two boxes and whiskers for FICO and LTV, for each category of default separately. As can be seen in Exhibit 3.9, the location of the box is higher for FICO and lower for LTV in the nondefault category compared to the default category, which again shows some interrelation between the variables in the sense that higher FICO scores correspond to a lower default frequency and higher LTVs correspond to a higher default frequency.

```
PROC SORT DATA= mortgage1;
BY default_time;
RUN;
```

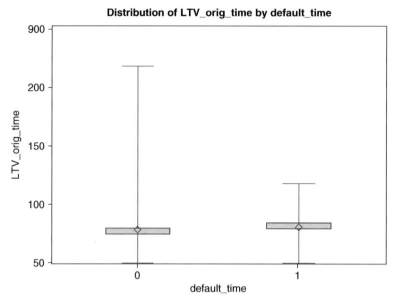

Exhibit 3.9 Box Plot of LTV Grouped by Default

```
ODS GRAPHICS ON;
PROC BOXPLOT DATA = mortgage1;
PLOT FICO_orig_time*default_time /IDSYMBOL=CIRCLE
IDHEIGHT=2 CBOXES=BLACK BOXWIDTH=10 ;
RUN;
ODS GRAPHICS OFF;

ODS GRAPHICS ON;
PROC BOXPLOT DATA = mortgage1;
PLOT LTV_orig_time*default_time / IDSYMBOL=CIRCLE
IDHEIGHT=2 CBOXES=BLACK BOXWIDTH=10 ;
RUN;
ODS GRAPHICS OFF;
```

The joint frequency tables and box plots allow us to draw conclusions about dependencies between variables from a visual perspective. To make stronger statements about dependence, one needs to compute numeric measures. To start, one first needs a reference point, which is obviously the case of independence. Statistically, two variables are empirically independent if the joint frequencies in the two-way table are given by the product of the respective marginal frequencies across the entire table; that is,

$$f_{ij} = \frac{h_{i.}h_{.j}}{n^2}$$

$$h_{ij} = \frac{h_{i \cdot} h_{\cdot j}}{n}$$

Having defined a reference point, we can now start to make assessments about the direction and the strength of the dependence by measuring the deviation from independence. This is done via correlation and dependence measures.

Correlation Measures

The first measure is the χ^2-coefficient, which can be applied to two-way tables and is defined as:

$$\chi^2 = \sum_{i=1}^{k} \sum_{j=1}^{l} \frac{\left(h_{ij} - \frac{h_{i \cdot} h_{\cdot j}}{n}\right)^2}{\frac{h_{i \cdot} h_{\cdot j}}{n}} = n \sum_{i=1}^{k} \sum_{j=1}^{l} \frac{(f_{ij} - f_{i \cdot} f_{\cdot j})^2}{f_{i \cdot} f_{\cdot j}}$$

It measures the sum across all cells in the table of the squared deviations of the observed frequencies from those that would result if the two variables were independent. Thus, in the case of perfect independence a value of $\chi^2 = 0$ would result. It has a lower reference point of zero but is unbounded from above. We can now compute related measures, such as the *ϕ-coefficient*

$$\phi = \sqrt{\frac{\chi^2}{n}}$$

the *contingency coefficient*

$$cc = \sqrt{\frac{\chi^2}{\chi^2 + n}}$$

and *Cramer's V*

$$V = \sqrt{\frac{\chi^2 / n}{m}}$$

where $m = \min(k - 1, l - 1)$ and k and l are the numbers of rows and columns of the table. It holds that $V \in [0, 1]$. The measures (plus two other measures that are not discussed here) can be computed using PROC FREQ with the command CHISQ as shown in the following code. All measures show dependence, and a statistical test conducted for χ^2 signals that the value is statistically different from zero (independence). In other words, this gives evidence of dependence between FICO and default. Note that due to the large number of observations n and the minimum of row and column numbers of two, ϕ, cc, and V coincide. (See Exhibit 3.10.)

```
PROC FREQ DATA=new;
TABLES default_time*FICO_ORIG_TIME / CHISQ;
RUN;
```

The χ^2 and related measures can be used for categorical ordered, or grouped metric variables. If we group metric variables, however, this means a partial loss of

The FREQ Procedure

Statistics for Table of default_time by FICO_orig_time

Statistic	DF	Value	Prob
Chi-Square	4	1881.6127	<.0001
Likelihood Ratio Chi-Square	4	2037.4607	<.0001
Mantel-Haenszel Chi-Square	1	1848.1334	<.0001
Phi Coefficient		0.0550	
Contingency Coefficient		0.0549	
Cramer's V		0.0550	

Exhibit 3.10 Chi-Square-Related Measures of Association

information in the data. If we want to compute dependency measures for metric variables, we can take account of the full information in the data by using every raw variable value. This can be done by the first metric measure of association, the sample covariance defined as:

$$s_{xy} = \frac{1}{n-1} \sum_{i=1}^{n} (x_i - \bar{x})(y_i - \bar{y})$$

The *sample covariance* is (as is the variance) scale dependent. A standardized measure is the sample correlation defined as:

$$r_{xy} = \frac{\sum_{i=1}^{n} (x_i - \bar{x})(y_i - \bar{y})}{\sqrt{\sum_{i=1}^{n} (x_i - \bar{x})^2 \cdot \sum_{i=1}^{n} (y_i - \bar{y})^2}}$$

$$= \frac{\sum x_i y_i - n\bar{x}\bar{y}}{\sqrt{\left(\sum x_i^2 - n\bar{x}^2\right)\left(\sum y_i^2 - n\bar{y}^2\right)}} = \frac{s_{xy}}{s_x \cdot s_y}$$

r_{xy} is sometimes called the *Bravais-Pearson correlation* (or *product-moment correlation*) and takes on values $-1 \leq r_{xy} \leq +1$. It is a measure for *linear* dependence, that is, $r_{xy} = \pm 1 \iff y_i = a + b \cdot x_i$. A coefficient of $r_{xy} \approx 0$ does not necessarily mean that the variables are not dependent, only that there is no linear relation.

Another measure for ordered (ranked) data is the *Spearman rank correlation*. Let $rk(x_i)$ be the rank of x_i in the ordered list of X, and $rk(y_i)$ be the rank of y_i in the ordered list of Y. Then we can compute the correlation by applying the Bravais-Pearson correlation to the ranked values $(rg(x_i), rg(y_i))$:

$$r_{sp} = \frac{\sum_{i=1}^{n}(rk(x_i) - \overline{rk}(x))(rk(y_i) - \overline{rk}(y))}{\sqrt{\sum_{i=1}^{n}(rk(x_i) - \overline{rk}(x))^2 \cdot \sum_{i=1}^{n}(rk(y_i) - \overline{rk}(y))^2}}$$

which yields:

$$r_{sp} = 1 - \frac{6 \cdot \sum_{i=1}^{n} (rk(x_i) - rk(y_i))^2}{n \cdot (n^2 - 1)}$$

Another frequently used measure of nonlinear dependence is *Kendall's* τ_b. It is based on the number of concordances and discordances in paired observations. Concordance occurs when paired observations vary together, and discordance occurs when paired observations vary differently. It is defined as:

$$\tau_b = \frac{\sum_{i<j}(sign(x_i - x_j))(sign(y_i - y_j))}{\sqrt{(T_0 - T_1)(T_0 - T_2)}}$$

where $T_0 = n(n - 1)/2$, $T_1 = \sum_k t_k(t_k - 1)/2$, and $T_2 = \sum_l u_l(u_l - 1)/2$. t_k is the number of tied *x*-values in the *k*th group of tied *x*-values and u_l is the number of tied *y*-values in the *l*th group of tied *y*-values, and *sign(z)* is defined as:

$$sign(z) = \begin{cases} 1 & \text{if } z > 0 \\ 0 & \text{if } z = 0 \\ -1 & \text{if } z < 0 \end{cases}$$

The dependence can also be represented graphically using a scatter plot where each symbol in the plot gives the two-dimensional location of an observation. As the total data set consists of more than 600,000 observations, a scatter plot would be very time consuming. We therefore draw a random sample of 1 percent of observations, and compute the correlation measures (Exhibit 3.11) and show the scatter plot (Exhibit 3.12) using PROC CORR for FICO and LTV. An observation is included if a uniform variable (equal distribution between zero and one) generated by RANUNI with the seed 123456 is less than 1 percent. Alternatively, PROC SURVEYSELECT may be used for random sampling.

The options Kendall and Spearman request these measures to be computed. As can be seen, all three measures return a negative correlation, which means that a higher FICO score corresponds to a lower LTV. The size of the measures (around −0.2) and the scatter plot, however, show that the strength of this relation is not very strong, revealing that both variables provide self-contained information.

```
DATA sample;
SET data.mortgage;
IF RANUNI(123456) < 0.01;
RUN;

ODS GRAPHICS ON;
PROC CORR DATA=sample
PLOTS(MAXPOINTS=NONE)=SCATTER(NVAR=2 ALPHA=.20 .30)
```

The CORR Procedure

Pearson Correlation Coefficients, *N* = 6073 Prob > |r| under H0: Rho=0				
	FICO_orig_time	LTV_orig_time	PFICO_orig_time	PLTV_orig_time
FICO_orig_time	1.00000	−0.14063		<.0001
LTV_orig_time	−0.14063	1.00000	<.0001	
Spearman Correlation Coefficients, *N* = 6073 Prob > |r| under H0: Rho=0				
	FICO_orig_time	LTV_orig_time	PFICO_orig_time	PLTV_orig_time
FICO_orig_time	1.00000	−0.17170		<.0001
LTV_orig_time	−0.17170	1.00000	<.0001	
Kendall Tau b Correlation Coefficients, *N* = 6073 Prob > |tau| under H0: Tau=0				
	FICO_orig_time	LTV_orig_time	PFICO_orig_time	PLTV_orig_time
FICO_orig_time	1.00000	−0.12363		<.0001
LTV_orig_time	−0.12363	1.00000	<.0001	

Exhibit 3.11 Correlation Measures

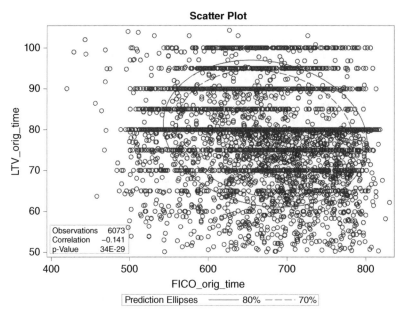

Exhibit 3.12 Scatter Plot of FICO versus LTV (Sample)

```
KENDALL SPEARMAN;
VAR FICO_orig_time LTV_orig_time;
RUN;
ODS GRAPHICS OFF;
```

HIGHLIGHTS OF INDUCTIVE STATISTICS

Sampling

The former two sections provided graphical and mathematical measures for exploring data. These data can be from an entire population or from a sample of the population only. Actually, most data at hand are only sample data that are drawn from a larger population. Even the huge data set of mortgage loans can be interpreted as a sample from the entire population of all mortgages in the United States or the whole world. There are various types of sampling designs, which can be roughly divided into:

- *Probability sampling:* Here each unit in the population has a chance (greater than zero) of being selected in the sample, and this probability can be accurately determined.

- *Nonprobability sampling:* Some units in the population have no chance of being selected or the probability cannot be accurately determined. This gives an exclusion bias. Examples are voluntary sampling or convenience sampling where people are selected either by their own or by the surveyor's will to participate.

In most applications one assumes probability sampling. This can be further divided into:

- *Simple random sampling:* It is assumed that the population consists of N objects. The sample consists of n objects, and all possible samples of n objects are equally likely to occur. An example is the lottery method. If the probability of each object is not equal, it is simply named "random sampling."

- *Stratified sampling:* The population is divided into groups (also called strata), based on some characteristic (e.g., sex or age). Then, within each group, a probability sample (often a simple random sample) is selected.

- *Cluster sampling:* Every member of the population is assigned to one, and only one, group (called a cluster), for example a municipality. Then a sample of clusters is chosen, using a probability method (often simple random sampling). Only individuals within sampled clusters are surveyed.

- Others, which we do not explain explicitly (e.g., multistage sampling, systematic random sampling).

Let us have a closer look at random sampling. We denote by Ω the population of individuals or objects $(\omega_1,...,\omega_N)$ with attribute X (e.g., age). Next, consider n random draws from that population, so that:

$$\text{1st draw delivers:} \quad \omega_1 \xrightarrow[\text{measurement}]{} X_1(\omega_1) = x_1$$

$$\text{2nd draw delivers:} \quad \omega_2 \xrightarrow[\text{measurement}]{} X_2(\omega_2) = x_2$$

$$\vdots \qquad\qquad\qquad \vdots$$

$$n\text{th draw delivers:} \quad \omega_n \xrightarrow[\text{measurement}]{} X_n(\omega_n) = x_n$$

That is, the objects are randomly selected, and their attributes are measured (e.g., age of the drawn person). The data $x_1, \ldots, x_n$ are realizations of the random variables $X_1, \ldots, X_n$ and represent the same property X. Thus, $X_1, \ldots, X_n$ are *identically distributed* as X.

Hence, if objects and their variables (age, height etc.) are obtained via random sampling, their values can be interpreted as outcomes and realizations of the same random variables. If the random draws are also independent, then $X_1, \ldots, X_n$ are *independent and identically distributed (i.i.d.)*.

Point Estimation

Now, if one has sample data at hand, the goal is often to not only describe and explore the data, but also make inferences about distributions, parameters thereof, or relations between variables, such as correlations, in the underlying population using the sample data. For this, the sampling mechanism has to be taken into account.

The first goal is to infer one or more parameters of the distribution of a variable in the population using the sample. This is called *parameter* or *point estimation*. An example is computing the mean of the sample and taking it as an estimate for the mean (the expectation) in the population. There are various statistical techniques for parameter estimation, the most important of which are:

- *Ordinary least squares (OLS) method:* The parameter(s) are computed such that the sum of the squared differences of the observations from the predictions is minimized.
- *Method of moments (MM):* The parameters of the population are substituted by their counterparts in the sample.
- *Maximum-likelihood (ML) method:* The parameters are computed such that the likelihood (probability) of observing the sample at hand is maximal among the potential set of parameters.

Most of the methods in this book use the ML method. The method is described in more detail for models in the respective chapters (e.g., for PD models in the chapters on PDs).

Confidence Intervals

Once parameters are estimated, the sampling design comes into play. If we have a random sample, then the number of observations is typically much smaller than the size of the population. Therefore, we will not match the true (and unknown) parameter in the population exactly but instead have a random deviation from that parameter.

A popular way of constructing probability bounds around the parameter estimate is by computing confidence intervals. If one chooses an approach t delivers with probability, say, $1 - \alpha$, an interval that contains the true parameter, then this interval is called a *confidence interval*. Formally, let θ be the (unknown) parameter in the population of interest and let $\hat{\theta}$ be its estimate from a random sample. Then we construct lower and upper bounds B_l and B_u such that:

$$P(B_l \leq \theta \leq B_u) = 1 - \alpha$$

where α is called the error probability and $1 - \alpha$ is the confidence level.

Many models considered in this book result in approximately normally distributed parameter estimators. In particular, it can be shown that the ML estimation methods approximately yield normally distributed estimators that are furthermore unbiased (i.e., their expectation is the true parameter). Then, confidence intervals can be easily constructed. Let the estimator $\hat{\theta}$ be normally distributed with expectation θ and variance σ_θ^2; that is, $\hat{\theta} \sim N(\theta, \sigma_\theta^2)$. Then $\frac{\hat{\theta}-\theta}{\sigma_\theta}$ is standard normally distributed, and due to the properties of the standard normal distribution we obtain $P(-z_{1-\alpha/2} \leq \frac{\hat{\theta}-\theta}{\sigma_\theta} \leq z_{1-\alpha/2}) = 1 - \alpha$, where $z_{1-\alpha/2}$ is the $1 - \alpha/2$ percentile of the standard normal distribution. Rearranging yields:

$$P(\hat{\theta} - z_{1-\alpha/2} \cdot \sigma_\theta \leq \theta \leq \hat{\theta} z_{1-\alpha/2} \cdot \sigma_\theta) = 1 - \alpha$$

This gives the confidence interval

$$[\hat{\theta} - z_{1-\alpha/2} \cdot \sigma_\theta; \quad \hat{\theta} + z_{1-\alpha/2} \cdot \sigma_\theta]$$

Usually, however, the standard deviation σ_θ of the estimator is also unknown and has to be estimated from the sample. Let $\hat{\sigma}_\theta$ be the estimate (e.g., the sample standard error). Then the confidence interval becomes:

$$[\hat{\theta} - t_{n-1,1-\alpha/2} \cdot \hat{\sigma}_\theta; \quad \hat{\theta} + t_{n-1,1-\alpha/2} \cdot \hat{\sigma}_\theta]$$

where $t_{n-1,1-\alpha/2}$ is the $1 - \alpha/2$ percentile of Student's t-distribution with $n - 1$ degrees of freedom and n is the sample size. For large sample sizes, this converges toward the standard normal distribution.

In SAS, confidence intervals are typically automatically reported in the standard output when model parameters are estimated (e.g., for the PD models from the chapters on PDs). For sample means they can also be computed using PROC UNIVARIATE with option BASICINTERVALS, as shown in the following code for LTV; see SAS Institute Inc. (2015). The option cibasic(alpha=.01) produces a 99 percent confidence interval. (See Exhibit 3.13.)

```
ODS SELECT BASICINTERVALS;
PROC UNIVARIATE DATA=data.mortgage CIBASIC(ALPHA=.01);
VAR LTV_orig_time;
RUN;
```

The UNIVARIATE Procedure
Variable: LTV_orig_time

Basic Confidence Limits Assuming Normality			
Parameter	Estimate	99% Confidence Limits	
Mean	78.97546	78.94240	79.00852
Std Deviation	10.12705	10.10372	.
Variance	102.55718	102.08523	.

Exhibit 3.13 Basic Confidence Intervals

Due to the large sample size, the standard error of the mean (not the standard error of the total observations) is very low. Therefore, the confidence interval for the mean is very narrow. Moreover, note that SAS also produces intervals for the standard deviation and the variance (where it failed for numerical reasons to provide the upper bound). These intervals are not constructed using normal distributions. Because these are not often used throughout the book, we will not go into further detail here.

Hypothesis Testing

Another way of inferring from the sample to the population is hypothesis testing on one or more parameters in the population.

Step 1: Hypothesis Formulation
In a first step, one has to formulate a null hypothesis for the population, which will be tested using the sample data. For example, a hypothesis could be about a specific value for a parameter in the population and could be formulated as H_0: "The population parameter θ is exactly equal to a value θ_0", or in short $H_0 : \theta = \theta_0$. The null hypothesis also has an alternative, say H_1, which is valid if H_0 is not true. Here the alternative could be H_1: "The population parameter θ is not equal to a value θ_0," or in short $H_1 : \theta \neq \theta_0$. This is called a two-sided hypothesis.

There are also one-sided hypotheses, namely $H_0 : \theta \leq \theta_0$ versus $H_1 : \theta > \theta_0$, and $H_0 : \theta \geq \theta_0$ versus $H_1 : \theta < \theta_0$.

The hypotheses are usually derived from economic theories or intuition. For example, a null hypothesis could be that the mean LTV in the population is 60 whereas the alternative could be that it is different from 60.

Step 2: Choice of Test Statistic
In a second step, we determine an appropriate measure for testing the hypothesis, the so-called test statistic. If we want to test a hypothesis for the population mean, an obvious test statistic is the sample mean.

Step 3: Distribution of the Test Statistic

As a third step, we determine the probability distribution of the test statistic under the assumption that H_0 is true. As many model parameters are estimated via maximum likelihood, the estimators that serve as test statistics are approximately normally distributed. For example, if the null hypothesis were about a parameter $H_0 : \theta = \theta_0$ and the estimator $\hat{\theta}$ is normally distributed with variance σ_{θ}^2, then under the null hypothesis the distribution of $\hat{\theta}$ is $N(\theta_0, \sigma_{\theta}^2)$.

Step 4: Computing the p-Value

Next, given the distribution under the null hypothesis, and given the sample estimate $\hat{\theta}$, one computes the probability of observing exactly the value $\hat{\theta}$ or greater in the sample data when the null is true. In other words, under the normal distribution assumption one computes for our null hypothesis,

$$p - value = 2 \cdot \left[1 - \Phi \left(\frac{|\hat{\theta} - \theta_0|}{\sigma_{\theta}} \right) \right]$$

which is the so-called *p*-value. The term in brackets on the right-hand side of the equation is multiplied by 2 and the numerator is computed as the absolute deviation because we have a two-sided test here. For a one-sided test, the multiplicator and the absolute operator would be dropped. The *p*-value gives the probability of sampling the observed sample value (or a greater value) assuming the null hypothesis is true. The lower this probability, the more *p*-value evidence against the null hypothesis (and in favor of the alternative). For small values ($0.05 \leq p\text{-value} < 0.1$) we say that the result is weakly significant. For even smaller values ($0.01 \leq p\text{-value} < 0.05$) the result is significant, and for very small values ($p\text{-value} < 0.01$) the result is said to be strongly significant against the value under the null hypothesis. The borderline values are sometimes also called significance levels. This two-sided test can also be conducted as one-sided tests, similar to confidence intervals. Moreover, if the standard deviation has to be estimated in addition, the CDF of the standard normal distribution is replaced by the percentile of the Student's *t*-distribution as for the confidence intervals.

Step 5: Decision

Finally, we have to decide whether to support or reject the null hypothesis as a consequence of the test result (the *p*-value). This decision has consequences for the error that often occurs. Remember that the test decision is made from sample data only, which are random. That is, even if the data may provide evidence against the null hypothesis, another sample may yield the opposite result. Generally, given a null hypothesis H_0 and an alternative hypothesis H_1, we can differentiate between the true but unknown states of the world (either H_0 or H_1 is true), and the decision based on the statistical test (either rejection of H_0 or no rejection of H_0). Thus, four scenarios can arise:

1. H_0 is true but the test decision is *not* to reject H_0 → This is a correct decision.

2. H_0 is true but the test decision is to (erroneously) reject H_0 → This is a wrong decision.

The UNIVARIATE Procedure
Variable: LTV_orig_time

Tests for Location: Mu0=60				
Test		**Statistic**	**p Value**	
Student's t	t	1478.343	Pr > |t|	<.0001
Sign	M	277123	Pr >= |M|	<.0001
Signed Rank	S	9.452E10	Pr >= |S|	<.0001

Exhibit 3.14 Test for Location

3. H_0 is not true (and H_1 is true instead) and the test decision is to reject $H_0 \rightarrow$ This is a correct decision.

4. H_0 is not true (and H_1 is true instead) but the test decision is *not* to reject $H_0 \rightarrow$ This is a wrong decision.

Situations 1 and 3 are not problematic, but situations 2 and 4 might be, as a wrong decision occurs. We won't go into detail here but will follow up on this in the chapter on model validation.

Similar to confidence intervals, most standard procedures automatically compute p-values when a model is estimated. In PROC UNIVARIATE the p-values can be computed via the following code p-Value using the option TESTFORLOCATION. The option MU0=60 specifies the value under the null hypothesis.

```
ODS GRAPHICS ON;
ODS SELECT TESTSFORLOCATION ;
PROC UNIVARIATE DATA=data.mortgage MU0=60;
VAR LTV_orig_time;
RUN;
ODS GRAPHICS OFF;
```

PROC UNIVARIATE provides three different tests where only the first is of interest here. As can be seen in Exhibit 3.14, the p-value is lower than 0.0001 and therefore the mean LTV is significantly different from 60 and we should reject the null hypothesis that the LTV is 60 in the population.

There are huge numbers of different tests for various hypotheses (e.g., for medians, for standard deviations, for entire distributions) and we will not try to cover this in the introductory section. Most of the models estimated in this book and most of the SAS output will work with the standard tests as shown in this chapter.

REFERENCE

SAS Institute Inc. 2015. *SAS/STAT 14.1 User's Guide: Technical Report.* Cary, NC: SAS Institute.

CHAPTER 4

Data Preprocessing for Credit Risk Modeling

Data is the key ingredient for any credit risk model (Baesens 2014). Thus, it is vital to thoroughly consider and list all data sources of potential interest and relevance before modeling credit risk parameters such as probability of default (PD), loss given default (LGD), or exposure at default (EAD). Large experiments as well as a broad experience in different fields indicate that when it comes to data, bigger is better (Junqué de Fortuny, Martens, and Provost 2013). However, real-life credit risk data can be and typically is dirty because of inconsistencies, incompleteness, duplication, merging, and many other problems. Throughout the modeling steps, various data-filtering mechanisms will be applied to clean up and reduce the data to a manageable and relevant size. Worth mentioning here is the garbage in, garbage out (GIGO) principle, which essentially states that messy data will yield messy analytical models. It is of utmost importance that every data preprocessing step is carefully justified, carried out, validated, and documented before proceeding with further analysis; even the slightest mistake can make the data totally unusable for further analysis and the results invalid. In what follows, we will elaborate on the most important data preprocessing steps that should be considered during a credit risk modeling exercise. The activities discussed will apply to PD, LGD, and EAD modeling.

TYPES OF DATA SOURCES

First, let us have a closer look at what data to gather. Data can originate from a variety of different sources and provide different types of information that might be useful for the purpose of credit risk modeling, as will be further discussed in this section. The provided mixed discussion of different sources and types of data concerns a *broad*, *nonexhaustive*, and *non–mutually exclusive* categorization. We discuss the most prominent data sources and types of information available in a typical organization, but clearly not all possible data sources and types of information. Furthermore, some overlap may exist between the enlisted categories.

Transactional data is a first important source of data. It consists of structured and detailed information capturing the key characteristics of a customer transaction (e.g., cash transfer, installment payment). It is usually stored in massive online transaction processing (OLTP) relational databases. This data can also be summarized over longer time horizons by aggregating it into averages, absolute or relative trends, maximum or minimum values, and so forth.

Contractual, subscription, or account data may complement transactional data. Contractual data includes information about the type of product (e.g., loan) combined with customer characteristics. Examples of subscription data are the start date of the relationship, characteristics of a subscription such as type of services or products delivered, levels of service, cost of service, product guarantees, and insurances. The moment when a customer subscribes to a service offers a unique opportunity for the organization to get to know the customer—unique in the sense that it may be the only time when a direct contact exists between the bank and the customer, either in person, over the phone, or online—and as such it offers the opportunity to gather additional information that is nonessential to the contract but may be useful for credit risk modeling. Such information is typically stored in an account management or customer relationship management (CRM) database.

Subscription data may also be a source of **sociodemographic information**, since subscription or registration typically requires identification. Examples of socioeconomic characteristics of a population consisting of customers are *age, gender, marital status, income level, education level, occupation*, and *religion*. Although not very advanced or complex measures, sociodemographic information may significantly relate to credit risk behavior. For instance, it appears that both gender and age are very often related to an individual's likelihood to default: Women and older individuals are less likely to default than men and younger customers. Similar characteristics can also be defined when the basic entities for which default is to be detected do not concern individuals but instead companies or organizations. In such a setting one rather speaks of slow-moving data dimensions, factual data, or static characteristics. Examples include the address, year of foundation, industrial sector, and activity type. These do not change over time at all, or do not change as often as do other characteristics such as turnover, solvency, number of employees, and so on. These latter variables are examples of what we will call behavioral information. Several data sources may be consulted for retrieving sociodemographic or factual data, including subscription data sources as discussed previously, as well as data poolers, survey data, and publicly available data sources as discussed next.

In recent times, **data poolers** have increased in importance in the credit risk modeling industry. Examples are Experian, Equifax, CIFAS, Dun & Bradstreet, Thomson Reuters, and so on. The core business of these companies is to gather data (e.g., sociodemographic information) in particular settings or for particular purposes (e.g., credit risk assessment, fraud detection, and marketing) and sell it to interested customers looking to enrich or extend their data sources. In addition to selling data, these data poolers typically also build predictive models themselves and sell the outputs of these models as risk scores. This is a common practice in credit risk; for instance, in the United States the FICO score is a credit score ranging between 300 and 850 provided by the three most important credit data poolers or credit bureaus: Experian, Equifax, and TransUnion.[1] Many financial institutions as well as commercial vendors that give credit to customers use these FICO scores either as their final internal model to assess creditworthiness or to benchmark it against an internally developed credit scorecard to better understand the weaknesses of the latter.

Surveys are another source of data, and this information is gathered via offline methods such as mail, or via online modes including telephone, website, and social media interactions (e.g., Facebook, LinkedIn, or Twitter). Surveys may aim at gathering sociodemographic data, but also behavioral information.

Behavioral information concerns any information describing the behavior of an individual or an entity in the particular context under study. Such data is also called fast-moving data or dynamic characteristics. Examples of behavioral variables include information with regard to preferences of customers, usage information, frequencies of events, and trend variables. When dealing with organizations, examples of behavioral characteristics or dynamic characteristics are *turnover*, *solvency*, or *number of employees*. Marketing data results from monitoring the impact of marketing actions on the target population, and concerns a particular type of behavioral information.

Also, **unstructured data** embedded in text documents (e.g., e-mails, web pages, claim forms) or multimedia content can be interesting to analyze. However, these sources typically require extensive preprocessing before they can be successfully included in a credit risk modeling exercise. Analyzing textual data is the goal of a particular branch of analytics (i.e., text analytics). Given the high level of specialization involved, this book does not provide an extensive discussion of text mining techniques. For more information on this topic, you could consult academic textbooks on the subject (Chakraborty, Murali, and Satish 2013; Miner et al. 2012).

A second type of unstructured information is **contextual or network information**, meaning the context of a particular entity. An example of such contextual information concerns relations of a particular type that exist between an entity and other entities of the same or a different type. An example in credit risk modeling could be liquidity dependencies between corporate counterparts. Taking into account these complex network relationships allows us to model system risk whereby the default of one company may create a knock-on effect in the network of interconnected companies.

Another important source of data is **qualitative, expert-based data**. An expert is a person with a substantial amount of subject matter expertise within a particular setting (e.g., credit portfolio manager, brand manager). The expertise stems from both common sense and business experience, and it is important to elicit this knowledge as much as possible before the credit risk model building exercise commences. It will allow for steering the modeling in the right direction and interpreting the analytical results from the right perspective. A popular example of applying expert-based validation is checking the univariate signs of a regression model. For instance, an example already discussed relates to the observation that a higher age often results in a lower credit risk. Consequently, a negative sign is expected when including age in a default risk model yielding the probability of an individual being a defaulter. If this turns out not to be the case (e.g., due to bad data quality or multicollinearity), the expert or business user will not be tempted to use the credit risk model at all, since it contradicts prior expectations.

A final source of information concerns **publicly available** data sources, which can provide **external information**. This is contextual information that is not related to a particular entity, such as macroeconomic data (e.g., gross domestic product [GDP], inflation, unemployment). By enriching the data set with such information, you may see, for example, how the model and the model outputs vary as a function of the state of the economy. This information can then be used to calibrate or stress test the credit risk model.

Also, social media data from publicly available sources like Facebook, Twitter, or LinkedIn can be an important source of information. However, you need to be careful when both gathering and using such data and ensure that local and international privacy regulations are respected at all times.

MERGING DATA SOURCES

Building a credit risk model typically requires or presumes the data to be presented in a single table containing and representing all the data in a structured manner. A structured data table allows straightforward processing and analysis.

The rows of a data table typically represent the basic entities to which the analysis applies (e.g., customers, companies, and countries). The rows are referred to as instances, observations, or lines. The columns in the data table contain information about the basic entities. Many synonyms are used to denote the columns of the data table, such as (explanatory) variables, fields, characteristics, attributes, indicators, or features.

In order to construct the aggregated, nonnormalized data table to facilitate further analysis, often several normalized source data tables have to be merged. Merging tables involves selecting information from different tables related to an individual entity, and copying it to the aggregated data table. The individual entity can be recognized and selected in the different tables by making use of *keys*, which are attributes that have been included in the table exactly to allow identifying and relating observations from different source tables pertaining to the same entity. Exhibit 4.1 illustrates the process of merging two tables (i.e., transaction data and customer data) into a single nonnormalized data table by making use of the key attribute *ID*, which allows connecting observations in the transactions table with observations in the customer table. The same approach can be taken to merge as many tables as required, but clearly, the more tables that are merged, the more duplicate data might be included in the resulting table.

When merging data tables, it is crucial that no errors occur, so some checks should be applied to control the resulting table and to make sure that all information is correctly integrated.

Transactions		
ID	Date	Amount
XWV	2/01/2015	52 €
XWV	6/02/2015	21 €
XWV	3/03/2015	13 €
BBC	17/02/2015	45 €
BBC	1/03/2015	75 €
VVQ	2/03/2015	56 €

Customer data		
ID	Age	Start date
XWV	31	1/01/2015
BBC	49	10/02/2015
VVQ	21	15/02/2015

Non-normalized data table				
ID	Date	Amount	Age	Start date
XWV	2/01/2015	52 €	31	1/01/2015
XWV	6/02/2015	21 €	31	1/01/2015
XWV	3/03/2015	13 €	31	1/01/2015
BBC	17/02/2015	45 €	49	10/02/2015
BBC	1/03/2015	75 €	49	10/02/2015
VVQ	2/03/2015	56 €	21	15/02/2015

Exhibit 4.1 Aggregating Normalized Data Tables into a Non-normalized Data Table

Data sets can be merged in SAS after sorting by the key variable using the DATA/MERGE command. Other ways to combine data sets in Base SAS include concatenating (DATA/SET command), appending (PROC APPEND), and updating (DATA/UPDATE command).

SAMPLING

We already discussed sampling in Chapter 3, Exploratory Data Analysis. Within the context of building scorecards, the aim of sampling is to take a subset of historical data (e.g., past customers), and use that to build the credit risk model. A first obvious question that comes to mind concerns the need for sampling. With the availability of high-performance computing facilities (e.g., grid and cloud computing), you could also try to directly analyze the full data set. However, a key requirement for a good sample is that it should be representative for the future entities on which the credit risk model will be run. Hence, the timing aspect becomes important since customers of today are more similar to customers of tomorrow than customers of yesterday are. Choosing the optimal time window of the sample involves a trade-off between lots of data (and hence a more robust credit risk model) and recent data (which may be more representative). The sample should also be taken from a representative business period to produce a picture of the target population that is as accurate as possible.

It speaks for itself that sampling bias should be avoided as much as possible. However, this is not always that straightforward. Let's take the example of credit scoring. Assume you want to build an application scorecard to score mortgage applications. The future population then consists of all customers who knock on the door of the bank and apply for a mortgage—the so-called through-the-door (TTD) population. You then need a subset of the historical through-the-door population to build an analytical model. However, in the past the bank was already applying a credit policy (either expert based or based on a previous analytical model). This implies that the historical TTD population has two subsets: the customers who were

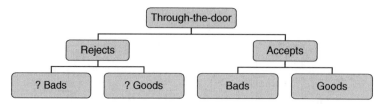

Exhibit 4.2 The Reject Inference Problem in Credit Scoring

accepted with the old policy, and the ones who were rejected (see Exhibit 4.2). Obviously, for the latter, we don't know the target value since they were never granted the credit. When building a sample, you can then only make use of the accepts, which clearly implies a bias. Procedures to deal with reject inference have been suggested in the literature (Thomas, Edelman, and Crook 2002). We discuss some of these in Chapter 5 on credit scoring.

Another potential bias concerns seasonality effects. Since every month may in fact deviate from *normal*, if normal is defined as average, it could make sense to build separate models for different months, or for *homogeneous* time frames. This is a rather complex and demanding solution from an operational perspective, since multiple models have to be developed, run, maintained, and monitored. Alternatively, a sample may be gathered by sampling observations over a period covering a full business cycle. Then only a single model has to be developed, run, maintained, and monitored, which may possibly come at a cost of reduced performance since it's less tailored to a particular time frame. However, this approach will be less complex and costly to operate.

In stratified sampling, a sample is taken according to predefined strata. In a default risk context, data sets are typically very skewed (e.g., 99 percent nondefaulters and 1 percent defaulters). When stratifying according to the target default indicator, the sample will contain exactly the same percentages of default and nondefault customers as in the original data. Additional stratification can be applied on predictor variables as well, for instance in order for the number of observations across different industry categories to closely resemble the real industry category distribution. However, as long as no large deviations exist with respect to the sample and observed distribution of predictor variables, it will usually be sufficient to limit stratification to the target variable.

In Base SAS, PROC SURVEYSELECT can be used to create a stratified sample as follows:

```
PROC SORT DATA=data.hmeq;
    BY bad;
RUN;


PROC SURVEYSELECT DATA=data.hmeq
METHOD=SRS N=1000 SEED=12345 OUT=data.mySample;
STRATA bad / ALLOC=PROP;
RUN;
```

Before a stratified sample can be created, the data needs to be sorted on the stratification variable using PROC SORT. The options of PROC SURVEYSELECT can be explained as follows:

- METHOD=SRS: Applies simple random sampling.
- N=1000: Creates a sample of 1,000 observations.
- SEED=12345: The seed needed to randomly sample the observations.
- OUT=data.mySample: The result will be stored in the data set mySample.
- STRATA bad / ALLOC=PROP: The stratification variable is bad and the allocation method used is proportional.

We can now use PROC FREQ to contrast the bad distribution of the sample with the original data as follows:

```
PROC FREQ DATA=data.hmeq;
TABLES bad;
RUN;


PROC FREQ DATA=data.mySample;
TABLES bad;
RUN;
```

For the original data HMEQ, this gives the result shown in Exhibit 4.3.

For the sample mySample, this gives the result shown in Exhibit 4.4.

It can be seen that, thanks to the stratification, the percentage of defaults is similar in the sample and the original data.

In SAS Enterprise Miner, a sample can be created using the Sample node from the Sample tab (see Exhibit 4.5). Various sample methods are supported such as First N, Stratify, Random, Cluster, and Systematic. In case a class variable is present (e.g., in case of modeling default risk), the default setting is to stratify based on the class variable. The random seed is used for randomly selecting the observations. The same

The FREQ Procedure

BAD	Frequency	Percent	Cumulative Frequency	Cumulative Percent
0	4771	80.05	4771	80.05
1	1189	19.95	5960	100.00

Exhibit 4.3 The FREQ Procedure

The FREQ Procedure

BAD	Frequency	Percent	Cumulative Frequency	Cumulative Percent
0	801	80.10	801	80.10
1	199	19.90	1000	100.00

Exhibit 4.4 The FREQ Procedure

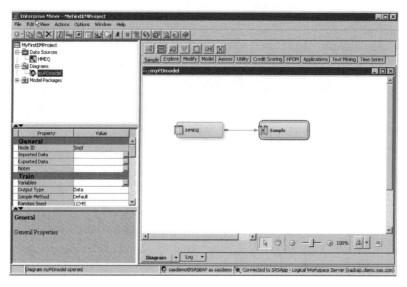

Exhibit 4.5 Sampling in SAS Enterprise Miner

random seed will result in the same random sample. The size of the sample can be specified as the number of observations or as a percentage of the total number of observations.

TYPES OF DATA ELEMENTS

It is important to appropriately consider the different types of data elements at the start of each credit risk modeling exercise. The following types of data elements can be considered:

- Continuous data

    These are data elements that are defined on an interval that can be either limited or unlimited.

    A distinction is sometimes made between continuous data with and without a natural zero value; they are respectively referred to as ratio data (e.g., amounts) and interval data (e.g., temperature in degrees Celsius or Fahrenheit). In the latter case, the interval between values is interpretable. However, it does not make sense to take the ratio of two values and make statements such as "It is double or twice as hot as last month." Most continuous data in a credit risk modeling setting concerns ratio data, since we are often dealing with amounts.

    Examples: loan-to-value (LTV) ratio; income; balance on checking/savings account.

- Categorical data

    - Nominal. These are data elements that can only take on a limited set of values with no meaningful ordering in between.

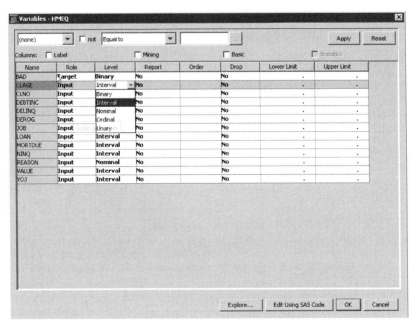

Exhibit 4.6 Setting the Measurement Level of Variables in SAS Enterprise Miner

Examples: payment type; industry sector.

■ Ordinal. These are data elements that can only take on a limited set of values with a meaningful ordering in between.

Examples: credit rating; age coded as young, middle-aged, or old.

■ Binary. These are data elements that can only take on one of two values.

Examples: default (yes/no); employed (yes/no).

Appropriately distinguishing between these different data elements is of key importance to start the analysis when importing the data into SAS. For example, if marital status were incorrectly specified as a continuous data element, then SAS would calculate its mean, standard deviation, and so on, which is obviously meaningless and may perturb the analysis. In SAS Enterprise Miner, the type of variable can be specified by setting the measurement level as Binary, Interval, Nominal, Ordinal, or Unary (see Exhibit 4.6). Note that the last level represents a variable with only one value, which is meaningless for modeling.

VISUAL DATA EXPLORATION AND EXPLORATORY STATISTICAL ANALYSIS

Visual data exploration is a very important step in getting to know your data in an informal way. It allows you to gain some initial insights into the data that can then be usefully adopted throughout the modeling stage. Different plots/graphs can be useful here. Bar charts represent the frequency of each of the values (either absolute

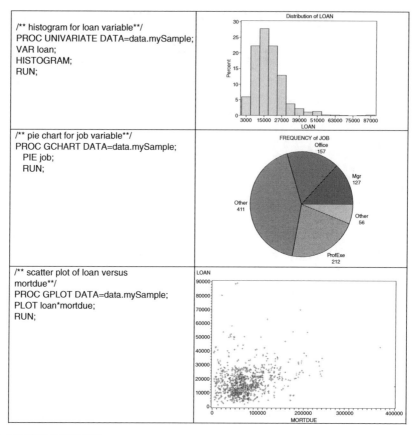

Exhibit 4.7 Plots in Base SAS

or relative) as bars. A bar chart or histogram provides an easy way to visualize the central tendency and to determine the variability or spread of the data. It also allows you to contrast the observed data with standard known distributions (e.g., the normal distribution). A pie chart represents a variable's distribution as a pie, whereby each section represents the percentage taken by each value of the variable. The total of all pie slices is equal to 100 percent.

Other handy visual tools are scatter plots. Plots such as these allow you to visualize one variable against another to see whether there are any correlation patterns in the data. Also, online analytical processing (OLAP)-based multidimensional data analysis can be usefully adopted to explore patterns in the data.

Exhibit 4.7 illustrates how to create histograms, pie charts, and scatter plots in Base SAS using PROC UNIVARIATE, PROC GCHART, and PROC GPLOT.

In SAS Enterprise Miner, the MultiPlot node from the Explore tab is a handy node to visually explore your data (see Exhibit 4.8). It allows you to create both histograms and scatter plots for each of the variables. Exhibit 4.9 displays the histogram of job status versus good/bad status.

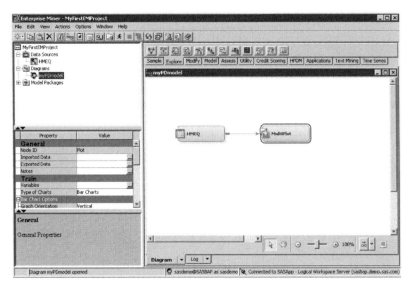

Exhibit 4.8 The Multiplot Node in SAS Enterprise Miner

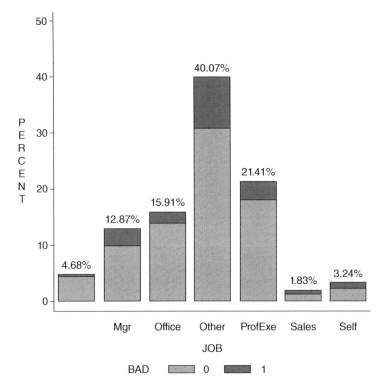

Exhibit 4.9 Histogram of Job Status versus Good/Bad Status

DESCRIPTIVE STATISTICS

In addition to the preparatory visual data exploration, several descriptive statistics might be calculated that provide basic insight or *feeling* for the data. Plenty of descriptive statistics exist that all summarize or provide information with respect to a particular characteristic of the data, and therefore descriptive statistics should be assessed together (i.e., in support and completion of each other). We have already discussed most of these in the exploratory data analysis chapter, and quickly refresh them here.

Basic descriptive statistics are the mean and median value of continuous variables, with the median value being less sensitive to extreme values (i.e., outliers), but not providing as much information with respect to the full distribution. Complementary to the mean value, the variation or the standard deviation provides insight with respect to how much the data is spread around the mean value. Likewise, percentile values such as the 10th, 25th, 75th, and 90th percentile provide further information with respect to the distribution and as a complement to the median value.

Specific descriptive statistics exist to express the symmetry or asymmetry of a distribution, such as the *skewness* measure, as well as the peakedness or flatness of a distribution (e.g., the *kurtosis* measure). However, the exact values of these measures are likely a bit harder to interpret than the value of the mean and the standard deviation, for instance. This limits their practical use. Instead, you could more easily assess these aspects by inspecting visual plots of the distributions of the involved variables.

When dealing with categorical variables, instead of the median and the mean value you may calculate the mode, which is the most frequently occurring value. In other words, the mode is the most typical value for the variable at hand. The mode is not necessarily unique, since multiple values can result in the same maximum frequency.

Descriptive statistics can be calculated in Base SAS using PROC UNIVARIATE as follows:

```
PROC UNIVARIATE DATA=data.mySample;
VAR loan;
RUN;
```

The results are displayed in Exhibit 4.10.

In SAS Enterprise Miner, the StatExplore node from the Explore tab can be used to calculate the descriptive statistics (see Exhibit 4.11). This node will calculate various descriptive statistics for each of the variables (see Exhibit 4.12) and also report these for each of the target classes individually (see Exhibit 4.13).

MISSING VALUES

Missing values can occur for various reasons. The information can be nonapplicable. For example, when modeling the amount of loss for obligors, then this information is available only for the defaulters and not for the nondefaulters since it is not applicable there. The information can also be undisclosed, such as when a customer decides

The UNIVARIATE Procedure
Variable: LOAN

Moments			
N	1000	Sum Weights	1000
Mean	17898.3	Sum Observations	17898300
Std Deviation	10331.742	Variance	106744892
Skewness	1.92510314	Kurtosis	7.2790685
Uncorrected SS	4.26987E11	Corrected SS	1.06638E11
Coeff Variation	57.7247111	Std Error Mean	326.718368

Basic Statistical Measures			
Location		Variability	
Mean	17898.30	Std Deviation	10332
Median	16000.00	Variance	106744892
Mode	15000.00	Range	87200
		Interquartile Range	11750

Tests for Location: Mu0=0				
Test	Statistic		p Value	
Student's t	t	54.78204	Pr > |t|	<.0001
Sign	M	500	Pr >= |M|	<.0001
Signed Rank	S	250250	Pr >= |S|	<.0001

Quantiles (Definition 5)	
Level	Quantile
100% Max	89200
99%	51900
95%	36350
90%	28250
75% Q3	22500
50% Median	16000
25% Q1	10750
10%	7200
5%	5600
1%	3800
0% Min	2000

Exhibit 4.10 Results of PROC Univariate

Extreme Observations			
Lowest		Highest	
Value	Obs	Value	Obs
2000	803	62900	797
2000	802	69700	798
2400	804	80300	799
3000	805	88500	800
3000	1	89200	801

Exhibit 4.10 (*Continued*)

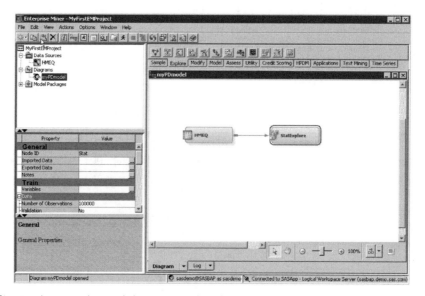

Exhibit 4.11 The StatExplore Node in SAS Enterprise Miner

Variable	Role	Mean	Standard Deviation	Non Missing	Missing	Minimum	Median	Maximum	Skewness	Kurtosis
CLAGE	INPUT	179.7663	85.81009	5652	308	0	173.4667	1168.234	1.343412	7.599549
CLNO	INPUT	21.2961	10.13893	5738	222	0	20	71	0.775052	1.157673
DEBTINC	INPUT	33.77992	8.601746	4693	1267	0.524499	34.81696	203.3121	2.852353	50.50404
DELINQ	INPUT	0.449442	1.127266	5380	580	0	0	15	4.02315	23.56545
DEROG	INPUT	0.25457	0.846047	5252	708	0	0	10	5.32087	36.87276
LOAN	INPUT	18607.97	11207.48	5960	0	1100	16300	89900	2.023781	6.93259
MORTDUE	INPUT	73760.82	44457.61	5442	518	2063	65017	399550	1.814481	6.481866
NINQ	INPUT	1.186055	1.728675	5450	510	0	1	17	2.621984	9.786507
VALUE	INPUT	101776	57385.78	5848	112	8000	89231	855909	3.053344	24.3628
YOJ	INPUT	8.922268	7.573982	5445	515	0	7	41	0.98846	0.372072

Exhibit 4.12 Descriptive Statistics for the HMEQ Data Set

Data Role=TRAIN Variable=CLAGE

Target	Target Level	Median	Missing	Non Missing	Minimum	Maximum	Mean	Standard Deviation	Skewness	Kurtosis
BAD	0	180.2841	230	4541	0.486711	649.7471	187.0024	84.46522	0.901459	2.191917
BAD	1	132.8667	78	1111	0	1168.234	150.1902	84.95229	3.480899	35.27536
OVERALL		173.4667	308	5652	0	1168.234	179.7663	85.81009	1.343412	7.599549

Exhibit 4.13 Class Conditional Descriptive Statistics for the HMEQ Data Set

not to disclose his or her income for privacy reasons. Missing data can also originate because of an error during merging (e.g., typos in name or ID).

Some analytical techniques (e.g., decision trees) can deal directly with missing values. Other techniques need some additional preprocessing. The following are the most popular schemes that deal with missing values (Little and Rubin 2002, 408):

- **Replace (impute).** This implies replacing the missing value with a known value. For example, consider the example in Exhibit 4.14. You could impute the missing credit bureau scores with the average or median of the known values. For marital status the mode can then be used. You could also apply regression-based imputation whereby a regression model is estimated to model a target variable (e.g., credit bureau score) based on the other information available (e.g., age, income). The latter is more sophisticated, although the added value from an empirical viewpoint (e.g., in terms of model performance) is questionable.

- **Delete.** This is the most straightforward option and consists of deleting observations or variables with lots of missing values. This of course assumes that information is missing at random and has no meaningful interpretation and/or relationship to the target.

ID	Age	Income	Marital Status	Credit Bureau Score	Default
1	34	1,800	?	620	Yes
2	28	1,200	Single	?	No
3	22	1,000	Single	?	No
4	60	2,200	Widowed	700	Yes
5	58	2,000	Married	?	No
6	44	?	?	?	No
7	22	1,200	Single	?	No
8	26	1,500	Married	350	No
9	34	?	Single	?	Yes
10	50	2,100	Divorced	?	No

Exhibit 4.14 Dealing with Missing Values

■ **Keep.** Missing values can be meaningful. For example, if a customer did not disclose his or her income because he or she is currently unemployed, this fact may have a relationship with default and needs to be considered as a separate category.

As a practical way of working, you can first start by statistically testing whether missing information is related to the target variable (using, e.g., a chi-square test, discussed later). If yes, then you can adopt the keep strategy and make a special category for it. If not, depending on the number of observations available, you can decide to either delete or impute.

In Base SAS, PROC STANDARD can be used to replace missing values. Consider the following statement:

```
PROC STANDARD DATA =data.mysample REPLACE OUT=data.mysamplenomissing;
RUN;
```

This will replace all missing values of the continuous variables with the mean. The missing values for the categorical variables will remain untreated. Note that PROC STANDARD cannot be used to impute with the median or other values. In this case, this should be manually programmed using a set of data manipulation statements.

In SAS Enterprise Miner, missing values can be treated using the Impute node from the Modify tab (see Exhibit 4.15). This node provides separate treatment options for the class and interval variables. In our example, the missing categorical variables will be replaced with the mode (indicated by Default Input Method=Count in the Class Variables section), and missing interval variables will be replaced by the median (indicated by Default Input Method=Median in the Interval Variables section).

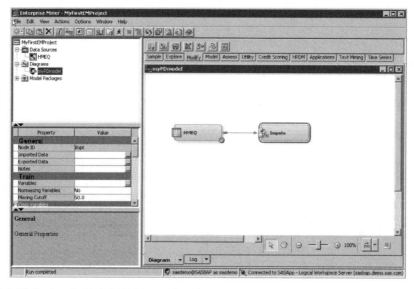

Exhibit 4.15 The Impute Node in SAS Enterprise Miner

OUTLIER DETECTION AND TREATMENT

Outliers are extreme observations that are very dissimilar to the rest of the population. Actually, two types of outliers can be considered:

1. Valid observations (e.g., salary of boss is $1 million)
2. Invalid observations (e.g., age is 300 years)

Both are univariate outliers in the sense that they are outlying on one dimension. However, outliers can be hidden in unidimensional views of the data. Multivariate outliers are observations that are outlying in multiple dimensions. Exhibit 4.16 gives an example of two outlying observations considering the dimensions of both income and age.

Two important steps in dealing with outliers are detection and treatment. A first obvious check for outliers is to calculate the minimum and maximum values for each of the data elements. Various graphical tools can be used to detect outliers. Histograms are a first example. Exhibit 4.17 presents an example of a distribution for age whereby the circled areas clearly represent outliers.

Box plots (see Chapter 3, Exploratory Data Analysis) can also be used to detect outliers. Another way is to calculate z-scores, measuring how many standard deviations an observation lies away from the mean, as follows:

$$z_i = \frac{x_i - \overline{x_i}}{s},$$

whereby $\overline{x_i}$ represents the average of the variable and s its standard deviation. An example is given in Exhibit 4.18. Note that by definition the z-scores will have a mean of zero and standard deviation of one.

A practical rule of thumb then defines outliers when the absolute value of the z-score $|z|$ is bigger than 3. Note that the z-score method relies on the normal distribution.

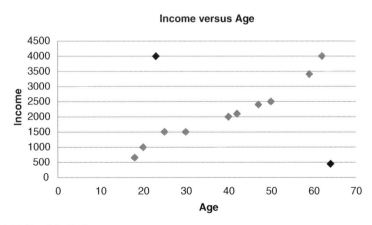

Exhibit 4.16 Multivariate Outliers

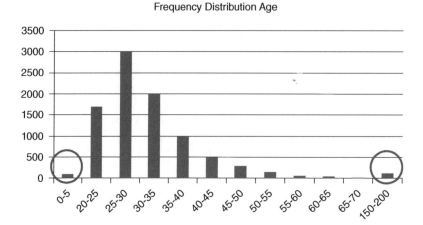

Exhibit 4.17 Histogram for Outlier Detection

ID	Age	z-Score
1	30	$(30 - 40)/10 = -1$
2	50	$(50 - 40)/10 = +1$
3	10	$(10 - 40)/10 = -3$
4	40	$(40 - 40)/10 = 0$
5	60	$(60 - 40)/10 = +2$
6	80	$(80 - 40)/10 = +4$
...	...	...
	$\overline{x_i} = 40 \ s = 10$	$\overline{x_i} = 0 \ s = 1$

Exhibit 4.18 z-Scores for Outlier Detection

The preceding methods all focus on univariate outliers. Multivariate outliers can be detected by fitting regression lines and inspecting the observations with large errors (e.g., using a residual plot). Alternative methods are clustering or calculating the Mahalanobis distance. Note, however, that although potentially useful, multivariate outlier detection is typically not considered in many modeling exercises due to the typically marginal impact on model performance.

Some analytical techniques (e.g., decision trees, neural networks, support vector machines [SVMs]) are fairly robust with respect to outliers. Others (e.g., linear/logistic regression) are more sensitive to them. Various schemes exist to deal with outliers. It highly depends upon whether the outlier represents a valid or an invalid observation. For invalid observations (e.g., age is 300 years), you could treat the outlier as a missing value using any of the schemes discussed in the previous section. For valid observations (e.g., income is $1 million), other schemes are needed. A popular scheme is truncation/capping/winsorizing. You hereby impose both a lower limit and an upper limit on a variable and any values below/above are brought back to these limits. The limits can be calculated using the z-scores (see Exhibit 4.19) or the

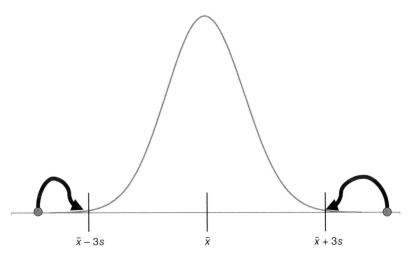

Exhibit 4.19 Using the z-Scores for Truncation

interquartile range (IQR) (which is more robust than the z-scores), as follows (see Van Gestel and Baesens 2009):

Upper/lower limit $= M \pm 3s$, with $M =$ median and $s = IQR/(2 \times 0.6745)$

A sigmoid transformation ranging between 0 and 1 can also be used for capping, as follows:

$$f(x) = \frac{1}{1 + e^{-x}}$$

Also, expert-based limits based on business knowledge and/or experience can be imposed.

An important remark concerning outliers is the fact that not all invalid values are outlying, and as such may go unnoted if not explicitly looked into. For instance, a clear issue exists when observing customers with values *gender = male* and *pregnant = yes*. Which value is invalid, either the value for gender or the value for pregnant, cannot be determined, but neither value is outlying and therefore such a conflict will not be noted by the analyst unless some explicit precautions are taken. In order to detect particular invalid combinations, you may construct a set of rules that are formulated based on expert knowledge and experience, which is applied to the data to check and alert for issues. In this particular context a network representation of the variables may be of use to construct the rule set and reason upon relationships that exist between the different variables, with links representing constraints that apply to the combination of variable values and resulting in rules added to the rule set.

In Base SAS, we can filter outliers based on the z-scores by using PROC STANDARD as follows:

```
PROC STANDARD DATA =data.mysample MEAN=0 STD=1 OUT=data.zscores;
VAR clage clno debtinc delinq derog loan mortdue ninq value yoj;
RUN;
```

The preceding statement will calculate the z-scores for each of the continuous variables. We can then filter out the outliers by requiring that all z-scores should be less than 3 in absolute value, as follows:

```
DATA data.filteredsample;
SET data.zscores;
WHERE ABS(clage) < 3 & ABS(clno) <3  & ABS(debtinc) < 3 & ABS(delinq)<3
  & ABS(derog) < 3
& ABS(loan) < 3 & ABS(mortdue)< 3 & ABS(ninq)<3 & ABS(value) < 3 & ABS(yoj)
 < 3;
RUN;
```

The resulting data set, filteredsample, will have 890 observations; in other words, 110 observations have been removed.

In SAS Enterprise Miner, the Filter node from the Sample tab can be used to filter or remove the outliers (see Exhibit 4.20). In our example, we will remove observations with class values that occur less than 1 percent for class variables with fewer than 25 values. We will also remove observations with interval variables that are more than 3 standard deviations away from the mean (the latter can be specified in the Tuning Parameters property).

The Replacement node from the Modify tab can be used for outlier truncation (see Exhibit 4.21). In the example, interval variables will be truncated to the mean ± 3 standard deviations (specified by the Default Limits method and Cutoff Values properties in the Interval Variables section). For class variables, a replacement editor is provided where the user can manually enter the new values for each of the class variables.

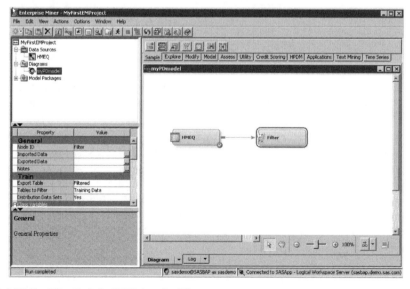

Exhibit 4.20 The Filter Node in SAS Enterprise Miner

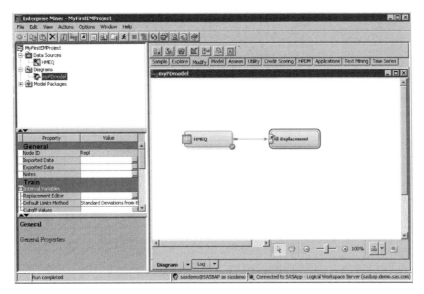

Exhibit 4.21 The Replacement Node in SAS Enterprise Miner

STANDARDIZING DATA

Standardizing data is a data preprocessing activity targeted at scaling variables to a similar range. Consider, for example, two variables gender (coded as 0/1) and income (ranging between zero and $1 million). When building logistic regression models using both information elements, the coefficient for income might become very small. Hence, it could make sense to bring them back to a similar scale. The following standardization procedures could be adopted:

- Min/max standardization
  - $x_{new} = \frac{x_{old} - \min(x_{old})}{\max(x_{old}) - \min(x_{old})}(newmax - newmin) + newmin$, whereby *newmax* and *newmin* are the newly imposed maximum and minimum (e.g., 1 and 0).
- z-score standardization
  - Calculate the z-scores (see the previous section).
- Decimal scaling
  - Dividing by a power of 10, as follows: $x_{new} = \frac{x_{old}}{10^n}$, with n the number of digits of the maximum absolute value.

Again note that standardization is especially useful for regression-based approaches but is not needed for some approaches like decision trees.

As we already illustrated in the section on outliers, the z-scores can be calculated using PROC STANDARD in Base SAS.

In SAS Enterprise Miner, the Transform Variables node from the Modify tab can be used to standardize or transform the data. In our example, all interval variables will be standardized to zero mean and unit standard deviation by calculating

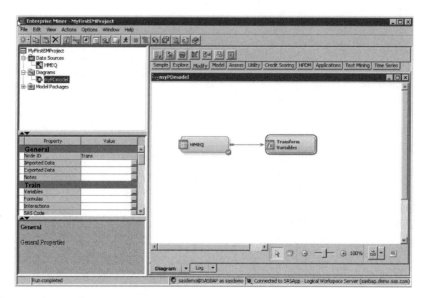

Exhibit 4.22 The Transform Variables Node in SAS Enterprise Miner

the z-scores (specified by the Interval Inputs=Standardize property in the Default Methods section).

CATEGORIZATION

Categorization (also referred to as coarse classification, classing, grouping, or binning) can be done for various reasons. For categorical variables, it is needed to reduce the number of categories. Consider, for example, the variable *industry sector* having 50 different values. When this variable is put into a (logistic) regression model, you would need 49 dummy variables (50 – 1 because of the collinearity), which would necessitate the estimation of 49 parameters for only one variable. With categorization, you create categories of values such that fewer parameters will have to be estimated and a more robust model is obtained.

For continuous variables, categorization may also be beneficial. Consider, for example, the age variable and the observed default rate as depicted in Exhibit 4.23. Clearly, there is a nonmonotonous relationship between risk of default and age. If a nonlinear model (e.g., neural network, support vector machine) were used, then the nonlinearity could be perfectly modeled. However, if a regression model were used (which is typically more common because of its interpretability), then since it can only fit on a line, it would miss out on the nonmonotonicity. By categorizing the variable into ranges, part of the nonmonotonicity can be taken into account in the regression. Hence, categorization of continuous variables can be useful to model nonlinear effects in linear models.

Various methods can be used to do categorization. Two very basic methods are equal-interval binning and equal-frequency binning. Consider, for example, the

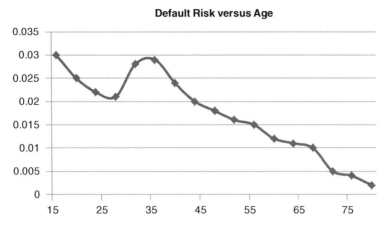

Exhibit 4.23 Default Risk versus Age

income values 1,000, 1,200, 1,300, 2,000, 1,800, 1,400. Equal-interval binning would create two bins with the same range (Bin 1: 1,000, 1,500, and Bin 2: 1,500, 2,000), whereas equal-frequency binning would create two bins with the same number of observations (Bin 1: 1,000, 1,200, 1,300, and Bin 2: 1,400, 1,800, 2,000). However, both methods are quite basic and do not take into account the target variable or default risk. We provide further examples in the context of rating class formation in the chapters on exploratory data analysis and discrete time hazard models.

Most analytics software tools have built-in facilities to perform categorization. A very handy and simple approach (available in Microsoft Excel) is to use pivot tables. Consider the example shown in Exhibit 4.24.

We can then construct a pivot table and calculate the odds as shown in Exhibit 4.25.

We can then categorize the values based on similar odds. One example would be category 1 (travel, house), category 2 (study), and category 3 (car, furniture).

Customer ID	Age	Purpose of Loan	...	Default
C1	44	Travel		No
C2	20	House		No
C3	58	Car		Yes
C4	26	Travel		No
C5	30	Study		Yes
C6	32	Furniture		No
C7	48	House		Yes
C8	60	Travel		No
...	...	...		

Exhibit 4.24 Coarse Classifying the Purpose of Loan Variable

	Travel	Car	Furniture	House	Study	...
Good	1,000	2,000	3,000	100	5,000	
Bad	500	100	200	80	800	
Odds	2	20	15	1.25	6.25	

Exhibit 4.25 Pivot Table for Coarse Classifying the Purpose of Loan Variable

Attribute	Owner	Rent Unfurnished	Rent Furnished	With Parents	Other	No Answer	Total
Good	6,000	1,600	350	950	90	10	9,000
Bad	300	400	140	100	50	10	1,000
Good/Bad Odds	20:1	4:1	2.5:1	9.5:1	1.8:1	1:1	9:1

Exhibit 4.26 Coarse Classifying the Residential Status Variable

Chi-square analysis is a more sophisticated way to perform categorization. Consider the example depicted in Exhibit 4.26 for coarse classifying a residential status variable.[2]

Suppose we want three categories and consider the following options:

- Option 1: owners; renters; others
- Option 2: owners; with parents; others

Both options can now be investigated using chi-square analysis. The purpose is to compare the empirically observed with the independence frequencies. For Option 1, the empirically observed frequencies are depicted in Exhibit 4.27.

The independence frequencies can be calculated as follows. The number of good owners given that the odds are the same as in the whole population is $6,300/10,000 * 9,000/10,000 * 10,000 = 5,670$. We then obtain Exhibit 4.28.

The more the numbers in both tables differ, the less independence and hence the more dependence and a better coarse classification. Formally, we can calculate the chi-square distance as follows:

$$\chi^2 = \frac{(6,000 - 5,670)^2}{5,670} + \frac{(300 - 630)^2}{630} + \frac{(1,950 - 2,241)^2}{2,241} + \frac{(540 - 249)^2}{249}$$
$$+ \frac{(1,050 - 1,089)^2}{1,089} + \frac{(160 - 121)^2}{121} = 583$$

Attribute	Owners	Renters	Others	Total
Good	6,000	1,950	1,050	9,000
Bad	300	540	160	1,000
Total	6,300	2,490	1,210	10,000

Exhibit 4.27 Empirical Frequencies Option 1 for Coarse Classifying Residential Status

Attribute	Owners	Renters	Others	Total
Good	5,670	2,241	1,089	9,000
Bad	630	249	121	1,000
Total	6,300	2,490	1,210	10,000

Exhibit 4.28 Independence Frequencies Option 1 for Coarse Classifying Residential Status

Likewise, for option 2, the calculation becomes:

$$\chi^2 = \frac{(6,000 - 5,670)^2}{5,670} + \frac{(300 - 630)^2}{630} + \frac{(950 - 945)^2}{945} + \frac{(100 - 105)^2}{105}$$
$$+ \frac{(2,050 - 2,385)^2}{2,385} + \frac{(600 - 265)^2}{265} = 662$$

So, based on the chi-square values, option 2 is the better categorization. Note that formally you need to compare the value with a chi-square distribution with $k - 1$ degrees of freedom, with k the number of values of the characteristic.

In Base SAS, we can start by first defining the data set as follows:

```
DATA residence;
    INPUT default$ resstatus$ count;
    DATALINES;
good owner 6000
good rentunf 1600
good rentfurn 350
good withpar 950
good other 90
good noanswer 10
bad owner 300
bad rentunf 400
bad rentfurn 140
bad withpar 100
bad other 50
bad noanswer 10
;
```

We can now also create the data sets for both categorization options:

```
DATA coarse1;
    INPUT default$ resstatus$ count;
    DATALINES;
good owner 6000
good renter 1950
good other 1050
bad owner 300
```

```
bad renter 540
bad other 160
;

DATA coarse2;
    INPUT default$ resstatus$ count;
    DATALINES;
good owner 6000
good withpar 950
good other 2050
bad owner 300
bad withpar 100
bad other 600
;
```

We can now run PROC FREQ on both options as follows:

```
PROC FREQ DATA=coarse1;
    WEIGHT count;
    TABLES default*resstatus / CHISQ;
RUN;
```

This will give the output depicted in Exhibit 4.29.
We can now also examine Option 2 as follows:

```
PROC FREQ DATA=coarse2;
    WEIGHT count;
    TABLES default*resstatus / CHISQ;
RUN;
```

This will give the output depicted in Exhibit 4.30.

WEIGHTS OF EVIDENCE CODING

Categorization reduces the number of categories for categorical variables. For continuous variables, categorization will introduce new variables. Consider a regression model with age characteristics (four categories, so three parameters) and purpose characteristics (five categories, so four parameters). The model then looks like the following:

$$D = \beta_0 + \beta_1 \text{Age}_1 + \beta_2 \text{Age}_2 + \beta_3 \text{Age}_3 + \beta_4 \text{Purp}_1 + \beta_5 \text{Purp}_2 + \beta_6 \text{Purp}_3 + \beta_7 \text{Purp}_4$$

with $D = 1$ for defaulters, and 0 otherwise.

Despite having only two characteristics, the model still needs eight parameters to be estimated. It would be handy to have a monotonic transformation $f(.)$ such that

The FREQ Procedure

default	resstatus			
	other	owner	renter	Total
Bad	160	300	540	1000
	1.60	3.00	5.40	10.00
	16.00	30.00	54.00	
	13.22	4.76	21.69	
Good	1050	6000	1950	9000
	10.50	60.00	19.50	90.00
	11.67	66.67	21.67	
	86.78	95.24	78.31	
Total	1210	6300	2490	10000
	12.10	63.00	24.90	100.00

Table of default by resstatus

The FREQ Procedure

Statistics for Table of default by resstatus

Statistic	DF	Value	Prob
Chi-Square	2	583.9019	<.0001
Likelihood Ratio Chi-Square	2	540.0817	<.0001
Mantel-Haenszel Chi-Square	1	199.5185	<.0001
Phi Coefficient		0.2416	
Contingency Coefficient		0.2349	
Cramer's V		0.2416	

Exhibit 4.29 Output for Categorization Option 1

our model could be rewritten as follows:

$$D = \beta_0 + \beta_1 f(\text{Age}_1, \text{Age}_2, \text{Age}_3) + \beta_2 f(\text{Purp}_1, \text{Purp}_2, \text{Purp}_3, \text{Purp}_4)$$

The transformation should have a monotonically increasing or decreasing relationship with D. Weights of evidence (WOE) coding is one example of a transformation that can be used for this purpose. This is illustrated in Exhibit 4.31.

The WOE is calculated as: ln(Dist Good/Dist Bad). Because of the logarithmic transformation, a positive WOE means Dist Good > Dist Bad; a negative WOE means Dist Good < Dist Bad. WOE coding thus implements a transformation that is monotonically related to the target variable.

The model can then be reformulated as follows:

$$D = \beta_0 + \beta_1 \text{WOE}_{\text{age}} + \beta_2 \text{WOE}_{\text{purpose}}$$

The FREQ Procedure

Table of default by resstatus

default	resstatus			
	other	owner	withpar	Total
Bad	600	300	100	1000
	6.00	3.00	1.00	10.00
	60.00	30.00	10.00	
	22.64	4.76	9.52	
Good	2050	6000	950	9000
	20.50	60.00	9.50	90.00
	22.78	66.67	10.56	
	77.36	95.24	90.48	
Total	2650	6300	1050	10000
	26.50	63.00	10.50	100.00

The FREQ Procedure

Statistics for Table of default by resstatus

Statistic	DF	Value	Prob
Chi-Square	2	662.8731	<.0001
Likelihood Ratio Chi-Square	2	594.0167	<.0001
Mantel-Haenszel Chi-Square	1	372.9141	<.0001
Phi Coefficient		0.2575	
Contingency Coefficient		0.2493	
Cramer's V		0.2575	

Exhibit 4.30 Output for Categorization Option 2

Age	Count	Distribution of Count	Goods	Distribution of Goods	Bads	Distribution of Bads	WOE
Missing	50	2.50%	42	2.33%	8	4.12%	−57.28%
18–22	200	10.00%	152	8.42%	48	24.74%	−107.83%
23–26	300	15.00%	246	13.62%	54	27.84%	−71.47%
27–29	450	22.50%	405	22.43%	45	23.20%	−3.38%
30–35	500	25.00%	475	26.30%	25	12.89%	71.34%
36–43	350	17.50%	339	18.77%	11	5.67%	119.71%
44+	150	7.50%	147	8.14%	3	1.55%	166.08%
	2,000		1,806		194		

Exhibit 4.31 Calculating Weights of Evidence (WOE)

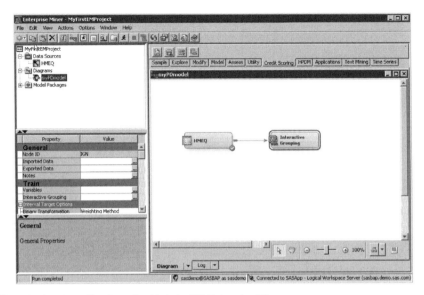

Exhibit 4.32 The Interactive Grouping Node in SAS Enterprise Miner

This gives a more concise model than the model we started this section with. However, note that the interpretability of the model becomes somewhat less straightforward when WOE variables are being used.

The technique can be programmed separately using a set of data manipulation statements, or alternatively PROC HPBIN can be used (we will illustrate this in the chapter on time-discrete hazard models).

The best and easiest way to perform categorization and weights of evidence coding in SAS Enterprise Miner is by using the Interactive Grouping node from the Credit Scoring tab (Exhibit 4.32). The latter is an extension to Enterprise Miner offering four nodes tailored to building credit scorecards. The Interactive Grouping node has various properties that can be inspected in the properties panel. As with many nodes in Enterprise Miner, the default settings usually work well. After the node has run, you can interactively inspect the results by clicking the button next to Interactive Grouping in the properties panel. This will give the output shown in Exhibit 4.33. Here you can see the variables listed, their measurement level, and their calculated role, which we will discuss in the next section. If you now click the Groupings tab in the upper left corner, you will obtain the output of Exhibit 4.34. In the upper left corner, you can see the variable distribution and how it has been categorized. The upper right corner depicts the corresponding weights of evidence plot. The lower left corner shows the variable values. It is possible to adjust the grouping by selecting multiple values using SHIFT followed by right-click to decide which group the selected values should be assigned to. Obviously, all the plots will then change as well. The lower right corner shows some variable statistics, which will be discussed in the next section.

Variable	Label	Pre-Defined Grouping	Level	Calculated R...	New Role	Original Gini	Original Information Value	Gini Statistic	Information Value
DEBTINC			INTERVAL	Input	Default	65.238	1.87	65.238	1.87
DELINQ			INTERVAL	Input	Default	33.044	0.565	33.044	0.565
VALUE			INTERVAL	Input	Default	21.989	0.454	21.989	0.454
DEROG			INTERVAL	Input	Default	23.834	0.347	23.834	0.347
CLAGE			INTERVAL	Input	Default	25.331	0.227	25.331	0.227
NINQ			INTERVAL	Input	Default	19.911	0.171	19.911	0.171
LOAN			INTERVAL	Input	Default	19.55	0.159	19.55	0.159
JOB			NOMINAL	Input	Default	17.563	0.123	17.563	0.123
CLNO			INTERVAL	Rejected	Default	14.464	0.084	14.464	0.084
YOJ			INTERVAL	Rejected	Default	14.417	0.077	14.417	0.077
MORTDUE			INTERVAL	Rejected	Default	11.306	0.044	11.306	0.044
REASON			NOMINAL	Rejected	Default	4.311	0.009	4.311	0.009

Exhibit 4.33 Results of the Interactive Grouping Node in SAS Enterprise Miner

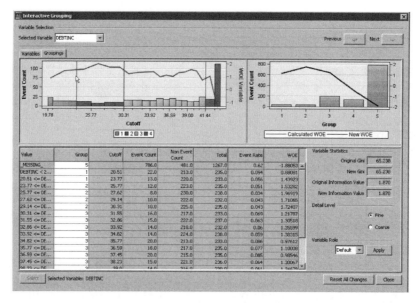

Exhibit 4.34 Results of the Interactive Grouping Node and Groupings Tab in SAS Enterprise Miner

VARIABLE SELECTION

Many analytical modeling exercises start with a broad selection of variables, of which typically only a few actually contribute to the prediction of the target variable. Common application or behavioral scorecards often have between 10 and 15 variables.

	Continuous Target (e.g., LGD, EAD)	Categorical Target (e.g., Default)
Continuous variable	Pearson correlation	Fisher score
Categorical variable	Fisher score/ANOVA	Information value Cramer's V Gain/entropy

Exhibit 4.35 Filters for Variable Selection

The key question is how to find these variables. Filters are a very handy variable selection mechanism. They work by measuring univariate correlations between each variable and the target. As such, they allow for a quick screening of which variables should be retained for further analysis. Various filter measures have been suggested in the literature. You can categorize them as depicted in Exhibit 4.35.

The Pearson correlation ρ_P is calculated as follows:

$$\rho_P = \frac{\sum_{i=1}^{n}(x_i - \bar{x})(y_i - \bar{y})}{\sqrt{\sum_{i=1}^{n}(x_i - \bar{x})^2}\sqrt{\sum_{i=1}^{n}(y_i - \bar{y})^2}}$$

It measures a linear dependency between two variables and always varies between −1 and +1. To apply it as a filter, you could select all variables for which the Pearson correlation is significantly different from 0 (according to the p-value), or, for example, the ones where $|\rho_P| > 0.50$.

The Fisher score can be calculated as follows:

$$\frac{|\bar{x}_{ND} - \bar{x}_D|}{\sqrt{s_{ND}^2 + s_D^2}},$$

whereby $\bar{x}_{ND}$ represents the average value of the variable for the nondefaulters (and $\bar{x}_D$ for the defaulters) and s_{ND}^2 (s_D^2) the corresponding variances. High values of the Fisher score indicate a predictive variable. To apply it as a filter, you could keep the top 10 percent. Note that the Fisher score may generalize to a well-known analysis of variance (ANOVA) when a variable has multiple categories.

The information value (IV) filter is based on weights of evidence and is calculated as follows:

$$IV = \sum_{i=1}^{k}(Dist\ Good_i - Dist\ Bad_i) * WOE_i$$

whereby k represents the number of categories of the variable. For the example presented in Exhibit 4.31 the calculation becomes as shown in Exhibit 4.36.

The following rules of thumb apply for the information value:

- <0.02: unpredictive
- 0.02–0.1: weakly predictive

Age	Count	Distribution of Count	Goods	Distribution of Goods	Bads	Distribution of Bads	WOE	IV
Missing	50	2.50%	42	2.33%	8	4.12%	−57.28%	0.0103
18–22	200	10.00%	152	8.42%	48	24.74%	−107.83%	0.1760
23–26	300	15.00%	246	13.62%	54	27.84%	−71.47%	0.1016
27–29	450	22.50%	405	22.43%	45	23.20%	−3.38%	0.0003
30–35	500	25.00%	475	26.30%	25	12.89%	71.34%	0.0957
36–43	350	17.50%	339	18.77%	11	5.67%	119.71%	0.1568
44+	150	7.50%	147	8.14%	3	1.55%	166.08%	0.1095
Information Value								0.6502

Exhibit 4.36 Calculating the Information Value Filter Measure

- 0.1–0.3: moderately predictive
- +0.3: strongly predictive

Note that the information value assumes that the variable has been categorized. It can also be used to adjust or steer the categorization so as to optimize the IV. Many software tools will provide interactive support to do this, whereby the modeler can adjust the categories and gauge the impact on the IV. To apply it as a filter, you can calculate the information value of all (categorical) variables and keep only those for which the IV > 0.1, or the top 10 percent.

Another filter measure based on chi-square analysis is Cramer's V. Consider the contingency table depicted in Exhibit 4.37 for employed/unemployed versus good/bad.

Similar to the example discussed in the section on categorization, the chi-square value for independence can then be calculated as follows:

$$\chi^2 = \frac{(500 - 480)^2}{480} + \frac{(100 - 120)^2}{120} + \frac{(300 - 320)^2}{320} + \frac{(100 - 80)^2}{80} = 10.41$$

This follows a chi-square distribution with k–1 degrees of freedom, with k being the number of classes of the characteristic. The Cramer's V measure can then be calculated as follows:

$$\text{Cramer's V} = \sqrt{\frac{\chi^2}{n}} = 0.10$$

	Good	Bad	Total
Employed	500	100	600
Unemployed	300	100	400
Total	800	200	1,000

Exhibit 4.37 Contingency Table for Employment Status versus Good/Bad Customer

with n the number of observations in the data set. Cramer's V is always bounded between 0 and 1, and higher values indicate better predictive power. As a rule of thumb, a cutoff of 0.1 is commonly adopted. You can then again select all variables where Cramer's V is bigger than 0.1, or consider the top 10 percent. Note that the information value and Cramer's V typically consider the same characteristics as most important.

Filters are very handy, as they permit a reduction of the number of variables of the data set early in the analysis in a quick way. Their main drawback is that they work univariately and typically do not consider correlation between the variables individually. Hence, a follow-up variable selection step during the modeling phase will be necessary to further refine the set of variables.

It is worth mentioning that other criteria may play a role in selecting variables, such as regulatory compliance and privacy issues. Note that different regulations may apply in different geographical regions and should be checked. Also, operational issues could be considered. For example, trend variables could be very predictive but may require too much time to be computed in a real-time, online credit scoring environment.

In Base SAS, the Pearson correlation can be calculated using PROC CORR, whereas the Cramer's V is available in PROC FREQ (see Exhibit 4.29). The information value can be computed by PROC HPBIN.

In SAS Enterprise Miner, the Pearson correlation and Cramer's V can be obtained from the StatExplore node (see Exhibit 4.11). The information value can be obtained from the Interactive Grouping node. In the right-hand column of Exhibit 4.33, you can see the information value for each of the variables. If the information value is bigger than 0.1, the variable's calculated role is set to Input; otherwise it is set to Rejected. The cutoff value for the information value can be set in the properties of the Interactive Grouping node. The original information value is the information value obtained by SAS Enterprise Miner using its default settings. The information value in the last column is the information value obtained when the user has changed the groupings. The two values are identical when the user does not adjust the groupings (see also Exhibit 4.34).

SEGMENTATION

Sometimes the data is segmented before the credit risk modeling starts. A first reason for this could be strategic. Banks might want to adopt special strategies for specific segments of customers. Segmentation could also be motivated from an operational viewpoint. Some new customers must have separate models because the characteristics in the standard model do not make sense operationally for them. Segmentation could also be needed to take into account significant variable interactions. If one variable strongly interacts with a number of others, it might be sensible to segment according to this variable.

The segmentation can be done using the experience and knowledge of a business expert, or it could be based on the results of a clustering analysis.

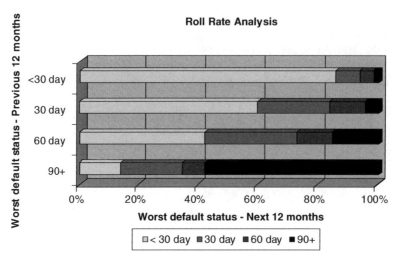

Exhibit 4.38 Roll-Rate Analysis

Segmentation is a very useful preprocessing activity since you can now estimate different analytical models, each tailored to a specific segment. However, you need to be careful with it since by segmenting you will increase the number of analytical models to estimate, which will obviously also increase the production, monitoring, and maintenance costs.

DEFAULT DEFINITION

Credit scoring systems have been implemented for many years and since long before the Basel Capital Accords were introduced. Banks were using their own proprietary default definition. Roll-rate analysis can be used in order to gauge the stability of the default definition adopted. In roll-rate analysis, you investigate how customers already in payment arrears in one period move to a more or less severe default status in the next period. Exhibit 4.38 provides an example of roll-rate analysis. It can be seen that once customers are 90 days in payment arrears, most of them will keep this delinquency status for the next period and only a small minority will recover. Hence, using 90 days as a cutoff for the default definition seems a stable and viable option. Markov chains are essentially a more advanced approach of doing roll-rate analysis where you model the transition probabilities of moving from one default state to another during one period of time.

PRACTICE QUESTIONS

1. Discuss how the FICO score can be used by banks and other companies.
2. Why is the reject inference problem a sampling problem?

3. Contrast the benefits of categorization for the continuous versus categorical variables.

4. Consider the following data:

Characteristic	No Children	1 or 2 Children	3+ Children
Number of goods	1,500	2,200	300
Number of bads	500	300	200

We are interested in the best coarse classification into two classes. One possibility is to split into no children versus children; another is two or fewer children versus three or more children. Find which of these splits is better using the chi-square statistic and PROC FREQ in SAS.

5. Preprocess the HMEQ data set in SAS Enterprise Miner as follows:
   - Draw a stratified sample of 10,000 observations (stratified based on the target).
   - Impute missing values by using the median for continuous variables and the mode for categorical variables.
   - Remove observations with outliers as follows: more than 3 standard deviations away from the mean for the continuous variables. For class variables with less than 20 different values, remove the values that occur in less than 5 percent of the observations.
   - Use a StatExplore node to determine the five most predictive variables based on Cramer's V.
   - Use an Interactive Grouping node to categorize all variables and code them using weights of evidence.

     Inspect the results. Which are the five most predictive variables according to the information value? Are these the same as according to Cramer's V?

NOTES

1. FICO is an acronym for the Fair Isaac Corporation, the developers of the FICO score.
2. The example is taken from Thomas, Edelman, and Crook (2002).

REFERENCES

Baesens, B. 2014. *Analytics in a Big Data World: The Essential Guide to Data Science and Its Applications*. Hoboken, NJ: John Wiley & Sons.

Chakraborty, G., P. Murali, and G. Satish. 2013. *Text Mining and Analysis: Practical Methods, Examples, and Case Studies Using SAS*. Cary, NC: SAS Institute.

Junqué de Fortuny, E., D. Martens, and F. Provost. 2013. "Predictive Modeling with Big Data: Is Bigger Really Better?" *Big Data* 1 (4): 215–226. doi:10.1089/big.2013.0037.

Little, R. J. A., and D. B. Rubin. 2002. *Statistical Analysis with Missing Data*. 2nd ed. New York: John Wiley & Sons.

Miner, G., J. Elder, A. Fast, T. Hill, B. Nisbet, and D. Delen. 2012. *Practical Text Mining and Statistical Analysis for Non-structured Text Data Applications*. Waltham, MA: Academic Press.

Thomas, L. C., D. B. Edelman, and J. N. Crook. 2002. *Credit Scoring and Its Applications*. Philadelphia, PA: Society for Industrial and Applied Mathematics.

Van Gestel, T., and B. Baesens. 2009. *Credit Risk Management: Basic Concepts: Financial Risk Components, Rating Analysis, Models, Economic and Regulatory Capital*. Oxford: Oxford University Press.

CHAPTER **5**

Credit Scoring

G ranting credit to both retail and nonretail (e.g., corporate) customers is the core business of a bank. In doing so, banks need to have adequate systems to decide to whom to grant credit. Credit scoring is a key risk assessment technique to analyze and quantify a potential obligor's credit risk. Essentially, credit scoring aims at quantifying the likelihood that an obligor will repay the debt. The outcome of the credit scoring exercise is a score reflecting the creditworthiness of the obligor.

In this chapter, you will learn the fundamentals of credit scoring. We start by introducing the basic idea of credit scoring. We then outline the differences between judgmental and statistical scoring, and discuss the advantages of the latter. Next, we zoom in on credit scoring for both retail and nonretail exposures. This is followed by a discussion of the potential of big data for credit scoring. Another section explains overrides whereby the result of the scorecard is overruled by the credit expert. Various criteria to evaluate scorecard performance are covered. We also review key business applications of credit scores. The chapter concludes by discussing the limitations of credit scoring.

BASIC CONCEPTS

Let's start by defining credit scoring. Throughout the past few decades banks have gathered plenty of information describing the default behavior of their customers. Examples are historical information about a customer's date of birth, gender, income, employment status, and so on. All this data has been nicely stored into huge (e.g., relational) databases or data warehouses. On top of this, banks have accumulated lots of business experience about their credit products. As an example, many credit experts do a pretty good job of discriminating between low-risk and high-risk mortgages using their business expertise only. It is now the aim of credit scoring to analyze both sources of data in more detail and come up with a statistically based decision model that allows scoring future credit applications and ultimately deciding which ones to accept and which to reject.

A key assumption made when building a credit scoring model (and all other credit risk models introduced in later chapters) is that the future resembles the past. By analyzing past repayment behavior of previous customers, it becomes possible to learn how future customers will behave in terms of default risk. More specifically, for the historical customers, we know which ones turned out to be good payers and which ones turned out to be bad payers. This good/bad status is now the binary target variable Y, which we will relate to all information available at scoring time about our obligors. The goal of credit scoring is now to quantify this relationship as precisely as possible to assist credit decisions, monitoring, and management. Banks score borrowers at loan application, as well as at regular times during the term of a financial contract (generally loans, loan commitments, and guarantees).

Once we have our credit scoring model built, we can then use it to decide whether the credit application should be accepted or rejected, or to derive the probability of a future default. To summarize, credit scoring is a key risk management tool for a bank to optimally manage, understand, and model the credit risk it is exposed to.

JUDGMENTAL VERSUS STATISTICAL SCORING

There are basically two main approaches to assessing credit risk: the judgmental approach and the statistical approach. Both rely on historical information, but the type of information they use is different.

The judgmental approach is a qualitative, expert-based approach whereby, based on business experience and common sense, the credit expert or credit committee, which is a group of credit experts, will make a decision about the credit risk. Usually, this is done based on inspecting the five Cs of the applicant and loan:

- **Character** measures the borrower's character and integrity (e.g., reputation, honesty, etc.).
- **Capital** measures the difference between the borrower's assets (e.g., car, house, etc.) and liabilities (e.g., renting expenses, etc.).
- **Collateral** measures the collateral provided in case payment problems occur (e.g., house, car, etc.).
- **Capacity** measures the borrower's ability to pay (e.g., job status, income, etc.).
- **Condition** measures the borrower's circumstances (e.g., market conditions, competitive pressure, seasonal character, etc.).

In analyzing this information, a qualitative or subjective evaluation of the credit risk is made. Although the judgmental approach might seem subjective and thus unsophisticated at first sight, it is still quite commonly used by banks for very specific credit portfolios such as project finance or new credit products.

With the emergence of statistical classification techniques at the beginning of the 1980s, banks became more and more interested in abandoning the judgmental approach and opting for a more formal data-based statistical approach.

The statistical approach is based on statistical analysis of historical data to find the optimal multivariate relationship between a customer's characteristics and the binary good/bad target variable (Baesens et al. 2003). It is less subjective than the judgmental approach since it is not tied to a particular credit expert's background knowledge and experience.

The statistical approach aims at building scorecards, which are based on multivariate correlations between inputs (such as age, marital status, income, savings amount) and a target variable that reflects the risk of default. In other words, a scorecard will assign scores to each of those inputs. In our example, scores will be assigned to age, marital status, income, and savings amount. All those scores will then be added up and compared with the critical threshold, which specifies the minimum level of required credit quality. If the aggregated score exceeds the threshold, then credit will be granted. If it falls below the threshold, then credit will be withheld.

In practice, hybrid approaches may be applied. In a first step, a bank may generate informational values by judgmental scoring. An example may be an expert opinion of a credit analyst on the payment ethics of a borrower (e.g., as a discrete number between 1 and 5). In a second step, the bank may aggregate this judgmental score and other hard information into a statistical score.

ADVANTAGES OF STATISTICAL CREDIT SCORING

Generally speaking, the statistical approach to credit scoring has many advantages compared with the judgmental approach. First, it is better in terms of speed and accuracy. We can now make faster decisions than we were able to do with the judgmental approach. This is especially relevant when working in an online environment where credit decisions need to be made quickly, possibly in real time. Because a credit scorecard is essentially a mathematical formula, it can be easily programmed and evaluated in an automated and fast way.

Another advantage of having statistical credit scoring models is consistency. We no longer have to rely upon the experience, intuition, or common sense of one or multiple business experts. Now it's just a mathematical formula, and the formula will always evaluate in exactly the same way if given the same set of inputs, like age, marital status, income, and so on.

Finally, statistical credit scoring models will typically also be more powerful than judgmental models. This performance boost will allow a reduction of bad debt loss and operating costs, and consequently it will also improve portfolio management.

To summarize, statistical credit scoring models have a lot of advantages compared with judgmental credit scoring models and are thus considered superior.

TECHNIQUES TO BUILD SCORECARDS

In this section, we discuss both logistic regression and decision trees, two classification techniques which are very powerful and popular to build application and/or behavioral scorecards.

Customer	Age	Income	Employed	...	Default	D
ABC	30	2,000	Yes		No	0
BCD	62	4,600	Yes		No	0
CDE	42	3,200	No		Yes	1
...						
XYZ	56	3,800	No		Yes	1

Exhibit 5.1 Example Credit Scoring Data Set

Logistic Regression

Basic Model Formulation

Consider a credit scoring data set in panel form as depicted in Exhibit 5.1.

When modeling the binary default target D using linear regression, we get:

$$D = \beta_0 + \beta_1 \text{Age} + \beta_2 \text{ Income} + \beta_3 \text{ Employed}$$

When estimating this using ordinary least squares (OLS), two key problems arise:

1. The errors/target are not normally distributed but follow a Bernoulli distribution with only two outcomes.

2. There is no guarantee that the target is between 0 and 1; it would be handy if it were, because then it could be interpreted as a probability.

Consider now the following bounding function:

$$f(z) = \frac{1}{1 + e^{-z}}$$

which looks like Exhibit 5.2.

For every possible value of z, the outcome is always between 0 and 1. By combining the linear regression with the bounding function, we get the following logistic regression model:

$$P(D = 1 | \text{Age, Income, Employed}) = \frac{1}{1 + e^{-(\beta_0 + \beta_1 \text{Age} + \beta_2 \text{Income} + \beta_3 \text{Employed})}}$$

The outcome of this model is always bounded between 0 and 1, no matter which values of age, income, and employed are being used, and can therefore be interpreted as a probability.

The general formulation of the logistic regression model then becomes (Allison 2001):

$$P(D = 1 | x_1, \ldots, x_N) = \frac{1}{1 + e^{-(\beta_0 + \beta_1 x_1 + \ldots + \beta_N x_N)}}$$

or alternatively,

$$P(D = 0 | x, \ldots, x_N) = 1 - P(D = 1 | x_1, \ldots, x_N)$$

$$= 1 - \frac{1}{1 + e^{-(\beta_0 + \beta_1 x_1 + \ldots + \beta_N x_N)}} = \frac{1}{1 + e^{(\beta_0 + \beta_1 x_1 + \ldots + \beta_N x_N)}}$$

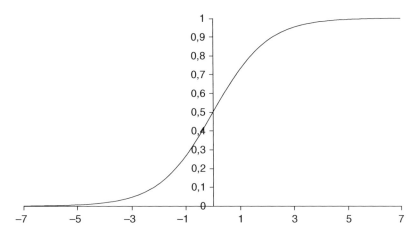

Exhibit 5.2 Bounding Function for Logistic Regression

whereby D equals 1 in case of default, and 0 otherwise.

Hence, both $P(D = 1|x_1, \ldots, x_N)$ and $P(D = 0|x_1, \ldots, x_N)$ are bounded between 0 and 1.

Reformulating in terms of the odds, the model becomes:

$$\frac{P(D = 1|x_1, \ldots, x_N)}{P(D = 0|x_1, \ldots, x_N)} = e^{(\beta_0 + \beta_1 x_1 + \ldots + \beta_N x_N)}$$

or in terms of the log odds (logit),

$$\ln\left(\frac{P(D = 1|x_1, \ldots, x_N)}{P(D = 0|x_1, \ldots, x_N)}\right) = \beta_0 + \beta_1 x_1 + \ldots + \beta_N x_N$$

The β_i parameters of a logistic regression model are then estimated using the idea of maximum likelihood. Maximum likelihood optimization chooses the parameters in such a way as to maximize the probability of getting the sample at hand. First, the likelihood function is constructed. For observation i, the probability of observing either class equals:

$$P(D = 1|x_{1i}, \ldots, x_{Ni})^{D_i}(1 - P(D = 1|x_{1i}, \ldots, x_{Ni})^{1-D_i}$$

whereby D_i represents the target value (either 0 or 1) for observation i. The likelihood function across all n observations then becomes:

$$\prod_{i=1}^{n} P(D = 1|x_{1i}, \ldots, x_{Ni})^{D_i}(1 - P(D = 1|x_{1i}, \ldots, x_{Ni})^{1-D_i}$$

To simplify the optimization, the logarithmic transformation of the likelihood function is taken and the corresponding log-likelihood can then be optimized using, for instance, the iteratively reweighted least squares procedure.

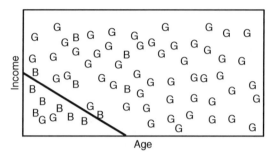

Exhibit 5.3 Linear Decision Boundary of Logistic Regression

Logistic Regression Properties

Since logistic regression is linear in the log odds (logit), it basically estimates a linear decision boundary to separate both classes. This is illustrated in Exhibit 5.3, whereby G represents the good customers and B the bad customers or defaulters.

To interpret a logistic regression model, one can calculate the odds ratio.

Suppose variable x_i increases with one unit with all other variables being kept constant (ceteris paribus); then the new logit becomes the old logit with β_i added. Likewise, the new odds become the old odds multiplied by $e^{\beta i}$. The latter represents the odds ratio—that is, the multiplicative increase in the odds when x_i increases by 1 (ceteris paribus). Hence,

- $\beta_i > 0$ implies $e^{\beta i} > 1$ and the odds and probability increase with x_i.
- $\beta_i < 0$ implies $e^{\beta i} < 1$ and the odds and probability decrease with x_i.

Another way of interpreting a logistic regression model is by calculating the doubling amount. This represents the amount of change required for doubling the primary outcome odds. It can be easily seen that for a particular variable x_i, the doubling amount equals $\log(2)/\beta_i$.

Variable Selection for Logistic Regressions

Variable selection aims at reducing the number of variables in a model. It will make the model more concise and faster to evaluate. Logistic regression has a built-in procedure to perform variable selection. It is based on a statistical hypothesis test to verify whether the coefficient of a variable i is significantly different from zero:

$$H_0: \ \beta_i = 0$$
$$H_A: \ \beta_i \neq 0$$

In logistic regression, the test statistic is:

$$\chi^2 = \left(\frac{\hat{\beta}_i}{s.e. \ (\hat{\beta}_i)} \right)^2$$

p-value < 0.01	Highly significant
0.01 < p-value < 0.05	Significant
0.05 < p-value < 0.10	Weakly significant
p-value > 0.10	Not significant

Exhibit 5.4 Reference Values for Variable Significance

and follows a chi-square distribution with 1 degree of freedom. This test statistic is intuitive in the sense that it will reject the null hypothesis H_0 if the estimated coefficient $\hat{\beta}_i$ is high in absolute value compared to its standard error $s.e.(\hat{\beta}_i)$. The latter can be easily obtained as a by-product of the optimization procedure. Based on the value of the test statistic, we calculate the p-value, which is the probability of getting a more extreme value than the one observed. In other words, a low p-value represents a significant variable, and a high p-value represents an insignificant variable. From a practical viewpoint, the p-value can be compared against a significance level. Exhibit 5.4 presents some commonly used values to decide on the degree of variable significance.

Various variable selection procedures can now be used based on the p-value. Suppose we have four variables, V_1, V_2, V_3, and V_4 (e.g., credit bureau score, income, years employed, and purpose of loan). The number of possible variable subsets equals $2^4 - 1$, or 15, as displayed in Exhibit 5.5.

When the number of variables is small, an exhaustive search among all variable subsets can be performed. However, as the number of variables increases, the search space grows exponentially and heuristic search procedures are needed. Using the p-values, the variable space can be navigated in three possible ways. Forward regression starts from the empty model and always adds variables based on low p-values.

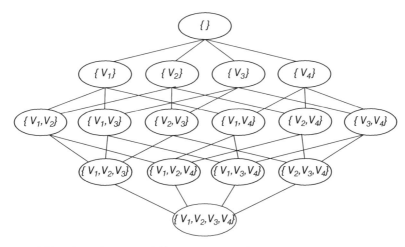

Exhibit 5.5 Variable Subsets for Four Variables, V_1, V_2, V_3, and V_4

Backward regression starts from the full model and always removes variables based on high p-values. Stepwise regression is a mix of both. It starts off like forward regression, but once the second variable has been added, it will always check the other variables in the model and remove them if they turn out to be insignificant according to their p-values. Obviously, all three procedures assume preset significance levels, which should be set by the user before the variable selection procedure starts.

In credit scoring, it is very important to be aware that statistical significance is only one evaluation criterion to consider in doing variable selection. As mentioned before, *interpretability* is also an important criterion (Martens et al. 2007). In logistic regression, this can be easily evaluated by inspecting the sign of the regression coefficient. It is highly preferable that a coefficient has the same sign as anticipated by the credit expert; otherwise he or she will be reluctant to use the model. Coefficients can have unexpected signs due to multicollinearity issues, noise, or small sample effects. Sign restrictions can be easily enforced in a forward regression setup by preventing variables with the wrong sign from entering the model.

Another criterion for variable selection is *operational efficiency*. This refers to the amount of resources needed for the collection and preprocessing of a variable. For example, although trend variables are typically very predictive, they require considerable effort to calculate and thus may not be suitable for use in an online credit scoring environment. The same applies to external data, where the latency might hamper a timely decision. In both cases, it might be worthwhile to look for a correlated, less predictive but easier to collect and calculate variable instead. Finally, *legal issues* also need to be properly taken into account. For example, in the United States, there is the Equal Credit Opportunity Act, which states that no one is allowed to discriminate based on gender, age, ethnic origin, nationality, beliefs, and so on. These variables must not be included in a credit scorecard. Other countries have other regulations, and it is important to be aware of this.

Building Logistic Regression Models in SAS

In Base SAS, a logistic regression model can be estimated using PROC LOGISTIC as follows:

```
PROC LOGISTIC DATA=mydata.hmeq;
CLASS job reason /PARAM=glm;
MODEL bad=clage clno debtinc delinq derog job loan mortdue ninq rea-
son value yoj/
SELECTION=stepwise SLENTRY=0.05 SLSTAY=0.01;
RUN;
```

The class statement is used to create dummy indicators for the categorical variables. The param=glm option indicates that we want these dummy indicators to be coded as 0/1. For example, since the job variable has five different values, four 0/1 dummy indicators will be created. The selection option indicates that we want to do stepwise logistic regression. The options slentry and slstay indicate that we will consider variables for entering the model at a significance level of 0.05, but in order to stay in the model their significance level should be below 0.01. SAS will report the output for each of the intermediate variable selection steps. The final output then looks like Exhibit 5.6.

From this output, we can decide the following:

- The final model consists of the variables CLAGE, CLNO, DEBTINC, DELINQ, DEROG, JOB, and NINQ. The LOAN, MORTDUE, VALUE, REASON, and YOJ variables have no impact on the default risk.

- The performance of the model is reported in the final table. The c-coefficient corresponds to the area under the receiver operating characteristic (ROC) curve. We will discuss this measure in more detail in the chapter on validation. For the moment, it suffices to say that the number 0.796 indicates a very good performance.

In SAS Enterprise Miner, the Regression node from the Model tab can be used to estimate a logistic regression model (see Exhibit 5.7). If this node is connected to a data set with a binary variable, it will perform logistic regression by default. The Model Selection section of the property panel can be used to specify the variable selection options.

Using Logistic Regression for Credit Scoring

Logistic regression is a very popular credit scoring classification technique due to its simplicity and good performance. Just as with linear regression, once the parameters have been estimated, the regression can be evaluated in a straightforward way, contributing to its operational efficiency. From an interpretability viewpoint, it can be easily transformed into an interpretable, user-friendly, points-based credit scorecard. Let's assume we start from the following logistic regression model whereby the explanatory variables have been coded using weights of evidence coding (see the chapter on data preprocessing):

$$P(default = yes|Age,\ Income,\ Employed,\ \ldots)$$
$$= \frac{1}{1 + e^{-(\beta_0 + \beta_1 WOE_{Age} + \beta_2 WOE_{Income} + \beta_3 WOE_{Employed} + \ldots)}}$$

As discussed earlier, this model can be easily reexpressed in a linear way in terms of the log odds as follows:

$$\log\left(\frac{P(default = yes|Age,\ Income,\ Employed,\ \ldots)}{P(default = no|Age,\ Income,\ Employed,\ \ldots)}\right)$$
$$= \beta_0 + \beta_1 WOE_{Age} + \beta_2 WOE_{Income} + \beta_3 WOE_{Employed} + \ldots$$

A scaling can then be introduced by calculating a credit score, which is linearly related to the log odds as follows:

$$Credit\ Score = offset + factor\ *\ \log(odds)$$

The LOGISTIC Procedure

	Summary of Stepwise Selection						
Step	Effect		DF	Number In	Score Chi-Square	Wald Chi-Square	Pr > ChiSq
	Entered	Removed					
1	DELINQ		1	1	254.2054		<.0001
2	DEBTINC		1	2	142.1980		<.0001
3	DEROG		1	3	105.4667		<.0001
4	CLAGE		1	4	40.4196		<.0001
5	JOB		5	5	23.6862		0.0002
6	NINQ		1	6	9.6436		0.0019
7	CLNO		1	7	7.2242		0.0072

Type 3 Analysis of Effects			
Effect	DF	Wald Chi-Square	Pr > ChiSq
CLAGE	1	30.6003	<.0001
CLNO	1	7.1820	0.0074
DEBTINC	1	94.3510	<.0001
DELINQ	1	121.3538	<.0001
DEROG	1	49.9766	<.0001
JOB	5	24.0728	0.0002
NINQ	1	10.2919	0.0013

Analysis of Maximum Likelihood Estimates						
Parameter		DF	Estimate	Standard Error	Wald Chi-Square	Pr > ChiSq
Intercept		1	4.5465	0.5633	65.1386	<.0001
CLAGE		1	0.00574	0.00104	30.6003	<.0001
CLNO		1	0.0204	0.00762	7.1820	0.0074
DEBTINC		1	−0.0996	0.0103	94.3510	<.0001
DELINQ		1	−0.7584	0.0688	121.3538	<.0001
DEROG		1	−0.7213	0.1020	49.9766	<.0001
JOB	Mgr	1	0.6078	0.3894	2.4372	0.1185
JOB	Office	1	1.1626	0.3983	8.5193	0.0035
JOB	Other	1	0.6241	0.3655	2.9163	0.0877
JOB	ProfExe	1	0.6390	0.3788	2.8464	0.0916
JOB	Sales	1	−0.8330	0.5253	2.5148	0.1128
JOB	Self	0	0			
NINQ		1	−0.1199	0.0374	10.2919	0.0013

Exhibit 5.6 Output of PROC LOGISTIC

Odds Ratio Estimates			
Effect	Point Estimate	95% Wald Confidence Limits	
CLAGE	1.006	1.004	1.008
CLNO	1.021	1.006	1.036
DEBTINC	0.905	0.887	0.924
DELINQ	0.468	0.409	0.536
DEROG	0.486	0.398	0.594
JOB Mgr vs Self	1.836	0.856	3.939
JOB Office vs Self	3.198	1.465	6.981
JOB Other vs Self	1.867	0.912	3.821
JOB ProfExe vs Self	1.895	0.902	3.980
JOB Sales vs Self	0.435	0.155	1.217
NINQ	0.887	0.824	0.954

Association of Predicted Probabilities and Observed Responses			
Percent Concordant	79.3	Somers' D	0.593
Percent Discordant	20.0	Gamma	0.597
Percent Tied	0.7	Tau-a	0.096
Pairs	919200	c	0.796

Exhibit 5.6 (*Continued*)

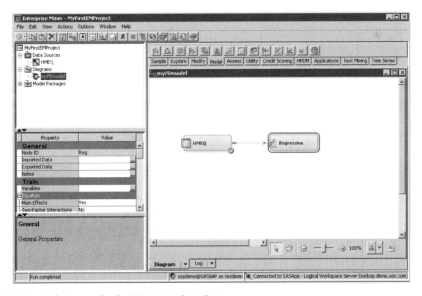

Exhibit 5.7 Logistic Regression in SAS Enterprise Miner

Assume that we want a credit score of 100 for odds of 50:1, and a credit score of 120 for odds of 100:1. This gives the following:

$$100 = \text{offset} + \text{factor} * \log 50$$
$$120 = \text{offset} + \text{factor} * \log 100$$

The offset and factor then become:

$$\text{Factor} = 20/\ln(2) = 28.85$$
$$\text{Offset} = 100 - \text{factor} * \ln(50) = -12.87$$

Once these values are known, the credit score becomes:

$$\text{Credit Score} = \left(\sum_{i=1}^{N} (WOE_i * \beta_i) + \beta_0 \right) * \text{factor} + \text{offset}$$

$$\text{Credit Score} = \left(\sum_{i=1}^{N} \left(WOE_i * \beta_i + \frac{\beta_0}{N} \right) \right) * \text{factor} + \text{offset}$$

$$\text{Credit Score} = \left(\sum_{i=1}^{N} \left(WOE_i * \beta_i + \frac{\beta_0}{N} \right) * \text{factor} + \frac{\text{offset}}{N} \right)$$

The points for each attribute are calculated by multiplying the weight of evidence of the attribute with the regression coefficient of the characteristic, then adding a fraction of the regression intercept, multiplying the result by the factor, and finally adding a fraction of the offset. The corresponding credit scorecard can then be visualized as depicted in Exhibit 5.8.

Characteristic Name	Attribute	Points
Age 1	Up to 30	80
Age 2	30–45	120
Age 3	45–60	160
Age 4	65+	240
Income 1	Up to $2,000	5
Income 2	$2,000–$3,500	20
Income 3	$3,500+	80
Employed	No	100
Employed	Yes	140
...		

Exhibit 5.8 Example Credit Scorecard

The credit scorecard is very easy to work with. Suppose a new customer with the following characteristics needs to be scored:

$$\text{Age} = 48, \text{ Income} = \$2{,}500, \text{ Employed} = \text{Yes}, \dots$$

The score for this customer can then be calculated as follows: 160 + 20 + 140 + ... This score can then be compared with a critical cutoff to help decide whether the customer is a defaulter. A key advantage of this credit scoring model is its interpretability. We can clearly see which are the most risky categories and how they contribute to the overall credit score. This is a very useful technique in credit scoring settings where interpretability is a key concern (Martens et al. 2007).

Logistic regression models can also be estimated in SAS/STAT. We will discuss this and other nonlinear regressions such as probit and cloglog model in the next chapter (Probabilities of Default: Discrete-Time Hazard Models).

Building Logistic Regression Scorecards in SAS Enterprise Miner

As part of the Credit Scoring tab, SAS offers a Scorecard node, which allows building scorecards using the procedure outlined in the previous section (see Exhibit 5.9). First, we added an Interactive Grouping node from the Credit Scoring tab to do the categorization and weights of evidence coding. We accepted the default settings for this node. For the Scorecard node, we set the Odds to 50, the Scorecard Points to 600, and the Points to Double Odds to 20. This will ensure that if the odds are 50,

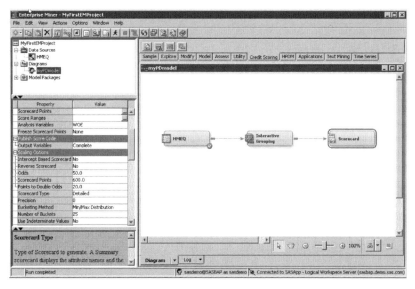

Exhibit 5.9 The Scorecard Node in SAS Enterprise Miner

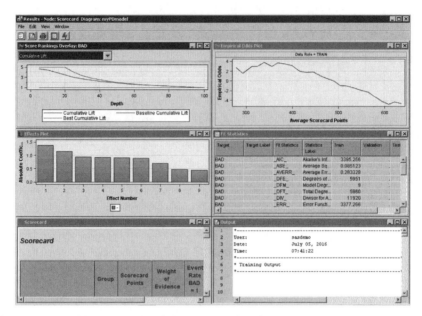

Exhibit 5.10 Output of the Scorecard Node in SAS Enterprise Miner

600 points will be assigned, and 620 in case the odds double to 100. We also set the Scorecard Type property to Detailed. The output is given in Exhibit 5.10, and the corresponding scorecard is shown in Exhibit 5.11.

Decision Trees

Basic Concepts

Decision trees are recursive partitioning algorithms (RPAs) that develop a tree-like structure representing patterns in an underlying data set (Duda, Hart, and Stork 2001). Exhibit 5.12 provides an example of a decision tree for credit scoring.

The top node is the root node specifying a testing condition of which the outcome corresponds to a branch leading up to an internal node. The terminal nodes of the tree assign the classifications (in our case good or bad) and are also referred to as the leaf nodes. Many algorithms have been suggested in the literature to construct decision trees. Among the most popular are: C4.5 (See5) (Quinlan 1993), CART (Breiman et al. 1984), and CHAID (Hartigan 1975). These algorithms differ in their way of answering the key decisions to build a tree, which are:

- **Splitting decision:** Which variable to split and at what value (e.g., Income is > $3,500 or not, Known Customer is yes or no, etc.)
- **Stopping decision:** When to stop adding nodes to the tree
- **Assignment decision:** What class (e.g., good or bad) to assign to a leaf node

	Group	Scorecard Points	Weight of Evidence	Event Rate BAD = 1	Percentage of Population	Coefficient	
CLAGE	CLAGE< 84.55	1.00	41	−0.75	34.51	9.48	−1.15
	84.55<= CLAGE< 173.47	2.00	57	−0.27	24.54	37.95	−1.15
	173.47<= CLAGE< 247.1	3.00	79	0.39	14.46	28.42	−1.15
	247.1<= CLAGE	4.00	92	0.78	10.26	18.98	−1.15
	MISSING	5.00	56	−0.31	25.32	5.17	−1.15
DEBTINC	_MISSING_	5.00	16	−1.88	62.04	21.26	−0.91
	DEBTINC< 23.77	1.00	96	1.13	7.48	7.85	−0.91
	23.77<= DEBTINC< 30.31	2.00	111	1.72	4.26	15.77	−0.91
	30.31<= DEBTINC< 41.44	3.00	98	1.20	6.96	47.23	−0.91
	41.44<= DEBTINC	4.00	54	−0.45	28.09	7.89	−0.91
DELINQ	_MISSING_	4.00	80	0.56	12.41	9.73	−0.89
	DELINQ< 1	1.00	77	0.43	13.95	70.12	−0.89
	1<= DELINQ< 2	2.00	47	−0.72	33.94	10.97	−0.89
	2<= DELINQ	3.00	23	−1.67	57.04	9.18	−0.89
DEROG	_MISSING_	3.00	77	0.58	12.29	11.88	−0.70
	DEROG< 1	1.00	70	0.22	16.66	75.96	−0.70
	1<= DEROG	2.00	39	−1.31	48.00	12.16	−0.70
JOB	OFFICE	1.00	79	0.50	13.19	15.91	−0.94
	PROFEXE	2.00	72	0.22	16.61	21.41	−0.94
	MGR, OTHER	3.00	61	−0.19	23.23	52.94	−0.94

Exhibit 5.11 Credit Scorecard for HMEQ Data Set

	Group	Scorecard Points	Weight of Evidence	Event Rate BAD = 1	Percentage of Population	Coefficient	
	SALES, SELF	4.00	49	−0.63	31.79	5.07	−0.94
	MISSING, _UNKNOWN_	5.00	94	1.02	8.24	4.68	−0.94
LOAN	LOAN< 7600	1.00	54	−0.92	38.49	9.98	−0.44
	7600<= LOAN< 10000	2.00	68	0.17	17.38	8.98	−0.44
	10000<= LOAN< 15300	3.00	64	−0.12	21.87	26.01	−0.44
	15300<= LOAN< 40000, _MISSING_	4.00	70	0.31	15.39	49.93	−0.44
	40000<= LOAN	5.00	63	−0.18	23.03	5.10	−0.44
NINQ	_MISSING_	5.00	71	0.37	14.71	8.56	−0.48
	NINQ< 1	1.00	70	0.30	15.65	42.47	−0.48
	1<= NINQ< 2	2.00	67	0.06	18.97	22.47	−0.48
	2<= NINQ< 4	3.00	62	−0.27	24.57	19.66	−0.48
	4<= NINQ	4.00	51	−1.11	43.14	6.85	−0.48
VALUE	_MISSING_	5.00	−43	−4.10	93.75	1.88	−0.92
	VALUE< 48800	1.00	49	−0.65	32.25	9.78	−0.92
	48800<= VALUE< 89235.5	2.00	68	0.08	18.75	39.28	−0.92
	89235.5<= VALUE< 132297	3.00	77	0.41	14.20	29.43	−0.92
	132297<= VALUE	4.00	70	0.14	17.78	19.63	−0.92

Exhibit 5.11 (Continued)

Assignment Decision

Usually, the assignment decision is the most straightforward to make since we typically look at the majority class within the leaf node to make the decision. This idea is also referred to as winner-take-all learning. The other two decisions are less straightforward and are elaborated on next.

Splitting Decision

In order to answer the splitting decision, one needs to define the concept of impurity or chaos. Consider, for example, the three data sets of Exhibit 5.13, each containing

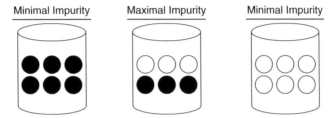

Exhibit 5.12 Example Decision Tree for Credit Scoring

Exhibit 5.13 Example Data Sets for Calculating Impurity

good customers (unfilled circles) and bad customers (filled circles). Quite obviously the good customers are nondefaulters, whereas the bad customers are defaulters. Minimal impurity occurs when all customers are either good or bad. Maximal impurity occurs when one has the same number of good and bad customers (i.e., the data set in the middle).

Decision trees will now aim at minimizing the impurity in the data. In order to do so appropriately, one needs a measure to quantify impurity. Various measures have been introduced in the literature, and the most popular are:

- Entropy: $E(S) = -p_G \log_2(p_G) - p_B \log_2(p_B)$ (C4.5/See5)
- Gini: $\text{Gini}(S) = 2p_G p_B$ (CART)
- Chi-square analysis (CHAID)

with p_G (p_B) being the proportions of good and bad, respectively. Both measures are depicted in Exhibit 5.14, where it can be clearly seen that the entropy (Gini) is minimal when all customers are either good or bad, and maximal in cases of the same number of good and bad customers.

In order to answer the splitting decision, various candidate splits will now be evaluated in terms of their decrease in impurity. Consider, for example, a split on age as depicted in Exhibit 5.15.

The original data set had maximum entropy since the amount of goods and bads were the same. The entropy calculations now become:

- Entropy top node $= -1/2 \times \log_2(1/2) - 1/2 \times \log_2(1/2) = 1$
- Entropy left node $= -1/3 \times \log_2(1/3) - 2/3 \times \log_2(2/3) = 0.91$
- Entropy right node $= -1 \times \log_2(1) - 0 \times \log_2(0) = 0$

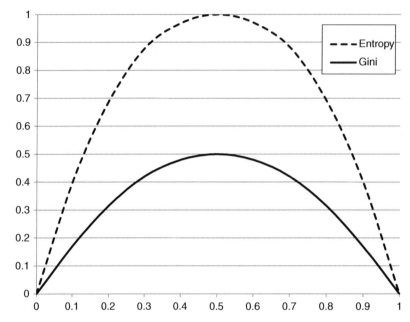

Exhibit 5.14 Entropy versus Gini

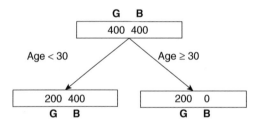

Exhibit 5.15 Calculating the Entropy for Age Split

The weighted decrease in entropy, also known as the gain, can then be calculated as follows:

$$\text{Gain} = 1 - (600/800) \times 0.91 - (200/800) \times 0 = 0.32$$

The gain measures the weighted decrease in entropy thanks to the split. It speaks for itself that a higher gain is to be preferred. The decision tree algorithm will now consider different candidate splits for its root node and adopt a greedy strategy by picking the one with the biggest gain. Once the root node has been decided upon, the procedure continues in a recursive way, each time adding splits with the biggest gain. In fact, this can be perfectly parallelized and both sides of the tree can grow in parallel, hereby increasing the efficiency of the tree construction algorithm.

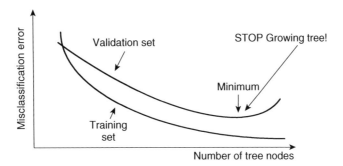

Exhibit 5.16 Using a Validation Set to Stop Growing a Decision Tree

Stopping Decision

The third decision relates to the stopping criterion. Obviously, if the tree continues to split, it will become very detailed with leaf nodes containing only a few observations. In the most extreme case, the tree will have one leaf node per observation and as such perfectly fit the data. However, by doing so, the tree will start to fit the specificities or noise in the data, which is also referred to as *overfitting*. In other words, the tree has become too complex and fails to correctly model the noise-free pattern or trend in the data. As such, it will generalize poorly to new unseen data. In order to prevent this from happening, the data will be split into a training sample and a validation sample. The training sample will be used to make the splitting decision. The validation sample is an independent sample, set aside to monitor the misclassification error (or any other performance metric such as a profit-based measure) as the tree grows. A commonly used split is a 70 percent training sample and a 30 percent validation sample. We then typically observe a pattern as depicted in Exhibit 5.16.

The error on the training sample keeps on decreasing as the splits become more and more specific and tailored toward it. On the validation sample, the error will initially decrease, which indicates that the tree splits generalize well. However, at some point the error will increase since the splits become too specific for the training sample as the tree starts to memorize it. Where the validation set curve reaches its minimum, the procedure should be stopped, as otherwise overfitting will occur. Note that, as already mentioned, besides classification error, we might also use accuracy or profit-based measures on the *y*-axis to make the stopping decision. Also note that sometimes simplicity is preferred above accuracy, and one can select a tree that does not necessarily have minimum validation set error, but a lower number of nodes.

Decision Tree Properties

In the example of Exhibit 5.12, every node had only two branches. The advantage of this is that the testing condition can be implemented as a simple yes/no question. Multiway splits allow for more than two branches and can provide trees that are

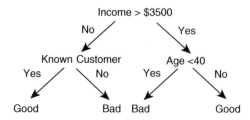

Exhibit 5.17 Example Decision Tree.

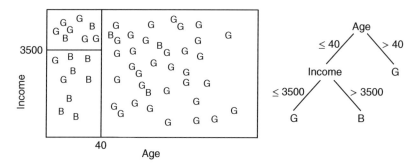

Exhibit 5.18 Decision Boundary of a Decision Tree

wider but less deep. In a read-once decision tree, a particular attribute can be used only once in a certain tree path.

Every tree can also be represented as a rule set since every path from a root node to a leaf node makes up a simple "If–Then" rule. For the tree depicted in Exhibit 5.17, the corresponding rules are:

If Income > $3,500 = Yes **And** Age < 40 = No **Then** Good

If Income > $3,500 = Yes **And** Age < 40 = Yes **Then** Bad

If Income > $3,500 = No **And** Known Customer = No **Then** Bad

If Income > $3,500 = No **And** Known Customer = Yes **Then** Good

These rules can then be easily implemented in all kinds of software packages (e.g., Microsoft Excel).

Decision trees essentially model decision boundaries orthogonally to the axes. This is illustrated in Exhibit 5.18 for an example decision tree.

Building Decision Trees in SAS Enterprise Miner

There are no readily available procedures to build decision trees in Base SAS. In SAS Enterprise Miner, decision trees can be built using the Decision Tree node from the Model tab. This is illustrated in Exhibit 5.19. Note that we also added a Data Partition node between the HMEQ data source and the Decision Tree node. This node

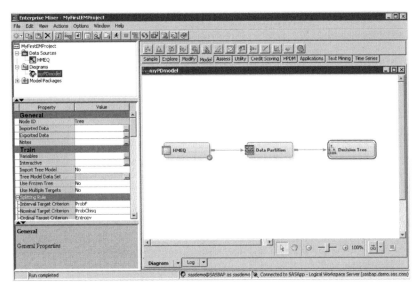

Exhibit 5.19 Decision Tree Node in SAS Enterprise Miner

will split the data into a training set (40 percent of the observations), a validation set (30 percent of the observations), and a test set (30 percent of the observations). The validation set will be used to make the stopping decision as we discussed earlier. The output of the node is given in Exhibit 5.20, whereas the tree is represented in Exhibit 5.21. Note that the nodes are colored according to the impurity, where a darker node corresponds to greater impurity. The thickness of the branches is proportional to the amount of training observations that follow them.

Logistic Regression versus Decision Trees

Logistic regression is the most popular scorecard construction technique used in industry. Its key advantage, when compared to decision trees, is that a continuous range of scores is provided between 0 and 1. For decision trees, every leaf node corresponds to a particular score (i.e., the proportion of goods in the leaf node). Hence, only a limited set of score values is provided, which may not be sufficient to provide a fine, granular distinction between obligors in terms of default risk. Decision trees are, however, often used during the data preprocessing step for variable selection, categorization, or segmentation (as discussed in the chapter on data preprocessing).

Other Classification Techniques

Other classification techniques have been developed to build scorecards, such as discriminant analysis, neural networks, and support vector machines (SVMs), as well

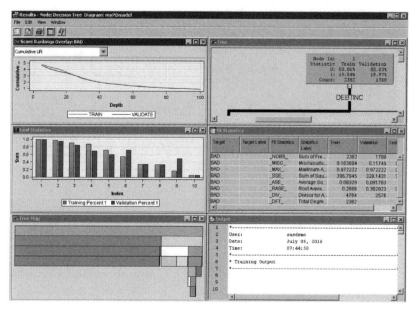

Exhibit 5.20 Output of the Decision Tree Node

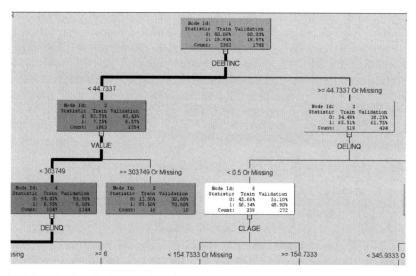

Exhibit 5.21 Decision Tree for HMEQ Data Set

as ensemble methods such as bagging, boosting, and random forests (Baesens 2014). Especially the last-named methods have proven to be very powerful in terms of classification performance. However, despite their potential, these techniques yield very complex models that are hard to understand and hence not useful for building credit scoring models, where model interpretability is a key concern (Martens et al. 2007).

CREDIT SCORING FOR RETAIL EXPOSURES

Popular examples of retail portfolios are mortgages, revolving exposures such as credit cards or overdraft accounts, and installment loans such as car loans. Three key statistical approaches for credit scoring in retail portfolios are application scoring, behavioral scoring, and dynamic scoring. All three approaches rely on historical data to build scorecards. A scorecard then provides a score whereby a higher score typically indicates less credit risk and a lower score a riskier obligor. The three approaches differ in the way they construct their historical data and set their prediction horizons. Let's go into these three approaches in more detail.

Application Scoring

Application scoring is the first important statistical credit scoring approach. The purpose of application scoring is to come up with a credit score that reflects the default risk of a customer at the moment of loan application. This is a very important scoring mechanism, as it will help the lender decide whether the credit application should be accepted or rejected.

In order to build an application scorecard, one first needs to define the concept of default. Multiple definitions of default can be adopted. It could be based on profit, amount owed, negative net present value, or number of months in payment arrears. A popular definition of default in the earlier days of credit scoring was that a customer was considered to be a defaulter if he or she ran into more than three months of payment arrears. With the introduction of the Basel Capital Accords, the default definition has now been set to 90 days in payment arrears, which is similar (Van Gestel and Baesens 2009). Note, however, that in some countries this definition has been overruled. In the United States, for example, in retail credit for residential mortgages the default definition is 180 days, for qualifying revolving exposures it's also 180 days, and for other retail exposures it's 120 days.

Let's assume now that we have our definition of default set. The next step is then to identify the information that can be used to predict default. Two different types of information can be distinguished: application variables and bureau variables.

Let's first discuss the application variables. This is the information provided to the bank by the applicant upon loan application. Popular examples are age, gender, marital status, income, time at residence, time at employment, time in industry, first digit of postal code, geographical (urban/rural/regional/provincial), residential status, employment status, lifestyle code, existing client (Y/N), number of years as client, number of products internally, total liabilities, total debt, total debt service ratio, gross debt service ratio, revolving debt/total debt, and number of credit cards. All these variables are internally available to the bank. They can be complemented by bureau variables.

Bureau variables are obtained from credit bureaus (also called credit reference agencies), which are external to the bank. A credit bureau is an organization that assembles and aggregates credit information from various financial institutions or banks. It can collect both positive and negative credit information, depending upon the country in which it operates. Usually, credit bureaus provide two sources of information. A first example is raw bureau data such as number of previous delinquencies, total amount of credit outstanding, previous delinquency history, time at credit bureau, total credit bureau inquiries, time since last credit bureau inquiry, inquiries in the past 3/6/12 months, inquiries in the past 3/6/12 months as percentage of total, and so on.

Using this raw bureau data, credit bureaus can now build bureau credit scores. These bureau scores can then be sold to banks, which can then use them in their application scoring models. Credit bureaus are all around these days. In the United States, popular bureaus are Experian, Equifax, and TransUnion, each of which covers its own geographical region. All three provide a FICO score, which ranges between 300 to 850 with higher scores reflecting better credit quality. A FICO score essentially relies on the following five data sources to determine creditworthiness:

1. Payment history: Has the customer any delinquency history? This accounts for 35 percent of the FICO score.

2. Amount of current debt: How many credits does the customer have in total? This accounts for 30 percent of the FICO score.

3. Length of credit history: How long has the customer been using credit? This accounts for 15 percent of the FICO score.

4. Types of credit in use: What kind of loans does the customer currently have (e.g., credit cards, installment loans, mortgage, etc.)? This accounts for 10 percent of the FICO score.

5. Pursuit of new credit: How many new credits is the customer applying for? This accounts for 10 percent of the FICO score.

These FICO scores are commonly used in the United States, not only by banks, but also by insurance providers, telecommunications firms, utilities companies, and others. Other countries obviously also have their own credit bureaus. In Australia, there is Baycorp Advantage, Germany has the Schufa, Netherlands BKR, and Belgium CKP. Dun & Bradstreet is a popular credit bureau targeting the midsize corporation and small to medium-sized enterprise market.

Exhibit 5.22 shows an example of an application scorecard. It includes three characteristics: age, known customer, and salary. Each of these characteristics has been categorized or coarse classified into several categories. For example, age has been categorized into four categories: the first is up to 26 years, the second between 26 and 35 years, and so on. Each of these categories has points assigned to it: The more points, the higher the credit quality. We can see that within the age characteristic the points are monotonically increasing from 100 to 225. We can also see that unknown customers are considered more risky than known customers since they receive only 90 points instead of 180. For salary, we again see a monotonic increase.

Let's now imagine that a new application for credit is submitted by a known customer whose age is 32 and salary is $1,150. We can now look up the points for each of these three characteristics. For age, the customer gets 120 points, for known customer 180 points, and for salary 160 points. This all adds up to 460 points, which

Characteristic Name	Attribute	Scorecard Points
Age 1 (years)	Up to 26	100
Age 2	26–35	120
Age 3	35–37	185
Age 4	37+	225
Known customer	No	90
Known customer	Yes	180
Salary 1	Up to $500	120
Salary 2	$501–$1,000	140
Salary 3	$1,001–$1,500	160
Salary 4	$1,501–$2,000	200
Salary 5	$2,000+	240

Exhibit 5.22 Example Application Scorecard

represents the total credit quality of this particular customer. This now needs to be compared against a cutoff of 500, which represents the minimum required credit quality set by the bank. We can see that this particular customer falls below the cutoff and will thus be rejected. Imagine now that we consider the same customer, but with a salary of $2,500 instead of $1,150. Do you think this customer will be accepted or rejected? Well, let's verify. The new score now becomes 120 + 180 + 240, which equals 540. This is above the cutoff of 500, so the customer will be accepted.

The purpose of application scoring is now to build a scorecard like the one you see in Exhibit 5.22. Note that this encompasses many decisions that need to be made during the scorecard development process. For example:

- Why do we select the characteristics age, known customer, and salary? Why don't we include other ones like employment status or number of years living at current address?
- Why do we categorize age into four categories?
- How do we decide on the points assigned to each category?
- Why do we set the cutoff at 500? If it had been set at 400, the customer would have been accepted with the lower salary.

When building an application scorecard, you are actually taking two snapshots of customer behavior (see Exhibit 5.23).

The first snapshot is taken at loan origination where you will gather both the application and credit bureau data. This is the information that will then be used to predict default. The second snapshot is taken at some later point during the loan at which the default behavior will be determined. Ideally, you should wait until the end of the loan to be absolutely certain about whether a customer defaulted. However, for mortgages this would imply having to wait 15, 20, or even more years to do this, and

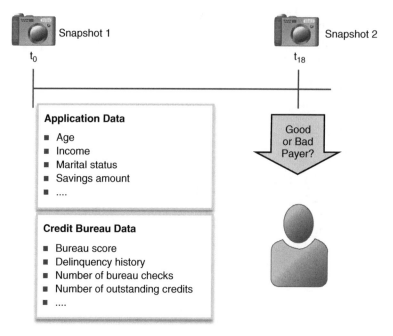

Exhibit 5.23 Application Scoring: Snapshot to Snapshot

obviously this is not feasible. Empirical analysis has shown that the majority of customers who default do so in the first 18 months. Hence, many firms take the second snapshot 18 months after loan origination to see whether the customer defaulted. In this way, they construct a data set and build an application scorecard from it.

Application scorecards provide scores. A score is a measure that allows lenders to rank customers from high risk (low score) to low risk (high score) and as such provides a relative measure of credit risk. Scores are unlimited and can be measured within any range; they can even be negative. A score is not the same as a probability. A probability also allows us to rank, but on top of that, since it is limited between 0 and 1, it also gives an absolute interpretation of credit risk. Hence, probabilities provide more information than scores do. For application scoring, one does not need well-calibrated probabilities of default. However, for other application areas such as regulatory capital calculation in a Basel setting, as we will discuss later, calibrated default probabilities are needed (Van Gestel and Baesens 2009). In later sections, we will discuss how to transform scores to probabilities.

Behavioral Scoring

Behavioral scoring is another statistical credit scoring approach, in this case one that analyzes the behavior of existing credit customers. Imagine that customer Bart applies for credit at your bank. First you are going to put this borrower through an application scoring model, and let's say that you decide to accept his application. At some point, you want to reassess the borrower's credit risk, taking into account all his recent behavior. That recent information could be his checking account behavior summarized by the average of the checking account balance, the maximum or minimum thereof, or the trend during the previous 12 months. Other interesting information could be delinquency information like whether the borrower had already incurred payment delays. Also, changes in his job status or home address could be considered. All this behavioral information can then be combined into a behavioral credit score, which provides the bank with a new and better assessment of the credit risk for the already existing obligor.

Behavioral scoring models are typically constructed using a 24-month time frame. Twelve months are taken to measure and quantify all the information that will be used as predictors, and the subsequent 12 months to determine the default status.

Behavioral scoring is dynamic since it summarizes the behavior into various dynamic variables such as average checking account balance, maximum checking account balance, trend in checking account balance, and more. As such, it is as if we construct a video clip of customer behavior during a period of 12 months. This video clip is then again summarized using a snapshot to determine the good/bad status 12 months after the observation point. Hence, behavioral scoring is often referred to as a video clip to snapshot problem (see Exhibit 5.24).

When compared to application scoring, behavioral scoring starts from a much bigger data set in terms of the number of variables. Behavioral scoring data sets typically have a few hundred variables to consider. Some examples are maximum and minimum levels of balance, credit turnover, trend in payments, trend in balance, number of missed payments, times exceeded credit limit, times changed home address, and so forth. Hence, during scorecard construction, it will be very important to carefully select the variables that contribute to predicting default risk.

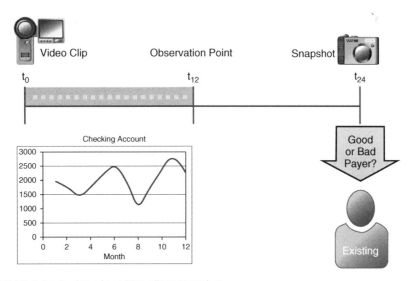

Exhibit 5.24 Behavioral Scoring: Video Clip to Snapshot

When creating a behavioral scoring data set, it is really important to carefully think about the definitions of the variables. These variables should as much as possible be related to the financial solvency of the customer. In doing so, a first issue to thoroughly consider is the roles that a customer can take for a particular product. A customer can be the primary debtor, secondary debtor, or guarantor of the credit. When defining a behavioral variable such as the number of credits of a customer, all these roles should be taken into account. Furthermore, a customer can have both private and professional products. Also, the behavior can be measured at various levels in a product taxonomy. Think about a behavioral variable such as average, maximum, or minimum savings amount. When quantifying this variable, various savings-related products could be considered simultaneously such as checking accounts, saving accounts, term accounts, and so on.

When defining behavior, the same variable can be measured multiple times during the observation period. Think about variables such as checking account, credit balance, or bureau score. During a 12-month observation period, multiple values for these variables will be available. Hence, aggregate functions need to be used to aggregate these variables. Popular aggregate functions are the mean, which is sensitive to outliers; the median, which is robust to outliers; the minimum; and the maximum. Think of variables such as the worst delinquency status during the past six months, or the highest credit utilization during the past 12 months. Also, trend variables can be computed, such as the absolute or relative trend. The latter takes into account the starting value of the variable. These trends can be computed during the previous six or 12 months, as illustrated. Trend variables are usually very predictive but require more time to be computed. It may also be worthwhile to add variables such as the most recent value, the value one month ago, and so on. The aggregate functions can also be used for ratio variables, which are very popular in behavioral scoring. One example is the obligation/income ratio, which is calculated by adding the monthly house payment and any regular monthly installment or revolving debt and dividing by the monthly income. Another example could be the ratio of the current credit balance to the credit limit.

Just as with application scoring, the aim of behavioral scoring is to provide a score that is, as explained earlier for application scores, a relative credit assessment allowing banks to rank order customers from low risk to high risk in terms of their default likelihood.

A final issue concerns the migration from an application to a behavioral score. A sudden move from an application to a behavioral score can cause big fluctuations (e.g., in terms of expected or unexpected losses) and is thus discouraged. Many banks will work with a transition period of about six months during which a weighted combination of both scores is used. The transition score then becomes $\alpha \times AS + (1 - \alpha) \times BS$. During the transition period, the weight α is gradually decreased such that at the end of the period the customer has fully migrated to the behavioral score.

Dynamic Scoring

We already discussed application scoring as a snapshot to snapshot problem, and behavioral scoring as a video clip to snapshot problem, and in what follows we will now discuss dynamic scoring as a video clip to video clip statistical credit scoring approach.

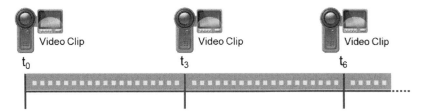

Exhibit 5.25 Dynamic Scoring: Video Clip to Video Clip

In dynamic scoring, a risk assessment is provided for any future moment in time (see Exhibit 5.25). Contrary to application and behavioral scoring, where the risk assessment is provided for a fixed time horizon (e.g., 18 or 12 months), in dynamic scoring risk assessments will be provided for 3, 4, 5, 6, 12, or 18 months (or more) into the future. As such it gives a lot more information than an application scorecard or a behavioral scorecard. However, it is a lot harder to construct since we need to use special statistical techniques such as survival analysis, which can be difficult. Basically, these techniques allow us to model not just if a borrower will default, but also when. The key advantages of using survival analysis techniques for credit scoring are:

- They provide a natural way to model the loan default process and also incorporate obligors who have not defaulted during the observation period.
- They do not necessitate the definition of a fixed performance window during which default is measured.
- They can easily accommodate time-varying behavioral and economic factors.
- The survival probabilities can be easily used for profit scoring.

We do see a growing interest in dynamic credit scoring models in the industry, and some banks have already started to experiment with them. The outcomes of these models not only are useful for credit risk assessment but also can be used to model customer lifetime value (CLV), for example.

REJECT INFERENCE

The problem of reject inference refers to the fact that the data available to build application scorecards concerns only the past accepts and not the rejects since we don't know their default or nondefault behavior. Not including the rejects in the application scorecard development process will create a bias. Various methods for handling reject inference have been suggested, as we will discuss in what follows.

Classifying the Rejects as Bads

A first method to perform reject inference is to classify all rejects as bad payers. Obviously, this method will reinforce the credit scoring policy and prejudices of the past. It is also a conservative approach since it is plausible to assume that not all rejects would have turned out to be bad payers. Hence, by classifying all rejects as bads, the

Reject	Score	Inferred G/B
R1	0.46	B
R2	0.22	B
R3	0.58	G
R4	0.04	B

Exhibit 5.26 Hard Cutoff Augmentation

bad rate in the sample will be too high. A softer version can also be adopted whereby only a subsample of the rejects is classified as bads based on expert knowledge.

Hard Cutoff Augmentation

The hard cutoff augmentation method starts by building a scorecard on the accepts only. It then uses this scorecard to calculate scores for the rejects. An assumption is then made about the bad rate in the rejects. Consider, for example, Exhibit 5.26 with four rejects and their scores.

If the assumed bad rate equaled 75 percent, that would mean that there were three bads among the four rejects. The three rejects with the lowest scores would then be considered as bad payers. In our case, this would mean rejects R1, R2, and R4 would be considered as bad payers. Once all the rejects have been labeled as good or bad payers, they are added to the accepts data set. The final scorecard can then be built on this combined data set. Although this method looks quite appealing at first sight, a key input parameter is the bad rate in the rejects, which is usually not known.

Parceling

Parceling is another method that works similarly to hard cutoff augmentation. It starts by building a scorecard on the accepts only. This model is then also used to score the rejects. The score range is then categorized, and for the accepts the percentages of goods and bads within each category are calculated. These percentages are then used to allocate the rejects to the good and bad classes.

In the example depicted in Exhibit 5.27, this would mean that for the 654 rejects in the score range 100 to 199, 21.6 percent or 141 will be classified as bad, and 78.4

Score	Accepts				Rejects		
	# Bad	# Good	% Bad	% Good	# Rejects	# Bad	# Good
0–99	24	10	70.3%	29.7%	342	240	102
100–199	54	196	21.6%	78.4%	654	141	513
200–299	43	331	11.5%	88.5%	345	40	305
300–399	32	510	5.9%	94.1%	471	28	443
400+	29	1,232	2.3%	97.7%	778	18	760

Exhibit 5.27 Parceling

Accepts/Rejects	Customer ID	Age	Income	...	Weight	Good/Bad
Accepts	John	56	$3,400		1	Bad
Accepts	Sara	38	$2,200		1	Good
					...	
Rejects	Dan	44	$2,500		0.80	Good
Rejects	Dan	44	$2,500		0.20	Bad

Exhibit 5.28 Fuzzy Augmentation

percent or 513 will be classified as good. This allocation can then be done randomly. Obviously, the proportion of bads for the rejects and accepts cannot be the same. Hence, an alternative could be to use a scaling factor to allocate a higher proportion of the rejects to the bad class. As an example rule of thumb when determining this scaling factor, the bad rate for the rejects could be 2 to 4 times higher than the bad rate for the accepts.

Fuzzy Augmentation

Fuzzy augmentation also starts by first creating a model based on the accepts, and then using that model to score the rejects. Every reject now gets a probability of being good, $p(\text{Good})$, and a probability of being bad, $p(\text{Bad})$. Every reject will now be duplicated into two observations with target good and bad and corresponding weights $p(\text{Good})$ and $p(\text{Bad})$, respectively. In Exhibit 5.28, you can see that the reject customer Dan has been duplicated into a first observation with target good and weight 0.80, and a second observation with target bad and weight 0.20. The rejects can then be combined with the accepts and a new model can be estimated on this combined data set. Ideally, the classification technique that is being used to build the model should take into account the weights set for the rejects.

Nearest Neighbor Methods

Nearest neighbor methods can also be used to do reject inference. They work very intuitively as follows. For every reject, look at the k most similar accepts in the Euclidean sense. These are also called the k nearest neighbors. k can be set to 1, 10, 100, or even more. You can then assign the most common class among those nearest neighbors to the reject. For example, if you consider the 100 nearest neighbors of a reject and it turns out that 80 of them are good payers and 20 are bad payers, then the reject will be considered as a good payer. Once all rejects have been classified as good or bad, they can be added to the accepts and a new model on the combined data set can be estimated. Although the nearest neighbor method to do reject inference looks quite appealing, instability problems can occur when the rejects are too far away from the accepts. In this case, the classes assigned to the rejects will be very uncertain and unstable.

Grant Credit to All Customers

A controversial approach to do reject inference is granting credit to all customers, including the rejects, during a specific period of time. This is motivated by a statement made by professor David Hand (2001):

> … There is no unique best method of universal applicability, unless extra information is obtained.

> That is, the best solution is to obtain more information (perhaps by granting loans to some potential rejects) about those applicants who fall in the reject region.

The idea here is to grant credit to some but not all rejects by evaluating the trade-off between the cost of granting credit to rejects and the benefit of obtaining a better scoring model. Banasik, Crook, and Thomas (2001) were in the exceptional situation of being able to observe the repayment behavior of customers who would normally have been rejected. They were able to contrast the effect on scorecard performance of both using and not using reject inference procedures. They concluded that the scope for improving scorecard performance by including the rejected applicants in the model development process is present but modest. However, note that this was studied on only one data set and can thus not be generalized.

Credit Bureau Based Inference

Another way to get more information about the rejects is via the credit bureau. Remember that a credit bureau or credit reference agency gathers information from various financial institutions about the delinquency behavior of their customers. So what you could do is also ask the bureau if some past rejects received credit elsewhere, and also inquire after their performance at these other financial institutions. Actually, you can ask the credit bureau for two pieces of information. You can give the credit bureau a sample of your past rejects and ask the bureau to classify them as good or bad. Or, if privacy regulations would not allow you to do so, you could also provide the credit bureau with a sample of your past rejects and ask the bureau about the bad rate in that sample. This bad percentage can then be used in the hard cutoff augmentation method, for example. One problem with bureau-based reject inference is that customers that were previously rejected by your bank may have received credit elsewhere but under other conditions, making the comparison not strictly apples to apples.

Other Methods

Other methods to do reject inference have also been developed but are less popular. Some examples are a three-group approach, iterative reclassification, and mixture distribution modeling (Thomas, Edelman, and Crook 2002). We will not consider those any further since they are less frequently used in the industry.

Withdrawal Inference

In this section, we have discussed the reject inference problem. Remember, the reject inference problem is essentially a sampling problem because no information about the target good/bad class is available for the previously rejected customers. However, when you think a bit more closely about the historical through-the-door population, you will see that you also have withdrawals in there. These are customers who decided themselves to not take up the offer because they found a better offer elsewhere. In other words, these are the shoppers. Also for these withdrawals, we may not know the true good/bad class, and procedures for withdrawal inference should be adopted. One easy way to do withdrawal inference could again be via the credit bureau, whereby a sample of past withdrawals is given to the credit bureau so as to obtain information about their good/bad status at other financial institutions. However, it needs to be noted that not many firms consider the withdrawals in their scorecard development.

Reject Inference in SAS Enterprise Miner

As part of the Credit Scoring tab, SAS Enterprise Miner offers the Reject Inference node to perform reject inference using hard cutoff augmentation, parceling, or fuzzy augmentation.

CREDIT SCORING FOR NONRETAIL EXPOSURES

In this section, we will discuss four credit scoring approaches for nonretail credit portfolios such as corporate exposures, sovereign exposures, and bank exposures. As opposed to retail portfolios, a key issue in these portfolios is the availability of data. The four approaches covered differ in the type of data that they use. Let's continue and discuss these approaches in more detail.

Prediction Approach

The prediction approach assumes that there is historical data available about the obligors (e.g., firms) and their default (e.g., bankruptcy) status. This data can then be analyzed by statistical techniques to predict default behavior. As an example, popular data to be used for bankruptcy prediction are accounting information such as balance sheet and financial statement ratios, and stock price behavior if the firm is publicly listed.

A well-known model for bankruptcy prediction is the Altman z-model for manufacturing firms. It was built in the late 1960s using a statistical technique called linear discriminant analysis. Separate versions exist for public and private industrial companies:

- For public industrial companies: $z = 1.2 \times 1 + 1.4 \times 2 + 3.3 \times 3 + 0.6 \times 4 + 1.0 \times 5$ (healthy if $z > 2.99$, unhealthy if $z < 1.81$)
- For private industrial companies: $z = 6.56 \times 1 + 3.26 \times 2 + 6.72 \times 3 + 1.05 \times 4$ (healthy if $z > 2.60$, unhealthy if $z < 1.1$)

The x1, ... x5 variables are the following accounting ratios: x1: working capital/total assets; x2: retained earnings/total assets; x3: earnings before interest and taxes (EBIT)/total assets; x4: market (book) value of equity/total liabilities; x5: net sales/total assets.

Essentially, the z-score is a linear combination of these five accounting ratios. A higher z score reflects a healthier firm and thus a lower bankruptcy risk. Extensions of the original z-score model have been provided for privately held and nonmanufacturing firms. The z-score can be used by a bank as its internal bankruptcy prediction model. It can also be used to benchmark other bankruptcy prediction models. Note, however, that the z-score model has been built using U.S. corporates, and care should be taken when applying it to other countries.

Expert-Based Approach

As discussed previously, the prediction approach necessitates the availability of data, and you may not always have data available in a nonretail setting. So in the absence of data, the expert-based approach is also used in nonretail credit risk modeling. Basically, the expert-based approach builds a scorecard in a qualitative way using the business experience, intuition, and common sense of one or more credit experts.

Exhibit 5.29 shows an example of an expert-based scorecard for corporate credit risk modeling. You can see that it considers various characteristics, such as industry position, market share trends and prospects, and so on. Each of these characteristics has been defined in a qualitative way. They also have scores assigned to them. These scores have not been estimated from historical data, since this is not available here, but have been determined by the business experts themselves in a subjective way. Expert-based scorecards are often written down as a set of "If–Then" business rules. Although they might seem inferior to statistically based scorecards at first sight, they are still quite commonly used in the industry for specific corporate portfolios where no historical data is available.

Business Risk	Score
Industry Position	6
Market Share Trends and Prospects	2
Geographical Diversity of Operations	2
Diversity Product and Services	6
Customer Mix	1
Management Quality and Depth	4
Executive Board Oversight	2
...	...

Exhibit 5.29 Expert-Based Scorecard (Ozdemir and Miu 2009)

Agency Ratings Approach

We already discussed the prediction approach, which assumes the availability of historical data, and the expert-based approach, which assumes the availability of expert-based knowledge or experience. The agency ratings approach is an approach that can be adopted if none of these is available. In other words, if the bank cannot come up with an internal approach to do credit risk assessment, it needs to look externally. Rating agencies are interesting partners to collaborate with in this case since they provide credit ratings for almost any type of nonretail exposure. These ratings typically vary from AAA, which represents excellent credit quality, to AA, A, … and down to D, which represents the default status. The ratings also come with default rates measured across different time horizons such as one, two, three, or even five years. Banks can then purchase these credit ratings to score their nonretail exposures. Popular rating agencies are Moody's, Standard & Poor's, and Fitch. They provide ratings to almost any type of debt or fixed income securities. Examples are ratings for companies (both private and public), countries and governments (sovereign ratings), local authorities, and banks. Retail exposures are typically not covered by the rating agencies. The methodology behind the rating assignment is obviously not disclosed, but it is based on a combination of both quantitative and qualitative modeling. Exhibit 5.30 shows the list of ratings adopted by these three agencies.

Shadow Ratings Approach

The shadow ratings approach starts from a data set with ratings for a particular set of obligors. In a next step, information will be collected for each obligor that might have an influence on the rating. Example data that can be considered in a corporate setting are accounting ratios, firm characteristics, and stock price behavior. The aim is then to combine all this information in one data set (see Exhibit 5.31) and build an analytical model to predict the ratings (Van Gestel et al. 2005, 2007). Exhibit 5.32 shows an example of a decision tree predicting ratings. The advantage of this approach is that we obtain a "white box" understandable model that clearly indicates how the various characteristics of an obligor contribute to the rating. It will also provide clear advice to corporates on how to improve their ratings. Furthermore, in the long term, this approach allows the bank to become independent from the rating agency, since the internal statistical model can now be used to rate any obligor given its characteristics.

BIG DATA FOR CREDIT SCORING

Data are everywhere these days. IBM projects that every day we generate 2.5 quintillion bytes of data. In relative terms, this means 90 percent of the data in the world has been created in the past two years. These massive amounts of data yield an unprecedented treasure of information, ready to be analyzed using state of the art analytical

Moody's	S&P	Fitch	Credit Quality
Aaa	AAA	AAA	Extremely strong
Aa1	AA+	AA+	
Aa2	AA	AA	Very strong
Aa3	AA−	AA−	
A1	A+	A+	
A2	A	A	Strong
A3	A−	A−	
Baa1	BBB+	BBB+	
Baa2	BBB	BBB	Adequate
Baa3	BBB−	BBB−	
Ba1	BB+	BB+	
Ba2	BB	BB	Speculative
Ba3	BB−	BB−	
B1	B+	B+	
B2	B	B	Highly speculative
B3	B−	B−	
Caa1	CCC+	CCC+	
Caa2	CCC	CCC	Vulnerable
Caa3	CCC−	CCC−	
Ca	CC	CC	Highly vulnerable
C	C	C	Extremely vulnerable
RD	SD	RD	Selective, restrictive default
D	D	D	Default

Exhibit 5.30 Credit Ratings by Moody's, S&P, and Fitch (Van Gestel and Baesens 2009)

Company	Solvency	Liquidity	Stock Price	...	Rating
ABC	10%	66%	100		B
CDE	5%	90%	16		A
DEF	78%	12%	225		A
FGH	24%	58%	88		C
...					

Exhibit 5.31 Example Data Set for the Shadow Rating Approach

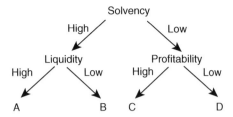

Exhibit 5.32 Example Shadow Rating Model

techniques to build better credit scorecards. Before we illustrate its potential in a credit scoring context, let's first get a closer look at big data.

Big data is often characterized in terms of its four Vs: volume, variety, velocity, and veracity. To illustrate this, let's briefly zoom in on some key sources or processes generating big data. Traditional sources are large-scale transactional enterprise systems such as online transaction processing (OLTP), enterprise resource planning (ERP), and customer relationship management (CRM) applications. Companies have been deploying these systems for about two decades now. Classic credit scorecards are typically constructed using data extracted from these transactional systems.

The online social graph is a more recent example. Think about the major social networks such as Facebook, Twitter, LinkedIn, Weibo, and WeChat. All together, these networks capture information on close to two billion people about their friends, preferences, and other behavior, leaving a massive digital trail of data. With close to five billion handsets worldwide and with the mobile channel serving as the primary gateway to the Internet in many developed and developing countries, this is another source of big data, as every action taken by the user can be tracked and potentially geo-tagged. Also think about the Internet of Things (IoT) or the emerging sensor-enabled ecosystem that is going to connect various objects (e.g., homes, cars) with each other and with humans. Finally, we see more and more open or public data such as data about weather, traffic, maps, and the macroeconomy.

All these data-generating processes can be characterized in terms of the sheer *volume* of data that is being generated. Clearly, this poses serious challenges in terms of setting up scalable storage architectures combined with a distributed approach to data manipulation and querying.

Big data usually comes in a great *variety* of various formats. Traditional data types or structured data such as customer name, customer birth date, and the like are more and more complemented with unstructured data such as images, fingerprints, tweets, e-mails, Facebook pages, sensor data, and GPS data. Although the former can be easily stored in traditional (e.g., relational) databases, the latter needs to be accommodated using the appropriate database technology facilitating the storage, querying, and manipulation of each of these types of unstructured data. This also requires a substantial effort since it is claimed that at least 80 percent of all data is unstructured.

Velocity refers to the speed at which the data is generated and needs to be stored and analyzed. Think about streaming applications such as online trading platforms, YouTube, SMS messages, credit card swipes, phone calls, and the like, which are all examples where high velocity is a key concern.

Veracity indicates the quality or trustworthiness of the data. Unfortunately, more data does not automatically imply better data, so the quality of the data-generating process must be closely monitored and guaranteed.

As the volume, variety, velocity, and veracity of data continue to grow, so do the new opportunities for building better credit scoring models. Think about Facebook or Twitter as examples. It is quite obvious that knowing a credit applicant's hobbies, followers, friends, likes, education, and workplace could be very beneficial to better quantify his or her creditworthiness. In other words, a customer's social standing, online reputation, and professional connections are likely to be related to his or her credit quality. Another useful data source concerns call detail records (CDR) data, which capture the mobile phone usage of an applicant. Also, surfing behavior could be a nice add-on. Obviously, any privacy concerns surrounding the usage of this data should be properly addressed.

Clearly, the availability of these big data sources creates both opportunities as well as challenges for credit scoring. For example, the availability of social network and CDR data may be beneficial in various settings. First, it may be useful to score customers who lack borrowing experience (e.g., because it's their first loan or they recently moved to a new country) and would be automatically perceived as risky according to traditional credit scoring models that rely on historical information. By using these alternative data sources, a lender can make a better assessment of the credit risk, which can then be translated into a more favorable interest rate. This obviously gives an incentive to the customer to disclose his or her social network, CDR, or other relevant data to the bank. Another example is developing countries. In these countries, banks often lack historical credit information and no local credit bureaus may be available. Other data sources should be used to optimize access to credit. Given the widespread use of social networks and mobile phones (even in developing countries), the data gathered might be an interesting alternative to undertaking credit scoring.

Obviously, using the aforementioned data sources also comes with various challenges. The first one concerns privacy. It is important that customers are properly informed about what data is used to calculate their credit score. An opt-out option should always be provided. Furthermore, using social network data for credit scoring can trigger new default behavior whereby customers strategically construct their social network to artificially and maliciously brush up their credit quality. One example is that customers can easily buy Twitter followers to boost their credit scores. Finally, regulatory compliance might become an important issue. Many countries prohibit the use of gender, age, marital status, national origin, ethnicity, and beliefs for credit scoring. Much of this information can be easily scraped from social networks. It may be harder to oversee regulatory compliance when using social network or other big data for credit scoring.

OVERRIDES

Decisions made by a scorecard may be overruled by human judgment when extra information is present that has not been captured by the scorecard, or because of specific bank policies or strategies. A low-side override or upgrade override occurs when a customer is rejected by the scorecard but accepted anyway because recent information indicates that the customer has improved (or is expected to improve) his solvency status. The default status of the low-side override can then be subsequently tracked in order to determine whether it was the right decision to accept the customer. A high-side override or downgrade override occurs when a customer is accepted by the scorecard but rejected by the credit officer because new information shows, for example, that this customer is expected to change his or her employment status in the near future. Since credit is rejected, the true default status of the customer will never be known unless the customer receives credit elsewhere and his or her default status can be tracked via the credit bureau.

Exhibit 5.33 provides an example of an override report wherein the italic numbers indicate overrides. It is important to note that an excessive number of overrides is a sign that there is no longer confidence in the scorecard, and rebuilding should be considered. Financial regulators discourage financial institutions from doing ad hoc overrides, but instead insist on having clear, well-articulated override policies. Note that an override is sometimes also referred to as an overruling.

EVALUATING SCORECARD PERFORMANCE

Before bringing a scorecard into production, it needs to be thoroughly evaluated. Depending on the exact setting and usage of the model, different aspects may need to be assessed during evaluation in order to ensure the model is acceptable for

Score Range	Accepts	Rejects
<400	*2*	10
400–425	*5*	50
425–450	*10*	80
450–475	*20*	100
475–500	*25*	120
500–525	200	*5*
525–550	500	*5*
550–575	400	*4*
575–600	300	*2*
>600	200	*2*

Exhibit 5.33 Example Override Report for an Application Scorecard with Cutoff Equal to 500

implementation. A number of key characteristics of successful scorecards, which may or may not apply depending on the exact application, are defined and explained in Exhibit 5.34.

BUSINESS APPLICATIONS OF CREDIT SCORING

The most important usage of application scores is to decide on loan approval. The scores can also be used for pricing purposes. Risk-based pricing (sometimes also referred to as risk-adjusted pricing) sets the price or other characteristics (e.g., loan term, collateral) of the loan based on the perceived risk as measured by the application score. A lower score will imply a higher interest rate. Hence, subprime loans (e.g., having a FICO score of less than 620) will come with higher rates and fees.

Behavioral scores can be used for various business purposes. First, they can be used for marketing applications. The behavioral scores can be segmented and each of the segments can then be individually approached with targeted mailings. Another usage is for up-, down-, or cross-selling. Up-selling means that you want to sell more of the same product. Think about credit cards or lines of credit, for example. In the case of a good behavioral score and thus low credit risk, the bank may consider increasing the credit limit, thereby generating more revenue. Down-selling means selling less of the same product. So, in case of a bad behavioral score, the bank may consider mitigating its potential loss by lowering the credit limit. Finally, cross-selling means selling other products. For example, if the customer has a good behavioral score on his or her mortgage, the bank may try to sell some additional insurance products.

Although the idea of using behavioral scores to set credit limits sounds reasonable, there has been some debate in the literature about whether this is appropriate. In their book *Credit Scoring and Its Applications* (2002), Thomas et al. argue that one should be careful when using behavioral scores for limit setting. Their reasoning goes as follows. A behavioral credit score is calculated using a given operating policy and credit limit. Hence, using the behavioral score to change the credit limit basically invalidates the effectiveness of the score. To further illustrate this, they came up with an analogy. Suppose it is proposed that only those people who have no or few accidents when they drive a car at 30 miles per hour in town be allowed to drive at 70 miles per hour on the highways. Clearly, this is not a good reasoning since other skills may be required to drive faster. Similarly, it's not because a customer has a good behavioral score with a low credit limit that his or her behavioral score will remain good with a high credit limit, since other characteristics or skills might be needed to manage accounts with large credit limits. However, despite this argument, behavioral scores are commonly used in the industry to manage credit limits. Typically, the behavioral score will be categorized into bands, whereby each band will correspond to a specific credit limit.

Behavioral scores can also be used to authorize accounts to go in excess of their credit limit A gradually decreasing behavioral score could be an early warning signal

Statistical accuracy	Refers to the detection power and the correctness of the scorecard in labeling customers as defaulters. Several statistical evaluation criteria exist and may be applied to evaluate this aspect, such as the hit rate, lift curves, area under the curve (AUC), and so on. Statistical accuracy may also refer to statistical significance, meaning that the patterns that have been found in the data have to be valid and not the consequence of noise. In other words, we need to make sure that the model generalizes well and is not overfitted to the historical data set.
Interpretability	A scorecard needs to be interpretable. In other words, a deeper understanding of the detected default behavior is required, for instance to validate the scorecard before it can be used. This aspect involves a certain degree of subjectivism, since interpretability may depend on the credit expert's knowledge. The interpretability of a model depends on its format, which in turn is determined by the adopted analytical technique. Models that allow the user to understand the underlying reasons why the model signals a customer to be a defaulter are called white box models, whereas complex, incomprehensible, mathematical models are often referred to as black box models.
Operational efficiency	Operational efficiency refers to the time that is required to evaluate the scorecard, or in other words the time required to evaluate whether a customer is a defaulter. When customers need to be scored in real time, operational efficiency is crucial and is a main concern during model performance assessment. Operational efficiency also entails the efforts needed to collect and preprocess the data, evaluate the scorecard, monitor and back-test the scorecard, and reestimate it when necessary.
Economical cost	Developing and implementing a scorecard involves a significant cost to an organization. The total cost includes the costs to gather, preprocess, and analyze the data, and the costs to put the resulting scorecards into production. In addition, the software costs as well as human and computing resources should be taken into account. Possibly also external (e.g., credit bureau) data has to be bought to enrich the available in-house data. Clearly it is important to perform a thorough cost-benefit analysis at the start of the credit scoring project, and to gain insight into the constituent factors of the return on investment of building a scorecard system.
Regulatory compliance	A scorecard should be in line and compliant with all applicable regulations and legislation. In a credit scoring setting, the Basel Accords specify what information can or cannot be used and how the target (i.e., default) should be defined. Other regulations (e.g., with respect to privacy and/or discrimination) should also be respected.

Exhibit 5.34 Key Characteristics of Successful Scorecards

for looming credit problems, which can be very useful information from a proactive debt collection perspective. It allows time to develop a collection strategy by working out actions that might prevent default.

Both application and behavioral scores will also be used for risk management in a Basel II/III context (Van Gestel and Baesens 2009). More specifically, they will be used as key inputs to estimate the default rate on a loan portfolio, which will then be used to calculate the expected losses (covered by provisions) and unexpected losses (covered by capital). They can also be helpful for securitization purposes by slicing and dicing a credit portfolio into tranches with similar risk.

Besides financial institutions, other organizations can also use credit scores to support their business decisions. For example, electricity and telecommunications companies can use credit scores in their pricing or contracting policies. Employers can use them to get a better idea of the profiles of job applicants, while landlords can get a better idea about the solvency of their future renters. Insurance companies can use credit scores to set insurance premiums or decide for whom to accept the insurance policy. Note that some of these applications are controversial and subject to debate.

The widespread use of both application and behavioral scorecards has made them a key decision support tool in modern risk measurement and management.

LIMITATIONS

Although credit scoring systems are being implemented and used by most banks nowadays, they do face a number of limitations. A first limitation concerns the data that is used to estimate credit scoring models. Since data is the major, and in most cases the only, ingredient to build these models, its quality and predictive ability is key to the models' success. The quality of the data refers, for example, to the number of missing values and outliers, and to the recency and representativity of the data. Data quality issues can be difficult to detect without specific domain knowledge, but have an important impact on the scorecard development and resulting risk measures. The availability of high-quality data is a very important prerequisite for building good credit scoring models. However, not only does the data need to be of high quality, but it should be predictive as well, in the sense that the captured characteristics are related to the customer's likelihood of defaulting. Before constructing a scorecard, we need to thoroughly reflect on why a customer defaults and which characteristics could potentially be related to this. Customers may default because of unknown reasons or information not available to the financial institution, thereby posing another limitation to the performance of credit scoring models. The statistical techniques used in developing credit scoring models typically assume a data set of sufficient size containing enough defaults. This may not always be the case for specific types of portfolios where only limited data is available, or only a low number of defaults is observed. For these types of portfolios, one may have to rely on alternative risk assessment methods using, for example, expert judgment based on the five Cs, as we discussed earlier.

Financial institutions should also be aware that scorecards have only a limited lifetime. The populations on which they were estimated will typically vary throughout time because of changing economic conditions or new strategic actions (e.g., new customer segments targeted, new credit products introduced) undertaken by the bank. This is often referred to as population drift and will necessitate the financial institution rebuilding its scorecards if the default risk in the new population is totally different from the one present in the population that was used to build the old scorecards.

Many credit bureaus nowadays start disclosing how their bureau scores (e.g., FICO scores) are computed in order to encourage customers to improve their financial profiles, and hence increase their success in getting credit. Since this gives customers the tools to polish up their scores and make them look good in future credit applications, this may trigger new types of default risk (and fraud), thereby invalidating the original scorecard and necessitating more frequent rebuilds.

Introducing credit scoring into an organization requires serious investments in information and communications technology (ICT) hardware and software, personnel training, and support facilities. The total cost needs to be carefully considered beforehand and compared with future benefits, which may be hard to quantify.

Finally, a last criticism concerns the fact that most credit scoring systems model only default risk (i.e., the risk that a customer runs into payment arrears on one of his or her financial obligations). Default risk is, however, only one type of credit risk. Besides default risk, credit risk also entails recovery risk and exposure risk.

PRACTICE QUESTIONS

1. Contrast the judgmental approach and the statistical approach to credit scoring. Give examples of situations where one is to be preferred over the other.

2. Contrast logistic regression to decision trees in terms of model formulation, model representation, and decision boundary. Give examples of situations where one is to be preferred over the other.

3. Discuss the criteria that should be considered when performing variable selection for credit scoring.

4. What decisions should be made when building a decision tree?

5. Discuss the approaches available to do credit scoring for retail portfolios.

6. Give some examples of modeling decisions that need to be made when building an application scorecard.

7. Discuss some issues that arise when defining variables for behavioral scoring.

8. What is reject inference? How can it be dealt with?

9. Discuss the approaches available to do credit scoring for nonretail portfolios.

10. Discuss the potential and risks of using social media data (e.g., Facebook, Twitter) for credit scoring.

11. What are the key characteristics of successful scorecards? Discuss which ones are important in what situations.

12. Discuss who is allowed to use credit scores in your country (e.g., utility companies, telecommunications firms, employers, landlords, etc.).

13. What is the importance of data quality in the context of credit scoring?

REFERENCES

Allison, P. D. 2001. *Logistic Regression Using the SAS System: Theory and Application*. New York: John Wiley & Sons–SAS.

Baesens, B., T. Van Gestel, S. Viaene, M. Stepanova, J. Suykens, and J. Vanthienen. 2003. "Benchmarking State of the Art Classification Algorithms for Credit Scoring." *Journal of the Operational Research Society* 54 (6): 627–635.

Baesens, B. 2014. *Analytics in a Big Data World*, Wiley.

Banasik, J., J. N. Crook, and L. C. Thomas. 2001. "Sample Selection Bias in Credit Scoring Models." In *Proceedings of the Seventh Conference on Credit Scoring and Credit Control (CSCCVII'2001)*, Edinburgh, Scotland.

Breiman, L., J. H. Friedman, R. A. Olshen, and C. J. Stone. 1984. *Classification and Regression Trees*. Monterey, CA: Wadsworth & Brooks/Cole Advanced Books & Software.

Duda, R. O., P. E. Hart, and D. G. Stork. 2001. *Pattern Classification*. New York: John Wiley & Sons.

Hand, D. J. 2001. "Reject Inference in Credit Operations: Theory and Methods." In *Handbook of Credit Scoring*, edited by Elizabeth Mays. Chicago: Glenlake Publishing Company.

Hartigan, J. A. 1975. *Clustering Algorithms*. New York: John Wiley & Sons.

Martens, D., B. Baesens, T. Van Gestel, and J. Vanthienen. 2007. "Comprehensible Credit Scoring Models Using Rule Extraction from Support Vector Machines." *European Journal of Operational Research* 183:1466–1476.

Ozdemir, B., and P. Miu. 2009. *Basel II Implementation: A Guide to Developing and Validating a Compliant, Internal Risk Rating System*. New York: McGraw-Hill.

Quinlan, J. R. 1993. *C4.5 Programs for Machine Learning*. San Francisco: Morgan Kaufmann.

Thomas, L. C., D. B. Edelman, and J. N. Crook. 2002. *Credit Scoring and Its Applications*. Monographs on Mathematical Modeling and Computation. Philadelphia: Society for Industrial and Applied Mathematics.

Van Gestel, T., and B. Baesens. 2009. *Credit Risk Management: Basic Concepts: Financial Risk Components, Rating Analysis, Models, Economic and Regulatory Capital*. Oxford: Oxford University Press.

Van Gestel, T., B. Baesens, P. Van Dijcke, J. Suykens, J. Garcia, and T. Alderweireld. 2005. "Linear and Nonlinear Credit Scoring by Combining Logistic Regression and Support Vector Machines." *Journal of Credit Risk* 1, no. 4.

Van Gestel, T., D. Martens, B. Baesens, D. Feremans, J. Huysmans, and J. Vanthienen. 2007. "Forecasting and Analyzing Insurance Companies' Ratings." *International Journal of Forecasting* 23 (3): 513–529.

CHAPTER 6

Probabilities of Default (PD): Discrete-Time Hazard Models

INTRODUCTION

In the previous chapter, we saw that credit scores are indicators of the credit risk of borrowers. Default probabilities or probabilities of default (PDs) are in essence credit scores that are standardized likelihood measures with a range between zero and one, whereby zero implies that an event is impossible to occur and one implies certainty. Realistic models generally assign PDs between zero and 30 percent to loans.

The PD is the most scrutinized parameter in credit risk analytics and subject to minimum standards imposed by prudential regulators. For example, banks are required to include and exclude specific risk factors. Furthermore, minimum floors such as three basis points are imposed (often to have a nonzero PD value for low default portfolios, which is a subject that we explore later). Banks are also required to validate their PD estimates with rigorous tests, which we discuss in the validation chapter.

Default Events

A PD describes the likelihood of a default event. Banks observe whether borrowers default, and generally indicate this with a default indicator:

$$D_{it} = \begin{cases} 1 & \text{borrower } i \text{ defaults at time } t \\ 0 & \text{otherwise} \end{cases}$$

with $i = 1, \ldots, I$ and $t = 1, \ldots, T$. We assume that the default event is random and use an uppercase letter D as the random variable and a lowercase letter d as its realization. A default event may be defined by any of the following events:

- Payment delinquency of a number of days or more; popular thresholds are 30, 60, and 90 days
- Bankruptcy of the borrower
- Collateral owned by a bank (e.g., real estate owned after an unsuccessful sale at a foreclosure auction)
- Foreclosure of loan
- Short sale of loan
- Loss/write-down amount
- Involuntary liquidation
- Debt modification as a positive interest, expense, or principal forgiveness

Alternative default definitions are possible, and one example may be the Basel definition, which is based on a payment delinquency of 90 days or more. In later sections, we discuss examples where banks observe other outcomes such as payoff, winsorizing, or competing default states (e.g., delinquency, liquidation, or receivership).

Conditional and Unconditional Default

Banks track the performance of loans over time and include dynamic information in their measurements. Time-varying information may include information about the borrower, loan, and collateral (idiosyncratic information), and macroeconomic conditions (systematic information). Common assessment periods may be a day, a month, a quarter, or a year. The choice of time period may depend on the availability of information and the needs of stakeholders such as depositors, investors, prudential regulators, or shareholders. The assessments of credit risk support various functional bank areas. Some areas (e.g., capital allocation and risk reporting under Basel) require risk estimates for the next period, whereas others (e.g., loan loss provisioning under IFRS 9) cover multiple periods, often the lifetime of financial instruments.

Exhibit 6.1 shows the conditionality of default events for two periods. Defaults are generally terminating events, and a default event in one period is therefore conditional on survival (i.e., nondefault) in prior periods.

Banks measure the probability of default (PD) for both counterparties and financial instruments. As mentioned, the terminology of default probability is generally

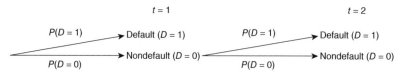

Exhibit 6.1 Conditionality of Default Events

used to refer to the one-period default probability. Other terms used are the conditional default probability (conditional on survival) and default intensity.

Furthermore, multiyear default probabilities may be computed as unconditional default probabilities and applied in multiyear evaluations, as is done in the context of computing expected present values or loss values for financial instruments. The unconditional probability of default is often used to measure the likelihood of default from the perspective of the loan's origination. The conditional probability of default measures the likelihood of default conditional on survival and is often used to measure the risk after origination. The conditional and unconditional default probabilities are identical for the first period.

Assuming that every borrower has the same conditional probability of default $PD_{t-1,t}$ at any period $t-1, t$, we can omit the borrower index i. The unconditional probability of default $UPD_{t-1,t}$ can then be computed as follows:

$$
\begin{aligned}
UPD_{t_1,t_2} &= S(t_1) - S(t_2) \\
&= \prod_{t=1}^{t_1}(1 - PD_{t-1,t}) - \prod_{t=1}^{t_2}(1 - PD_{t-1,t}) \\
&= \prod_{t=1}^{t_1}(1 - PD_{t-1,t}) - \prod_{t=1}^{t_1}(1 - PD_{t_1,t})\prod_{t=t_1}^{t_2}(1 - PD_{t-1,t}) \\
&= \prod_{t=1}^{t_1}(1 - PD_{t-1,t})\left(1 - \prod_{t=t_1}^{t_2}(1 - PD_{t-1,t})\right) \\
&= S(t_1)PD_{t_1,t_2}
\end{aligned}
$$

$S(t)$ is the cumulative survival probability to time t (i.e., no default by time t).

Real-World versus Risk-Neutral

Default probabilities are called real-world default probabilities if they are modeled for real-world default realization. The majority of a bank's credit risk exposures relate to illiquid loans (in particular mortgage loans) for which a bank estimates real-world default probabilities.

For marketable exposures, risk-neutral probabilities of default may be derived from observed market prices (e.g., share prices or credit default swap spreads). This approach is very popular in the finance literature but limited to a small fraction of total credit exposures, namely public and/or large counterparties for which equity, debt, or derivatives markets exist. Moreover, risk-neutral probabilities can be quite different from real-world probabilities due to premiums for risk aversion and are therefore of only limited value for risk management.

Basel Requirements

In order to determine regulatory capital requirements, banks often assign rating classes to borrowers and then compute default probabilities for these rating classes.

For corporates, central governments, and central banks, the default rating should exclusively reflect the risk of obligor default. At least seven ratings should be available for the nondefaulted obligors and one rating for the defaulters. For retail exposures, a credit rating needs to reflect both obligor and transaction risk. Hence, credit product characteristics and collateralization also need to be taken into account. An excessive concentration of obligors in a rating should be avoided. Instead, ratings should be as homogeneous as possible in terms of default risk. No minimum number of ratings for retail exposures is suggested.

For corporates, central governments, central banks, and retail exposures, a PD needs to be provided per rating. Note that depending upon geographical location, ratings may also be referred to as pools, segments, grades, classes, or clusters. A defaulter is defined as an obligor who is unlikely to pay his or her obligations or is past due more than 90 days. In the United States this has been set to either 120 or 180 days depending on the exposure class. In the United Kingdom, both 90 and 180 days are used. A lower bound has been set to the PD of three basis points. For obligors in default, it is obvious that the PD equals 100 percent. To calculate the PD, at least five years of historical data should be used, although not all data should receive equal weight in case older data is less relevant. The PD of a particular rating can then be estimated as the long-run average of the one-year default rates.

Parameter Estimation

It is common to assume that default events are driven by an unobservable data-generating process (DGP). The data-generating process is unknown and much research has focused on understanding its key components. Many different models have been proposed in the literature, and a popular one is the Merton (1974) model for corporate borrowers. In this model, default occurs if the market value of the assets (or the return) falls below the market value of the outstanding debt. Exhibit 6.2 shows the derivation of a one-year default probability from such a structural model.

The asset value is often assumed to follow a lognormal distribution, and the asset return a normal distribution. We define log (x) as the natural logarithm of x and exp (x) as e raised to the power of x throughout this chapter. The standardized asset return A_{it} of borrower i in time period t can be modeled as a latent process. A default event occurs if the asset return A_{it} falls below a threshold γ_{it}. The probability of default (PD) then becomes:

$$PD_{it} = P(D_{it} = 1) = P(A_{it} < \gamma_{it}) = \Phi(\gamma_{it})$$

with Φ the cumulative density function of the standard normal distribution. This simple credit model results in a probit model with the linear predictor γ_{it}. Similar models may be constructed for other distributions and other risk segments such as consumer loans. The latter include a consumer's asset value or credit score and a threshold, which if passed results in a default event. For example, Hamerle, Liebig, and

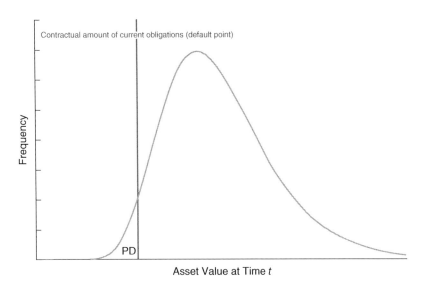

Contractual amount of current obligations (default point)

Frequency

PD

Asset Value at Time *t*

Exhibit 6.2 Merton Model

Scheule (2006) derive a logit regression model using an asset value return/threshold model. We will extend this model by a decomposition of the asset value returns into systematic and idiosyncratic components in our default correlation and credit portfolio risk chapter.

The observable outcome is the default event. In the banking industry, regression models have been introduced that link the observable default/nondefault outcome to information that is available at the time of the risk assessment. Credit risk modelers approximate the structural model (i.e., the comparison of asset value and debt value, also known as the distance to default) by using observable information such as the earnings, debt, liquidity of the creditor, and so on. Parameters explain the sensitivities for the impact of observable information on observable outcomes, and a link function (e.g., a linear combination or a nonlinear link) is assumed.

Econometric methods for parameter estimation are discussed later. More specifically, we will introduce both discrete-time and continuous-time (survival) models. Discrete-time models explain the default event within a certain time period, while survival models estimate the time to default. There are close linkages between these methodologies.

Popular examples of such estimation techniques are: the unconditional mean of the default indicators for single or multiple periods, regression techniques that condition the default probabilities on observable variables (e.g., linear regressions for averages of default indicators), and nonlinear regressions for the default indicator itself. These approaches are generally based on maximum likelihood estimation techniques that maximize a theoretical likelihood for the realized dependent variable given the observed information variables and estimated parameters.

Estimated parameters are subject to parameter uncertainty. Most estimation procedures report estimates for the parameters, their standard deviation (standard errors) and covariance/correlation matrices. These are typically based on the assumption of a normal distribution with the parameter estimate being the estimated mean and the standard error being the estimated standard deviation. We will follow up on this kind of model risk in our stress testing chapter.

DISCRETE-TIME HAZARD MODELS

Probabilities of default may be modeled with discrete-time hazard models. In order to estimate such models in SAS, the data should be arranged in panel form. Note that the word "panel" needs to be interpreted with care, as discrete-time hazard models are estimated by maximizing the product over the observational likelihoods (see later discussion). This implies that discrete-time hazard models treat the observations as conditionally (i.e., given the covariates) independent. For loan exposures, every loan is observed in periodic intervals to either default, payoff, or end of the observation period.

Every row in a panel data set represents the observation of one loan in a single period. The columns represent variables, which include information on the propensity of a borrower default, including borrower-specific variables, macroeconomic variables, origination variables, and collateral variables as well as the random outcome variable D_{it} with realization d_{it}, which is zero if a borrower does not default and one if a borrower does default.

The code and output in Exhibit 6.3 show the last three observations of three loans from our mortgage data set.

In our mortgage data set, the loans in the data are numbered consecutively (id = 1 to 50,000) and the observation periods (time = 1 to 60) are numbered consecutively from the first observation period. Loans may have originated prior to the first observation period and may carry negative values in such cases. Examples of loan-specific variables are the FICO score at origination and the loan-to-value (LTV) ratio at origination. The FICO mortgage score is a credit score with values between 300 and 850. LTV is the ratio of the outstanding loan amount to the collateral value, and banks

id	orig_ time	time	default_ time	payoff_ time	FICO_ orig_ time	LTV_ orig_ time	LTV_time	gdp_time	uer_time
46	19	27	0	0	581	80.0	67.5913	2.36172	4.4
46	19	28	0	0	581	80.0	68.2919	1.22917	4.6
46	19	29	1	0	581	80.0	68.8752	1.69297	4.5
47	19	25	0	0	600	80.0	66.7938	2.89914	4.7
47	19	26	0	0	600	80.0	66.9609	2.15136	4.7
47	19	27	0	1	600	80.0	67.5853	2.36172	4.4
56	-15	58	0	0	664	52.5	17.3599	2.86859	6.2
56	-15	59	0	0	664	52.5	17.2625	2.44365	5.7
56	-15	60	0	0	664	52.5	16.8980	2.83636	5.7

Exhibit 6.3 Panel Data

traditionally extend loans in the region of 80 percent. The unemployment rate is time-varying and has the same value for all loans in a given observation period.

The loans result in different outcomes over time. Loan 46 defaults in period *time* = 29, which is indicated by the binary variable default_time. Loan 47 is paid off in period *time* = 27, which is indicated by the binary variable payoff_time. Loan 56 survives until the end of our observation period (i.e., *time* = 60), and we will later refer to this as a right-censored observation (see Chapter 7).

Discrete-time hazard regression models establish a link between the probability of the binary default variable taking on a particular value (e.g., default) and the observable information through nonlinear link functions F: $P(D_{it} = 1) = F(lp_{it-1})$. Note that the models are generally formulated in terms of expectation due to the binary character of the dependent variable. Furthermore, lp_{it-1} is a linear predictor formulated in terms of $lp_{it-1} = \beta' x_{it-1}$, that is a linear combination of observable information and parameters that are estimated, as discussed in what follows.

Note that the probability of default is time-varying and that the explanatory variables need to be known at the beginning of the observation period (hence the index $it - 1$) to enable the models to provide out-of-time econometric forecasts (see fitting and forecasting section). Examples of papers that apply discrete-time hazard models to estimate borrower-specific default probabilities are Hamerle et al. (2006), Crook, Edelman, and Thomas (2007), Crook and Bellotti (2010), and Leow and Mues (2012).

In the following section, we discuss four discrete-time hazard models: the linear model, the logit model, the probit model, and the complementary log-log (cloglog) model. In the industry, the logit and probit models are the most popular.

Linear Model

Linear models are generally estimated with an ordinary least squares (OLS) technique in which the distances between the predicted outcome and realized outcome are squared and summed over all observations, and the parameters are chosen such that this deviation measure is minimized. The model equation is:

$$D_{it} = \beta' x_{it-1} + \epsilon_{it}$$

with a vector of appropriate covariates x_{it-1}, the corresponding sensitivities β and ϵ_{it}, which is normally distributed with mean zero and standard deviation σ. The models can be estimated in SAS with PROC REG:

```
PROC REG DATA=data.mortgage;
MODEL default_time = FICO_orig_time
LTV_orig_time gdp_time;
RUN;
```

We do not show all output tables for the various procedures but limit our presentation to the ODS tables of interest throughout the book. Exhibit 6.4 shows the parameter estimates and *R*-squared measures (adjusted and nonadjusted) for model accuracy.

The REG Procedure
Model: MODEL1
Dependent Variable: default_time

Root MSE	0.15349	R-Square	0.0083
Dependent Mean	0.02435	Adj R-Sq	0.0083
Coeff Var	630.33859		

Parameter Estimates					
Variable	DF	Parameter Estimate	Standard Error	t Value	Pr > |t|
Intercept	1	0.07957	0.00259	30.71	<.0001
FICO_orig_time	1	−0.00011544	0.00000275	−42.02	<.0001
LTV_orig_time	1	0.00038077	0.00001944	19.59	<.0001
gdp_time	1	−0.00545	0.00009914	−55.02	<.0001

Exhibit 6.4 Linear Model

The estimate for σ is given by root mean squared error (MSE). No additional link function is applied in a linear model, which implies that the parameter estimates can be interpreted in terms of the dependent variable. For example, the impact of a change in the FICO score can be assessed by multiplying the change by the parameter estimate. We have set up the data such that the covariates refer to the time stamp, and the dependent variable (here default_time) refers to the period that follows the observation of the covariates. In other words, the dependent variable and the covariates are time lagged $(t − 1)$. Various time lags may be chosen for all or a set of selected covariates.

The sign of the parameters indicates the directional impact on the default probability. The FICO score and GDP growth have negative signs, which implies that the default probability decreases with a higher FICO score or GDP growth. The LTV ratio has a positive sign, which implies that the default probability increases with a higher LTV ratio.

The linear model is not popular for estimating borrower/loan-level default probabilities, as the predicted probabilities of default are not constrained within the range of the defined default probabilities of zero and one. This has the caveat that in some instances probabilities of default that are negative or above one may result. These values are unreasonable and often cause problems in follow-up applications such as the computation of regulatory capital or loan pricing.

Note that the model fit as indicated by the R-squared is low. The low R-squared is common for binary models and a reflection of the data-generating process: The realization of default events is based on a random binary variable and the default probability as event likelihood. The random experiment explains the low fit, and better results are achieved when default rates (rather than default events) are modeled.

As a matter of fact, linear models and extensions thereof are very popular to model default rates for risk segments and time periods. The reason for this popularity is that the estimated parameters can now be interpreted in terms of the default probability, and advanced econometric modeling techniques, such as state space models, require a linear link.

Furthermore, a nonlinear transformation for the dependent variable default rate is often chosen. Popular transformation functions are inverse cumulative density functions such as the logit and probit functions. The transformation in essence increases the range of values to the range of possible outcomes (i.e., from minus infinity to plus infinity) to match the range of possible values for the sum of the linear predictor and residual terms.

Nonlinear Models: Probit, Logit, and Cloglog Models

Specifying the Link Function

In order to constrain the dependent variable to the defined range of zero to one, nonlinear link functions can be applied. The nonlinear link functions are generally inverse cumulative distribution functions of well-known distributions. The functions that we discuss in this and the following subsections are the probit, the logit, and the complementary log-log (cloglog) functions. These functions map the linear predictor into a default probability, which is shown in Exhibit 6.5, where the linear predictor is shown on the x-axis, and the default probability, which is bounded between zero and one, is shown on the y-axis.

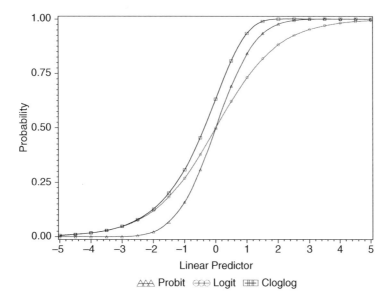

Exhibit 6.5 Nonlinear Link Functions

Creating Charts in SAS

Most credit risk analysts either export the data from SAS to other programs, in particular Excel, or directly draw the graphs in SAS. The graph in Exhibit 6.5 can be generated by the following code:

```
DATA graph;
DO x=-5 TO 5 BY 0.5;
logit=cdf('LOGISTIC',x);
probit=cdf('NORMAL',x);
cloglog=1-EXP(-EXP(x));
OUTPUT;
END;
RUN;


ODS GRAPHICS ON;
AXIS1 ORDER=(-5 to 5 BY 1) LABEL=('Linear predictor');
AXIS2 ORDER=(0 to 1 BY 0.25) LABEL=('Probability');
SYMBOL1 INTERPOL=SPLINE WIDTH=2 VALUE=TRIANGLE C=BLUE;
SYMBOL2 INTERPOL=SPLINE WIDTH=2 VALUE=CIRCLE C=RED;
SYMBOL3 INTERPOL=SPLINE WIDTH=2 VALUE=SQUARE C=BLACK;
LEGEND1 LABEL=NONE SHAPE=SYMBOL(4,2)
POSITION=(BOTTOM OUTSIDE);
PROC GPLOT DATA=test; PLOT logit*x probit*x cloglog*x
/ OVERLAY LEGEND=LEGEND1 HAXIS=AXIS1 VAXIS=AXIS2;
RUN;
ODS GRAPHICS OFF;
```

The shapes of the three link functions are comparable, yet distinct. Research has shown that different link functions result in different parameter estimates but the predicted values, here the probabilities of default, are comparable (see, e.g., Hamerle et al. 2006). Hence, practitioners may choose any of the presented link functions.

Probit Model

In what follows, we compare three models with different link functions: the logit model, the probit model, and the cloglog model. As we have already introduced the logit model in the credit scoring chapter, we now focus on the probit model, which can be estimated using PROC LOGISTIC or PROC PROBIT. We prefer PROC LOGISTIC as it has exactly the same syntax for all link functions and the link function can easily be changed for robustness checks.

As said, we generally find that the link function is of minor importance but different functions have important applications. For example, the logit link function has useful properties if the resulting mean PDs have to be calibrated to a different level. The probit link function is particularly useful for estimating parameters that are in line with the internal ratings based (IRB) models under the Basel regulations, as these assume the probit link.

The probit model equation is:

$$P(D_{it} = 1|X_{it-1}) = \Phi(\beta'x_{it-1})$$

with $\Phi(.)$ the cumulative density function of the standard normal distribution, β a vector of sensitivity parameters, and x_{it-1} a vector of time-lagged (with regard to the observable default event) covariates (i.e., risk factors). The following code estimates a logit model:

```
PROC LOGISTIC DATA=data.mortgage DESCENDING;
MODEL default_time =FICO_orig_time LTV_time gdp_time
/ LINK=PROBIT RSQUARE;
OUTPUT OUT=probabilities PREDICTED=PD_time;
RUN;
```

The PROC LOGISTIC statement invokes the procedure that estimates the probit, logit, as well as a range of other models. By default, SAS sorts the dependent variable from low to high and models the first category. The option DESCENDING reverses the default order and specifies that the probability of $y_{it} = 1$ is modeled.

The OUTPUT statement in combination with the PREDICTED= statement requests that the default probabilities are calculated for the estimation sample and stored in a separate variable in the input data set and also saved in the OUT= location. Alternatively, a STORE statement may be added that requests that the procedure parameter estimates are stored in the file specified by the name associated with the OUT= statement. This file cannot be modified but can be used for estimation and prediction of default probabilities, which we explain in detail later in the book. The contents of the item store can be processed with the PROC PLM procedure, which we will explain in more detail later in this chapter.

The Model Information section of the output (Exhibit 6.6) lists the reference data set, the dependent variable, and the number of response categories. Our dependent variable is default_time, which is binary and coded 0 for nondefault and 1 for default (other codes such as "Yes"/"No" are also possible). We use the suffix_time to indicate that the variable is time-varying. We use the suffix_orig_time to indicate that the variable is collected at loan origination and hence is constant over time. Furthermore, the number of observations and a breakdown by category of the dependent variable are provided. These are important descriptive statistics that are often included in risk reports.

Maximum Likelihood Estimation

In SAS, the Fisher's scoring method is used as a default method of iteratively estimating the regression parameters via maximization of the log-likelihood. The likelihood is defined as follows:

The LOGISTIC Procedure

Model Information	
Data Set	DATA.MORTGAGE
Response Variable	default_time
Number of Response Levels	2
Model	Binary probit
Optimization Technique	Fisher's scoring

Number of Observations Read	622489
Number of Observations Used	622219

Response Profile		
Ordered Value	**default_time**	**Total Frequency**
1	1	15153
2	0	607066

note	Probability modeled is default_time=1.

Model Convergence Status
Convergence criterion (GCONV=1E−8) satisfied.

Exhibit 6.6 Probit Model

$$L(\boldsymbol{\beta}, \boldsymbol{x}_{it-1}) = \prod_{i=1}^{I} \prod_{t=1}^{T} \left((P(D_{it} = 1)^{d_{it}} \cdot (1 - P(D_{it} = 1))^{(1-d_{it})} \right)$$

with $P(d_{it} = 1) = \Phi(\boldsymbol{\beta}' \boldsymbol{x}_{it-1})$. The likelihood function in essence multiplies all event probabilities by the probability for a default event of $P(d_{it} = 1)$ and the probability for a nondefault event of $1 - P(d_{it} = 1)$. The likelihood is then transformed by the monotone natural logarithm (i.e., log-likelihood):

$$\log\ L(\boldsymbol{\beta}, \boldsymbol{x}_{it-1}) = \sum_{i=1}^{I} \sum_{t=1}^{T} (d_{it} \log\ (P(D_{it} = 1)) + (1 - d_{it}) \log\ (1 - P(D_{it} = 1)))$$

The SAS algorithm then maximizes the natural logarithm, as the latter maintains monotonicity and results in the same parameter estimates with the merit that the sum of log-likelihoods is computationally simpler than the product of likelihoods.

Note that other optimization techniques may result in different standard errors. The Number of Observations Read and Number of Observations Used are the number of observations in the data set and the number of observations used in the analysis. The latter may be lower if values for the dependent or independent variables can not be processed, or if they are missing.

The Response Profile shows that the probability of a default event is modeled as we have applied the DESCENDING command, which sorts the dependent variable default_time in descending order (high to low). This implies that a positive parameter estimate (note that the logistic link function is monotone) increases the default probability. SAS models by default the probability of the lowest category, here the probability of a nondefault event, which is coded as zero. SAS confirms this in the output file with the sentence "Probability modeled is […]."

The next output section (Exhibit 6.7) includes the likelihood-based performance measures.

The model fit statistics are measures for model fit based on −2 times the log-likelihood (−2LogL). Both the Akaike information criterion (AIC) and the Schwartz criterion (SC) are based on −2 times the log-likelihood and include a penalty for the number of estimated parameters. A lower AIC/SC/−2LogL indicates a better fit, which holds for nested models. These measures are absolute measures, which depend on the sample size. In other words, these measures are not suitable to compare models based on different sample sizes, which may be a result of the availability of dependent and independent variables (see the previous comment on Number of Observations Used).

We have also requested the generalized R-squared measure (i.e., the likelihood-based pseudo R-squared measure and its rescaled variant) for the

Model Fit Statistics		
Criterion	Intercept Only	Intercept and Covariates
AIC	142525.57	134965.28
SC	142536.91	135010.64
−2 Log L	142523.57	134957.28

R-Square	0.0121	Max-rescaled R-Square	0.0590

Testing Global Null Hypothesis: BETA=0			
Test	Chi-Square	DF	Pr > ChiSq
Likelihood Ratio	7566.2941	3	<.0001
Score	7861.2257	3	<.0001
Wald	6854.6897	3	<.0001

Exhibit 6.7 Probit Model (cont.)

Analysis of Maximum Likelihood Estimates					
Parameter	DF	Estimate	Standard Error	Wald Chi-Square	Pr > ChiSq
Intercept	1	−1.0091	0.0354	814.0574	<.0001
FICO_orig_time	1	−0.00242	0.000050	2366.9776	<.0001
LTV_time	1	0.00781	0.000158	2447.5807	<.0001
gdp_time	1	−0.0496	0.00167	883.8005	<.0001

Exhibit 6.8 Probit Model (cont.)

model by using the RSQUARE option after the model statement. The measure is a relative performance measure, as it includes a comparison with a noninformative model that assigns all default observations the same average default rate and is defined between zero and one. A model with a higher R-squared value dominates models with lower R-squared values. Note that relative performance measures share the same critique as absolute performance measures and should be used with great care when models are estimated using different sample sizes (see Hamerle, Rauhmeier, and Rösch 2003, and the validation chapter).

The Global Null Hypothesis test that is included tests whether all parameter estimates are jointly equal to zero. As we primarily deal with large data, this hypothesis is generally rejected, implying that at least one explanatory variable is significant.

The next output section (Exhibit 6.8) includes the actual parameter estimates and hence the meat of our model analysis.

The column Estimate shows the parameter estimates and mean of the normal parameter distribution. Standard Error is the estimated standard deviation, and Wald Chi-Square is the test statistic for a test that verifies whether the parameter is equal to zero (i.e., the explanatory variable has no impact on the default behavior). A higher value generally indicates greater significance. The information is also included in the p-value, which is labeled Pr > ChiSq. An explanatory variable is considered to be significant if the p-value is less than or equal to a chosen significance level (often termed α), which effectively limits the type 1 error rate.

The sensitivities have to be interpreted in terms of the linear predictor. The sensitivity of the FICO score is −0.00242 and implies that the linear predictor and hence the PD decreases with the FICO score. A FICO score which is 100 points greater results in a linear predictor that is −0.242 lower (= −0.00242 ∗ 100). The interpretation for the LTV ratio and the GDP growth follows analogously.

The last output table (Exhibit 6.9) includes statistics that are of great interest to credit risk analysts.

```
        Association of Predicted Probabilities and Observed Responses

        Percent Concordant          69.5     Somers' D     0.422
        Percent Discordant          27.3     Gamma         0.436
        Percent Tied                 3.2     Tau-a         0.020
        Pairs                 9198871098     c             0.711
```

Exhibit 6.9 Probit Model (cont.)

Somers' D is the accuracy ratio (AR) and c is the area under the ROC curve (AUROC). Both measures can be transformed into one another: AR = 2 * AUROC − 1. The accuracy ratio is sometimes also referred to as the Gini coefficient. We will discuss these measures in more detail in the validation chapter.

Estimation of Default Probabilities

The PROC LOGISTIC has also generated a data set called probabilities with the OUTPUT command. The command adds an additional column (named PD_time) to the input data set. In other words, a default probability has been estimated for every observation based on the

- ▨ Model assumptions
- ▨ Estimated model parameters
- ▨ Historical data that was used to estimate the parameters

Calibration of Probit Models

An important consideration in estimating default probabilities is their calibration to the default rates. Discrete-time hazard models by definition are calibrated (see later analysis): The mean of the estimated default probabilities matches the default rate of the estimation sample. The intercept parameter captures any baseline risk that is not attributable to the explanatory variables.

Calibration of default rates is a "hard" requirement in building Basel-compliant credit risk models and models that do not meet this standard are not approved for capital allocation, loan loss provisioning, and stress testing. Furthermore, banks are unlikely to consider such models for internal economic purposes such as loan pricing. Note that because of this, the industry has hesitated to embrace risk-neutral credit risk models based on share prices. We test the calibration of the logistic model by comparing the mean estimated default probabilities with the default rate in the sample.

We run PROC MEANS for the default indicator and default probabilities and find that the mean of the in-sample PD estimates matches the default rate. Furthermore, the dispersion of the estimated default probabilities (i.e., the difference between the maximum and minimum estimates) is an indication of the ability of a PD model to predict default. This ability is highest if PDs with a value of zero are assigned to nondefault events and PDs with a value of one are assigned to default events. Note that this measure is also data dependent and the discriminatory power increases with the degree of discrimination in the data-generating process. We have estimated the in-sample default probabilities with the OUTPUT statement, which has evaluated the model equation and estimated parameters (indicated by a hat) as follows:

$$\widehat{P}(D_{it} = 1 | X_{it-1}) = \Phi(\widehat{\beta}_0 + \widehat{\beta}_1 * \text{FICO\_orig\_time} + \widehat{\beta}_2 * \text{LTV\_time} + \widehat{\beta}_3 * \text{gdp\_time})$$

with $\widehat{\beta}_0$ to $\widehat{\beta}_3$ the estimated parameters. A PROC MEANS provides the mean for the default indicators and the estimated PDs (Exhibit 6.10).

```
PROC MEANS DATA=probabilities MEAN NOLABELS;
VAR default_time PD_time;
RUN;
```

The MEANS Procedure

Variable	Mean	Variable	Mean
default_time	0.0243506	PD_time	0.0242548

Exhibit 6.10 Calibration of Probit Models: Comparison of Default Indicators and Estimated Default Probabilities

The calibration is clear, as the mean of the default event almost matches the mean of the estimated PD. The minor difference that we observe is due to the estimation algorithm that iteratively maximizes the likelihood and stops if a target function indicates a low model improvement.

We include a more detailed discussion of the estimation and forecasting of default probabilities using the data set generated by the STORE command and PROC PLM later in the book.

Logit Model

As mentioned in the credit scoring chapter, a logit model is the default option of PROC LOGISTIC and hence does not require the explicit specification of a link function:

```
PROC LOGISTIC DATA=data.mortgage DESCENDING;
MODEL default_time = FICO_orig_time LTV_time gdp_time;
RUN;
```

The parameter estimates have the same signs as the probit model but a different magnitude (see Exhibit 6.11).

The LOGISTIC Procedure

Analysis of Maximum Likelihood Estimates					
Parameter	DF	Estimate	Standard Error	Wald Chi-Square	Pr > ChiSq
Intercept	1	−1.6523	0.0832	394.8522	<.0001
FICO_orig_time	1	−0.00540	0.000116	2156.7605	<.0001
LTV_time	1	0.0184	0.000372	2446.3140	<.0001
gdp_time	1	−0.1094	0.00375	851.1896	<.0001

Association of Predicted Probabilities and Observed Responses			
Percent Concordant	69.4	Somers' D	0.423
Percent Discordant	27.1	Gamma	0.438
Percent Tied	3.5	Tau-a	0.020
Pairs	9198871098	c	0.711

Exhibit 6.11 Logit Model

The LOGISTIC Procedure

Analysis of Maximum Likelihood Estimates					
Parameter	DF	Estimate	Standard Error	Wald Chi-Square	Pr > ChiSq
Intercept	1	−0.8041	0.0761	111.6063	<.0001
FICO_orig_time	1	−0.00535	0.000112	2268.0798	<.0001
LTV_time	1	0.00885	0.000283	980.3850	<.0001
gdp_time	1	−0.1415	0.00355	1591.2030	<.0001

Association of Predicted Probabilities and Observed Responses			
Percent Concordant	67.7	Somers' D	0.396
Percent Discordant	28.1	Gamma	0.413
Percent Tied	4.2	Tau-a	0.019
Pairs	9198871098	c	0.698

Exhibit 6.12 Cloglog Model

The model fit as indicated by the accuracy ratio (Somers' D) and AUROC (c) is comparable to the probit model.

Cloglog Model

The following code estimates a cloglog model:

```
PROC LOGISTIC DATA=data.mortgage DESCENDING;
MODEL default_time = FICO_orig_time
LTV_time gdp_time/ LINK=CLOGLOG;
RUN;
```

Again, the parameter estimates have the same signs as the probit and logit models, but different magnitudes (see Exhibit 6.12). We will show that the combination of link function, parameter estimates, and covariates will result in very similar estimates for the probability of default, regardless of the choice of link function. The model fit as indicated by the accuracy ratio (Somers' D) and AUROC (c) is lower than the one by the probit and logit models.

Applications

Qualitative Information

Another important feature is the CLASS statement that enables the coding of categorical variables. It is common to control for origination periods (also known as vintages) and other qualitative variables by means of appropriate coding. Popular approaches include reference/dummy coding and effect coding. For both approaches, $K - 1$ new variables are created if the categorical variable has K categories.

Reference Coding

In reference coding, the respective variable is coded one if the category is given, and zero otherwise:

$$C_k = \begin{cases} 1 & \text{category } k \text{ is given} \\ 0 & \text{otherwise} \end{cases}$$

with $k = 1, \cdots K - 1$. The interpretation of the parameter estimates is in terms of the linear predictor where category k is given relative to the linear predictor where the reference category K is given.

Effect Coding

In effect coding, the respective variable is coded one if the category is given and minus one if the reference category is given:

$$C_k = \begin{cases} 1 & \text{category } k \text{ is given} \\ -1 & \text{reference category } K \text{ is given} \\ 0 & \text{otherwise} \end{cases}$$

with $k = 1, \dots K - 1$.

Controlling for Categorical Information in SAS

A popular categorical variable is the origination year, which is also known as the vintage. The data set has many vintages with different observation counts. To simplify the analysis, we restrict the number of categories to vintages with sufficient observation counts by generating a new variable called orig_time2:

```
data mortgage;
SET data.mortgage;
orig_time2=orig_time;
IF orig_time NOT IN (20,21,22,23,24,25) THEN orig_time2 =0;
RUN;
```

We then include orig_time2 and specify dummy coding (PARAM=REFERENCE, effect coding would be PARAM=EFFECT):

```
PROC LOGISTIC DATA=mortgage DESCENDING;
CLASS orig_time2/PARAM=REFERENCE;
MODEL default_time = FICO_orig_time
LTV_time gdp_time orig_time2 / LINK=PROBIT;
RUN;
```

The parameter estimates are reported in Exhibit 6.13. Note that the accuracy ratio has slightly increased as we add more meaningful variables to the model. We encourage the reader to identify and add more risk factors.

Through-the-Cycle (TTC) versus Point-in-Time (PIT)

We now analyze default probabilities generated by different modeling methodologies. Through-the-cycle (TTC) models generally abstract from the state of the overall economy by excluding macroeconomic risk drivers. Point-in-time (PIT) models explicitly control for the state of the economy. In reality, the distinction is not so easy, as many borrower-specific (i.e., idiosyncratic) risk factors are time-varying and often correlated with the economy. Various alternative definitions may be found in the literature for TTC and PIT models that are not considered here.

For a first comparison, we estimate two models: a TTC model and a PIT model.

The TTC model is based on application data (i.e., information that is observable at loan origination). The model is a logit model based on the FICO score at origination and LTV ratio at origination:

```
PROC LOGISTIC DATA=data.mortgage DESCENDING;
MODEL default_time = FICO_orig_time
LTV_orig_time / LINK=probit;
OUTPUT OUT=probabilities PREDICTED=PD_TTC_time;
RUN;
```

The PIT model is based on application data and time-varying information. It is a logit model based on the FICO score at origination and the LTV ratio at observation time, as well as the following macroeconomic indicators: (1) GDP growth rate, (2) unemployment rate, and (3) house price index.

```
PROC LOGISTIC DATA=probabilities DESCENDING;
MODEL default_time = FICO_orig_time
LTV_time gdp_time uer_time hpi_time / LINK=PROBIT;
OUTPUT OUT=probabilities2 PREDICTED=PD_PIT_time;
RUN;
```

Exhibit 6.14 compares the default rate and the mean estimated default probability for the TTC model and the PIT model over time. The chart is also known as an in-sample real-fit diagram.

```
DATA means;
SET means;
LABEL PD_TTC_time="PD_TTC_time";
LABEL PD_PIT_time="PD_PIT_time";
RUN;

ODS GRAPHICS ON;
AXIS1 ORDER=(0 to 60 by 5) LABEL=('Time');
AXIS2 order=(0 to 0.06 by 0.01) LABEL=('DR and PD');
```

The LOGISTIC Procedure

Class Level Information								
Class	Value	Design Variables						
orig_time2	0	1	0	0	0	0	0
	20	0	1	0	0	0	0
	21	0	0	1	0	0	0
	22	0	0	0	1	0	0
	23	0	0	0	0	1	0
	24	0	0	0	0	0	1
	25	0	0	0	0	0	0

Analysis of Maximum Likelihood Estimates						
Parameter		DF	Estimate	Standard Error	Wald Chi-Square	Pr > ChiSq
Intercept		1	−0.9670	0.0379	649.8974	<.0001
FICO_orig_time		1	−0.00241	0.000050	2329.3365	<.0001
LTV_time		1	0.00770	0.000162	2260.7985	<.0001
gdp_time		1	−0.0495	0.00167	877.8470	<.0001
orig_time2	0	1	−0.0365	0.0116	9.9937	0.0016
orig_time2	20	1	−0.1176	0.0213	30.4655	<.0001
orig_time2	21	1	−0.0528	0.0185	8.1113	0.0044
orig_time2	22	1	−0.0646	0.0169	14.6329	0.0001
orig_time2	23	1	−0.0101	0.0171	0.3475	0.5556
orig_time2	24	1	−0.0353	0.0164	4.6079	0.0318

Association of Predicted Probabilities and Observed Responses			
Percent Concordant	69.5	Somers' D	0.423
Percent Discordant	27.3	Gamma	0.437
Percent Tied	3.2	Tau-a	0.020
Pairs	9198871098	c	0.711

Exhibit 6.13 Probit Model with Categorical Covariates

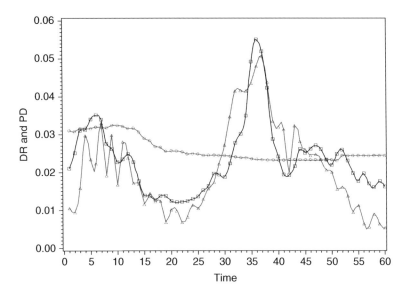

<AAA Default_time ⊖⊖⊖ PD_TTC_time ⊞⊞⊞ PD_PIT_time

Exhibit 6.14 Real-fit diagram for the TTC Probit Model and the PIT Probit Model

```
SYMBOL1 INTERPOL=SPLINE WIDTH=2 VALUE=TRIANGLE C=BLUE;
SYMBOL2 INTERPOL=SPLINE WIDTH=2 VALUE=CIRCLE C=RED;
SYMBOL3 INTERPOL=SPLINE WIDTH=2 VALUE=SQUARE C=BLACK;
LEGEND1 LABEL=NONE SHAPE=SYMBOL(4,2) POSITION=(bottom outside);

PROC GPLOT DATA=means;
PLOT (default_time PD_TTC_time PD_PIT_time)*time
/ OVERLAY HAXIS=AXIS1 VAXIS=AXIS2 LEGEND=LEGEND1;
RUN;
ODS GRAPHICS OFF;
```

The TTC model produces default probabilities that are mostly time-invariant. The only sources for time variation are changes in the loan population. For example, if the fraction of low-risk borrowers increases over time, then the model-implied mean default probability decreases; if the fraction of low-risk borrowers decreases, then the default probability increases. A hybrid TTC model may include time-varying borrower information that is correlated with the economy and may show a moderate time variation.

The PIT model includes the time-varying LTV ratio and a number of macroeconomic factors. Its mean default probability is closer to the realized default rate. From an econometric viewpoint, PIT models are closer to the data-generating process and hence more accurate. For examples in the literature, see Rösch and Scheule (2010) and Rösch and Scheule (2004).

Controversy Regarding Procyclical Risk Measures

The use of macroeconomic variables is sometimes of concern to prudential regulators as their use leads to time-varying risk measures and hence time-varying loan loss provisioning and regulatory capital requirements. Banks often find it challenging to raise capital during economic downturns, and the use of PIT models leads to procyclical capital requirements that may further exacerbate economic downturns. To avoid such situations, regulators may prohibit the use of macroeconomic indicators, mandate forward-looking (i.e., anticipating) risk measures, or offset the impact of procyclical capital requirements through other actions (e.g., countercyclical capital buffers).

Note that PIT models are more accurate than TTC models as they control for important (time-varying) covariates and should be considered for the measurement of economic risks.

Estimation of Rating Migration Probabilities

It is common in banking to estimate rating migration probabilities (often displayed in rating migration matrices) to simplify rating analytics. As with the case of default probabilities, multiyear rating migration probabilities can be computed by means of matrix multiplication.

We first define the rating classes for the current period $k = 1, 2,... K$ and the past period $k^* = 1, 2,... K$. The last rating class K may be defined as the terminating default event, in which case the number of past rating classes reduces to $k^* = 1, 2,... K - 1$ as only borrowers that did not default in the prior period can be observed.

We prepare the data set by categorizing the FICO score to derive rating classes. Various categorization techniques are discussed in the model validation chapter. We generate three rating classes and assume that the default event constitutes a fourth rating class:

```
PROC SORT DATA=data.mortgage OUT=mortgage;
BY id time;
RUN;

DATA mortgage;
SET mortgage;
IF FICO_orig_time>350 AND FICO_orig_time<=500 THEN rating=1;
IF FICO_orig_time>500 AND FICO_orig_time<=650 THEN rating=2;
IF FICO_orig_time>650 AND FICO_orig_time<850 THEN rating=3;
lagid=LAG(id);
lagrating=LAG(rating);
RUN;

DATA mortgage;
SET mortgage;
IF id NE lagid THEN lagrating=.;
IF default_time=1 THEN rating=4;
RUN;
```

The example should be read with care. Rating migration models do not generally provide for more accurate models than a loan-level PD model. PD models have an infinite number of possible values, while the aggregation of PDs or any metric score to rating classes implies a loss of information. However, we acknowledge that situations may exist within particular risk applications of a bank where ratings classes and rating migration probabilities provide added value.

Rating Matrix from Observed Migration Frequencies

A rating matrix tabulates the relative frequencies or estimated probabilities of migrating from a rating at the beginning of the period (generally indicated by the first column) to a rating including the terminal default state at the end of the period (generally indicated by the first row). It can be easily calculated using an actuarial method by PROC FREQ:

```
PROC FREQ DATA=mortgage(WHERE=(rating NE . AND lagrating NE .));
TABLES lagrating*rating /NOCOL NOPERCENT NOCUM;
RUN;
```

We cross-tabulate the rating at the beginning of the period and the rating at the end of the period. We are interested in the conditional rating migration probabilities (i.e., the rating migration probabilities conditional on a particular rating at the beginning of the period). Hence, we suppress the display of column percentages, percentages, and cumulative frequencies using the NOCOL, NOPERCENT, and NOCUM options. The resulting table shows the absolute and relative frequencies for the rating migrations (see Exhibit 6.15). Relative frequencies are conditional on the rating at the beginning of the period. As a result, all relative frequencies for a given rating at the beginning of the period add up to one.

```
                      The FREQ Procedure

                  Table of Lagrating by Rating

     Lagrating       Rating

     Frequency|
     Row Pct  |        1|        2|        3|        4|  Total
     ---------+--------+--------+--------+--------+
           1  |   2731 |      0 |      0 |    112 |   2843
              |  96.06 |   0.00 |   0.00 |   3.94 |
     ---------+--------+--------+--------+--------+
           2  |      5 | 193070 |     15 |   6978 | 200068
              |   0.00 |  96.50 |   0.01 |   3.49 |
     ---------+--------+--------+--------+--------+
           3  |      3 |     50 | 362080 |   7445 | 369578
              |   0.00 |   0.01 |  97.97 |   2.01 |
     ---------+--------+--------+--------+--------+
     Total       2739    193120   362095    14535   572489
```

Exhibit 6.15 Rating Migration Matrix Based on Observed Migration Frequencies

As default is a terminating state, ratings cannot be observed at the end of a period if the loan has defaulted at the beginning of the period. Therefore, the number of rows of the rating migration matrix (i.e., the rating at the beginning of the observation period) is one less than the number of columns (i.e., the rating at the end of the observation period).

Cumulative Probit Model

Discrete-time hazard models may be extended by cumulative probit models (also known as ordered probit models) to accommodate the probability of migrating from one state to another. Comparable extensions exist for continuous-time models such as a competing hazard model. We discuss these in the exposure at default (EAD) modeling chapter. We model the probability of migrating to rating R_{it} conditional on the realized rating of the previous period r_{it-1}:

$$
\begin{cases}
P(R_{it} = 1 | r_{it-1} = k^*) = \Phi(\theta_1 + \boldsymbol{\beta}' \boldsymbol{X}_{it-1}) \\
\ldots \\
P(R_{it} = k | r_{it-1} = k^*) = \Phi(\theta_k + \boldsymbol{\beta} \boldsymbol{X}_{it-1}) - \Phi(\theta_{k-1} + \boldsymbol{\beta} \boldsymbol{X}_{it-1}) \\
\ldots \\
P(R_{it} = K | r_{it-1} = k^*) = 1 - \Phi(\theta_{K-1} + \boldsymbol{\beta} \boldsymbol{X}_{it-1})
\end{cases}
$$

The parameters are determined by estimating one model for every starting rating class and maximizing the natural logarithm of the following likelihood:

$$
L = \prod_{k=1}^{K} \prod_{i=1}^{I} \prod_{t=1}^{T} P(R_{it} = k | r_{it-1} = k^*)^{I(R_{it}=k)}
$$

The indicator variable $I(R_{it} = k)$ equals one if R_{it} is equal to k and zero otherwise. We include the rating at the beginning of the period as a categorical control variable using PROC LOGISTIC with the CLASS statement.

```
PROC LOGISTIC DATA = mortgage;
CLASS lagrating(REF='3');
MODEL rating = lagrating /LINK=PROBIT;
OUTPUT OUT=probabilities PREDICTED=PROB_CUM;
RUN;
```

The code generates an output data set that includes the cumulative probability for rating migration from the rating at the beginning of the period to the ratings one to three. Note that the cumulative probability for the fourth rating class is per definition one.

The parameter estimates include the threshold estimates and the parameter estimate for the first and second class (see Exhibit 6.16).

The rating migration matrix can be derived from the cumulative probabilities generated by the OUTPUT command in the data set probabilities in a number of steps.

The LOGISTIC Procedure

Model Information	
Data Set	WORK.MORTGAGE
Response Variable	Rating
Number of Response Levels	4
Model	Cumulative probit
Optimization Technique	Fisher's scoring

Class Level Information		
Class	Value	Design Variables
Lagrating	1	1 0
	2	0 1
	3	−1 −1

c

Analysis of Maximum Likelihood Estimates						
Parameter		DF	Estimate	Standard Error	Wald Chi-Square	Pr > ChiSq
Intercept	1	1	−2.7377	0.0151	32904.2195	<.0001
Intercept	2	1	1.5819	0.0111	20178.6211	<.0001
Intercept	3	1	4.8703	0.0118	171445.072	<.0001
Lagrating	1	1	3.5768	0.0216	27410.2541	<.0001
Lagrating	2	1	−0.2444	0.0109	500.0602	<.0001

Exhibit 6.16 Cumulative Probit Model for Rating Migration Probabilities

First, we add rows for the rating class 4, which was not included in the output data set, as it is the reference category in the model:

```
DATA rating4;
INPUT lagrating _LEVEL_;
DATALINES;
1 4
2 4
3 4
;
RUN;

DATA probabilities2;
SET probabilities rating4;
RUN;
```

Second, we create a new data set that includes one observation per unique combination of lagrating and rating:

```
PROC SORT DATA=probabilities2 OUT=probabilities3(WHERE=(lagrating NE .))
NODUPKEY;
BY lagrating _LEVEL_;
RUN;
```

Third, we compute the cumulative migration probabilities for all ratings at the beginning of the observation and the marginal migration probabilities for all ratings at the beginning of the observation:

```
DATA probabilities3(KEEP =lagrating rating probability);
SET probabilities3;
lagprob_cum=LAG(prob_cum);
IF _LEVEL_=1 THEN probability=prob_cum;
IF _LEVEL_=2 THEN probability=prob_cum-lagprob_cum;
IF _LEVEL_=3 THEN probability=prob_cum-lagprob_cum;
IF _LEVEL_=4 THEN probability=1-lagprob_cum;
rating=_LEVEL_;
RUN;
```

Fourth, we transpose the data set to match the format of a rating migration matrix:

```
PROC TRANSPOSE DATA=probabilities3 OUT=probabilities4(DROP=_NAME_)
PREFIX=rating;
BY lagrating;
ID rating;
RUN;
```

The resulting data set, which includes the rating matrix, is presented in Exhibit 6.17.

This rating migration matrix is different from the empirical one presented earlier, as we have made some simplifying assumptions with regard to the parameter estimates. More specifically, we have assumed that the differences in rating migration probabilities are identical for all ratings at the beginning of the period.

Other ways to control for the rating at the beginning of a period exist. For example, a credit risk modeler may include interactions between the rating at the

Obs	Lagrating	rating1	rating2	rating3	rating4
1	1	0.79930	0.20070	0.00000	0.000000
2	2	0.00143	0.90804	0.09052	0.000002
3	3	0.00000	0.04001	0.89795	0.062039

Exhibit 6.17 Rating Migration Matrix

The LOGISTIC Procedure

Analysis of Maximum Likelihood Estimates						
Parameter		DF	Estimate	Standard Error	Wald Chi-Square	Pr > ChiSq
Intercept	1	1	−2.8034	0.0152	34027.7024	<.0001
Intercept	2	1	1.5275	0.0112	18574.9967	<.0001
Intercept	3	1	4.8284	0.0118	167505.368	<.0001
Lagrating	1	1	3.5811	0.0216	27435.3449	<.0001
Lagrating	2	1	−0.2448	0.0109	501.3024	<.0001
gdp_time		1	0.0430	0.00103	1728.8677	<.0001

Exhibit 6.18 Cumulative Probit Model for Rating Migration Probabilities with Time-Varying Covariates

beginning of an observation period and other control variables, or, alternatively, estimate separate equations for every rating class at the beginning of a period. In this extension, all parameters are conditional on $k^* = 1, 2, \ldots K - 1$. For example, the rating migration model can be extended by including other control variables such as macroeconomic effects. Both the resulting rating migration probabilities and rating migration matrix then become time-varying. The following model conditions on GDP growth:

```
PROC LOGISTIC DATA = mortgage;
CLASS lagrating(REF='3');
MODEL rating = lagrating gdp_time/LINK=PROBIT;
RUN;
```

The parameter estimates include the threshold estimates, the parameter estimate for the first and second classes, and GDP growth (see Exhibit 6.18).

Another interesting extension could be the inclusion of higher-order lags into the analysis.

WHICH MODEL SHOULD I CHOOSE?

Choice of Link Functions, Distributions, and Optimization Algorithms

Multiple distributional choices are often available within a model class. As a general rule, the empirical distribution should match the assumed distribution. However, it can be hard to determine which model is best due to data limitations. An important driver in credit risk analytics is the macroeconomy. Time series data are generally limited due to the evolution of data storage facilities (often from 2000 onward) and typically also include structural breaks such as changes in economies, financial markets, institutions, instruments, and borrowers. This implies that distributions and parameters may change over time and that the out-of-time validation of choices is limited.

Furthermore, different models lead to different estimates. However, the final estimation outputs are always calibrated on data histories, and the economic content is often comparable across model types (see Hamerle et al. 2006, for one example). In other words, these choices typically lead to very similar conclusions, as the aim to bring default probabilities close to default indicators with a scientific method is common to all approaches.

Variable Selection

The development of economically founded models that follow the thinking of borrowers, lenders, and the general economy provides strong improvements for model quality. The choice of variables is crucial, portfolio dependent, and often subject to a first-stage analysis that is executed prior to the actual model building. In granular retail portfolios (e.g., mortgage portfolios that consist of a large number of exposures with small to moderate exposure amounts), macro-economic variables such as house prices or bank lending standards may dominate idiosyncratic (i.e., borrower-specific) variables. In smaller portfolios such as corporate lending, borrower-specific variables may dominate macroeconomic variables.

Adding explanatory variables to increase the model fit (e.g., via a forward selection technique) is potentially dangerous, as one may risk overfitting by providing excellent fits that cannot be replicated in an out-of-sample context. Hence, statistical validation techniques should be applied in an out-of-sample context (see also the validation chapter).

An important consideration is the selection of good predictive variables as inputs to the model. It also means that only variables that can sufficiently discriminate between default and nondefault should be considered.

There are various statistical techniques to test discriminatory power of individual independent variables such as means comparison in different groups, information value, and accuracy ratio.

SAS provides a procedure to statistically test the difference between two means of independent groups (default and nondefault). For example:

```
PROC TTEST DATA=data.mortgage;
CLASS default_time;
VAR FICO_orig_time;
RUN;
```

The output is based on two methods: the Satterthwaite approximation, which does not assume equal variance between the default and nondefault samples, and the pooled method, which assumes equal variance in both samples (see Exhibit 6.19).

It can be seen that both tests indicate a difference in means for defaults and nondefaults. Furthermore, PROC HPBIN in SAS is useful for binning and computing weight-of-evidence values and the corresponding information value (see the credit scoring chapter). An example of this is:

The TTEST Procedure

Variable: FICO_orig_time

Method	Variances	DF	t Value	Pr > |t|
Pooled	Equal	622487	42.87	<.0001
Satterthwaite	Unequal	16027	45.52	<.0001

Exhibit 6.19 T-test for FICO_orig_time by default_time

```
PROC HPBIN DATA=data.mortgage NUMBIN=5;
INPUT FICO_orig_time;
ODS OUTPUT MAPPING=Mapping;
RUN;
PROC HPBIN DATA=data.mortgage WOE BINS_META=Mapping;
TARGET default_time/LEVEL=BINARY;
RUN;
```

Remember, as discussed in the credit scoring chapter, the weight of evidence (WOE) measures the relative risk of each variable bin (or category). The information value is the weighted sum of the weight of evidence measures across the bins and indicates the predictive strength of the variable. The weights of evidence and information value that are obtained are shown in Exhibit 6.20.

As discussed in the credit scoring chapter, SAS is able to help selecting variables with the SELECTION=BACKWARD, SELECTION=FORWARD, and SELECTION=STEPWISE statements. These techniques vary the number of variables included by adding variables that are significant and dropping variables that are insignificant. See the credit scoring chapter for more details. While these techniques provide a first way to identify reasonable variable sets, variable selection in credit risk models has to take into account particular economic aspects, as purely machine-based selections are often not robust in out-of-sample forecasting exercises.

Other Helpful SAS Features

Other useful features in SAS that you may be interested in exploring include:

- The ROC statement within PROC LOGISTIC allows receiver operating characteristic evaluation (see the validation chapter for more details).
- PROC SURVEYLOGISTIC provides for clustered standard errors. The parameter estimates are comparable with PROC LOGISTIC, but standard errors are now computed by assuming dependence between observations of the same cluster unit. Clustering variables can be defined by the CLUSTER command.
- PROC DISCRIM estimates a discriminant criterion to classify each observation into default or nondefault. Early scoring functions (e.g., the Altman z-score) were developed using discriminant analysis.

The HPBIN Procedure

Weight of Evidence

Variable	Binned Variable	Range	Nonevent Count	Nonevent Rate	Event Count	Event Rate	Weight of Evidence	Information Value
FICO_orig_time	[FICO...]		0	0	0	0	0	0
		FICO_orig_time<488	1533	0.95217391	77	0.04782609	-0.6993690	0.00178735
		488<=FICO_orig_time<576	59952	0.96482024	2186	0.03517976	-0.3790746	0.01724805
		576<=FICO_orig_time<664	196955	0.96836128	6435	0.03163872	-0.2693221	0.02699478
		664<=FICO_orig_time<752	251238	0.97860025	5494	0.02139975	0.13219861	0.00677210
		752<=FICO_orig_time	97653	0.99020473	966	0.00979527	0.92546632	0.08982732

Variable Information Value

Variable	Information Value
FICO_orig_time	0.14262960

Exhibit 6.20 Weights-of-Evidence and Information Value for FICO_orig_time with Regard to default_time

FITTING AND FORECASTING

Sampling strategy: training and validation sample

For large data sets, it is common to create cross-sectional random samples to reduce the data volume. Within a random sample, it is common to stratify the sample further into a training sample with regard to the cross-section and time series dimension and borrower, and a validation sample (for an example, see Lee, Rösch, and Scheule 2016).

With regard to the cross section, one may differentiate between in-sample validation if the borrowers of the training sample are analyzed, and out-of-sample validation if different borrowers than those in the training sample are analyzed.

With regard to the time series dimension, one may differentiate between in-time (if the same time periods of the training sample are analyzed), and out-of-time (if different time periods than those in the training sample are analyzed).

Exhibit 6.21 shows the various combinations of these classifications and resulting data samples.

In a rigorous model validation, validation samples are generally out-of-sample and out-of-time with regard to the training sample. The data sampling strategy may be simpler if data is limited.

Please note that it is possible that the training sample is not representative with regard to the population. Bayesian models are able to include prior assumptions with regard to the population and hence correct for this bias. These methods are discussed in the chapter on Bayesian methods.

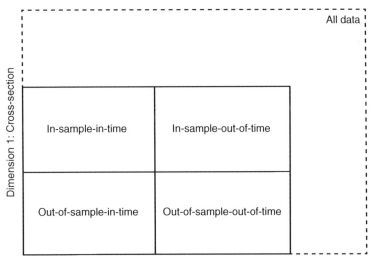

Exhibit 6.21 Data Sampling Strategies

Generation of Samples

We now illustrate the generation of a training sample. Here, we do not distinguish between in-time and out-of-time and use all available data (i.e., the four tiles in the above chart are equal to all data). PROC SURVEYSELECT generates random samples. By default, the output data set includes only those observations selected for the sample. If OUTALL is specified, then a selection indicator named Selected is added to the input data set. Furthermore, it is common in panel data sets to select by subjects (here borrowers/loans), which we achieve with the SAMPLINGUNIT command:

```
PROC SURVEYSELECT DATA=data.mortgage SAMPRATE=0.8 OUT-
ALL SEED=12345 OUT=mortgage;
SAMPLINGUNIT id;
RUN;
```

The command SEED=12345 fixes the random experiment so that the random draw results in the same outcome if executed another time. We note that the observed mortgage data experiences an increase in default risk at approximately time period 25. Hence, one may build a model that is estimated precrisis and apply the estimated parameters (out-of-sample) to periods during the crisis to assess whether the model is capable of predicting credit risk outcomes in severe economic downturns. Lee et al. (2016) perform such an analysis based on a larger number of risk factors.

In-Sample and Out-of-Sample Validation

We can now estimate a logit model using PROC LOGISTIC for the training sample:

```
PROC LOGISTIC DATA=mortgage(WHERE=(selected=1)) DESCENDING;
MODEL default_time = FICO_orig_time
LTV_time gdp_time;
STORE OUT=model_logistic;
RUN;
```

Next, we calculate the probabilities for the training and validation sample using PROC PLM. The procedure allows the post-modeling estimation of default probabilities. In case of out-of-time subsets, we actually forecast the default probabilities, as all covariates are time lagged with regard to the default indicator.

```
PROC PLM SOURCE=model_logistic;
SCORE DATA=mortgage OUT=mortgage2;
RUN;
```

As PROC PLM calculates the linear predictor, we need to convert the calculated linear predictor to a default probability using the logit link function; note that we would use the cumulative density function of the standard normal distribution for a probit model by replacing the line PD_time=... by PD_time= PROBNORM(predicted):

```
DATA mortgage2;
SET mortgage2;
```

```
PD_time=EXP(predicted)/(1+EXP(predicted));
RUN;
```

We then analyze the default rates and mean default probabilities in-sample and out-of-sample:

```
PROC SORT DATA=mortgage2;
BY selected time;
RUN;

PROC MEANS DATA=mortgage2;
BY selected time;
OUTPUT OUT=means MEAN(default_time PD_time)=default_time PD_time;
RUN;
```

Exhibits 6.22 and 6.23 show the real-fit diagrams (produced by PROC GPLOT), which include the default rate (DR) and the mean estimated default probabilities (PD) for the in-sample and out-of-sample.

```
ODS GRAPHICS ON;
AXIS1 ORDER=(0 TO 60 BY 5) LABEL=('Time');
AXIS2 ORDER=(0 TO 0.06 BY 0.01) LABEL=('DR and PD');
SYMBOL1 INTERPOL=SPLINE WIDTH=2 VALUE=TRIANGLE C=BLUE;
SYMBOL2 INTERPOL=SPLINE WIDTH=2 VALUE=CIRCLE C=RED;
LEGEND1 LABEL=NONE SHAPE=SYMBOL(4,2) POSITION=(BOTTOM OUTSIDE);
PROC GPLOT DATA=means;
```

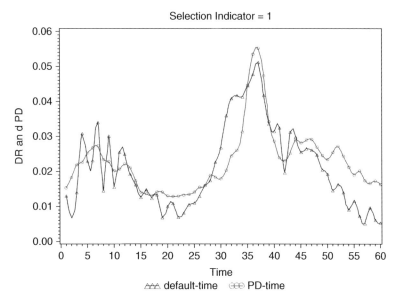

Exhibit 6.22 Real-Fit Diagram for In-Sample

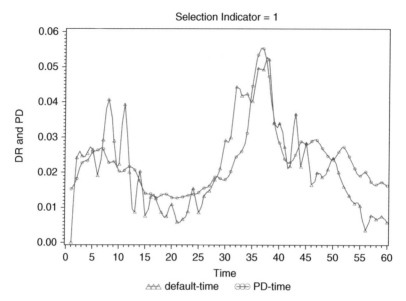

Exhibit 6.23 Real-Fit Diagram for Out-of-Sample

```
PLOT (default_time PD_time)*time / OVERLAY HAXIS=AXIS1 VAXIS=AXIS2
          LEGEND=LEGEND1;
BY selected;
RUN;
ODS GRAPHICS OFF;
```

Generally speaking, in-sample estimated default probabilities dominate out-of-sample estimates and in-time default probabilities dominate out-of-time estimates.

FORMATION OF RATING CLASSES

Model performance measurement often requires a large number of observations, and banks form rating classes, allocate observations to rating classes, and compute risk and risk model validation metrics for these rating classes. Observations (i.e., borrowers at a given time period) are assumed to be homogeneous for a given rating class. Rating classes not only are formed for model validation but may also match expectations of regulators (i.e., part of prudential regulation), or serve various risk applications of a bank, as ratings often simplify complicated measurement challenges.

Rating classes are generally created by (1) observing classes or (2) categorizing meaningful metric variables or metric credit scores. Classes may be observable if borrowers are rated by external credit rating agencies or similar service providers. External ratings are often available for only the largest corporates within an economy.

Various options are available to categorize scores into rating classes, and three popular examples are:

1. Set class intervals to have equal sizes.
2. Set class intervals so that classes are expected to have equal numbers of observations.
3. Set class intervals so that classes are expected to have equal numbers of default observations.

Other categorization techniques are also possible. For example, a mapping to an external rating agency scale can be adopted, or an exponential heuristic method, which says, for example, that the default rate should double from one rating to the next. In practice (based on our experience), ratings can be normally classified from the PD. There are a few points to consider when developing a rating system:

- Distribution of ratings: The distribution of ratings is often expected to follow a skewed bell curve. This implies that a large proportion of borrowers/loans concentrates in the medium-risk ratings, low-risk ratings are at one tail, and high-risk ratings at the other tail.

- Monotonicity of default rate curve: The default rate for the ratings should be monotonically increasing or decreasing over the ratings.

- Dispersion: The default rate difference between the lowest and the highest rating should be large (e.g., 20 to 30 percent).

- Master scale for ratings: Banks often develop multiple PD models for different products or segments within the whole credit portfolio. It would be handy if the ratings were aligned in terms of risk levels across risk segments. This can be accomplished by the definition of a master scale as a corporate-wide standard.

- Aligning with external rating agencies: Banks often assign internal credit ratings in line with the default rate of external rating agencies.

We now implement these three options in SAS to demonstrate the formation of rating classes from a credit score—here the FICO score.

Rating approach 1: Set class intervals to have equal sizes

In this application, we assume 10 rating classes (classes zero to nine), define lower and upper bounds of the rating classes with regard to the FICO score, and assign the observations/borrowers to the rating classes based on the observed FICO scores. The new variable FICO_orig_time_rank1 collects the rating classes for this approach.

```
DATA rank1;
SET data.mortgage;
IF FICO_orig_time>=300 AND FICO_orig_time<=400 THEN FICO_orig_time_rank1=0;
```

```
IF FICO_orig_time>400 AND FICO_orig_time<=450 THEN FICO_orig_time_rank1=1;
IF FICO_orig_time>450 AND FICO_orig_time<=500 THEN FICO_orig_time_rank1=2;
IF FICO_orig_time>500 AND FICO_orig_time<=550 THEN FICO_orig_time_rank1=3;
IF FICO_orig_time>550 AND FICO_orig_time<=600 THEN FICO_orig_time_rank1=4;
IF FICO_orig_time>600 AND FICO_orig_time<=650 THEN FICO_orig_time_rank1=5;
IF FICO_orig_time>650 AND FICO_orig_time<=700 THEN FICO_orig_time_rank1=6;
IF FICO_orig_time>700 AND FICO_orig_time<=750 THEN FICO_orig_time_rank1=7;
IF FICO_orig_time>750 AND FICO_orig_time<=800 THEN FICO_orig_time_rank1=8;
IF FICO_orig_time>800 AND FICO_orig_time<=850 THEN FICO_orig_time_rank1=9;
RUN;
```

Note that the FICO score is defined between 300 and 850 in this data set.

Rating approach 2: Set class intervals so that classes are expected to have equal numbers of observations

In this application, we use PROC RANK to assign the observations into 10 rating classes with an equal number of observations. The GROUPS command defines the number K of rating classes and assigns the $1/K$ observations with the lowest FICO score to class 0, $1/K$ observations with the second lowest FICO score to class 1, and so on. The new variable FICO_orig_time_rank2 collects the rating classes for this approach.

```
PROC RANK DATA=rank1 OUT=rank2 GROUPS=10;
VAR FICO_orig_time;
RANKS FICO_orig_time_rank2;
RUN;
```

Rating approach 3: Set class intervals so that classes are expected to have equal numbers of default observations

In this application, we use PROC RANK to assign the observations into 10 rating classes with an equal number of observations but stratify the ranking by the default indicator default_time. The new variable FICO_orig_time_rank3 collects the rating classes for this approach.

```
PROC SORT DATA=rank2;
BY default_time;
RUN;
```

```
PROC RANK DATA=rank2 OUT=rank3 GROUPS=10;
VAR FICO_orig_time;
RANKS FICO_orig_time_rank3;
BY default_time;
RUN;
```

We then sort according to the FICO scores and overwrite the ranking for stratum for nondefaults by the ranking of the previous default event.

```
PROC SORT DATA=rank3;
BY FICO_orig_time descending default_time;
RUN;

DATA rank3(DROP=temp);
SET rank3;
BY FICO_orig_time descending default_time;
IF first.default_time AND default_time = 1 THEN temp = FICO_orig_time_rank3;
ELSE IF default_time = 0 THEN DO;
FICO_orig_time_rank3 = temp;
END;
RETAIN temp;
RUN;

DATA rank3;
SET rank3;
IF FICO_orig_time_rank3 = . THEN FICO_orig_time_rank3 = 0;
RUN;
```

In this example, we created 10 rating classes. Various options within PROC RANK (option ties) are available to specify how tied values should be ranked and include the lowest, mean, or highest rank value of tied observations. Tied observations are of a lower importance if the number of ties is small relative to the total number of observations. An indication for this might be a mortgage loan book with a continuous score.

Exhibit 6.24 shows the relative frequencies of observations per rating class. We have generated the data points by computing the number of observations, the default rate, and the mean FICO score by rating class for the three approaches. We obtain three data sets and assign different names to them (_1, _2, and _3).

```
PROC SORT DATA=rank3;
BY FICO_orig_time_rank1;
RUN;

PROC MEANS DATA=rank3;
BY FICO_orig_time_rank1;
OUTPUT OUT=orank1 N(default_time)=N_1 MEAN(default_time)=DR_1
MEAN(FICO_orig_time)=FICO_1;
RUN;
```

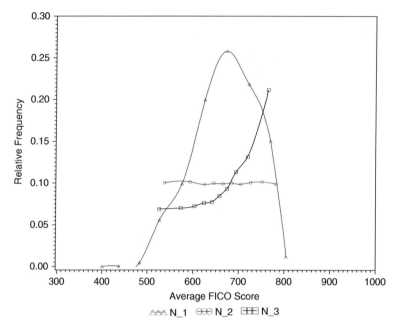

Exhibit 6.24 Relative Frequencies of Observations per Rating Class

```
PROC SORT DATA=rank3;
BY FICO_orig_time_rank2;
RUN;

PROC MEANS DATA=rank3;
BY FICO_orig_time_rank2;
OUTPUT out=orank2 N(default_time)=N_2 MEAN(default_time)=DR_2
MEAN(FICO_orig_time)=FICO_2;
RUN;

PROC SORT DATA=rank3;
BY FICO_orig_time_rank3;
RUN;

PROC MEANS DATA=rank3;
BY FICO_orig_time_rank3;
OUTPUT OUT=orank3 N(default_time)=N_3 MEAN(default_time)=DR_3
MEAN(FICO_orig_time)=FICO_3;
run;
```

We then rename the rating class variable to a joint name and merge the three data sets:

```
DATA orank1(KEEP= FICO_orig_time_rank FICO_1 N_1 DR_1);
SET orank1;
RENAME FICO_orig_time_rank1=FICO_orig_time_rank;
N_1=N_1/622489;
RUN;


DATA orank2(KEEP= FICO_orig_time_rank FICO_2 N_2 DR_2);
SET orank2;
RENAME FICO_orig_time_rank2=FICO_orig_time_rank;
N_2=N_2/622489;
RUN;


DATA orank3(KEEP= FICO_orig_time_rank FICO_3 N_3 DR_3);
SET orank3;
RENAME FICO_orig_time_rank3=FICO_orig_time_rank;
N_3=N_3/622489;
RUN;


DATA orank;
MERGE orank1 orank2 orank3;
BY FICO_orig_time_rank;
RUN;
```

We use PROC GPLOT to plot the relative frequencies of observations per rating class:

```
ODS GRAPHICS ON;
AXIS1 ORDER=(300 TO 1000 BY 100) LABEL=('Average FICO score');
AXIS2 ORDER=(0 TO 0.3 BY 0.05) LABEL=('Relative frequency');
SYMBOL1 INTERPOL=SPLINE WIDTH=2 VALUE=TRIANGLE C=BLUE;
SYMBOL2 INTERPOL=SPLINE WIDTH=2 VALUE=CIRCLE C=RED;
SYMBOL3 INTERPOL=SPLINE WIDTH=2 VALUE=SQUARE C=BLACK;
LEGEND1 LABEL=NONE SHAPE=SYMBOL(4,2) POSITION=(BOTTOM OUTSIDE);
PROC GPLOT DATA=orank; PLOT N_1*FICO_1 N_2*FICO_2 N_3*FICO_3 /
OVERLAY LEGEND=LEGEND1 HAXIS=AXIS1 VAXIS=AXIS2;
RUN;
ODS GRAPHICS OFF;
```

The number of observations follows a hump-shape distribution if rating class intervals are set by fixed intervals of equal length. The number of observations is per

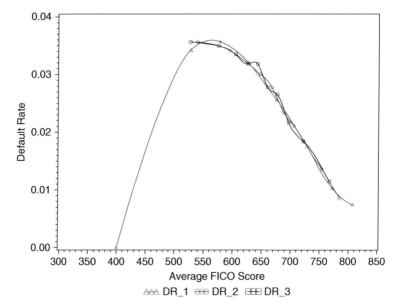

Exhibit 6.25 Default Rate per Rating Class

definition equally distributed for the second approach, and increases for equal numbers of default events per rating classes, as the credit risk of borrowers and hence frequency of default events is lower.

We use PROC GPLOT to plot the default rate per rating class (see Exhibit 6.25):

```
ods graphics on;
AXIS1 ORDER=(300 TO 850 BY 50) LABEL=('Average FICO score');
AXIS2 ORDER=(0 TO 0.04 BY 0.01) LABEL=('Default rate');
SYMBOL1 INTERPOL=SPLINE WIDTH=2 VALUE=TRIANGLE C=BLUE;
SYMBOL2 INTERPOL=SPLINE WIDTH=2 VALUE=CIRCLE C=RED;
SYMBOL3 INTERPOL=SPLINE WIDTH=2 VALUE=SQUARE C=BLACK;
LEGEND1 LABEL=NONE SHAPE=SYMBOL(4,2) POSITION=(BOTTOM OUTSIDE);
PROC GPLOT DATA=orank; PLOT DR_1*FICO_1 DR_2*FICO_2 DR_3*FICO_3 /
OVERLAY LEGEND=LEGEND1 HAXIS=AXIS1 VAXIS=AXIS2;
RUN;
ODS GRAPHICS OFF;
```

Generally speaking, the default rate decreases from low to high rating class. In the example, this is only the case for Options 2 and 3, but not for Option 1. Note that this property is based on our definition of risk ordering, which is consistent with the FICO score (low value: high risk to high value: low risk). External rating agencies like Fitch and Moody's have chosen letters to assign to rating classes (AAA/Aaa: low risk to C: high risk), +/−, (+: lower risk to −: higher risk), or numbers 1/2/3 (1: lower risk to 3: higher risk). Others may use traffic light approaches (red: high risk, yellow: medium risk, and green: low risk).

Trade-Off Effect

The first approach is more likely to result in a nonmonotone decline of the default rate by rating class. This is due to the random nature of default events. Lower rating classes have fewer observations and the default rate is volatile. Hence, there are trade-offs between these options that relate to the nature of the data set. Generally speaking, the number of default observations is small relative to the total sample size.

Option 1 may be preferable as it provides for an equally spaced coverage over the score range if the number of default events is sufficiently large. However, Option 2 or 3 may become suitable if default events are limited, as both approaches (Option 3 to a greater extent than Option 2) focus on ranges where reasonable numbers of default events are observed. Note that the first and last rating classes may encompass a large range of score values and are limited in terms of their informational value and interpretation. Therefore, we prefer in most of our empirical applications to use the third option.

PRACTICE QUESTIONS

1. Estimate a probit model for the default probability, and interpret the parameters with regard to the PD. Include the following risk factors: FICO_orig_time, LTV_time, REtype_CO_orig_time, REtype_PU_orig_time, and REtype_SF_orig_time. Use data set mortgage.

2. Categorize the current LTV ratio into 10 rating classes, and estimate the rating migration probabilities. Use data set mortgage.

3. Categorize the current LTV ratio and include the effect-coded LTV ratio next to the FICO score into a logit model for the PD. How do you interpret the parameter estimates for the LTV ratio, and what may be the advantages and disadvantages of including a metric variable in categories (relative to a stand-alone inclusion)? Use data set mortgage.

4. Estimate a probit model and a logit model based on the interest rate and FICO score at origination. Compare the parameter estimates. Estimate the minimum, maximum, mean, and median for the resulting PDs, and compare the moments. Which model dominates in your opinion? Use data set mortgage.

5. Compute a proxy for house price appreciation and include it next to the current LTV ratio in a probit model for PDs. Estimate the model and interpret the parameter estimates. Why would the house price appreciation be relevant next to the current LTV ratio that includes the price of the house collateral?

6. Show an example of a TTC model and a PIT model for PDs. What are the implications for both from a regulatory perspective?

REFERENCES

Crook, J., and T. Bellotti. 2010. "Time Varying and Dynamic Models for Default Risk in Consumer Loans," *Journal of the Royal Statistical Society: Series A (Statistics in Society)* 173 (2): 283–305.

Crook, J. N., D. B. Edelman, and L. C., Thomas. 2007. "Recent Developments in Consumer Credit Risk Assessment," *European Journal of Operational Research* 183 (3): 1447–1465.

Hamerle, A., T. Liebig, and H. Scheule. 2006. "Forecasting Credit Event Frequency—Empirical Evidence for West German Firms." *Journal of Risk* 9: 75–98.

Hamerle, A., R. Rauhmeier, and D. Rösch. 2003. "Uses and Misuses of Measures for Credit Rating Accuracy." Available at SSRN 2354877

Lee, Y., D. Rösch, and H. Scheule. 2016. "Accuracy of Mortgage Portfolio Risk Forecasts during Financial Crises." *European Journal of Operational Research* 249 (2): 440–456.

Leow, M., and C. Mues. 2012. "Predicting Loss Given Default (LGD) for Residential Mortgage Loans: A Two-Stage Model and Empirical Evidence for UK Bank Data." *International Journal of Forecasting* 28 (1): 183–195.

Merton, R. C. 1974. "On the Pricing of Corporate Debt: The Risk Structure of Interest Rates." *Journal of Finance* 29: 449–470.

Rösch, D., and H. Scheule. 2004. "Forecasting Retail Portfolio Credit Risk." *Journal of Risk Finance* 5 (2): 16–32.

Rösch, D., and H. Scheule. 2010. "Downturn Credit Portfolio Risk, Regulatory Capital and Prudential Incentives." *International Review of Finance* 10 (2), 185–207.

CHAPTER 7

Probabilities of Default: Continuous-Time Hazard Models

INTRODUCTION

Continuous-time hazard models in a credit risk context describe the survival time of a borrower or loan T_i ($T_i \geq 0$), which is known as time to default, as a random variable in continuous form. The survival time is generally measured from loan origination. Alternatively, you may measure survival time from the date of incorporation of a firm, if this information is available, or the time of the first observation. In our empirical analyses, we use the latter as the mortgage data set observes the loans after origination and to ensure that the PD models are calibrated with regard to the in-sample default rate.

CENSORING

Censoring is an important characteristic of survival analysis data. There are three types of censoring: right-censoring, left-censoring, and interval-censoring.

An observation on a variable T is right-censored if all that you know about T is that it is greater than some value. For example, suppose T is a firm's age at default, and you only know that the firm survived up to the age of 50 but do not know when it will default, as the firm is no longer observed. This situation is called right-censored at age 50.

An observation on a variable T is left-censored if all that you know about T is that it is smaller than some value. To illustrate this, suppose you are doing a study to analyze when people started smoking. Some smokers might not know the exact start

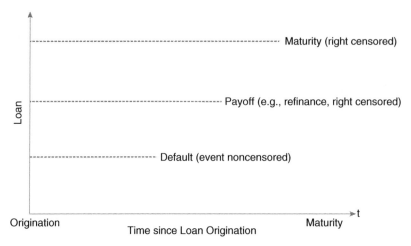

Exhibit 7.1 Observation Credit Outcomes: Default or Censoring

time but can give an upper bound. For example, someone mentions that he started smoking when he was younger than 16 years. This is an example of left-censoring.

An observation on a variable T is interval-censored if all that you know about T is that it is bigger than some value and smaller than some value. In other words, the time of the event is situated in a continuous interval. Let's reconsider the smoking example. For example, someone mentions that he started smoking when he was younger than 16 years, but older than 12 years. This is an example of interval-censoring.

Basically, the problem of censoring is that data is missing. In other words, we don't know the precise value of our target variable, which is the timing of the event, but we can specify a lower bound, upper bound, or both. Classical regression approaches always assume a precise value for the target. Hence, new techniques may be used to deal with censored data.

Right-censoring is a key concern for credit instruments that have a limited lifetime. Banks stop the collection of loan or borrower performance data at loan maturity or the early prepayment of a loan if borrowers no longer require the credit or refinance with a different lender. As a result, the observed outcome for a given time interval is:

$$\delta_{it} = 1_{\{T_i \leq t\}} = \begin{cases} 1, & \text{if } T_i \leq t, \text{ i.e., default} \\ 0, & \text{otherwise (i.e., censoring)} \end{cases}$$

Exhibit 7.1 shows the various outcomes.

Examples in the literature that have applied survival models include Quigley and Van Order (1991), Belotti and Crook (2009), Malik and Thomas (2010), Tong , Mues, and Thomas (2012), and Dirick, Bellotti, Claeskens, and Baesens (2015).

Generally speaking, following functions may represent the random variable T:

■ The probability density function (PDF) $f_i(t)$, with cumulative density function $F_i(t) = \int_{-\infty}^{t} f_i(u)du$

- The survival function $S_i(t) = 1 - F_i(t)$
- The hazard rate $\lambda_i(t) = \lim\limits_{\Delta t \to 0, \Delta t > 0} \frac{1}{\Delta t} P(t \le T_i < t + \Delta t | T_i \ge t) = \frac{f_i(t)}{S_i(t)}$
- The cumulative hazard rate $\int_0^t \lambda_i(u)du = \int_0^t \frac{f_i(u)}{1 - F_i(u)} du = -\log(1 - F_i(t)) = -\log S_i(t)$

with borrower $i = 1...,I$. The functions may be transformed into each other, and SAS offers a number of approaches to estimate these functions, which are discussed latter. We consider three approaches: nonparametric methods (section on life tables), semiparametric methods (section on Cox proportional hazard model), and parametric methods (section on accelerated failure time model).

Survival models control for censoring. We focus on right-censoring, which means that borrowers or loans are no longer observed for the reasons given.

LIFE TABLES

Life table models estimate a survival function, which measures the probability of survival based on the consideration of past default times (i.e., default has occurred within the observation window) and censoring times (i.e., default has not occurred within the observation window). The probability of default follows as one minus the probability of survival. Two approaches are common: Kaplan-Meier analysis (the product limit method) and the actuarial method.

Kaplan-Meier Analysis

Kaplan-Meier (KM) analysis is a first method for survival analysis. The KM estimator is also known as the product limit estimator. It is basically a nonparametric maximum likelihood estimator for the survival probability $S(t)$ as follows:

$$\hat{S}(t) = \hat{S}(t-1)(1 - \frac{d_t}{n_t}) = \hat{S}(t-1)(1 - \lambda(t)) = \prod_{j:t_j \le t}(1 - \frac{d_j}{n_j})$$

If there is no censoring, then the KM estimator for time t, $\hat{S}(t)$, is simply the proportion of observations in the sample with event times greater than t. If there is censoring, we start by ordering the event times in ascending order $t_1 \le t_2 \le ... \le t_T$. At each time t_j, there are n_j individuals who are at risk of the event. "At risk" means that they have not undergone the event, nor have they been censored prior to t_j. In other words, they will either undergo the event or become censored after t_j. Assume now that d_j represents the number of individuals who will default at t_j.

The KM estimator is then calculated as follows: $\hat{S}(t)$ equals $\hat{S}(t-1)$ times one minus d_t divided by n_t. This is very intuitive because it basically says that in order to survive time t, you must survive $t-1$ and cannot die during time t. d_t divided by n_t represents the hazard for time t. The expression can now be worked out recursively. This will bring us to the last term in the expression. That is, $\hat{S}(t)$ equals the product

ID	Time of Default or Censoring	Default or Censored
C1	6	Default
C2	3	Censored
C3	12	Default
C4	15	Censored
C5	18	Censored
C6	12	Default
C7	3	Default
C8	12	Default
C9	9	Censored
C10	15	Default

Exhibit 7.2 Example for Kaplan-Meier Analysis

across all j whereby t_j is less than or equal to t, of one minus d_j divided by n_j. The latter term is the conditional probability of surviving to time $t_j + 1$, given that the subject has survived to time t_j. For further details, we refer to the SAS documentation for PROC LIFETEST (Details/Computational Formulas).

Let's illustrate the Kaplan-Meier estimate with an example. In Exhibit 7.2 we have a data set of 10 customers: C1 through C10. The second column denotes the time of default or censoring. The third column indicates whether the customer is a defaulter or a censored observation.

We can now complete the table shown in Exhibit 7.3.

At time 0, all customers are still alive. Hence, the number of customers at risk, n_0, equals 10. The number of customers that defaulted, d_0, equals zero. The number of customers that were censored also equals zero. This results in a survival probability of one. The first default occurs at time 3. We started with 10 customers, so n_3 equals 10. Customer C7 defaulted so d_3 equals one. Customer C2 was censored. This results in a survival probability of 0.9. The next default happens at time 6. We still have eight customers, so n_6 equals eight. Customer C1 defaulted. No one was censored. In order

Time	At Risk at t n_t	Defaulted at t d_t	Censored at t	$S(t)$
0	10	0	0	1
3	10	1	1	0.9
6	8	1	0	0.9 * 7/8 = 0.79
9	7	0	1	0.79 * 7/7 = 0.79
12	6	3	0	0.79 * 3/6 = 0.39
15	3	1	1	0.39 * 2/3 = 0.26
18	1	0	1	0.26 * 1/1 = 0.26

Exhibit 7.3 Example for Kaplan-Meier Analysis (cont.)

to survive time 6, a customer must first survive time 3 and cannot default during time 6. Hence, this results in a survival probability of $0.9 * 7/8$ or 0.79. At time 9, we still have seven customers at risk, so n_9 equals seven. No one defaults, but customer C9 was censored. Hence, the survival probability becomes $0.79 * 7/7$, or thus 0.79. In other words, because censoring occurred only during time 9, the survival probability remains unaffected. At time 12, we still have six customers at risk, three of which will default. The survival probability thus becomes $0.79 * 3/6$ or 0.39. At time 15, we start with three customers. Customer C10 defaulted and customer C4 was censored. Hence, the survival probability becomes $0.39 * 2/3$ or 0.26. Finally, at time 18, no one defaults, so that the survival probability remains 0.26.

Actuarial Method

If there are many unique event times, we recommend using a life table or actuarial method to group the event times into intervals. The survival probability, $\hat{S}(t)$, then equals:

$$\hat{S}(t) = \prod_{j:t_j \leq t} (1 - \frac{d_j}{n_j - c_j/2})$$

Basically, this formula assumes that censoring occurs uniformly across a time interval. Because we started with n_j at the beginning of the time interval and ended with n_j minus c_j, the average number at risk equals $(n_j + (n_j - c_j))/2$ or $n_j - c_j/2$, which corresponds to the denominator in the expression. For further details, we refer to the SAS documentation for PROC LIFETEST (Details/Computational Formulas).

Reshaping the Data

Life tables do not generally condition on observable information (i.e., are nonparametric) and require a cross-sectional form (i.e., one observation per loan). Our mortgage data have to be reshaped by keeping the last observation and computing the time in months since the first observation time. Hence, the default indicator default_time is zero if an observation is censored and one if a default occurs.

We avoid left-censoring by assuming that all loans start from the first observation period onward and generate the new time stamp time2. Note that banks may also consider a time stamp from loan origination if loans are observed since origination.

```
PROC SORT DATA=data.mortgage;
BY id;
RUN;

DATA lifetest_temp1;
SET data.mortgage;
time2 = time-first_time+1;
BY id;
RETAIN id;
IF LAST.id THEN indicator=1;
RUN;
```

id	first_ time	time2	default_ time	payoff_ time	FICO_ orig_ time	LTV_ orig_ time
46	25	5	1	0	581	80.0
47	25	3	0	1	600	80.0
56	25	36	0	0	664	52.5

Exhibit 7.4 Cross-Sectional Data

```
DATA lifetest_temp2;
SET lifetest_temp1;
IF indicator = 1 OR default_time =1;
RUN;

DATA lifetest;
SET lifetest_temp2;
BY id;
RETAIN id;
IF FIRST.id THEN output;
RUN;
```

Exhibit 7.4 shows three borrower observations as an example. The time stamp time2 shows the time to default since the first observation period. This is contrary to the panel data set applied for discrete-time hazard models, where the time stamp time indicated the absolute time and loans were generally originated at different times. The first loan has defaulted in the fifth period after first observation, the second loan has been paid off in the third period after first observation, and the third loan is observed until the last observation period. The second and third loans are considered to be right-censored in the analyses shown in Exhibit 7.4.

Model Estimation Using PROC LIFETEST

In a first step, the survival function can be estimated with PROC LIFETEST using the product-limit method (also known as the Kaplan-Meier method, option method=PL in the PROC LIFETEST statement) or the life table method (also called the actuarial method, option method=LT in the PROC LIFETEST statement). We apply the life table method in the following:

```
ODS GRAPHICS ON;
PROC LIFETEST DATA=lifetest METHOD=LT INTERVALS=(0 TO 50 BY 10)
PLOTS=(ALL);
TIME time2*default_time(0);
RUN;
ODS GRAPHICS OFF;
```

The output presented in Exhibit 7.5 shows descriptive statistics for discrete time intervals including the numbers for failed observations, censored observations, and

The LIFETEST Procedure

Life Table Survival Estimates

Interval [L., U.)		No. Failed	No. Cens.	E. S. Size	C. P. Failure	S.E.	Survival	Failure	S.E.	M. R. Lifetime	S.E.	Evaluated at Midpoint				
												PDF	S.E.	Hazard	S.E.
0	10	8243	21300	39350.0	0.2095	0.00205	1.0000	0	0	28.6949	0.2715	0.0209	0.000205	0.023399	0.000256
10	20	4880	4139	18387.5	0.2654	0.00326	0.7905	0.2095	0.00205	.	.	0.0210	0.000263	0.0306	0.000433
20	30	1662	2083	10396.5	0.1599	0.00359	0.5807	0.4193	0.00298	.	.	0.00928	0.000214	0.017375	0.000425
30	40	353	6031	4677.5	0.0755	0.00386	0.4879	0.5121	0.00326	.	.	0.00368	0.000190	0.007843	0.000417
40	50	16	1286	666.0	0.0240	0.00593	0.4511	0.5489	0.00356	.	.	0.00108	0.000268	0.002432	0.000608
50	.	0	7	3.5	0	0	0.4402	0.5598	0.00438	.	.	.	.	.	.

Exhibit 7.5 Life Table Model

185

effective sample size (i.e., number of observations at the beginning of the time interval less 50 percent of the number of censored observations). We assume that censoring occurs uniformly across the time interval. Furthermore, the values for a number of functions are estimated (for METHOD = LT, detailed mathematical formulas are available in the SAS documentation for PROC LIFETEST):

- The default probability, which is labeled Conditional Probability of Failure. The estimator is the number of default events over the effective sample size for a given time interval. The standard deviation is computed for the default rate assuming a Bernoulli distribution of default events given the estimated default rate.

- The survival rate, which is labeled Survival. The estimator is one for the first time period and one minus the estimated default probability of the interval times the estimated survival rate in the previous time interval. The cumulative failure rate (Failure) is one minus the survival rate.

- The probability density function, which is labeled PDF. The estimator is the estimated survival rate times the estimated default probability relative to the length of the time interval.

- The hazard rate, which is labeled Hazard. The estimator is the estimated default rate over the midpoint of the survival rate relative to the length of the time interval.

The PLOTS command generates a number of plots, including the three estimated functions: PDF, survival function, and hazard rate (see Exhibits 7.6, 7.7, and 7.8).

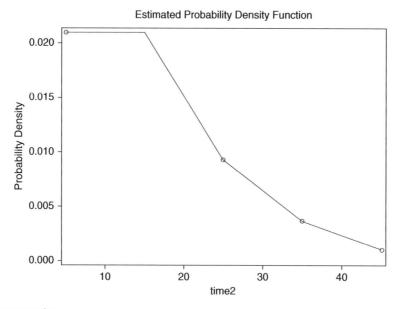

Exhibit 7.6 PDF plot

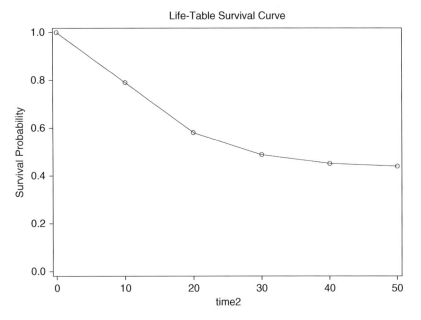

Exhibit 7.7 Survival Function Plot

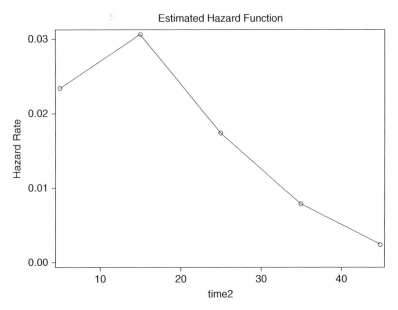

Exhibit 7.8 Hazard Rate Plot

Controlling for Information in Nonparametric Models

Life tables are nonparametric and as such do not condition on control information such as borrower, collateral, loan, or economic variables. Despite these limitations, there is a simple way to include (even time-varying) observable information by means of stratification. To demonstrate this point, we now stratify the results into five groups of equal size (i.e., 20 percent of all observations) using PROC RANK and the FICO score as discriminatory variable.

```
PROC RANK DATA=lifetest OUT=lifetest2 GROUPS=5;
VAR FICO_orig_time;
RANKS FICO_orig_time_rank;
RUN;

ODS GRAPHICS ON;
PROC LIFETEST DATA=lifetest2 METHOD=LT INTERVALS=(0 TO 50 BY 10)
PLOTS=(SURVIVAL);
TIME time2*default_time(0);
STRATA FICO_orig_time_rank;
RUN;
ODS GRAPHICS OFF;
```

We do not show the output for this model but present the survival plot, which is produced with the ODS GRAPHICS ON/ODS GRAPHICS OFF statements before and after the actual PROC LIFETEST code (see Exhibits 7.9).

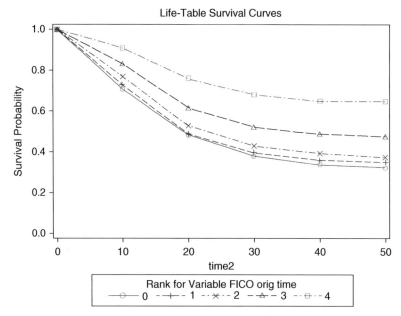

Exhibit 7.9 Survival Plot

It is clear that the FICO score and survival probability are positively correlated. A low FICO score has a greater default risk, which results in a low survival probability; a high score has less risk, and high survival probability.

Test of Equality over Groups

As mentioned, the Kaplan-Meier estimator does not account for the presence of covariates. It is a very useful tool for exploring and describing your survival data. However, other techniques are needed for building predictive survival analysis models, which is discussed in what follows.

A first extension of Kaplan-Meier analysis is to statistically test the equivalence of survival curves of different samples.

- ■ H_0: The survival curves are statistically the same.
- ■ H_1: The survival curves are statistically different.

As an example, suppose you want to test whether the survival curves for males and females are the same in a default setting. The null hypothesis then reads as follows: The survival curves for males and females are statistically the same. The alternative hypothesis is the following: the survival curves for males and females are statistically different. Various test statistics can be used to evaluate this, such as the log-rank test (sometimes also referred to as the Mantel-Haenszel test), the Wilcoxon test, and the likelihood ratio statistic. These three tests are closely related and usually give the same results. (See Exhibit 7.10.) They enable you to verify some basic insights about the survival data, which might further be elaborated on in the subsequent analysis. The STRATA statement reports these tests. This is useful in exploring data to see whether survival probabilities are significantly different across different segments.

Estimation of Survival Probabilities

With PROC LIFETEST we can export the survival probabilities using the OUTSURV command.

```
PROC LIFETEST DATA=lifetest METHOD=LT INTERVALS=(1 TO 102 BY 1)
   OUTSURV=SURVIVAL;
TIME time2*default_time(0);
RUN;
```

Test of Equality over Strata			
Test	**Chi-Square**	**DF**	**Pr > Chi-Square**
Log-Rank	1895.9755	4	<.0001
Wilcoxon	1962.9144	4	<.0001
-2Log(LR)	1963.3830	4	<.0001

Exhibit 7.10 PROC LIFETEST: Test of Equality over Groups

We convert the time stamp so that the measurement time is at the end of the period as OUTSURV computes the survival likelihood at the beginning of the period:

```
DATA survival;
SET survival;
time2=time2-1;
RUN;
```

Estimation of Default Probabilities

We have shown earlier that the conditional default probabilities between time t_1 and t_2 (PD_{t_1,t_2}), which are the quantities of interest for capital regulation, may be computed from the survival functions as the difference $S(t_1) - S(t_2)$ over $S(t_1)$:

$$PD_{t_1,t_2} = \frac{S(t_1) - S(t_2)}{S(t_1)}$$

We will apply variations of this formula later to derive discrete time default probabilities from the survival probability functions of continuous-time hazard models.

We can now compute default probabilities as follows: $(S(t1) - S(t2)/S(t1))$:

```
DATA survival2(WHERE=(PD_time NE .));
SET survival;
IF time2 >=1 THEN PD_time=(lag(survival)-survival)/lag(survival);
IF time2 =1 THEN PD_time=1-survival;
KEEP time2 PD_time;
RUN;
```

Finally, we add the default probabilities to the panel data set via match merging:

```
PROC SORT DATA=lifetest_temp1;
BY time2;
RUN;

PROC SORT DATA=survival2 NODUPKEY;
BY time2;
RUN;

DATA probabilities;
MERGE lifetest_temp1(IN=a) survival2;
BY time2;
IF a;
RUN;
```

Calibration of Life Tables

A PROC MEANS for the default indicator and the default probabilities shows that the mean of these in-sample PD estimates approximately matches the default rate. (see Exhibit 7.11).

The MEANS Procedure

Variable	Mean	Variable	Mean
default_time	0.0243506	PD_time	0.0249165

Exhibit 7.11 Calibration of Life Tables: Comparison of Default Indicators and Estimated Default Probabilities

```
PROC MEANS DATA=probabilities MEAN NOLABELS;
VAR default_time PD_time;
RUN;
```

COX PROPORTIONAL HAZARDS MODELS

Cox proportional hazards (CPH) models following Cox (1972) are regression models that link the survival time under consideration of censoring with predictive covariates. Hence, they are more flexible than the life table approach and stratification technique in controlling for observable information.

CPH models link the hazard rate with a baseline hazard rate and a transformation of the linear predictor (i.e., a linear combination of parameters with explanatory variables that exclude an intercept) as follows:

$$\lambda(t|\boldsymbol{x}_i) = \lambda_0(t) \exp\,(\boldsymbol{\beta}'\boldsymbol{x}_i)$$

where the baseline hazard rate $\lambda_0(t)$ is not specified ($\lambda_0(t) \geq 0$). CPH models are hence called semiparametric. We restrict the covariates to idiosyncratic information for now. From this equation, it becomes obvious that the covariates in a CPH model have a proportional impact on the hazard rate regardless of the base level of the hazard rate. In other words, if we take the ratio of the hazards of two individuals (i and j), we can see that the baseline hazard divides away, creating an expression that is independent of time as you can see in Exhibit 7.12.

This implies that the hazard of any individual is a fixed proportion of the hazard of any other individual; hence, the name proportional hazards. Put differently, the subjects most at risk at any one time remain the subjects most at risk at any other time, as you can see depicted in Exhibit 7.12.

The proportional hazards assumption can be tested by inspecting the survival functions for subgroups from the life table analysis. A good indication that the assumption holds is verifying that the survival functions do not cross.

The survival function of a CPH model is:

$$S(t|\boldsymbol{x}_i) = \exp\,\left(-\int_0^t \lambda(u|\boldsymbol{x}_i)du\right)$$

$$= \exp\,\left(-\int_0^t \lambda_0(u)\exp\,(\boldsymbol{\beta}'\boldsymbol{x}_i)du\right)$$

$$= S_0(t)^{\exp\,(\boldsymbol{\beta}'\boldsymbol{x}_i)}$$

with $S_0(t) = \exp\,\left(-\int_0^t \lambda_0(u)du\right)$

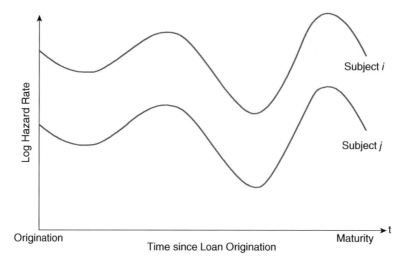

Exhibit 7.12 Proportional Hazards

The probability density function of the survival time T is given by:

$$f(t|x_i) = \lambda(t|x_i)\, S(t|x) = \lambda_0(t) \exp\, (\beta'x_i)\, S_0(t)^{\exp\, (\beta'x_i)}$$

If we now introduce an indicator variable for borrower i, δ_i, whereby $\delta_i = 0$ if censoring occurs and $\delta_n = 1$ if default occurs, then the likelihood for all observations becomes:

$$L(\lambda_0(t), \beta, x_i) = \prod_{i=1}^{N} f_i(t_i)^{\delta_i}\, S_i(t_i)^{1-\delta_i}$$

$$= \prod_{=1}^{N} [\lambda_0(t_i) \exp\, (\beta'x_{ii})]^{\delta_i} \exp\left[-\int_0^{t_i} \lambda_0(u) \exp\, (\beta'x_{ii}) du\right]$$

Partial Likelihood

Let's now discuss how the β parameters of a proportional hazards regression model can be estimated using the idea of partial likelihood (Cox, 1972, 1975). Suppose we have I individuals with i ranging from one to I. Each individual has three characteristics: x_i is the vector of covariates, t_i is the time of the event or censoring, and δ_i is one if the individual is uncensored and zero if the individual is censored. We start by ranking all the events of the noncensored subjects (t_1 up to t_T). Given the fact that one subject has event time t_i, the probability that this subject has inputs x_j is then given by:

$$\frac{\lambda(t_i x_i)\Delta t}{\sum_{l \in R(t_i)} h(t_i, x_l)\Delta t}$$

where $R(t_i)$ represents the subjects that are at risk at time t_i. Since the baseline hazard $\lambda_0(t_i)$ occurs in both the numerator and the denominator, it will cancel out. Hence, this gives us the following expression:

$$\frac{\exp\,(\boldsymbol{\beta}'\boldsymbol{x}_i)}{\displaystyle\sum_{l\in R(t_i)} \exp\,(\boldsymbol{\beta}'\boldsymbol{x}_l)}$$

which is independent of the baseline hazard.

The partial likelihood function then becomes:

$$\prod_{j=1}^{I} \frac{\exp\,(\boldsymbol{\beta}'\boldsymbol{x}_i)}{\displaystyle\sum_{l\in R(t_i)} \exp\,(\boldsymbol{\beta}'\boldsymbol{x}_l)}$$

Note that, for ease of notation, we assumed that individual j with covariates $\boldsymbol{x}_j$ has event time t_j. The $\boldsymbol{\beta}$ parameters can be optimized using the Newton-Raphson algorithm. It is important to observe how the censored observations enter the partial likelihood function. They will be included in the risk sets $R(t_j)$ until their censoring time.

Also, it is important to note that the $\boldsymbol{\beta}$ parameters can be estimated without having to specify the baseline hazard $\lambda_0(t)$. Furthermore, it can be shown that the partial likelihood estimates are consistent, which means that they converge to the true values as the sample increases, and are asymptotically normal. Moreover, the partial likelihood estimates depend only on the ranks of the event times and not on the numerical values. An important assumption made in deriving the partial likelihood function is that there are no tied event times. However, in many real-life settings, time is measured in a discrete way so that ties are likely to occur.

There are four common ways to deal with tied event times: the exact method, two approximations, and the discrete method. In case there are no ties, all four methods give the same estimates. The exact method assumes that ties occur because of imprecise time measurements and treats time as continuous. Hence, it considers all possible orderings of the event times and constructs a likelihood term for each ordering. When there are three ties, six orderings are possible, and thus six terms are added to the partial likelihood function. Obviously, this procedure is very time consuming for heavily tied data. It is recommended only when few ties occur. Two popular approximations are the Breslow and Efron likelihood methods. The Breslow likelihood method works well if ties occur rarely. Empirical evidence has shown that the Efron approximation is often superior to the Breslow approximation. A fourth option is the discrete method whereby time is treated in a discrete way so that multiple events can occur at the same time. Although this can also be addressed using the partial likelihood approach, it will become very time consuming for large, heavily tied survival data sets.

Cox Proportional Hazards Model in SAS Using PROC PHREG

CPH models can be estimated in SAS using life table data (see previous discussion) if estimated for information that is not time-varying (e.g., credit information at origination).

We first create a data set called covariates with the FICO score and the LTV ratio to plot the survival function for each. We then run PROC PHREG, including a command to generate the survival functions:

```
ODS GRAPHICS ON;
PROC PHREG data=lifetest PLOTS(OVERLAY)=SURVIVAL;
MODEL time2*default_time(0)=FICO_orig_time LTV_orig_time / TIES=EFRON;
BASELINE COVARIATES=covariates_orig_time / ROWID=set;
RUN;
ODS GRAPHICS OFF;
```

The structure of PROC PHREG is very similar to PROC LOGISTIC. The dependent variable in the model is the (survival) observation time and an indicator variable, which indicates default (coded by one), or whether the borrower is no longer observed (i.e., censored, coded by zero). The censoring state is specified in brackets and the two variables connected by "*".

The model output is presented in Exhibit 7.13.

The output is similar to PROC LOGISTIC with the distinction that rank-correlation measures between default probability and default events are no longer provided and a hazard ratio is included. The hazard ratio minus 100 percent shows the increase in default risk for a unit change in the explanatory variable.

Remember, we included only information that is, not time-varying, that is the FICO score and LTV ratio at origination. As in the PROC LOGISTIC results, FICO has a negative impact on the hazard rate and LTV a positive impact.

Similar to the PROC LIFETEST statement, various plots (here the survival function) can be generated with the (1) ODS GRAPHICS ON/ODS GRAPHICS OFF statements before and after the actual PROC PHREG code, (2) the PLOTS (OVERLAY) command whereby (OVERLAY) indicates that all curves are displayed in a single chart, and (3) the BASELINE command. The COVARIATES statement indicates reference values for the plot of the survival function given. The ROWID command indicates the names of the various reference value sets. We have created the following data set in SAS:

```
DATA covariates_orig_time;
INPUT set $ FICO_orig_time LTV_orig_time;
DATALINES;
high 600 90
low 800 60
;
```

If a data set is not explicitly specified, then a single survival function is plotted based on the average default values for the metric variables and the reference categories for the categorical variables as specified by the class statement. The survival functions for the two observations included in the data set covariates are depicted in Exhibit 7.14.

The PHREG Procedure

Model Information	
Data Set	WORK.LIFETEST
Dependent Variable	time2
Censoring Variable	default_time
Censoring Value(s)	0
Ties Handling	EFRON

Number of Observations Read	50000	Number of Observations Used	50000

Convergence Status
Convergence criterion (GCONV=1E−8) satisfied.

Model Fit Statistics		
Criterion	Without Covariates	With Covariates
-2 LOG L	303232.75	301068.64
AIC	303232.75	301072.64
SBC	303232.75	301087.89

Testing Global Null Hypothesis: BETA = 0			
Test	Chi-Square	DF	Pr > ChiSq
Likelihood Ratio	2164.1072	2	<.0001
Score	2198.7891	2	<.0001
Wald	2183.5710	2	<.0001

Analysis of Maximum Likelihood Estimates						
Parameter	DF	Parameter Estimate	Standard Error	Chi-Square	Pr > ChiSq	Hazard Ratio
FICO_orig_time	1	−0.00442	0.0001114	1571.3114	<.0001	0.996
LTV_orig_time	1	0.01554	0.0008019	375.6040	<.0001	1.016

Exhibit 7.13 CPH Model

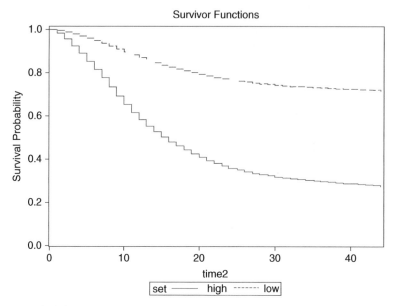

Exhibit 7.14 Survival Plot

As an extension, the baseline hazard function can be parameterized and the parameters estimated. Popular examples are the exponential, Weibull, and Gompertz distributions. Furthermore, PROC SURVEYPHREG estimates clustered standard errors by assuming dependence between observations of the same cluster unit. Clustering variables can be defined by the CLUSTER command.

Time-Varying Information

Time-varying information is a key concern in credit risk modeling. CPH models are able to accommodate time-varying explanatory variables as discrete-time hazard models:

$$\lambda(t|x_{it-1}) = \lambda_0(t) \exp\left(\boldsymbol{\beta}' x_{it-1}\right)$$

There are two main ways to include time-varying covariates: first, the aggregation of time-varying information and second, counting process data. We discuss both in what follows. SAS also offers an option for inclusion of time-varying covariates by programming statements. However, this assumes that the time variation occurs along the life cycle of a loan (time stamp time2) and not along the line of the economy (time stamp time). As a result, we do not discuss this technique in more detail.

Time-Varying Covariates: Aggregation of Time-Varying Information

In a first setting one can aggregate time-varying information to compute a moment of the distribution of the covariates per borrower for the period during which a subject is at risk using a PROC MEANS statement or, alternatively, using the last value that is observed (we use this as an example, as the PROC MEANS by borrower can be time consuming):

```
PROC SORT DATA=data.mortgage OUT=mortgage;
BY DESCENDING id;
RUN;

PROC SORT DATA=mortgage OUT=moment NODUPKEY;
BY id;
RUN;

DATA moment(KEEP=id LTV gdp);
SET moment;
RENAME LTV_time=LTV;
RENAME gdp_time=gdp;
RUN;

PROC SORT DATA=lifetest;
BY id;
RUN;

DATA lifetest2;
MERGE lifetest(IN=a) moment;
BY id;
RUN;
```

We then run the PROC PHREG for the lifetime data set

```
PROC PHREG data=lifetest2;
MODEL time2*default_time(0)=FICO_orig_time LTV gdp/ TIES=EFRON;
RUN;
```

which gives the parameter estimates presented in Exhibit 7.15.

The PHREG Procedure

Analysis of Maximum Likelihood Estimates						
Parameter	DF	Parameter Estimate	Standard Error	Chi-Square	Pr > ChiSq	Hazard Ratio
FICO_orig_time	1	−0.00461	0.0001132	1656.0392	<.0001	0.995
LTV	1	0.01772	0.0006075	850.5519	<.0001	1.018
gdp	1	−0.14956	0.00839	317.8000	<.0001	0.861

Exhibit 7.15 CPH Model

Time-Varying Covariates: Counting Process Data

The counting process data style of input requires the data to be in panel form (as for discrete-time hazard models) and two additional time stamps relative to the first observation time. These time stamps are (1) the time from first loan observation (alternatively, loan origination) to the beginning of an observation period, and (2) the time from the first loan observation to the end of an observation period.

```
DATA phreg;
SET data.mortgage;
time1 = time-first_time;
time2 = time-first_time+1;
RUN;
```

The data set looks as shown in Exhibit 7.16.

We now include one additional variable into our model, the GDP growth rate, and change the MODEL statement in PROC PHREG to accommodate the panel structure of the data with the two time stamps. The dependent variable in the MODEL statement is the two time stamps separated by a comma in brackets and an indicator variable, which indicates default (coded by one) or whether the borrower is no longer observed (i.e., censored, coded by zero). The censoring state is specified in brackets. The time stamps and censoring indicator are connected by "*".

The remaining code is identical to the life table data:

```
ODS GRAPHICS ON;
PROC PHREG DATA=phreg PLOTS(OVERLAY)=SURVIVAL;
MODEL (time1,time2)*default_time(0)=FICO_orig_time LTV_time gdp_time
   TIES=EFRON;
BASELINE COVARIATES=covariates_time/ ROWID=set;
RUN;
ODS GRAPHICS OFF;
```

id	first_ time	time	time1	time2	default_ time	payoff_ time	FICO_ orig_ time	LTV_ orig_ time	LTV_time	gdp_time
46	25	27	2	3	0	0	581	80.0	67.5913	2.36172
46	25	28	3	4	0	0	581	80.0	68.2919	1.22917
46	25	29	4	5	1	0	581	80.0	68.8752	1.69297
47	25	25	0	1	0	0	600	80.0	66.7938	2.89914
47	25	26	1	2	0	0	600	80.0	66.9609	2.15136
47	25	27	2	3	0	1	600	80.0	67.5853	2.36172
56	25	58	33	34	0	0	664	52.5	17.3599	2.86859
56	25	59	34	35	0	0	664	52.5	17.2625	2.44365
56	25	60	35	36	0	0	664	52.5	16.8980	2.83636

Exhibit 7.16 Counting Process Data

The PHREG Procedure

		Parameter	Standard			Hazard
Parameter	DF	Estimate	Error	Chi-Square	Pr > ChiSq	Ratio
FICO_orig_time	1	−0.00520	0.0001126	2129.1414	<.0001	0.995
LTV_time	1	0.00874	0.0001258	4823.3346	<.0001	1.009
gdp_time	1	−0.10285	0.00395	678.0251	<.0001	0.902

Exhibit 7.17 CPH Model

The counting process style of input invoked by the MODEL statement assumes that every line in the panel data is a stand-alone line. This corresponds to the assumption that every observation and subject is observed for one period in which default or nondefault occurs. This situation is comparable with discrete-time hazard models. Exhibit 7.17 shows the parameter estimates of the model and Exhibit 7.18 the survival plots for the upturn and downturn sets of covariates.

The data set covariates are the basis of an analysis for two borrowers corresponding to an economic downturn (GDP growth of −3 percent) and an economic upturn state (GDP growth of 3 percent):

```
DATA covariates_time;
INPUT set $ FICO_orig_time LTV_orig_time gdp_time;
DATALINES;
downturn 800 60 -3
upturn 800 60 3
;
```

Estimation of Survival Probabilities

Computing default probabilities is not accommodated by design in CPH models. Remember, to simplify the parameter estimation, CPH models are based on the maximization of the partial likelihood that relates to the parameters of the explanatory variables and not to the baseline hazard function. To enable the computation of the probability density function, survival function, and hazard rate, SAS has added the BASELINE command to PROC PHREG, where the baseline hazard rate is estimated in a second stage using the approximate likelihood provided in Breslow (1974) as a default technique or the optional Kaplan and Meier (1958) technique. The survival probabilities are then estimated as follows:

$$\hat{S}(t|x_i) = \exp\left(-\int_0^t \hat{\lambda}_0(u)\exp\left(\hat{\beta}' x_i\right)du\right)$$

The BASELINE command is computationally expensive as it computes the probability of default for all interactions of the explanatory variables and time2. Different

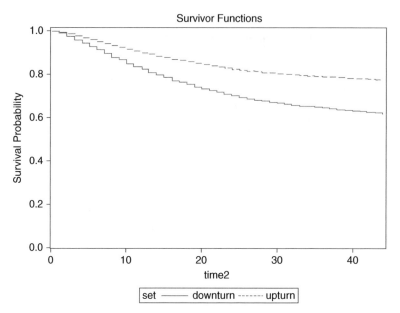

Exhibit 7.18 Survival Plot

ways to reduce the complexity exist. For example, you may:

- Generate mutually exclusive subsets of data using PROC SURVEYSELECT.
- Estimate the full model using all data multiple times but with different subsets for the COVARIATES and OUT commands in the BASELINE specification.
- Append the various subsets from the OUT commands in the BASELINE specification to obtain a complete collection of default probabilities.
- Select the observations that reflect explanatory variables and time stamps (time2) of the original data set.

Alternatively, you may restrict the data set to observations with a certain time stamp (here time2) and/or draw a random sample using PROC SURVEYSELECT:

```
DATA phreg2;
SET phreg;
WHERE time2<=10;
KEEP time1 time2
default_time FICO_orig_time LTV_time gdp_time;
RUN;

PROC SURVEYSELECT DATA=phreg2 SAMPRATE=0.05 OUT=PHREG3 SEED=12345;
RUN;
```

PROC SURVEYSELECT randomly draws 5 percent of all remaining observations. The command SEED = 12345 fixes the random experiment so that the random draw results in the same outcome if executed another time. We now create a new data set called "survival", which stores the survival probabilities for the first three periods (note that this step may take a few minutes despite the small sample size):

```
PROC PHREG data=phreg3;
MODEL (time1,time2)*default_time(0)=FICO_orig_time LTV_time gdp_time /
  TIES=EFRON;
BASELINE COVARIATES=phreg3 OUT=survival
SURVIVAL=SURVIVAL;
RUN;
```

Estimation of Default Probabilities

We then compute the PD as the first-order difference of the cumulative hazard rate of the current observation and the observation in the previous period $(S(t1) - S(t2)/S(t1))$:

```
DATA survival2(WHERE=(PD_time NE .));
SET survival;
IF time2 >=1 THEN PD_time=(lag(survival)-survival)/lag(survival);
IF time2 =1 THEN PD_time=1-survival;
KEEP FICO_orig_time LTV_time gdp_time time2 PD_time;
RUN;
```

Finally, we merge the default probabilities of the initial estimation data set for all observations:

```
PROC SORT DATA=phreg3;
BY time2 FICO_orig_time LTV_time gdp_time;
RUN;

PROC SORT DATA=survival2 nodupkey;
BY time2 FICO_orig_time LTV_time gdp_time;
RUN;

DATA probabilities;
MERGE phreg3(IN=a) survival2;
BY time2 FICO_orig_time LTV_time gdp_time;
IF a;
RUN;
```

Calibration of CPH Models

We test the calibration of the CPH model with a comparison of the mean estimated default probability by the CPH model and the default rate in the sample. PROC

The MEANS Procedure

Variable	Mean	Variable	Mean
default_time	0.0266877	PD_time	0.0260356

Exhibit 7.19 Calibration of CPH Models: Comparison of Default Indicators and Estimated Default Probabilities

MEANS for the default indicator and default probabilities shows that the mean of the in-sample PD estimates approximately matches the default rate (See Exhibit 7.19).

```
PROC MEANS DATA=probabilities MEAN NOLABELS;
VAR default_time PD_time;
RUN;
```

Note that the default rate for the data subset (based on the restriction *time2* ≤ 10 and the random sampling using PROC SURVEYSELECT) is a little higher than for the complete data set.

ACCELERATED FAILURE TIME MODELS

Accelerated failure time (AFT) models are parametric survival models that link the (log) transformed survival time to a linear predictor of the sum of parameter-weighted covariates:

$$\log (T_i) = \beta' x_i + \sigma \epsilon$$

with T_i the time to failure. We restrict the covariates to idiosyncratic information for now. The models are called AFT models as they assume that the parameters $\beta_1, \cdots, \beta_p$ and hence the impact of the independent variables are multiplicative on the event time. The parameters indicate how strongly the survival time accelerates or decelerates when a covariate changes by one unit. Krüger et al. (2015) apply AFT models.

The survival time is generally positive, and the transformation of the log-link function is defined from minus infinity to infinity, which matches the range of the model-implied estimated dependent variable that results from the weighted sum of the predictors and the volatility-weighted residual.

PROC LIFEREG fits these models for failure time data that can be uncensored, right-censored, left-censored, or interval-censored. The models for the dependent variable consist of a linear effect composed of the covariates and a random disturbance term. Common distributions for the residual are the exponential, Weibull (two parameters), lognormal, log-logistic, and gamma (three parameters) distributions. There are both graphical and likelihood procedures to choose the appropriate distribution.

Graphical Procedures

Let's reconsider some of the relationships that were introduced earlier. Remember that we have $\lambda(t)$ equals minus the derivative of $\log S(t)$ to t, or stated differently, minus $\log S(t)$ is equal to the integral from 0 to t of $\lambda(u)du$. Because of this relationship, the log survivor function is commonly referred to as the cumulative hazard function, which can be interpreted as the sum of the risks that are faced when going from time 0 to time t. If the survival times are exponentially distributed, then the hazard is constant and the cumulative hazard rate is equal to $\lambda * t$. Hence a plot of $-\log(S(t))$ versus t should yield a straight line through the origin at 0. Similarly, it can be shown that if the survival times are Weibull distributed, then a plot of $\log(-\log(S(t)))$ versus $\log(t)$ yields a straight line, not through the origin. In the case of a lognormal distribution, a plot of $N^{-1}(1 - S(t))$ versus $\log(t)$ should yield a straight line, whereby N^{-1} represents the inverse, cumulative, standard normal distribution. Finally, in the case of a log-logistic distribution, a plot of $\log((1 - S(t))/S(t))$ versus $\log(t)$ should be a straight line. Notice that in all these cases, the survival probabilities $S(t)$ to be plotted can be obtained from a Kaplan-Meier analysis. The plots of $-\log(S(t))$ and $\log(-\log(S(t)))$ can be easily asked for in SAS using PROC LIFETEST with the PLOTS(LS,LLS) option. (See Exhibits 7.20 and 7.21.)

```
ODS GRAPHICS ON;
PROC LIFETEST DATA=lifetest METHOD=LT INTERVALS=(1 to 102 BY 1)
  PLOTS=(LS LLS);
TIME time2*default_time(0);
RUN;
ODS GRAPHICS OFF;
```

Likelihood Procedure

A more formal approach to evaluate model fit is based on a likelihood procedure. More specifically, the likelihood ratio test statistic can be used to compare models and test if one model is a special case of another. Let's start from the generalized gamma distribution, which you can see defined right here.

$$f(t) = \frac{\beta}{\Gamma(\kappa)\theta} \left(\frac{t}{\theta}\right)^{\kappa\beta-1} \exp\left(-\left(\frac{t}{\theta}\right)^{\beta}\right)$$

Note that it has three parameters: β, θ, and κ. If we now define $\sigma = 1/(\beta\sqrt{\kappa})$ and $\delta = 1/\sqrt{\kappa}$, then the Weibull, exponential, standard gamma, and lognormal distributions are all special versions of the generalized gamma distribution as follows: If σ equals δ, we have a standard gamma distribution; if δ equals one, we have a Weibull distribution; if both σ and δ equal one, we have an exponential distribution; and if δ equals zero, we have a lognormal distribution.

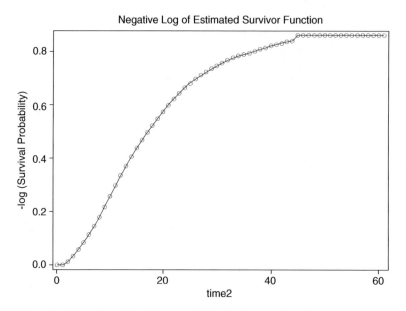

Exhibit 7.20 Graphical Procedures: Negative Log of Estimated Survivor Functions versus Time

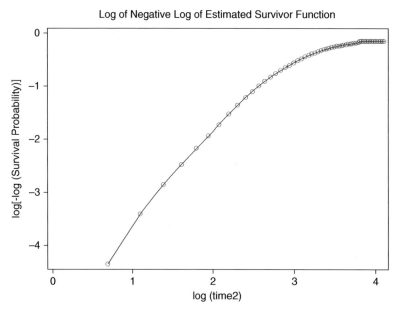

Exhibit 7.21 Graphical Procedures: Log of Negative Log of Estimated Survivor Functions versus the Log of Time

Parameters	Degrees of Freedom
Freedom	
Exponential versus Weibull	1
Exponential versus standard gamma	1
Exponential versus generalized gamma	2
Weibull versus generalized gamma	1
Lognormal versus generalized gamma	1
Standard gamma versus generalized gamma	1

Exhibit 7.22 Degrees of Freedom for Likelihood Ratio Test

We can now use this to perform a likelihood ratio test. Let L_{full} be the likelihood of the full model (such as a generalized gamma distribution) and L_{red} be the likelihood of the reduced or specialized model (such as an exponential distribution). If both are very similar, then, of course, the reduced or specialized model will be selected. More formally, a chi-square statistic can be computed as $-2log\ (L_{red}/L_{full})$. The degrees of freedom correspond to the number of reduced parameters. You can see the various options listed in Exhibit 7.22:

Accelerated Failure Time Models with PROC LIFEREG

As a simple first example, we choose an AFT model with an exponential distribution function for the residual (i.e., command / D = EXPONENTIAL in the MODEL statement). The exponential model has a constant hazard rate and the SAS code is:

```
PROC LIFEREG DATA = lifetest;
MODEL time2*default_time(0)
   = FICO_orig_time LTV_orig_time / D = EXPONENTIAL;
RUN;
```

We obtain the parameter estimates shown in Exhibit 7.23, which refer to the dependent variable of the survival time that is transformed by the natural logarithm. Contrary to PROC LOGISTIC (with the dependent variable default_time descending) and PROC PHREG, the parameter estimates have to be interpreted in the opposite way: An increase in the FICO score implies a higher survival time and hence lower probability of default. A higher LTV ratio at origination implies a lower survival time and hence higher probability of default. A higher GDP growth rate implies a higher survival time and hence lower probability of default.

We show in Exhibit 7.23 that the exponential distribution is a special case of the popular Weibull distribution with the two parameters Scale and Weibull shape being equal to one. Note that CPH models are identical to AFT models if the baseline hazard rate is Weibull distributed in a full likelihood estimation. The parameters can be

The LIFEREG Procedure

Model Information	
Data Set	WORK.LIFETEST
Dependent Variable	Log(time2)
Censoring Variable	default_time
Censoring Value(s)	0
Number of Observations	50000
Noncensored Values	15154
Right-Censored Values	34846
Left-Censored Values	0
Interval-Censored Values	0
Number of Parameters	3
Name of Distribution	Exponential
Log Likelihood	−39088.58288

Number of Observations Read	50000
Number of Observations Used	50000

Fit Statistics	
−2 Log Likelihood	78177.17
AIC (smaller is better)	78183.17
AICC (smaller is better)	78183.17
BIC (smaller is better)	78209.63

Algorithm converged.

Analysis of Maximum Likelihood Parameter Estimates							
Parameter	DF	Estimate	Standard Error	95% Confidence Limits		Chi-Square	Pr > ChiSq
Intercept	1	2.1137	0.1037	1.9105	2.3169	415.84	<.0001
FICO_orig_time	1	0.0043	0.0001	0.0041	0.0045	1499.23	<.0001
LTV_orig_time	1	−0.0155	0.0008	−0.0171	−0.0139	371.68	<.0001
Scale	0	1.0000	0.0000	1.0000	1.0000		
Weibull Shape	0	1.0000	0.0000	1.0000	1.0000		

Exhibit 7.23 LIFEREG Model

estimated by maximum likelihood. The constituents of the likelihood are the hazard rate, the survival function, and the probability density function.

These functions are for the exponential distribution:

- Hazard rate: $\lambda_i = \exp(-\boldsymbol{\beta}'\boldsymbol{x}_i)$
- Survival function: $S_i(t_i) = \exp(-\exp(-\boldsymbol{\beta}'\boldsymbol{x}_i * t_i))$
- Probability density function: $f_i(t_i) = \exp(-\boldsymbol{\beta}'\boldsymbol{x}_i)\exp(-\exp(\boldsymbol{\beta}'\boldsymbol{x}_i t_i))$

The hazard rate, survival function, and probability density function are derived in a similar way for the other distributions. The likelihood becomes:

$$
\begin{aligned}
L(\boldsymbol{\beta}, \boldsymbol{x}) &= \prod_{i=1}^{I} f(t_i)^{\delta_i} S(t_i)^{1-\delta_i} \\
&= \prod_{i=1}^{I} \lambda_i^{\delta_i} S(t_i) \\
&= \prod_{i=1}^{I} (\exp(-\boldsymbol{\beta}'\boldsymbol{x}_i))^{\delta_i} \exp(-\exp(-\boldsymbol{\beta}'\boldsymbol{x}_i * t_i))
\end{aligned}
$$

SAS then maximizes the logarithm of this likelihood.

Estimation of Default Probabilities

The estimation of default probabilities is not straightforward for AFT models in PROC LIFEREG. This is similar to the SAS implementation of the Cox proportional hazard model in PROC PHREG. We follow the methodology discussed previously and estimate the default probabilities from the survival probabilities.

First, we compute the hazard rate (λ_i). Remember that the hazard rate is time-invariant with regard to the life cycle (i.e., the baseline hazard rate) in the exponential model. This is also referred to as the memoryless property of the exponential distribution. Second, we compute default probabilities as the first-order difference of the cumulative hazard rate at the end of the current observation period and at the beginning of the current observation period. This is the same as the difference between the survival function at the beginning of the current period and the survival function at the end of the current period relative to the survival function at the beginning of the current period ($S_i(t1) - S_i(t2)/S_i(t1)$). Note that it is important that $S_i(t1)$ and $S_i(t2)$ are based on the same realizations of the time-varying covariates, as otherwise negative default probabilities are likely to result if the covariates indicate a lower risk at the end of a period than at the beginning of a period. We now compute the survival probabilities, which is somewhat different from the Cox proportional hazard model where we estimated default probabilities based on the PROC PHREG-generated survival probabilities:

$$
\hat{S}(t_i) = \exp(-\exp(-(\hat{\beta}_0 + \hat{\beta}_1 * \text{FICO\_orig\_time} + \hat{\beta}_2 * \text{LTV\_orig\_time}) * t_i))
$$

This is implemented in the following data step:

```
DATA probabilities;
SET phreg;
xbeta=2.0998+0.0044*FICO_orig_time-0.0159*LTV_orig_time;
lambda = EXP(-xbeta);
S1 = 1-CDF('EXPONENTIAL', time1 ,1/lambda);
S2 = 1-CDF('EXPONENTIAL', time2 ,1/lambda);
PD_time = (S1-S2)/(S1);
RUN;
```

Calibration of AFT Models: Comparison of Default Indicators and Estimated Default Probabilities

A PROC MEANS for the default indicator and default probabilities shows that the mean of the in-sample PD estimates approximately matches the default rate. (See Exhibit 7.24.)

```
PROC MEANS DATA=probabilities MEAN NOLABELS;
VAR default_time
PD_time;
RUN;
```

Time-Varying Covariates

The estimation of time-varying covariates for AFT models is as challenging as it is for Cox proportional hazard models, and you may choose to refer to some of the solutions presented in the previous section on the CPH models. When estimating default probabilities based on time-varying information, care must be taken in the presence of time-varying covariates, in the sense that the survival probabilities are based on the same covariates, and no lag function is applied to derive the survival probability at the beginning/end of the prior period.

EXTENSION: MIXTURE CURE MODELING

A key assumption in survival analysis is that, in the long run, everyone will experience the event. In a medical setting, everybody will die at some point and the survival probability becomes 0. This is not true in a credit-risk modeling setting because a large part of the population never defaults. Hence, the survival probability

The MEANS Procedure

Variable	Mean	Variable	Mean
default_time	0.0243506	PD_time	0.0235128

Exhibit 7.24 Calibration of AFT Models: Comparison of Default Indicators and Estimated Default Probabilities

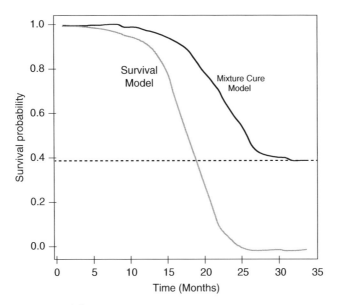

Exhibit 7.25 Mixture Cure Modeling

of the population will not be zero, but levels out at some value. You can see this visualized in the figure shown in Exhibit 7.25.

The survival model function goes to zero and the mixture cure model function goes to 0.4. Mixture cure modeling offers a solution to this problem by modeling distinct subpopulations.

Let us continue the example of a time-to-default prediction to illustrate the idea of mixture cure modeling. Let $Y = 1$ when an account is susceptible to default and $Y = 0$ otherwise. Let x and z be customer characteristics. You can think of characteristics such as age, income, marital status, and so on. The mixture cure model then becomes $S(t|x, z) = \pi(z)S(t|Y = 1, x) + 1 - \pi(z)$. As you can see, this model has two components. $\pi(z)$ is the probability of being susceptible to default, given characteristics z. It represents the incidence component and can be modeled using a binary logistic regression model, or any other classification technique. $S(t|Y = 1, x)$ is the latency model component and can be modeled using any survival analysis technique such as proportional hazards regression.

The parameters of the mixture cure model can then be estimated by formulating a combined likelihood function, which can be optimized by using the expectation maximization (EM) algorithm. This makes the mixture cure model computationally more intensive than the other survival models previously discussed. For more information, refer to Tong et al. (2012) and Dirick, Claeskens, and Baesens (2015).

DISCRETE-TIME HAZARD VERSUS CONTINUOUS-TIME HAZARD MODELS

In practice, discrete-time hazard models (in particular logit and probit regression models) are far more popular than continuous-time models. These models directly estimate the probability of default for the given data periodicity. Recent advances in regulation, in particular loan loss provisions under the International Financial Reporting Standards (IFRS 9), require the estimation of lifetime and life cycle effects (i.e., the baseline hazard rates). These effects can be included through controls that indicate the life cycle stage. Examples are lifetime dummies, time since origination, or time to maturity. Furthermore, interactions with other information may be added to the models. We generally recommend using these models as a first step.

Continuous-time hazard models may provide for more efficient and accurate default risk estimation, but come at the cost of complexity and loss of transparency. The analysis of these trade-off effects is an important consideration for the credit analyst. We recommend using these models in advanced applications.

PRACTICE QUESTIONS

1. Form five categories for the current LTV ratio. Estimate a life table model that is stratified by these five current LTV categories. Perform a statistical test for the equivalence of survival curves in the five samples.

2. Estimate a CPH model for PDs based on the FICO score and the LTV ratio at origination. Compute the survival function for a loan with a FICO score of 670 and an LTV ratio at origination of 90 percent. What is the PD for a loan five years from origination? Use data set mortgage.

3. Draw a random sample of 5,000 loans. Estimate two CPH models: one based on the FICO score and the LTV ratio at origination and another based on FICO score, the LTV ratio at origination, and the macro variable GDP growth. Estimate the probabilities of default, plot the default rate, and calculate the mean of the estimated default probabilities for both models by time. Use data set mortgage.

4. Estimate the probabilities of default for an AFT model based on the interest rate at origination. Use data set mortgage.

REFERENCES

Bellotti, T., and J. Crook. 2009. "Credit Scoring with Macroeconomic Variables Using Survival Analysis." *Journal of the Operational Research Society* 60 (12): 1699–1707.

Breslow, N. 1974. "Covariance Analysis of Censored Survival Data." *Biometrics* 30: 89–99.

Cox, D. R. 1972. "Regression Models and Life Tables (with Discussion)." *Journal of the Royal Statistical Society* 34: 187–220.

Cox, D. R. 1975. "Partial Likelihood." *Biometrika* 62 (2): 269–276.

Dirick, L., T. Bellotti, G. Claeskens, and B. Baesens. 2015. "The Prediction of Time to Default for Personal Loans Using Mixture Cure Models: Including Macro-economic Factors." *Proceedings of the Credit Scoring and Credit Control XIII Conference.*

Dirick, L., G. Claeskens, and B. Baesens. 2015. "An Akaike Information Criterion for Multiple Event Mixture Cure Models." *European Journal of Operational Research* 241 (2): 449–457.

Kaplan, E. L., and P. Meier. 1958. "Nonparametric Estimation from Incomplete Observations." *Journal of the American Statistical Association* 53 (282): 457–481.

Krüger, S., T. Oehme, D. Rösch, and H. Scheule. 2015. "Expected Loss Over Lifetime." *Working Paper, University of Regensburg and University of Technology Sydney.*

Malik, M., and L. C. Thomas. 2010. "Modelling Credit Risk of Portfolio of Consumer Loans." *Journal of the Operational Research Society* 61: 411–420.

Quigley, J. M., and R. Van Order. 1991. "Defaults on Mortgage Obligations and Capital Requirements for US Savings Institutions: A Policy Perspective." *Journal of Public Economics* 44 (3): 353–369.

Tong, E. N., C. Mues, and L. C. Thomas. 2012. "Mixture Cure Models in Credit Scoring: If and When Borrowers Default." *European Journal of Operational Research* 218 (1): 132–139.

CHAPTER 8

Low Default Portfolios

INTRODUCTION

In this chapter, we discuss low default portfolios (LDPs). We begin by discussing the modeling problem and provide some regulatory perspectives. We then elaborate on the development of predictive models for skewed data sets and cover the following approaches: varying the time window, undersampling and oversampling, and synthetic minority oversampling technique (SMOTE). The next subsections feature discussions on how to adjust the posterior probabilities to the original class distribution and perform cost-sensitive learning. We then focus on the shadow ratings approach, where the aim is to develop an internal credit risk model predicting external agency ratings. The confidence level approach is reviewed next, followed by some other methods to deal with LDPs. The chapter concludes by providing some thoughts on how to model loss given default (LGD) and exposure at default (EAD) for LDPs.

BASIC CONCEPTS

The Basel Accord provides no formal definition of a low default portfolio. The Bank of England earlier suggested 20 as the minimum number of required defaults to begin modeling (Prudential Regulation Authority 2013). Hence, if you have fewer than 20 defaults, you definitely have a low default portfolio. The definition of a low default portfolio strongly depends not only on the quantity, but also on the quality of the data. More specifically, to what extent is the data predictive for the given (limited) number of defaults? Put differently, if you have high-quality and highly predictive data, you don't need that many defaults in order to derive a meaningful default risk model.

When thinking about low default portfolios, a distinction needs to be made between a low number of defaults in an absolute and in a relative sense. For example, when you have a portfolio of 100,000 observations with a default rate of 1 percent (i.e., 1,000 defaulters), then the relative default rate is low, but the absolute number of defaulters is quite high. When the portfolio has 100 observations and 10 defaulters, then the relative default rate is high, but the absolute number of defaulters is low. Obviously, there can also be situations where both the absolute number and the relative number of defaulters are low.

Low default portfolios are quite common in a financial setting. A popular example is exposures to sovereigns; very few countries have gone into default in the past. Other examples are exposures to banks, insurance companies, and project finance, which is finance for large projects such as building highways or nuclear reactors. Exposures to large corporations and/or specialized lending are additional examples. When you bring new products to the market, it will also take some time before you have the necessary number of defaults to estimate standard credit risk models.

As already mentioned, for low default portfolios, typically you have a lack of modeling data, especially default data, which makes it very difficult to apply the advanced internal ratings based (IRB) approach, in which case you need to estimate the probability of default (PD), the LGD, and the EAD. Historical average default rates are not appropriate since they have been calculated on only a few observations. Because of data scarcity, the credit risk can thus be substantially underestimated or overestimated. This is a significant problem, especially given the fact that a substantial portion of a bank's assets might consist of low default portfolios.

Here you can see some statements made by the Basel Committee Accord Implementation Group's Validation Subgroup on the issue of low default portfolios (Basel Committee on Banking Supervision 2005):

- "LDPs should not, by their very nature, automatically be excluded from IRB treatment."
- "... an additional set of rules or principles specifically applying to LDPs is neither necessary nor desirable."
- "... relatively sparse data might require increased reliance on alternative data sources and data-enhancing tools for quantification and alternative techniques for validation."
- "... LDPs should not be considered or treated as conceptually different from other portfolios."

The Financial Services Authority (FSA), which was the predecessor of the Prudential Regulation Authority (PRA) in the United Kingdom, earlier also explicitly confirmed that it should be possible to include a firm's LDPs in the IRB approach (see Financial Services Authority 2006a, Section 7).

It needs to be noted, though, that given their intrinsic characteristics, LDPs do require special modeling and calibration approaches. We discuss these further in what follows. First, we take a look at the case where we have a skewed data set with a low number of defaults in a relative sense, but a sufficient number of defaults in an absolute sense.

DEVELOPING PREDICTIVE MODELS FOR SKEWED DATA SETS

Default risk data sets often have a very skewed target class distribution where typically only about 1 percent or even less of the transactions are defaulters. Obviously, this creates problems for the analytical techniques discussed earlier since they are being flooded by all the nondefault observations and will thus tend toward classifying every observation as nondefault. Think about decision trees, for example: If they start from a data set with 99 percent/1 percent nondefault/default observations, then the entropy is already very low and hence it is very likely that the decision tree does not find any useful split and classifies all observations as nondefault, thereby achieving a classification accuracy of 99 percent, but essentially detecting none of the defaulters. It is thus recommended to increase the number of default observations or their weight, such that the analytical techniques can pay better attention to them. Various procedures are possible to do this and will be outlined in what follows.

Varying the Sample Window

A first way to increase the number of defaulters is by increasing the time horizon for prediction. For example, instead of predicting default with a 12-month forward-looking time horizon, an 18- or 24-month time horizon can be adopted. This is likely to add more defaulters to the sample and thus enable the analytical techniques to find a meaningful discrimination. An ex post recalibration step may then be added to obtain Basel-compliant 12-month PDs. An example application may be the determination of default rates for investment-grade rating classes, which are often zero or close to zero for one year but become positive in cumulative terms over the longer term (say 20 to 30 years).

Another approach works by sampling every defaulter twice (or more), as depicted in Exhibit 8.1. Let's assume we predict default with a one-year forward-looking time horizon using information from a one-year backward-looking time horizon (e.g., as in behavioral scoring). By shifting the observation point earlier or later, the same default observation can be sampled twice. Obviously, the variables collected will be similar but not perfectly the same, since they are measured on a different (although overlapping) time frame. This added variability can then come in handy for the analytical techniques to better discriminate between the defaulters and nondefaulters. Note that depending on the skewness of the target, multiple observation points can be considered such that the number of defaulters is multiplied by 2, 3, 4, and so on. Finding the optimal number is subject to a trial-and-error exercise. Note that a disadvantage of this method is that the characteristics of the duplicated observations may be overstated.

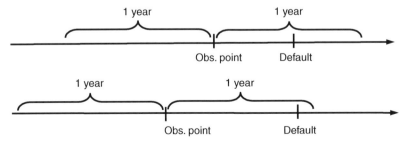

Exhibit 8.1 Varying the Time Window to Deal with Skewed Data Sets

Undersampling and Oversampling

Another way to increase the weight of the defaulters is by either oversampling them or by undersampling the nondefaulters. Oversampling is illustrated in Exhibit 8.2. Here, the idea is to replicate the defaulters two or more times so as to make the distribution less skewed. In our example, observations 1 and 4, both defaulters, have been replicated so as to create an equally balanced training sample having the same number of defaulters and nondefaulters.

Undersampling is illustrated in Exhibit 8.3. Here, observations 2 and 5, which are both nondefaulters, have been removed so as to create an equally balanced training sample. The undersampling can be done based on business experience where

Original data

	ID	Variables	Class
Train	1		Defaulter
	2		Non-Defaulter
	3		Non-Defaulter
	4		Defaulter
	5		Non-Defaulter
	6		Non-Defaulter
Test	7		Non-Defaulter
	8		Non-Defaulter
	9		Defaulter
	10		Non-Defaulter

Oversampled data

	ID	Variables	Class
Train	1		Defaulter
	1		**Defaulter**
	2		Non-Defaulter
	3		Non-Defaulter
	4		Defaulter
	4		**Defaulter**
	5		Non-Defaulter
	6		Non-Defaulter
Test	7		Non-Defaulter
	8		Non-Defaulter
	9		Defaulter
	10		Non-Defaulter

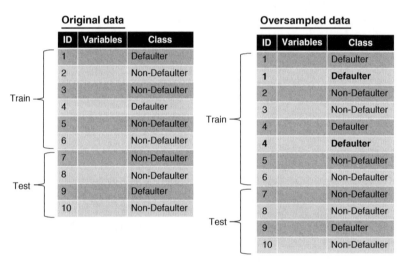

Exhibit 8.2 Oversampling the Defaulters

Original data

	ID	Variables	Class
Train	1		Defaulter
	2		Non-Defaulter
	3		Non-Defaulter
	4		Defaulter
	5		Non-Defaulter
	6		Non-Defaulter
Test	7		Non-Defaulter
	8		Non-Defaulter
	9		Defaulter
	10		Non-Defaulter

Undersampled data

	ID	Variables	Class
Train	1		Defaulter
	3		Non-Defaulter
	4		Defaulter
	6		Non-Defaulter
Test	7		Non-Defaulter
	8		Non-Defaulter
	9		Defaulter
	10		Non-Defaulter

Exhibit 8.3 Undersampling the Nondefaulters

obviously legitimate observations are removed. Also, low-value transactions or inactive accounts can be considered for removal.

Under- and oversampling can also be combined. In the literature, it has been shown that undersampling usually results in better classifiers than oversampling (Chawla et al. 2002).

Note that both undersampling and oversampling should be conducted on the training data and not on the test data. Remember, the latter should remain untouched during model development in order to give an unbiased view on model performance. A practical question concerns the optimal nondefaulter/defaulter odds that should be aimed for by doing under- or oversampling. Although working toward a balanced sample with the same number of defaulters and nondefaulters seems attractive, it severely biases the probabilities that will be output by the analytical technique. Hence, it is recommended to stay as close as possible to the original class distribution to avoid unnecessary bias. One practical approach to determining the optimal class distribution works as follows. In the first step, an analytical model is built on the original data set with the skew class distribution (e.g., 95 percent/5 percent nondefaulters/defaulters). The area under the curve (AUC) of this model is recorded (possibly on an independent validation data set). In a next step, over- or undersampling is used to change the class distribution by 5 percent (e.g., 90 percent/10 percent). Again, the AUC of the model is recorded. Subsequent models are built on samples of 85 percent/15 percent, 80 percent/20 percent, 75 percent/25 percent, and so on, each time recording their AUCs. Once the AUC starts to stagnate (or drop), the procedure stops and the optimal odds ratio has been found. Although it does depend on the data characteristics and quality, practical experience has shown that the ratio 80 percent/20 percent is quite commonly used in the industry.

In SAS, PROC SURVEYSELECT can be used to compose a sample with the required target distribution as follows:

```
PROC SORT DATA=data.mortgage out=mortgage;
BY default_time;
RUN;


PROC SURVEYSELECT DATA=mortgage
METHOD=SRS N=(1000,1000) SEED=12345 OUT=data.mySample;
STRATA default_time;
RUN;
```

The preceding statement will create a balanced sample of 2,000 observations by randomly selecting 1,000 defaulters and 1,000 nondefaulters. We can verify this as follows:

```
PROC FREQ DATA=data.mySample;
TABLE default_time;
RUN;
```

The output will be as shown in Exhibit 8.4.

The FREQ Procedure				
default_time	Frequency	Percent	Cumulative Frequency	Cumulative Percent
0	1000	50.00	1000	50.00
1	1000	50.00	2000	100.00

Exhibit 8.4 Creating a balanced sample using PROC FREQ

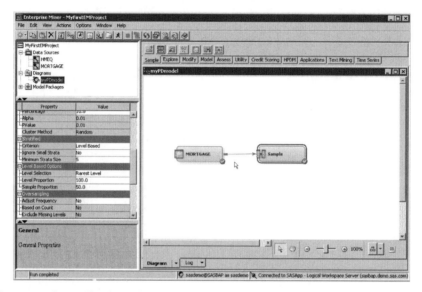

Exhibit 8.5 Creating a Tailored Sample in SAS Enterprise Miner

In SAS Enterprise Miner, the Sample node can be used to specify the desired properties of the sample (see Exhibit 8.5). In the stratification section, set the criterion property to level based and in the level based options section set the level section to rarest level (which is default in our case) and the sample proportion to 50 percent. This will create a sample with 50 percent defaulters and 50 percent nondefaulters. Running the sample node will give the output as displayed in Exhibit 8.6.

Synthetic Minority Oversampling Technique (SMOTE)

Rather than replicating the minority observations (i.e., defaulters), synthetic minority oversampling works by creating synthetic observations based on the existing minority observations (Chawla et al. 2002). This is illustrated in Exhibit 8.7, where the circles represent the majority class (e.g., nondefaulters) and the squares the minority class (e.g., defaulters). For each minority class observation, SMOTE calculates the k nearest neighbors. Let's assume we consider the crossed square and pick the five nearest neighbors represented by the black squares. Depending on the amount of

```
Output                                                                    _ □ ×
39   * Report Output
40   *----------------------------------------------------------------*
41
42
43
44   Summary Statistics for Class Targets
45   (maximum 500 observations printed)
46
47   Data=DATA
48
49                   Numeric    Formatted    Frequency
50      Variable      Value       Value        Count      Percent   Label
51
52   default_time        0           0         607331     97.5649
53   default_time        1           1          15158      2.4351
54
55
56   Data=SAMPLE
57
58                   Numeric    Formatted    Frequency
59      Variable      Value       Value        Count      Percent   Label
60
61   default_time        0           0          15158        50
62   default_time        1           1          15158        50
63
```

Exhibit 8.6 Creating a Tailored Sample in SAS Enterprise Miner: Results

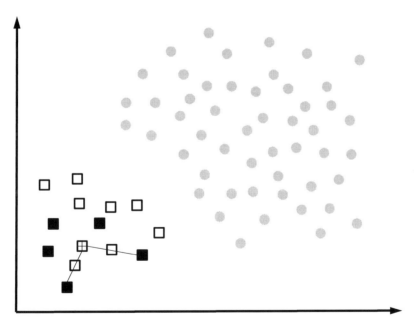

Exhibit 8.7 Synthetic Minority Oversampling Technique (SMOTE)

oversampling needed, one or more of the k nearest neighbors are selected to create the synthetic examples. Let's say our oversampling percentage is set at 200 percent. In this case, two of the five nearest neighbors are selected at random. The next step is then to randomly create two synthetic examples along the line connecting the observation under investigation (crossed square) with the two random nearest neighbors. These two synthetic examples are represented by dashed squares in Exhibit 8.7. As an example, consider an observation with characteristics (e.g., age and income) of 30 and 1,000, and its nearest neighbor with corresponding characteristics 62 and 3,200. We generate a random number between zero and one; let's say 0.75. The synthetic example then has age $30 + 0.75 * (62 - 30)$ or 54, and income $1,000 + 0.75 * (3,200 - 1,000) = 2,650$. SMOTE then combines the synthetic oversampling of the minority class with undersampling the majority class. Note that in their original paper, Chawla et al. (2002) also developed an extension of SMOTE to work with categorical variables. Empirical evidence has shown that SMOTE usually works better than either under- or oversampling. It has also proven to be very valuable for fraud detection (Van Vlasselaer et al. 2016).

Adjusting Posterior Probabilities

The key idea of undersampling, oversampling, and SMOTE is to adjust the class priors to enable the analytical technique to come up with a meaningful model discriminating the defaulters from the nondefaulters. By doing so, the class posteriors will also become biased. This is not a problem in the case where the credit analyst is interested only in ranking the observations in terms of their default risk. However, if well-calibrated probabilities of default are needed (e.g., for Basel II/III), then the posterior probabilities need to be adjusted. One straightforward way to do this is by using the following formula (Saerens, Latinne, and Decaestecker 2002):

$$p(C_i|x) = \frac{\frac{p(C_i)}{p_r(C_i)} p_r(C_i|x)}{\sum_{j=1}^{2} \frac{p(C_j)}{p_r(C_j)} p_r(C_j|x)}$$

where C_i represents class i (e.g., class 1 for the defaulters and class 2 for the nondefaulters); $p(C_i)$ the prior probability (e.g., $p(C_1) = 1\%$ and $p(C_2) = 99\%$); $p_r(C_i)$ the resampled prior probability due to oversampling, undersampling, or other resampling procedures (e.g., $p_r(C_1) = 20\%$ and $p_r(C_2) = 80\%$); and $p_r(C_i|x)$ represents the posterior probability for observation x as calculated by the analytical technique using the resampled data. Note that the formula can be easily extended to more than two classes (e.g., in case of predicting ratings).

Exhibit 8.8 shows an example of adjusting the posterior probability, where $p(C_1) = 0.01, p(C_2) = 0.99, p_r(C_1) = 0.20$, and $p_r(C_2) = 0.80$. It can be easily verified that the rank ordering of the customers in terms of their default risk remains preserved after the adjustment.

	Posteriors Using Resampled Data		Posteriors Recalibrated to Original Data	
	P (Default)	P (Nondefault)	P (Default)	P (Nondefault)
Customer 1	0.1	0.9	0.004	0.996
Customer 2	0.3	0.7	0.017	0.983
Customer 3	0.5	0.5	0.039	0.961
Customer 4	0.6	0.4	0.057	0.943
Customer 5	0.85	0.15	0.186	0.814
Customer 6	0.9	0.1	0.267	0.733

Exhibit 8.8 Adjusting the Posterior Probability

The preceding calculation can be implemented in Base SAS as follows:

```
DATA posteriors;
INPUT probdef;
DATALINES;
0.1
0.3
0.5
0.6
0.85
0.9
;

DATA posteriors2;
SET posteriors;
probnondef=1-probdef;
oldprior=0.20;
newprior=0.01;
temp1=probdef/oldprior*newprior;
temp2=(1-probdef)/(1-oldprior)*(1-newprior);
newprobdef=temp1/(temp1+temp2);
newprobnondef=temp2/(temp1+temp2);
DROP temp1 temp2 oldprior newprior;
RUN;

/*Print data set*/
Proc PRINT DATA= posteriors2;
RUN;
```

The output will be as shown in Exhibit 8.9.

Obs	probdef	probnondef	newprobdef	newprobnondef
1	0.10	0.90	0.00447	0.99553
2	0.30	0.70	0.01702	0.98298
3	0.50	0.50	0.03883	0.96117
4	0.60	0.40	0.05714	0.94286
5	0.85	0.15	0.18630	0.81370
6	0.90	0.10	0.26667	0.73333

Exhibit 8.9 Adjusting the Posterior Probability in Base SAS

Cost-Sensitive Learning

Cost-sensitive learning is another alternative for dealing with highly skewed data sets. The idea is to assign higher misclassification costs to the minority class, which in our case is the defaulters. These costs are then taken into account during classifier estimation or evaluation. Exhibit 8.10 gives the overview of the costs in a binary classification setting where $C(i,j)$ represents the cost of misclassifying an example from class j into class i.

Note that usually $C(+,+) = C(-,-) = 0$, and $C(-,+) > C(+,-)$, with + referring to the defaulters and – to the nondefaulters. The costs are typically also determined on an aggregated basis, rather than on an observation-by-observation basis.

A first straightforward way to make a classifier cost-sensitive is by adopting a cost-sensitive cutoff to map the posterior class probabilities to class labels. In other words, an observation x will be assigned to the class that minimizes the expected misclassification cost:

$$argmin_i \left(\sum_{j \in \{-,+\}} P(j|x) \times C(i,j) \right)$$

where $P(j|x)$ is the posterior probability of observation x to belong to class j. As an example, consider a default risk setting where class 1 consists of the defaulters

		Predicted Class	
		Positive	**Negative**
Actual Class	**Positive**	$C(+,+)$	$C(-,+)$
	Negative	$C(+,-)$	$C(-,-)$

Exhibit 8.10 Misclassification Costs

and class 2 the nondefaulters. An observation x will be classified as a defaulter (class 1) if:

$$P(1|x) \times C(1,1) + P(2|x) \times C(1,2) < P(1|x) \times C(2,1) + P(2|x) \times C(2,2)$$

$$P(1|x) \times C(2,1) > P(2|x) \times C(1,2)$$

$$P(1|x) \times C(2,1) > (1 - P(1|x)) \times C(1,2)$$

$$P(1|x) > \frac{C(1,2)}{C(1,2) + C(2,1)}$$

$$P(1|x) > \frac{1}{1 + \dfrac{C(2,1)}{C(1,2)}}$$

As a result, the cutoff depends only on the ratio of the misclassification costs, which may be easier to determine than the individual misclassification costs themselves.

Another approach to cost-sensitive learning works by directly minimizing the misclassification cost during classifier learning. Again assuming there is no cost for correct classifications, the total misclassification cost is then:

$$\text{Total cost} = C(-,+) \times FN + C(+,-) \times FP$$

where FN represents the number of false negatives, and FP the positives. Various cost-sensitive versions of existing classification techniques have been introduced in the literature. Ting (2002) introduced a cost-sensitive version of the C4.5 decision tree algorithm where the splitting and stopping decisions are based on the misclassification cost. Veropolous et al. (1999) developed a cost-sensitive version of support vector machines (SVMs) where the misclassification costs are taken into account in the objective function of the SVM. Domingos (1999) introduced MetaCost, which is a meta-algorithm capable of turning any classifier into a cost-sensitive classifier by first relabeling observations with their estimated minimal-cost classes and then estimating a new classifier on the relabeled data set. Fan et al. (1999) developed AdaCost, a cost-sensitive variant of AdaBoost that uses the misclassification costs to update the weights in successive boosting runs.

To summarize, cost-sensitive learning approaches are usually more complex to work with than the sampling approaches discussed earlier. López et al. (2012) conducted a comparison of sampling versus cost-sensitive learning approaches for imbalanced data sets and found that both methods are good and equivalent. From a pragmatic viewpoint, it is recommended to use sampling approaches.

MAPPING TO AN EXTERNAL RATING AGENCY

Another approach is to purchase external ratings from a rating agency, such as Moody's, Standard & Poor's, or Fitch. These rating agencies generate issuer ratings (corporate and sovereign), ratings of issues (loan and bond), and structured finance ratings (e.g., asset-backed security [ABS], collateralized debt obligation [CDO], and residential mortgage-backed security [RMBS]). Let's assume we want to build a sovereign rating system and obtain country ratings. A next step is then to collect predictors that could potentially have an influence on the rating. In our country rating example, one could think here of predictors such as gross domestic product (GDP), inflation, unemployment, imports, and exports. These predictors can then be put into a cumulative logistic regression model with the rating as the target variable. For each rating, the default rates reported by the rating agencies can then be used to determine the final calibrated PD. Earlier we referred to this approach as the shadow rating approach.

Cumulative logistic regression, also called ordinal logistic regression, is an extension of logistic regression to deal with ordinal multiclass targets such as credit ratings. Remember, as discussed previously, when adopting the shadow rating approach, you want to build a classification model predicting ratings. Ratings are ordinal and have an ordering between them: AAA is better than AA, AA is better than A, and so on. In other words, when thinking about cumulative probabilities, we then have:

$$P(C \leq AAA) \geq P(C \leq AA) \geq P(C \leq A) \geq P(C \leq BBB)\ldots$$

In cumulative logistic regression, the cumulative probabilities are modeled using a logit type of transformation. The formulation goes as follows: the probability that a firm with characteristics $x_1,\ldots, x_N$ has a particular rating AAA, AA,... is calculated as (Allison 2001):

$$P(Y \leq AAA) = \frac{1}{1 + e^{-\theta_{AAA} + \beta_1 x_1 + \ldots + \beta_N x_N}}$$

$$P(Y \leq AA) = \frac{1}{1 + e^{-\theta_{AA} + \beta_1 x_1 + \ldots + \beta_N x_N}}$$

...

$$P(Y \leq D) = \frac{1}{1 + e^{-\theta_D + \beta_1 x_1 + \ldots + \beta_N x_N}}$$

In a corporate setting, the x variables can represent firm characteristics such as accounting ratios, profitability information, and stock price information. This can then also be reformulated in terms of the odds as follows:

$$\frac{P(Y \leq AAA)}{1 - P(Y \leq AAA)} = e^{-\theta_{AAA} + \beta_1 x_1 + \ldots + \beta_N x_N}$$

$$\frac{P(Y \leq AA)}{1 - P(Y \leq AA)} = e^{-\theta_{AA} + \beta_1 x_1 + \ldots + \beta_N x_N}$$

...

$$\frac{P(Y \leq D)}{1 - P(Y \leq D)} = e^{-\theta_D + \beta_1 x_1 + \ldots + \beta_N x_N}$$

Note that since $P(Y \leq AAA) = 1$, $\theta_{AAA} = +\infty$. Taking the logarithm gives linear expressions as follows:

$$\frac{P(Y \leq AAA)}{1 - P(Y \leq AAA)} = -\theta_{AAA} + \beta_1 x_1 + \ldots + \beta_N x_N$$

$$\frac{P(Y \leq AA)}{1 - P(Y \leq AA)} = -\theta_{AA} + \beta_1 x_1 + \ldots + \beta_N x_N$$

$\ldots$

$$\frac{P(Y \leq D)}{1 - P(Y \leq D)} = -\theta_D + \beta_1 x_1 + \ldots + \beta_N x_N$$

The logit functions for all ratings are parallel since they differ only in the intercept. Hence, this model is also referred to as the proportional odds model (see Allison, 2001).

Just as with binary logistic regression, the β parameters of the cumulative logistic regression model can be estimated using the maximum likelihood procedure. In SAS, this is implemented by PROC LOGISTIC. The individual rating probabilities can then be obtained as follows:

$$P(Y = AA) = P(Y \leq AAA) - P(Y \leq AA)$$

$$P(Y = 1) = P(Y \leq AA) - P(Y \leq A)$$

$\ldots$

$$P(Y = D) = P(D \leq 1)$$

When assigning a rating to a new observation using the cumulative logistic regression model, you can calculate all the rating probabilities and assign the observation to the rating with the highest probability (winner-take-all learning).

Exhibit 8.11 shows some examples of rating probability distributions for a model predicting insurance ratings in terms of the z-score, which is (see Van Gestel et al. 2007):

$$z = -\theta_R + \beta_1 x_1 + \ldots + \beta_N x_N$$

It can be clearly seen that, depending on the z-score, every rating pops up at least once as the winner.

In SAS, cumulative logistic regression can be implemented using PROC LOGISTIC. The ratings data set contains ratings of 197 corporates where the target rating is numerically coded as 1 (= AAA), 2 (= AA), 3 (= A), ... 9 (= C), and 10 (= Default). The predictors are the well-known CAMELS variables, encoded as follows:

- COMMEQTA = common equity to total assets (capital adequacy)
- LLPLOANS = loan loss provision to total loans (asset quality)
- COSTTOINCOME = operating costs to operating income (management quality)

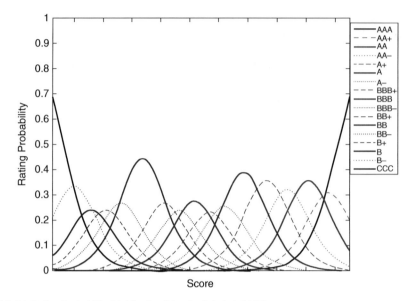

Exhibit 8.11 Rating Probability Distribution (Van Gestel et al. 2007)

- ROE = return on equity (earnings performance)
- LIQASSTA = liquid assets to total assets (liquidity)
- SIZE = natural logarithm of total assets (size)

We invite the reader to explore this data set using PROC MEANS and PROC UNIVARIATE.

We can now estimate a cumulative logistic regression model as follows:

```
PROC LOGISTIC DATA=data.ratings;
MODEL rating= COMMEQTA LLPLOANS COSTTOINCOME ROE LIQASSTA SIZE;
OUTPUT OUT =ratingsout PREDPROBS=INDIVIDUAL;
RUN;
```

The output statement specifies that the output should be written to the data set ratingsout. The PREDPROBS=INDIVIDUAL option indicates that we want to include estimated probabilities for each of the ratings individually.

Running the preceding PROC LOGISTIC gives the maximum likelihood estimates shown in Exhibit 8.12.

From Exhibit 8.12, it can be seen that all variables are significant. The performance can be evaluated by measuring the association between the predicted probabilities and the observed responses as indicated in Exhibit 8.13.

The table in Exhibit 8.13 shows that the model has good performance. As discussed earlier, the ratingsout data set contains the predicted probabilities for each of

The LOGISTIC Procedure						
Analysis of Maximum Likelihood Estimates						
Parameter		DF	Estimate	Standard Error	Wald Chi-Square	Pr > ChiSq
Intercept	1	1	−18.5764	2.1870	72.1484	<.0001
Intercept	2	1	−17.5111	2.1331	67.3889	<.0001
Intercept	3	1	−16.3356	2.0981	60.6218	<.0001
Intercept	4	1	−15.0194	2.0588	53.2212	<.0001
Intercept	5	1	−13.8925	2.0231	47.1553	<.0001
Intercept	6	1	−12.3558	1.9753	39.1261	<.0001
Intercept	7	1	−11.4118	1.9525	34.1625	<.0001
Intercept	8	1	−10.3187	1.9381	28.3453	<.0001
Intercept	9	1	−8.5034	1.9856	18.3402	<.0001
COMMEQTA		1	10.1167	3.5110	8.3024	0.0040
LLPLOANS		1	−29.4204	11.6879	6.3362	0.0118
COSTTOINCOME		1	−3.3613	0.7982	17.7350	<.0001
ROE		1	3.2776	1.2446	6.9345	0.0085
LIQASSTA		1	3.8190	0.9057	17.7802	<.0001
SIZE		1	0.7807	0.1078	52.4427	<.0001

Exhibit 8.12 Maximum Likelihood Estimates from PROC LOGISTIC

Association of Predicted Probabilities and Observed Responses			
Percent Concordant	75.2	Somers' D	0.508
Percent Discordant	24.3	Gamma	0.511
Percent Tied	0.5	Tau-a	0.432
Pairs	16386	c	0.754

Exhibit 8.13 Association Statistics from PROC LOGISTIC

the ratings, combined with the predicted rating where the latter is decided based on the largest probability (winner-take-all learning). We can now evaluate the performance of this model by creating a notch difference table and corresponding graph. We first create the following temporary SAS data set:

```
DATA temp;
SET ratingsout;
notchdiff= ABS(_FROM_ - _INTO_);
RUN;
```

The _FROM_ and _INTO_ variables contain the original rating and the predicted rating, respectively. The notchdiff variable then calculates the absolute value of the difference between them. We can now run PROC FREQ as follows:

```
ODS GRAPHICS ON;
PROC FREQ DATA=temp;
TABLES notchdiff / PLOTS=CUMFREQPLOT(SCALE=PERCENT);
RUN;
ODS GRAPHICS OFF;
```

This will give the output shown in Exhibit 8.14.

The FREQ Procedure				
notchdiff	Frequency	Percent	Cumulative Frequency	Cumulative Percent
0	63	31.98	63	31.98
1	77	39.09	140	71.07
2	34	17.26	174	88.32
3	17	8.63	191	96.95
4	3	1.52	194	98.48
5	2	1.02	196	99.49
6	1	0.51	197	100.00

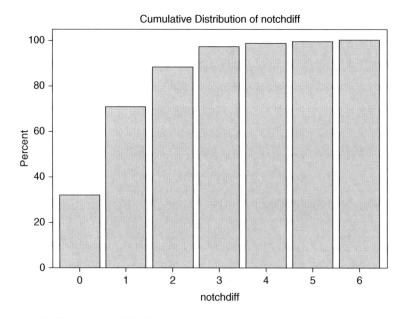

Exhibit 8.14 Notch Difference Graph for the Ratings Data Set

From Exhibit 8.14 we can see that at a 0-notch difference level, the model obtains a classification accuracy of 31.98 percent. By allowing a 1-notch difference between the predicted and target ratings, the cumulative accuracy increases to 71.07 percent.

CONFIDENCE LEVEL BASED APPROACH

Another interesting approach for working with a low number of defaulters is the confidence level based approach developed by Pluto and Tasche (2005).

Let's start with the most extreme example of a skewed data set, which is a data set with no defaulters at all. Obviously, none of the sampling approaches discussed so far will work for this. Assume now that we have an expert-based credit risk model that can discriminate the observations into default risk classes A, B, and C using a set of predefined business rules. Although these three classes allow us to discriminate among the observations in terms of their default risk, it would also be handy to accompany each of these classes with default probability estimates. These probabilities can then be used to calculate both the expected and the unexpected credit losses.

In a first step, we calculate the probability of default (PD) for class A, PD_A. A key assumption we make is that default occurs independently. Although this assumption might seem naive at first sight, it allows us to derive probability estimates in a fairly straightforward way given this complex setting with no data about defaulters. More specifically, we first assume that the ranking of the observations across the three default risk classes is correct, or, in other words, $PD_A \leq PD_B \leq PD_C$. The most prudent estimate (sometimes also referred to as the most conservative estimate) is then obtained under the temporary assumption that $PD_A = PD_B = PD_C$. Hence, the probability of default equals PD_A for every observation. Given that we have n_A observations in rating A, n_B observations in rating B, and n_C observations in rating C, and that default occurs independently, the probability of not observing any defaulter in the total data set equals:

$$(1 - PD_A)^{n_A+n_B+n_C}$$

We can now specify a confidence region for PD_A, which is the region of all values of PD_A such that the probability of not observing any defaulter is higher than $1 - \alpha$, or, in other words:

$$1 - \alpha \leq (1 - PD_A)^{n_A+n_B+n_C}$$

or

$$PD_A \leq 1 - (1 - \alpha)^{1/(n_A+n_B+n_C)}$$

Assume we have 100 observations in rating A, 200 in rating B, and 50 in rating C. Exhibit 8.15 illustrates the values obtained for PD_A by varying the confidence level from 50 percent to 99.9 percent. As can be observed, PD_A increases as the confidence level increases.

We can now continue this same procedure to compute PD_B. We have $n_B + n_C$ observations left. The most prudent estimate of PD_B is obtained by again assuming

α	50%	75%	90%	95%	99%	99.9%
PD_A	0.20%	0.39%	0.65%	0.85%	1.31%	1.95%

Exhibit 8.15 Values for PD_A for a Data Set with No Defaulters

α	50%	75%	90%	95%	99%	99.9%
PD_B	0.28%	0.55%	0.92%	1.19%	1.82%	2.72%

Exhibit 8.16 Values for PD_B for a Data Set with No Defaulters

α	50%	75%	90%	95%	99%	99.9%
PD_C	1.38%	2.73%	4.50%	5.81%	8.80%	12.90%

Exhibit 8.17 Values for PD_C for a Data Set with No Defaulters

$PD_B = PD_C$. Hence, we have:

$$1 - \alpha \leq (1 - PD_B)^{n_B + n_C}$$

or

$$PD_B \leq 1 - (1 - \alpha)^{1/(n_B + n_C)}$$

For our data set, this gives the values reported in Exhibit 8.16. Finally, we can calculate PD_C as follows:

$$1 - \alpha \leq (1 - PD_C)^{n_C}$$

or

$$PD_C \leq 1 - (1 - \alpha)^{1/n_C}$$

This gives the values reported in Exhibit 8.17.

Note that despite having no defaulters in the data, PD_C at the 99.9 percent confidence level equals 12.90 percent, which is quite high. Also observe that for a given confidence level, $PD_A \leq PD_B \leq PD_C$ as required at the outset. An obvious question is what confidence level should be adopted. Before answering this question, we illustrate how this approach can be implemented in SAS.

Assume we have a portfolio with three ratings as follows: A (100 obligors), B (150 obligors), and C (80 obligors):

```
%LET nA=100;
%LET nB=150;
%LET nC=80;


/*Set the confidence level to 99%*/
%LET sig=0.99;
```

```
/*Create a data set LDP with the calculations*/
DATA LDP;
PDA=1-(1-&sig)**(1/(&nA+&nB+&nC));
PDB=1-(1-&sig)**(1/(&nB+&nC));
PDC=1-(1-&sig)**(1/(&nC));
RUN;


/*Print data set*/
Proc PRINT DATA=LDP;
RUN;
```

Running and inspecting this data set then yields the results reported in Exhibit 8.18.

Let's now assume we have one defaulter in rating A, two in rating B, and four in rating C (seven in all). We first determine PD_A using again the most prudent estimate principle: $PD_A = PD_B = PD_C$. By using the binomial distribution to calculate the probability of observing less than or equal to seven defaulters, PD_A can be found as follows:

$$1 - \alpha \leq \sum_{i=0}^{7} \binom{n_A + n_B + n_C}{i} PD_A^i (1 - PD_A)^{n_A + n_B + n_C - i}$$

Likewise, PD_B and PD_C can be found as follows:

$$1 - \alpha \leq \sum_{i=0}^{6} \binom{n_B + n_C}{i} PD_B^i (1 - PD_B)^{n_B + n_C - i}$$

$$1 - \alpha \leq \sum_{i=0}^{4} \binom{n_C}{i} PD_C^i (1 - PD_C)^{n_C - i}$$

Exhibit 8.19 displays the values obtained depending upon the confidence levels. Again, note that the probabilities increase for increasing confidence levels. Just as in the previous examples, also observe that $PD_A \leq PD_B \leq PD_C$ as required at the outset.

Obs	PDA	PDB	PDC
1	0.013858	0.019823	0.055939

Exhibit 8.18 Example of Confidence Level Based Approach in Base SAS

α	50%	75%	90%	95%	99%	99.9%
PD_A	2.19%	2.76%	3.34%	3.72%	4.51%	5.51%
PD_B	2.66%	3.41%	4.17%	4.68%	5.73%	7.05%
PD_C	9.28%	12.26%	15.35%	17.38%	21.50%	26.56%

Exhibit 8.19 Values for PD_A, PD_B, and PD_C for a Data Set with Defaulters

As already mentioned, a key question to answer when adopting this approach is the setting of the confidence level. Obviously, this depends on how conservative the estimates should be. As illustrated, a higher confidence level results in a higher probability of default estimate. In their original paper, Pluto and Tasche (2005) suggest not to exceed 95 percent. Benjamin, Cathcart, and Ryan (2006) suggest adopting confidence levels between 50 percent and 75 percent.

Various extensions of this standard approach have been developed. A first extension takes into account correlated default events by using the Basel single-factor model and the asset correlations mentioned in the Basel Accord. More specifically, in the case of our earlier example (one defaulter in rating A, two in rating B, and four in rating C), the confidence region at level α for PD_A corresponds to the set of values of PD_A that satisfy the following inequality:

$$1 - \alpha \le \int_{-\infty}^{+\infty} \phi(x) \sum_{i=0}^{7} \binom{n_A + n_B + n_C}{i} CDF(PD_A, \rho, x)^i (1 - CDF(PD_A, \rho, x))^{n_A + n_B + n_C - i} dx$$

where $\phi(x)$ is the standard normal density and $CDF(PD_A, \rho, x)$ represents the conditional PD based on the unconditional average PD_A, asset correlation ρ, and systematic factor x, and is calculated as follows:

$$CDF(PD_A, \rho, x) = \Phi\left(\frac{\Phi^{-1}(PD_A) - \sqrt{\rho}x}{\sqrt{1 - \rho}}\right)$$

with Φ the cumulative standard normal distribution and Φ^{-1} its inverse. Note that the right-hand side of the inequality represents the one-period probability of not observing any default among the $n_A + n_B + n_C$ obligors with default probability PD_A. Following the Basel Accord, the asset correlation ρ for corporate exposures can be set to 12 percent. The preceding inequality can then be solved numerically (Pluto and Tasche 2005) or by using a simulation approach (Clifford, Marianski, and Sebestyen 2013). Similar expressions can then be derived for PD_B and PD_C as follows:

$$1 - \alpha \le \int_{-\infty}^{+\infty} \phi(x) \sum_{i=0}^{6} \binom{n_B + n_C}{i} CDF(PD_B, \rho, x)^i (1 - CDF(PD_B, \rho, x))^{n_B + n_C - i} dx$$

$$1 - \alpha \le \int_{-\infty}^{+\infty} \phi(x) \sum_{i=0}^{4} \binom{n_C}{i} CDF(PD_C, \rho, x)^i (1 - CDF(PD_C, \rho, x))^{n_C - i} dx$$

As illustrated in Pluto and Tasche (2005), the effect of including correlations is that the probabilities $PD_A, PD_B,$ and PD_C will increase. Given the increased complexity of taking into account default correlation, one might consider using the uncorrelated case with a higher confidence level instead.

Another extension proposed in Pluto and Tasche (2005) ensures that the average estimated portfolio PD equals the observed portfolio PD by introducing a scaling factor K as follows:

$$\frac{\widehat{PD}_A n_A + \widehat{PD}_B n_B + \widehat{PD}_C n_C}{n_A + n_B + n_C} K = PD_{Portfolio}$$

where $PD_{Portfolio}$ represents the observed portfolio PD. The scaled PD estimates then become:

$$\widehat{PD}_{A,scaled} = K \cdot \widehat{PD}_A; \widehat{PD}_{B,scaled} = K \cdot \widehat{PD}_B; \widehat{PD}_{C,scaled} = K \cdot \widehat{PD}_C$$

Note that this scaling will obviously make the estimates less conservative. One way to deal with this is by scaling according to the upper bound of the overall portfolio PD, which is also determined using the most prudent estimation principle.

This approach can also be extended to a multiperiod setting. See Pluto and Tasche (2005) for more details.

OTHER METHODS

Other methods can also be adopted for modeling low default portfolios. A first popular approach is to pool your low default portfolio data with other banks or market participants, such as credit bureaus, for example. Another approach is to aggregate subportfolios with similar risk characteristics to increase the default history. Suppose you have a portfolio with U.S.-based small and medium-sized enterprises (SMEs), which would be a low default portfolio. If you also happen to have a portfolio with Canadian SMEs, which also are low default, you could consider combining the two portfolios, thereby increasing the number of defaulters and facilitating the modeling. You could also consider combining rating categories and analyzing the PDs of the combined category in a manner consistent with the Basel Accord, for corporates, sovereigns, and banks. Alternatively, you could use an upper bound on the PD estimate as input to the capital requirement formulas, or infer the PD estimates with a horizon of more than one year and then annualize the resulting figure. Finally, you can also use the lowest nondefault rating as a proxy for default. Note, however, that here it is still necessary to calibrate the ratings to a PD in a manner that is consistent with the Basel definition.

Another statistical approach for LDPs can be applied via Bayesian statistics. We will describe this technique in the chapter on Bayesian methods for credit risk modeling and will revisit computing PDs for LDPs there.

LGD AND EAD FOR LOW DEFAULT PORTFOLIOS

In this chapter, we have discussed various methods for modeling PD in the case of low default portfolios. An obvious question is: What about LGD and EAD? In fact, for LGD and EAD, the problem becomes more challenging as you are restricted to the use of the defaulters only, whereas in the case of PD you can at least use both the defaulters and the nondefaulters to build the model. Here you can see a statement from the FSA in the United Kingdom (Financial Services Authority 2006b):

> It is accepted that the U.K. and international community are not well advanced in their thinking on EADs, and as a consequence estimation for LDPs adds further difficulty. As a result the EG fully endorses implementation to be pragmatic, flexible, and principle based.

However, this quote doesn't give precise input on how to deal with LGD and EAD in the presence of low default portfolios.

One approach might be to make use of a relationship between PD and LGD, as suggested by Frye (2013). In line with the capital requirements formulas in the Basel Accord, the latter assumes that the conditional default rate follows a Vasicek distribution. Suppose we now also assume that the conditional expected loss rate (cLoss) has a Vasicek distribution with the same value of ρ:

$$
\begin{aligned}
\text{cLoss} = CDF^{-1}_{cLoss}(q) &= \Phi\left(\frac{\Phi^{-1}(EL) + \sqrt{\rho}\,\Phi^{-1}(q)}{\sqrt{1-\rho}}\right) \\
&= \Phi\left(\Phi^{-1}(cDR) - \frac{\Phi^{-1}(PD) - \Phi^{-1}(EL)}{\sqrt{1-\rho}}\right)
\end{aligned}
$$

with CDF the cumulative distribution and CDF^{-1} its inverse, Φ the cumulative standard normal distribution and Φ^{-1} its inverse, q the quantile considered, EL the unconditional expected loss, PD the unconditional PD, and cDR the conditional default rate. The conditional LGD can then be obtained by dividing this equation by cDR as follows:

$$
cLGD = \frac{\Phi(\Phi^{-1}(cDR) - k)}{cDR} \text{ with } k = \frac{\Phi^{-1}(PD) - \Phi^{-1}(EL)}{\sqrt{1-\rho}}
$$

This relationship allows us to calculate the $cLGD$ based on a loan's PD, ρ, and EL. The PD can be determined using any of the methods discussed before, the asset correlation ρ can be set as specified in the Basel Accord (e.g., between 12 percent and 24 percent for corporate loans), and the EL can be determined based on the spread of the loan. Other relationships between PD and LGD have been developed in Frye and Jacobs (2012), Frye (2000), Pykhtin (2003), Tasche (2004), Giese (2005), Hillebrand (2006), and Rösch and Scheule (2012). Note that each of these approaches starts from making some assumptions and introduces additional parameters that need to be set in either a quantitative way (i.e., based on statistical analysis) or an expert-based way.

Another option to determine LGD and EAD for LDPs is to use the reference values set in the foundation internal ratings based (IRB) approach. Remember, in the foundation IRB approach the LGD is set to 45 percent for senior claims and 75 percent for subordinated claims. This approach is also suggested by the European Banking Authority (EBA) in its 2015 discussion paper, as the following quote illustrates (European Banking Authority 2015):

> It proved particularly difficult to calculate LGD for LDP. As a result in such cases the LGD values for unsecured senior exposures are often close to the regulatory value under the FIRB Approach (45%) for credit institutions and large corporate portfolios.

For EAD, the foundation IRB credit conversion factor (CCF) is set to 20 percent for commitments less than one year, and 50 percent for commitments more than one year.

PRACTICE QUESTIONS

1. What is the difference between SMOTE and undersampling/oversampling?
2. Consider the following table with logistic regression probabilities:

	Posteriors Using Resampled Data	
	P(Default)	P(Nondefault)
Customer 1	0.1	0.9
Customer 2	0.3	0.7
Customer 3	0.5	0.5
Customer 4	0.6	0.4
Customer 5	0.85	0.15
Customer 6	0.9	0.1

where $p(C_1) = 0.10, p(C_2) = 0.90, p_r(C_1) = 0.20,$ and $p_r(C_2) = 0.80.$ Calculate the posteriors recalibrated to the original data.

Build a decision tree for the ratings data set in Enterprise Miner and compare it to a cumulative logistic regression model in terms of model representation, significant variables, and performance.

3. Let's assume we have an LDP with three ratings: A (200 obligors), B (100 obligors), and C (50 obligors). Use the confidence level based approach to calculate $PD_A, PD_B,$ and PD_C for confidence levels 90 percent, 95 percent, and 99 percent.

4. Discuss some approaches that could be used to determine LGD and EAD for LDPs.

REFERENCES

Allison, P. D. 2001. *Logistic Regression Using the SAS System: Theory and Application.* New York: John Wiley & Sons–SAS.

Basel Committee on Banking Supervision. 2005. "Validation of Low-Default Portfolios in the Basel II Framework." *Basel Committee Newsletter no. 6*, September.

Benjamin, N., A. Cathcart, and K. Ryan. 2006. "Low Default Portfolios: A Proposal for Conservative Estimation of Default Probabilities." Discussion paper, Financial Services Authority.

Chawla, N. V., K. W. Bowyer, L. O. Hall, and W. P. Kegelmeyer. 2002. "SMOTE: Synthetic Minority Over-Sampling Technique." *Journal of Artificial Intelligence Research* 16:321–357.

Clifford, T., A. Marianski, and K. Sebestyen. 2013. "Low Default Portfolio Modeling–Probability of Default–Calibration Conundrum." Deloitte.

Domingos, P. 1999. "MetaCost: A General Method for Making Classifiers Cost-Sensitive." In *Proceedings of the Fifth International Conference on Knowledge Discovery and Data Mining,* 155–164. New York: ACM Press.

European Banking Authority. 2015. "Future of the IRB Approach." Discussion Paper 2015/01.

Fan, W., S. J. Stolfo, J. Zhang, and P. K. Chan. 1999. "AdaCost: Misclassification Cost-Sensitive Boosting." In *Proceedings of the Sixteenth International Conference on Machine Learning (ICML)*, 97–105. Waltham, MA: Morgan Kaufmann.

Financial Services Authority (FSA). 2006a. "CP06/3 Strengthening Capital Standards 2."

Financial Services Authority (FSA). 2006b. "Expert Group Paper on Exposure at Default."

Frye, J. 2000. "Depressing Recoveries." *Risk*, 108–111.

Frye, J., 2013. "Loss Given Default as a Function of the Default Rate," Federal Reserve Bank of Chicago.

Frye, J., and M. Jacobs. 2012. "Credit Loss and Systematic Loss Given Default." *Journal of Credit Risk* 8 (1): 1–32.

Giese, G. 2005. "The Impact of PD/LGD Correlations on Credit Risk Capital." *Risk*, 79–84.

Hillebrand, M. 2006. "Modeling and Estimating Dependent Loss Given Default." *Risk*, 120–125.

López, V., A. Fernández, J. Moreno-Torres, and F. Herrera. 2012. "Analysis of Preprocessing vs. Cost-Sensitive Learning for Imbalanced Classification: Open Problems on Intrinsic Data Characteristics." *Expert Systems with Applications* 39:6585–6608.

Pluto, K., and D. Tasche. 2005. "Estimating Probabilities of Default for Low Default Portfolios." In *The Basel II Risk Parameters*, edited by B. Engelmann and R. Rauhmeier. New York: Springer.

Prudential Regulation Authority. 2013. "Internal Ratings Based Approaches." SS 11/13, December.

Pykhtin, M. 2003. "Unexpected Recovery Risk." *Risk*, 74–78.

Rösch, D., and H. Scheule. 2012. "Forecasting Probabilities of Default and Loss Rates Given Default in the Presence of Selection." *Journal of the Operational Research Society* 65 (3): 393–407.

Saerens, M., P. Latinne, and C. Decaestecker. 2002. "Adjusting the Outputs of a Classifier to New a Priori Probabilities: A Simple Procedure." *Neural Computation* 14 (1): 21–41.

Tasche, D. 2004. "The Single Risk Factor Approach to Capital Charges in the Case of Correlated Loss Given Default Rates." Working paper.

Ting, K.M. 2002. "An Instance-Weighting Method to Induce Cost-Sensitive Decision Trees," IEEE Transactions on Knowledge and Data Engineering, 14(3):659–665, 2002.

Van Gestel, T., D. Martens, B. Baesens, D. Feremans, J. Huysmans, and J. Vanthienen. 2007. "Forecasting and Analyzing Insurance Companies' Ratings." *International Journal of Forecasting* 23 (3): 513–529.

Van Vlasselaer, V., T. Eliassi-Rad, L. Akoglu, M. Snoeck, and B. Baesens. 2016. GOTCHA! Network-Based Fraud Detection for Social Security Fraud." *Management Science*, forthcoming.

Veropoulos, K., C. Campbell, and N. Cristianini. 1999. "Controlling the Sensitivity of Support Vector Machines," *In Proceedings of the International Joint Conference on AI*, 55–60.

CHAPTER 9

Default Correlations and Credit Portfolio Risk

INTRODUCTION

Banks hold large portfolios of loans and, similarly to asset management, correlations or more generally dependencies are the main drivers of the risk of the portfolio. A bank commonly uses credit portfolio models to make assessments about the risks of a portfolio in terms of probability distributions of potential credit losses. Popular approaches used in the industry include actuarial and mathematical, as well as models that use computer simulations for generating the loss distribution. Usually, the outcome of such a model is a highly skewed probability distribution for the potential losses of the portfolio, as shown in Exhibit 9.1. The distribution is often characterized by some important parameters, namely the expected loss (EL), the value at risk (VaR, which is a quantile), and the conditional value at risk (CVaR) or expected shortfall(ES), which is the expectation of the losses that are greater than the value at risk. The expected loss is typically covered by provisions. The required economic capital for the bank to stay solvent is then the difference between the VaR and the expected loss (or CVaR and expected loss).

Let L_i be the random loss for a credit risky instrument i where $i = 1, \ldots, n$ in a certain time period. The portfolio loss is then the sum over the losses of all instruments (i.e., $L = \sum_{i=1}^{n} L_i$). Let $F(L)$ be the cumulative distribution function (CDF) of L. The risk measures then become:

- Expected loss:

$$E(L) = E\left(\sum_{i=1}^{n} L_i\right)$$

237

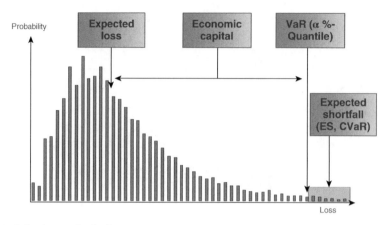

Exhibit 9.1 Stylized Loss Distribution

■ Value at risk (α-quantile):

$$VaR_\alpha(L) = \inf\{F^{-1}(\alpha)\}$$

where $F^{-1}(\cdot)$ is the generalized inverse of the CDF.

■ Economic capital:

$$EC_\alpha = VaR_\alpha(L) - E(L)$$

■ Expected shortfall:

$$ES_\alpha(L) = E(L|L > VaR_\alpha(L))$$

Although there are different models used in the industry, a seminal paper by Gordy (2000) showed that the most widely applied approaches can be unified and, if adequately parameterized, yield very similar results. Therefore, in this chapter we focus on one particular specification, which is widely used in practice and also implemented in the Basel Accord for regulatory capital. At the end of the chapter, we briefly show, similarly to Gordy (2000), that the risk of choosing the wrong model is not a big issue on a portfolio level. Hence, we focus in this chapter on ways to estimate correlations from empirical data, which is often a key shortcoming of industry models.

MODELING LOSS DISTRIBUTIONS WITH CORRELATED DEFAULTS

In order to show the issue with correlation, let the loss of instrument i, $i = 1, \ldots, n$, be:

$$L_i = EAD_i \cdot LGD_i \cdot D_i$$

where EAD_i and LGD_i are the exposure at default and the loss given default, and D_i is a default indicator variable. Let us for now assume that EAD and LGD are deterministic. The randomness of the loss is then driven by the default indicator, which is given as in the earlier chapter by:

$$D_i = \begin{cases} 1 & \text{borrower } i \text{ defaults} \\ 0 & \text{otherwise} \end{cases}$$

Now consider a simple portfolio of two obligors with portfolio loss

$$L = L_1 + L_2 = EAD_1 \cdot LGD_1 \cdot D_1 + EAD_2 \cdot LGD_2 \cdot D_2$$

Let $P(D_i = 1)$ be the probability of borrower i defaulting $(i \in \{1,2\})$ and let $P(D_i = 1 \cap D_j = 1)$ be the joint probability of both borrowers defaulting $(i \neq j)$. There are four potential scenarios for the default behavior of both borrowers (and therefore for the portfolio loss), as depicted in the following table.

	Borrower 2		
Borrower 1	No Default	Default	
No Default	$P(D_1 = 0 \cap D_2 = 0)$	$P(D_1 = 0 \cap D_2 = 1)$	$P(D_1 = 0)$
Default	$P(D_1 = 1 \cap D_2 = 0)$	$P(D_1 = 1 \cap D_2 = 1)$	$P(D_1 = 1)$
	$P(D_2 = 0)$	$P(D_2 = 1)$	1

The outcome combinations are: (1) neither borrower defaults, (2) Borrower 1 defaults, (3) Borrower 2 defaults, or (4) both borrowers default. The respective probabilities for these events are given in the table. The probabilities at the margins of the table are the marginal probabilities of default and nondefault for each borrower. In the special case of independence of the two borrowers, the probability that both borrowers default (i.e., their joint default probability $P(D_1 = 1 \cap D_2 = 1)$) equals the product of their marginal probabilities (which is per definition of independence). However, if the defaults are positively dependent (e.g., due to macroeconomic factors, which are the same for all borrowers in a given period), the joint default probability is higher than in the case of independence. As the joint default probability gives the probability for the highest possible loss of the portfolio (namely a total loss), we can see that, ceteris paribus, the extreme risk of the bank increases with default dependence. The default correlation can be computed as:

$$\rho^D = Corr(D_1, D_2) = \frac{E(D_1 \cdot D_2) - E(D_1) \cdot E(D_2)}{\sqrt{Var(D_1)Var(D_2)}}$$

$$= \frac{P(D_1 = 1 \cap D_2 = 1) - P(D_1 = 1) \cdot P(D_2 = 1)}{\sqrt{P(D_1 = 1)(1 - P(D_1 = 1))P(D_2 = 1)(1 - P(D_2 = 1))}}$$

For two borrowers, it is hard to empirically quantify a value for the default correlation or the joint default probability in practice. For a higher number of borrowers this becomes burdensome, if not impossible. For two borrowers, there are four probabilities in the table. For n borrowers, this would require 2^n probabilities, which is challenging for most credit portfolios. Therefore, we introduce a model that makes some simplifying assumptions.

Basic Model Framework

The Bernoulli default indicator variable can be characterized using some underlying metric variable that renders $D_i = 1$ if it crosses some threshold, and $D_i = 0$ otherwise. Let R_i be a metric variable following a continuous distribution. We then have:

$$D_i = \begin{cases} 1 & \text{if } R_i < c_i \\ 0 & \text{if } R_i \geq c_i \end{cases}$$

where c_i is the threshold value. The probability of default can then be expressed as $PD_i = P(D_i = 1) = P(R_i < c_i)$. If one assumes a structural default model and interprets R_i as a normalized asset return (i.e., normally distributed and standardized), then the PD is simply given as $PD_i = P(R_i < c_i) = \Phi(c_i)$, which is obviously the approach taken in the probit model as discussed in the PD chapter.

To introduce correlation of defaults, we let the underlying metric variables be correlated by a common stochastic variable. The R_i variable is split into an idiosyncratic component ϵ_i and a (systematic) component X (common to all i) via

$$R_i = \sqrt{\rho}X + \sqrt{1 - \rho}\epsilon_i$$

where $X \sim N(0, 1)$, $\epsilon_i \sim N(0, 1)$ i.i.d. The correlation between R_i and $R_j, j \neq i$, is given by the parameter ρ. Because R_i can be thought of as the asset return in an underlying structural framework, ρ is often called the "asset (return) correlation." The PD can still be given by $PD_i = P(R_i < c_i)$, as R_i is standard normally distributed.

Under this extension, a stochastic, conditional PD (CPD), can be given that is conditioned on the systematic random factor X as

$$CPD_i(X) = \Phi\left(\frac{c_i - \sqrt{\rho}X}{\sqrt{1 - \rho}}\right)$$

Analytical Solution

The CPD has expectation

$$E(CPD_i(X)) = \int_{-\infty}^{\infty} \Phi\left(\frac{c_i - \sqrt{\rho}x}{\sqrt{1 - \rho}}\right) \phi(x)dx$$

$$= PD_i$$

where $\phi(\cdot)$ is the standard normal probability density function (PDF), and variance

$$Var(CPD_i(X)) = E(CPD_i(X)^2) - [E(CPD_i(X))]^2$$

$$= \Phi(c_i, c_i, \rho) - PD_i^2$$

where $\Phi(c_i, c_i, \rho)$ is the bivariate normal CDF with correlation ρ and standardized margins; see Gordy (2000). The density $g(p_i)$ of $P_i = CPD_i(X)$ is given by:

$$g(p_i) = \frac{\sqrt{1-\rho}}{\sqrt{\rho}} \cdot \frac{\phi\left(\frac{c_i - \Phi^{-1}(p_i)\sqrt{1-\rho}}{\sqrt{\rho}}\right)}{\phi(\Phi^{-1}(p_i))}$$

$$= \frac{\sqrt{1-\rho}}{\sqrt{\rho}} \cdot \exp\left(\frac{1}{2}(\Phi^{-1}(p_i))^2 - \frac{1}{2\rho}(c_i - \sqrt{1-\rho} \cdot \Phi^{-1}(p_i))^2\right)$$

(see Vasicek 1987, 1991; Koyluoglu and Hickman 1998). The CDF $G(p_i)$ and α-quantile are:

$$G(p_i) = \Phi\left(\frac{\sqrt{1-\rho} \cdot \Phi^{-1}(p_i) - c_i}{\sqrt{\rho}}\right)$$

$$q_\alpha = \Phi\left(\frac{c_i + \sqrt{\rho}\Phi^{-1}(\alpha)}{\sqrt{1-\rho}}\right)$$

The joint probability of default for two obligors now becomes:

$$P(D_1 = 1 \cap D_2 = 1) = \int_{-\infty}^{\infty} \Phi\left(\frac{c_1 - \sqrt{\rho}x}{\sqrt{1-\rho}}\right) \Phi\left(\frac{c_2 - \sqrt{\rho}x}{\sqrt{1-\rho}}\right) \phi(x) dx$$

$$= \Phi(c_1, c_2, \rho)$$

where $\phi(x)$ is the standard normal PDF. The default correlation is:

$$\rho^D = Corr(D_1, D_2) = \frac{\Phi(c_1, c_2, \rho) - PD_1 PD_2}{\sqrt{PD_1(1 - PD_1)}\sqrt{PD_2(1 - PD_2)}}$$

It can be shown that if a portfolio has homogeneous parameters (i.e., PD and correlation) and infinitely many borrowers, the density $g(p_i)$ represents its default rate distribution (see Vasicek 1987, 1991). This model is sometimes called the asymptotic single risk factor (ASRF) model or Vasicek model. It is implemented in the internal ratings based approach (IRBA) of the Basel Accord and has some nice properties. The risk contribution of any loan to the risk of a portfolio can be computed by considering the properties of the loan only and does not require considering the portfolio in which the loan is held; for technical details see Gordy (2003). Thus, risk contributions are portfolio invariant. Hence, the risk contribution of a loan in terms of value at risk is directly given by q_α. So, if the correlation and the confidence level α are given, the risk contribution and hence capital can be computed as a function of the probability of default (PD). This is exactly the approach followed in the Basel IRBA formula, which uses q_α as the key constituent (see Basel Committee on Banking Supervision 2006, 2011). There the capital requirements are computed via

$$C = LGD \cdot \left[\Phi\left(\frac{\Phi^{-1}(PD) + \sqrt{\rho}\Phi^{-1}(0.999)}{\sqrt{1-\rho}}\right) - PD\right] \cdot \frac{1 + (M - 2.5)b}{1 - 1.5b}$$

where the last factor is a maturity adjustment with $b = (0.11852 - 0.05478 \cdot \ln(PD))$ to account for the fact that long-term credits are more risky than short-term credits and maturity effects are more pronounced for obligors with low PDs. In the capital requirement formula for corporates, sovereigns, and banks, the correlation is a function of the PD as follows:

$$\rho \equiv \rho(PD) = 0.12 \frac{1 - \exp^{-50 \cdot PD}}{1 - \exp^{-50}} + 0.24 \left(1 - \frac{1 - \exp^{-50 \cdot PD}}{1 - \exp^{-50}}\right)$$

The first expression in square brackets of the capital formula is the 99.9th percentile of the CPD from which the expected loss is subtracted. The result is then multiplied by the loss given default (LGD) and the maturity adjustment. The correlation is assumed to be a decreasing function of the PD with lower bound of 12 percent for high PDs and upper bound of 24 percent for low PDs. The decreasing form of the correlation leads to a flattening of the capital curve for higher PDs. Risk-weighted assets (RWA) are then computed as:

$$RWA = C \cdot 12.5 \cdot EAD$$

The maturity M represents the nominal or effective maturity and is between 1 and 5 years. For exposures to large financial sector entities, ρ is multiplied by 1.25. For retail exposures, there is no maturity adjustment. For residential mortgages, the asset correlation has been set to 15 percent, for qualifying revolving exposures to 4 percent. For other retail exposures the asset correlation is a decreasing function of the PD with lower bound of 3 percent for high PDs and upper bound of 16 percent for low PDs.

$$\rho \equiv \rho(PD) = 0.03 \frac{1 - \exp^{-35 \cdot PD}}{1 - \exp^{-35}} + 0.16 \left(1 - \frac{1 - \exp^{-35 \cdot PD}}{1 - \exp^{-35}}\right)$$

In the United States, the latter has been set to: $\rho = 0.03 + 0.13 \exp^{-35 \cdot PD}$. We analyze these asset correlations further in our stress testing chapter.

It is important to emphasize again that the risk weight functions cover unexpected loss, since expected loss should be covered by provisions. Also note that the risk-weighted assets are not explicitly calculated. They can, however, be backed out using the relationship that regulatory capital equals 8 percent of the risk-weighted assets. This implies that the risk-weighted assets are equal to 12.50 times the regulatory capital. Also, as a result of various quantitative impact studies run by the Basel group, an additional scaling factor of 1.06 is applied to the risk-weighted assets. See Articles 153 and 154 of the EU directive for more details (European Union 2013).

Remember the crucial role of the asset correlation term in the capital requirements formula. The question is: How are these values determined? For corporates, the assets can be unambiguously quantified by inspecting balance sheets, and various financial models have been introduced to quantify asset correlations in this context. For retail exposures, it becomes considerably more difficult, as the assets are less tangible, with the exception of real estate values, which are generally reasonably well described. The asset correlations have been determined using some empirical but not published procedure. They reflect a combination of supervisory judgment and empirical evidence. It is assumed that they are set based on reverse engineering of economic capital models from a selection of large banks worldwide. Note that, as you can see in the Vasicek model, the asset correlations also measure how the asset class is dependent upon the state of the economy.

The loss density of the model can be computed for two homogeneous portfolios in SAS by the following IML code. The PDs are 1 percent and 5 percent and the asset correlations are 10 percent and 20 percent for portfolio 1 and portfolio 2.

```
PROC IML;

/*Set parameters portfolio 1*/
PD1 = 0.01;
rho1 = 0.1;

/*Set parameters portfolio 2*/
PD2 = 0.05;
rho2 = 0.2;

/*Generate skeleton for loss distribution*/
DO p_i = 0.0001 TO 0.2 BY 0.0001;

/*Density portfolio 1*/
g_p_i1 = SQRT(1-rho1)/ SQRT(rho1)
* EXP(0.5*(PROBIT(p_i)**2) -0.5/rho1
* (PROBIT(PD1)-SQRT(1-rho1) * PROBIT(p_i))**2 );

/*Density portfolio 2*/
g_p_i2 = SQRT(1-rho2)/ SQRT(rho2)
* EXP(0.5*(PROBIT(p_i)**2) -0.5/rho2
* (PROBIT(PD2)-SQRT(1-rho2) * PROBIT(p_i))**2 );

/*Generate output data*/
out = out//(p_i||g_p_i1||g_p_i2);
END;

/*Name output variables*/
x={'loss','PD_1', 'PD_5'};

/*Export output data set*/
CREATE  analytic FROM out [colname=x];
APPEND FROM out;
QUIT;
```

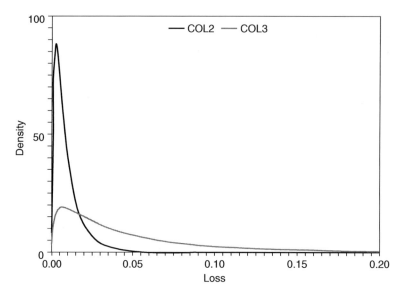

Exhibit 9.2 Analytical Loss Distributions

The following code generates the PDF for the portfolio loss. The vertical axis plots the density as the loss is continuous. (See also Exhibit 9.2.)

```
ODS GRAPHICS ON;
GOPTIONS RESET=GLOBAL GUNIT=PCT NOBORDER CBACK=WHITE
COLORS=(BLACK BLUE GREEN RED)
FTITLE=SWISSB FTEXT=SWISS HTITLE=3 HTEXT=3;
SYMBOL1 COLOR=RED INTERPOL=JOIN WIDTH=3 VALUE=NONE HEIGHT=0;
SYMBOL2 VALUE=NONE COLOR=BLUE INTERPOL=JOIN WIDTH=3 HEIGHT=0;
AXIS1 ORDER=(0 TO 0.2 BY 0.05) OFFSET=(0,0)
LABEL=('Loss')
MAJOR=(HEIGHT=1) MINOR=(HEIGHT=1)
WIDTH=3;
AXIS2 ORDER=(0 TO 100 BY 50) OFFSET=(0,0)
LABEL=('Density')
MAJOR=(HEIGHT=1) MINOR=(HEIGHT=1)
WIDTH=3;
LEGEND1 LABEL=NONE
SHAPE=SYMBOL(4,2)
POSITION=(TOP CENTER INSIDE)
MODE=SHARE;

PROC GPLOT DATA=analytic;
PLOT PD_1*loss PD_5*loss / OVERLAY LEGEND=LEGEND1
```

```
HAXIS=AXIS1
VAXIS=AXIS2;
RUN;
ODS GRAPHICS OFF;
```

Numerical Solution

In a portfolio with a finite number of borrowers, idiosyncratic risk is not canceled out, which means it must be taken into account when the loss distribution is computed. We condition again on the systematic factor and assume homogeneous borrowers (i.e., $PD_i = PD, \forall i$). Note that the remaining stochastic variables ϵ_i are independent. Assume further that defaults are independent for a given realization of the systematic factor $X = x$. The number of defaults $D = \sum_{i=1}^{n} D_i$ is conditionally binomially distributed:

$$P(D = d|x) = \binom{n}{d} CPD(x)^d (1 - CPD(x))^{n-d}, d = 0, \ldots, n$$

The final unconditional distribution is then found by mixing (integrating) over the distribution of the random factor X as

$$P(D = d) = \int_{-\infty}^{\infty} \binom{n}{d} CPD(x)^d (1 - CPD(x))^{n-d} \phi(x)dx, d = 0, \ldots, n$$

The integral can be calculated using IML, as shown in the following code using CALL QUAD within PROC IML. CALL QUAD solves integrals that are included in a separate module in PROC IML numerically. CALL QUAD has a number of inputs, of which we use the first four in the statement "CALL QUAD(z,"fun",a,eps);":

- z is a numeric vector containing the results of the integration.
- "fun" specifies the name of an IML module that contains the integral to be solved.
- "a" contains the limits of the integral. We specify "a = .M .P;" which implies integration from $-\infty$ to ∞.
- eps is a specification of accuracy of the numerical process, and we specify: "eps = 1.34E-15;" The choice of eps is optional and involves a trade-off between computing time and accuracy: The smaller this number, the longer the numerical solution takes and the more accurate the result will be.

More details on numerical integration using SAS can be found in the SAS manual; see SAS Institute Inc. (2015).

```
ODS GRAPHICS ON;

PROC IML SYMSIZE=10000000 WORKSIZE = 10000000;

/*Set asset correlation*/
rho = 0.2;
```

```
/*Set number of borrowers*/
N = 100;

/*Set PD*/
p = 0.05;

/*Define output matrix*/
out = J(1,7,0);

/*Create module fun - name is arbitrary*/
START fun(x) GLOBAL(k,p,N,rho);
pi = CONSTANT('PI');

/*Compute the CPD and multiply with the standard normal pdf */
CPD = PROBNORM((1/SQRT(1-rho)) * (PROBIT(p)-SQRT(rho)*x));
v   = PROBBNML(CPD,n,k) * (EXP(-(x*x)/2))/(SQRT(2*pi));
RETURN(v);
FINISH fun;

/*Increase k up to desired percentile*/
k=0;
DO UNTIL(z>0.9999);

/*Call QUAD to compute the integral */
a   = {.M .P};
eps = 1.34E-15;
CALL QUAD(z,"fun",a,eps);
quantile=k;
default_rate= quantile/N;
IF k = 0 THEN DO;
prob = z;
out = out//(N||rho||p||quantile||default_rate||z||prob);
END;
IF k > 0 THEN DO;
prob = z-out[k+1,6];
out = out//(N||rho||p||quantile||default_rate||z||prob);
END;
k=k+1;
END;
out = out[2:NROW(out),];
```

```
/*Export output data set*/
CREATE  numeric FROM out;
APPEND FROM out;
QUIT;
```

The following code generates the histogram for the loss distribution. (See Exhibit 9.3.)
The vertical axis plots probabilities, as we have discrete loss observations.

```
GOPTIONS RESET=GLOBAL GUNIT=PCT NOBORDER CBACK=WHITE
COLORS=(BLACK BLUE GREEN RED)
FTITLE=SWISSB FTEXT=SWISS HTITLE=3 HTEXT=3;
SYMBOL1 COLOR=BLUE INTERPOL=NEEDLE VALUE=NONE HEIGHT=0 WIDTH=3;
AXIS1 ORDER=(0 TO 0.5 BY 0.05) OFFSET=(0,0)
LABEL=('Loss') MAJOR=(HEIGHT=1) MINOR=(HEIGHT=1) WIDTH=3;
AXIS2 ORDER=(0 TO 0.2 BY 0.05) OFFSET=(0,0)
LABEL=('Probability') MAJOR=(HEIGHT=1) MINOR=(HEIGHT=1) WIDTH=3;

ODS GRAPHICS ON;
PROC GPLOT DATA=numeric;
PLOT COL7*COL5 /
HAXIS=AXIS1
VAXIS=AXIS2;
RUN;
ODS GRAPHICS OFF;
```

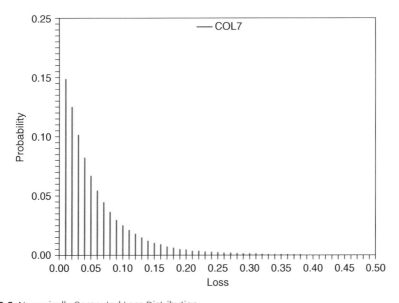

Exhibit 9.3 Numerically Computed Loss Distribution

Monte Carlo Simulation

The most flexible way of deriving loss distributions is via Monte Carlo simulations (e.g., using PROC IML). Here, the random variables of the model are drawn by a random number generator according to the specified distributions. In the preceding model, the model parameters have to be given, and standard normally distributed random variables are simulated from which the variable R_i is computed (denoted as "lnV" in the code). R_i is then compared to the default threshold c_i and a default variable is set to 1 if $R_i < c_i$ and 0 otherwise. The data are adequately stored and can be analyzed for instance by PROC UNIVARIATE, as shown in the following code.

```
PROC IML SYMSIZE=10000000 WORKSIZE = 10000000;

/*Set number of simulations*/
N_sim = 100000;

/*Set number of borrowers*/
N   = 10000;

/*Set homogeneous PDs*/
p = 0.05;

/*Create vector of PDs - may easily be extended to individual PDs*/
PD = J(N,1,p);

/*Set asset correlations*/
w_2 = 0.2 ;
w = SQRT(w_2);
ksi = SQRT(1-w_2);

/*Beginning of simulation loop*/
DO sim = 1 TO N_sim;
x1   = J(1,1,0);
x2   = J(N,1,0);

/*Simulation standard normal random numbers*/
z   = RANNOR (x1);
eps = RANNOR (x2);

/*Generation of asset returns*/
lnV = J(N,1,w) * z  + J(N, 1,ksi) #  eps;
threshold   =   PROBIT(PD);
defaults = lnv<threshold;
```

```
default_rate    = defaults[+]/N;
out= out//(sim||N||defaults[+]||default_rate);
END;

/*Name variables*/
x={'sim', 'N', 'D', 'Loss'};

/*Export output data*/
CREATE sim FROM out [colname=x];
APPEND FROM out;
QUIT;
```

We obtain 100,000 realizations of the default rate. (See Exhibit 9.4.) The default rate can be interpreted as a loss rate under the assumption of an EAD and a LGD of unity. We generate a histogram (Exhibit 9.5) using PROC UNIVARIATE for the rather large number of observations in our output data set:

```
ODS GRAPHICS ON;
PROC UNIVARIATE DATA = sim ;
VAR Loss;
OUTPUT OUT=sim_univariate PCTLPRE=P_
pctlpts=50, 95, 97.5, 99, 99.5, 99.9, 100;
HISTOGRAM / MIDPOINTS=0 TO 0.2 BY 0.01 HOFFSET=0 NOFRAME
CBARLINE=CYAN CFILL=CYAN
OUTHISTOGRAM = sim_histogram;
RUN;
ODS GRAPHICS OFF;
```

ESTIMATING CORRELATIONS

For parameter estimation, we consider some of the most popular estimation techniques such as the method of moments (MM), maximum likelihood (ML), and probit-linear regressions. The last technique will be divided into a special case for the ASRF model where closed formulas exist, and more general cases with finite numbers of borrowers where we consider various extensions, dependent upon the data and the objective.

Method of Moments

The method of moments technique replaces population moments by their empirical counterparts. In credit risk, this technique has been derived and applied by Gordy (2000). It requires a time series of defaults in a homogeneous segment where

The UNIVARIATE Procedure

Variable: Loss

Moments			
N	100000	**Sum Weights**	100000
Mean	0.05001205	**Sum Observations**	5001.2053
Std Deviation	0.05223872	**Variance**	0.00272888
Skewness	2.30169689	**Kurtosis**	7.77479974
Uncorrected SS	523.006189	**Corrected SS**	272.885645
Coeff Variation	104.452258	**Std Error Mean**	0.00016519

Basic Statistical Measures			
Location		**Variability**	
Mean	0.050012	**Std Deviation**	0.05224
Median	0.033100	**Variance**	0.00273
Mode	0.007500	**Range**	0.62720
		Interquartile Range	0.05180

Quantiles (Definition 5)	
Level	**Quantile**
100% Max	0.62720
99%	0.24905
95%	0.15530
90%	0.11560
75% Q3	0.06670
50% Median	0.03310
25% Q1	0.01490
10%	0.00650
5%	0.00390
1%	0.00130
0% Min	0.00000

Exhibit 9.4 Monte Carlo Simulation

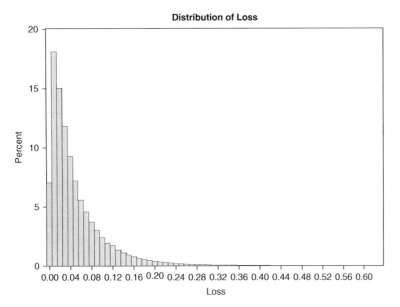

Exhibit 9.5 Simulated Loss Distribution

$d_t = \sum_{i=1}^{N_t} d_{it}$ $(i = 1,\ldots,n_t; t = 1,\ldots,T)$ is the number of defaults and n_t is the number of borrowers observed in year t. The estimator for the default probability is simply given by the average yearly default rate as

$$\widehat{PD} = \frac{1}{T} \sum_{t=1}^{T} \frac{d_t}{n_t}$$

and the variance of the default rate is estimated by the historical mean squared error (MSE) as

$$\hat{\sigma}^2 = \frac{1}{T} \sum_{t=1}^{T} \left(\frac{d_t}{n_t} - \widehat{PD} \right)^2$$

An estimator for the variance of the CPD is given by

$$\widehat{Var}(CPD) = \frac{\hat{\sigma}^2 - \frac{1}{T} \sum_{t=1}^{T} \frac{1}{n_t} \widehat{PD}(1 - \widehat{PD})}{1 - \frac{1}{T} \sum_{t=1}^{T} \frac{1}{n_t}}$$

Finally, the estimator $\hat{\rho}$ for the asset correlation is obtained as a (numerical) solution for

$$\widehat{Var}(CPD) = \Phi_2(\Phi^{-1}(\widehat{PD}), \Phi^{-1}(\widehat{PD}), \hat{\rho}) - \widehat{PD}^2$$

where $\Phi_2(., ., \hat{\rho})$ denotes the CDF of the bivariate standardized normal distribution with correlation $\hat{\rho}$.

This can be implemented in SAS as follows. First, we generate the mean gross domestic product (GDP) growth rate and default rate by time by sorting the data using PROC SORT and computing the averages of GDP growth rate and default indicator using PROC MEANS by time. Then, we compute the lagged and probit transformed default rate in a data step:

```
DATA tmp;
SET data.mortgage;
RUN;


PROC SORT DATA = tmp;
BY time;
RUN;


PROC MEANS DATA = tmp;
VAR default_time gdp_time;
BY time;
OUTPUT OUT = means;
RUN;


DATA tmp2;
SET means;
IF _STAT_ = "MEAN";
n_default = default_time * _FREQ_;
default_time_1 = LAG(default_time);
Probit_dr = PROBIT(default_time);
RUN;
```

Note that the resulting data set tmp2 is the basis for this and the following two sections (Maximum-Likelihood ASRF and Probit-Linear Regression).

```
PROC IML;
USE tmp2;
READ ALL Var _NUM_ INTO data;
default_rate = data[,4];

/* Average default rate */
lambda_hat = default_rate[:];

/* Average default rate squared*/
lambda_hat2 = lambda_hat**2;
```

```
/* 1 divided by N_t*/
N_inverse = 1/data[,3];


/* Probit of the default rate*/
threshold = PROBIT(lambda_hat);


/* Historical mean squared error*/
MSE = (default_rate-lambda_hat)`*(default_rate-lambda_hat)
/ NROW(data);


/* Variance of the CPD*/
Var_lambda_hat = (MSE - N_inverse` * J(Nrow(data),1,1)
*lambda_hat * (1-lambda_hat) / NROW(data))
/ (1- N_inverse` * J(Nrow(data),1,1)/NROW(data));


PRINT lambda_hat MSE Var_lambda_hat threshold lambda_hat2;
out =   lambda_hat||threshold||Var_lambda_hat;
CREATE output_MM FROM out;
APPEND FROM out;
QUIT;
```

The following code uses CALL NLPNRA to perform a nonlinear optimization by the Newton-Raphson method. (See Exhibit 9.6.) A more detailed description of this routine can be found in the SAS manual; see SAS Institute Inc. (2015).

```
PROC IML;
USE output_MM ;
READ ALL Var _NUM_ INTO data;


/* Read the data required for backing out the asset correlation*/
threshold = data[1,2];
lambda_hat = data[1,1];
Var = data[1,3];


START optim(x) GLOBAL(threshold, lambda_hat, Var);


/* Formula for the variance of the CPD
with argument x as asset correlation*/
/* Difference between left-hand and right-hand side
of the formula is denoted by f
and should be close to zero*/
f = ABS((PROBBNRM(threshold, threshold, x) - lambda_hat**2 - Var));
RETURN (f);
```

Optimization Start				
Parameter Estimates				
N	Parameter	Estimate	Gradient Objective Function	Lower Bound Constraint	Upper Bound Constraint
1	X1	0.990000	0.142121	0.000000100	1.000000
Value of Objective Function = 0.0177221014				

Newton-Raphson Optimization with Line Search
Without Parameter Scaling
Gradient Computed by Finite Differences
CRP Jacobian Computed by Finite Differences

Parameter Estimates	1
Lower Bounds	1
Upper Bounds	1

Optimization Start			
Active Constraints	0	Objective Function	0.0177221014
Max Abs Gradient Element	0.1421210742		

Iteration	Restarts	Function Calls	Active Constraints	Objective Function	Objective Function Change	Max Abs Gradient Element	Step Size	Slope of Search Direction
1	0	3	0	0.01568	0.00204	0.0812	1.000	−0.0028
2	0	4	0	0.01235	0.00333	0.0454	1.000	−0.0046
3	0	5	0	0.00752	0.00483	0.0238	1.000	−0.0068
4	0	6	0	0.00250	0.00503	0.0103	1.000	−0.0075
5	0	7	0	0.0000171	0.00248	0.00315	1.000	−0.0041
6	0	10	0	1.63156E-6	0.000015	0.00308	0.0228	−0.0008
7 *	0	16	0	1.56846E-7	1.475E-6	0.00309	0.00006	−167.8
8 *	0	21	0	2.1182E-11	1.568E-7	0.000368	0.00098	−0.0002
9 *	0	33	0	2.1182E-11	0	0.00368	1E-9	−14E-11

Optimization Results			
Iterations	9	Function Calls	34
Hessian Calls	10	Active Constraints	0
Objective Function	2.118166E-11	Max Abs Gradient Element	0.0003680843
Slope of Search Direction	−1.39024E-10	Ridge	0.1899715969

Exhibit 9.6 Parameter Estimates

Optimization Results			
Parameter Estimates			
N	Parameter	Estimate	Gradient Objective Function
1	X1	0.045432	0.000368
Value of Objective Function = 2.118166E-11			

Exhibit 9.6 *(Continued)*

```
FINISH optim;
x = 0.99;
optn = {0, 2};
con = {0.0000001 , 0.9999999};
CALL NLPNRA(rc,xres,"optim",x,optn, con) ;

QUIT;
```

The output shows the starting value of 0.99 together with the value of the objective function. Then the algorithm iterates a number of times and improves the value of the objective functions. It stops after further improvement is impossible and returns the value for the asset correlation of 4.5 percent.

Maximum-Likelihood ASRF

Another widely used estimation technique is the maximum likelihood method. A special simple case of the likelihood is obtained under the assumption that the model has exactly one systematic risk factor and is homogeneous and asymptotic (i.e., has infinitely many identical borrowers). This is called the asymptotic single risk factor (ASRF) model. Under these assumptions, the CPD becomes the default rate of the asymptotic portfolio, which stochastically depends on only the systematic random factor and has two parameters: the PD and the correlation. Düellmann, Klaus, Trapp, and Monika (2004) show that the ML estimator for the PD and the asset correlation are given by

$$\widehat{PD} = \Phi\left(\frac{\hat{c}}{\sqrt{1 + \widehat{Var}(\hat{c}_t)}} \right) \tag{9.1}$$

and

$$\hat{\rho} = \frac{\widehat{Var}(\hat{c}_t)}{1 + \widehat{Var}(\hat{c}_t)} \tag{9.2}$$

where $\hat{c} = \frac{1}{T} \sum_{t=1}^{T} \hat{c}_t$, $\widehat{Var}(\hat{c}_t) = \frac{1}{T} \sum_{t=1}^{T} \hat{c}_t^2 - \hat{c}^2$, and $\hat{c}_t = \Phi^{-1}\left(\frac{d_t}{n_t} \right)$.

This can be implemented in SAS as follows:

```
ODS GRAPHICS ON;
PROC IML;
USE tmp2;
READ all Var _NUM_ INTO data;

/* Probit of the yearly default rate*/
c_t  = PROBIT(data[,4]);

/* Average of theses Probits */
c_bar = c_t[:];

/* Variance of these Probits */
Var_c = c_t'*c_t / NROW(data) - c_bar**2;

/* Estimate for the PD */
PD_ML = PROBNORM(c_bar / (SQRT(1+Var_c)));

rho_ML = Var_c / (1+Var_c);
/* Estimate for the asset correlation */
PRINT c_bar Var_c rho_ML PD_ML;
RUN;
ODS GRAPHICS OFF;
```

The output returns the computed quantities (Exhibit 9.7); in the particular case, the asset correlation is estimated as 5.4 percent and the PD is estimated as 2.11 percent.

Probit-Linear Regression

Probit-Linear Regression without Covariates

The ASRF model can also be estimated in a simple way using a probit-linear regression model. In the ASRF model, it holds that the default rate $dr_t = \frac{d_t}{n_t}$ in time t equals the

c_bar	Var_c	rho_ML	PD_ML
−2.086967	0.057137	0.0540488	0.0211892

Exhibit 9.7 ASRF Maximum Likelihood Method

CPD. Then after transformation we have the regression model:

$$\Phi^{-1}(dr_t) = \frac{c - \sqrt{\rho}X}{\sqrt{1-\rho}}$$

$$= \frac{c}{\sqrt{1-\rho}} - \frac{\sqrt{\rho}}{\sqrt{1-\rho}}X$$

$$= a + \sigma \quad \epsilon$$

where $a = \frac{c}{\sqrt{1-\rho}}$, $\sigma = -\frac{\sqrt{\rho}}{\sqrt{1-\rho}}$, and $X = \epsilon \sim N(0, 1)$ i.i.d.

Note that we assume an infinitely granular portfolio (i.e., the assumption underlying the ASRF), which implies an infinitely large number of exposures with infinitely small exposure amounts. The result of this is that all idiosyncratic risk is diversified and that the portfolio default rates are exposed only to systematic risk, which is modeled by X in the ASRF and constitutes the error in a linear model. A linear regression model plots the MSE, which can be transformed into an estimate for the asset correlation (see later discussion).

The following code shows the implementation via PROC MODEL in SAS (see Exhibits 9.8 and 9.9).

```
/*Probit-Linear Regression*/
ODS GRAPHICS ON;
PROC MODEL DATA = tmp2;
Probit_dr = a;
FIT Probit_dr /  OUTEST=outest;
RUN;
ODS GRAPHICS OFF;
```

The code estimates two parameters, namely the constant a and the variance of the residual b^2, which is the mean squared error (MSE). From $\sigma^2 = \frac{\rho}{1-\rho}$ it follows that $\hat{\rho} = \frac{\sigma^2}{1+\sigma^2}$. Thus, the estimate for the asset correlation is $\hat{\rho} = \frac{0.0581}{1+0.0581} = 0.055 = 5.5\%$. The estimate for the default probability is obtained by noting that $c = a\sqrt{1-\rho}$ and $PD = \Phi(c)$. Thus, $\hat{c} = -2.0870 \cdot \sqrt{0.945} = -2.0288$, and therefore $\widehat{PD} = 0.0212 = 2.12\%$.

The procedure also returns some fit diagnostics for the regression model. The figures show that the residuals, which are the realizations of the systematic effects over time, exhibit a clear autocorrelation pattern. This is because the model does not include any explanatory, exogenous variables, such as macroeconomic variables, and therefore the time variation of default rates is fully captured by the residual. In the next model, we show that it is quite easy to account for this and include time-varying covariates.

The MODEL Procedure

Equation	DF Model	DF Error	SSE	MSE	Root MSE	*R*-Squared	Adj *R*-Sq
			Nonlinear OLS Summary of Residual Errors				
Probit_dr	1	59	3.4282	0.0581	0.2411	−0.0000	−0.0000

Parameter	Estimate	Approx Std Err	*t* Value	Approx Pr > |*t*|
	Nonlinear OLS Parameter Estimates			
a	−2.08697	0.0311	−67.06	<.0001

Number of Observations		Statistics for System	
Used	60	Objective	0.0571
Missing	0	Objective*N	3.4282

Exhibit 9.8 Probit-Linear Regression

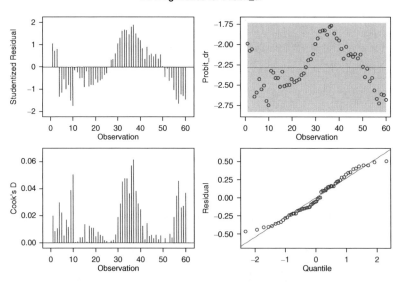

Fit Diagnostics for Probit_dr

Observations 60 MSE 0.073712 Model DF 1

Exhibit 9.9 Probit-Linear Regression

Probit-Linear Regression with Covariates

An important extension of the probit-linear regression model and an advantage over the analytical solutions is that covariates, particularly autoregressive (AR) effects and/or macroeconomic covariates, can be included. As an example, we include the realized one-year lagged default rate in the regression model (see Exhibits 9.10 and 9.11).

```
/*Probit-Linear Regression with covariates*/
ODS GRAPHICS ON;
PROC MODEL DATA = tmp2;
Probit_dr = a + b * PROBIT(default_time_1);
FIT Probit_dr / OUTEST=outest;
RUN;
ODS GRAPHICS OFF;
```

The model now has an additional coefficient b, which measures the impact of the lagged default rate on the current default risk. It is significantly positive and captures some of the autocorrelation of the default rates. The PD is now time-dependent and the residual is the difference between the time-dependent PD and the realized default rate, and is the remainder of the unexplained systematic risk. Therefore, the remaining asset correlation after including autocorrelated PDs is only $\hat{\rho} = \frac{0.0135}{1+0.0135} = 0.0133 = 1.33\%$. The regression diagnostics show that the fit is much better than without covariates. Instead, or in addition to the lagged transformed default rate, other (particularly macroeconomic) covariates can also be included. In the next

The MODEL Procedure

Nonlinear OLS Summary of Residual Errors							
Equation	DF Model	DF Error	SSE	MSE	Root MSE	*R*-Squared	Adj *R*-Sq
Probit_dr	2	57	0.7687	0.0135	0.1161	0.7726	0.7686

Nonlinear OLS Parameter Estimates				
Parameter	**Estimate**	**Approx Std Err**	***t* Value**	**Approx Pr > |*t*|**
a	−0.2078	0.1356	−1.53	0.1310
b	0.902061	0.0648	13.92	<.0001

Number of Observations		Statistics for System	
Used	59	**Objective**	0.0130
Missing	1	**Objective*N**	0.7687

Exhibit 9.10 Probit-Linear Regression

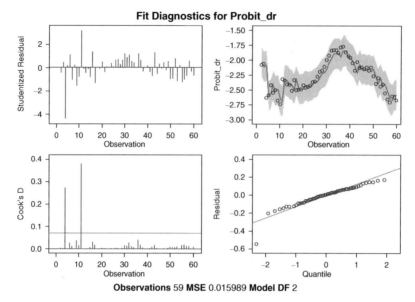

Exhibit 9.11 Probit-Linear Regression with Lagged Default Rate

example, shown in Exhibits 9.12 and 9.13, we include GDP. However, as most of the time variation is already captured by the lagged effect, the GDP is not significant for this data set.

The MODEL Procedure

Nonlinear OLS Summary of Residual Errors							
Equation	DF Model	DF Error	SSE	MSE	Root MSE	R-Squared	Adj R-Sq
Probit_dr	3	56	0.7395	0.0132	0.1149	0.7812	0.7734

Nonlinear OLS Parameter Estimates				
Parameter	Estimate	Approx Std Err	t Value	Approx Pr > |t|
a	−0.36139	0.1693	−2.13	0.0372
b	0.813225	0.0877	9.28	<.0001
c	−0.01739	0.0117	−1.49	0.1426

Number of Observations		Statistics for System	
Used	59	**Objective**	0.0125
Missing	1	**Objective*N**	0.7395

Exhibit 9.12 Probit-Linear Regression with Macroeconomic Variable

Fit Diagnostics for Probit_dr

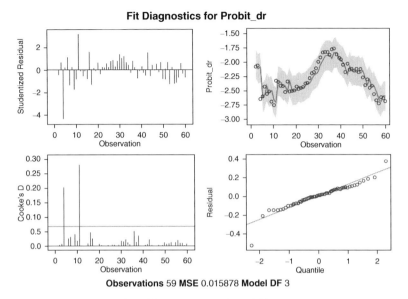

Observations 59 MSE 0.015878 Model DF 3

Exhibit 9.13 Probit-Linear Regression with Macroeconomic Variable

```
/*Probit-Linear Regression with covariates*/
ODS GRAPHICS ON;
PROC MODEL DATA = tmp2;
Probit_dr = a + b * PROBIT(default_time_1) + c * gdp_time;
FIT Probit_dr / /*out = resid outresid*/ OUTEST=outest;
RUN;
ODS GRAPHICS OFF;
```

As an alternative to including the lagged default rate as covariate, one might also directly estimate an autoregressive (AR) model using PROC AUTOREG. In the example shown in Exhibits 9.14 and 9.15, we include an AR(3) effect (i.e., with three lags) and GDP. The output shows that only the first lag is significant. Without AR effect, GDP is significant. After including the AR effect, GDP is still significant. The AR models can easily be extended in PROC AUTOREG to various GARCH family types. We refer to the SAS manual for a detailed description and leave it up to the interested reader to specify more advanced econometric models. For a general introduction and overview of time series models, see, for example, Box (2015).

```
/*AR model*/
ODS GRAPHICS ON;
PROC AUTOREG DATA=tmp2 ;
ar_1 :   MODEL Probit_dr = gdp_time /   NLAG=3 METHOD=ML;
RUN;
ODS GRAPHICS OFF;
```

The AUTOREG Procedure

Ordinary Least Squares Estimates			
SSE	1.88259464	DFE	58
MSE	0.03246	Root MSE	0.18016
SBC	−29.240303	AIC	−33.428993
MAE	0.14427436	AICC	−33.218466
MAPE	6.91479828	HQC	−31.790566
Durbin-Watson	0.4941	Total R-Squared	0.4509

Parameter Estimates					
Variable	DF	Estimate	Standard Error	t Value	Approx Pr > |t|
Intercept	1	−1.9211	0.0334	−57.45	<.0001
gdp_time	1	−0.0899	0.0130	−6.90	<.0001

Estimates of Autocorrelations			
Lag	Covariance	Correlation	-1 9 8 7 6 5 4 3 2 1 0 1 2 3 4 5 6 7 8 9 1
0	0.0314	1.000000	| |******************** |
1	0.0224	0.714006	| |************** |
2	0.0182	0.578784	| |************ |
3	0.0152	0.483873	| |********** |

Estimates of Autoregressive Parameters			
Lag	Coefficient	Standard Error	t Value
1	−0.605246	0.134606	−4.50
2	−0.104585	0.156781	−0.67
3	−0.058893	0.134606	−0.44

Maximum Likelihood Estimates			
SSE	0.64109687	DFE	55
MSE	0.01166	Root MSE	0.10796
SBC	−79.932239	AIC	−90.403962
MAE	0.08140146	AICC	−89.292851
MAPE	3.89550756	HQC	−86.307895
Log Likelihood	50.2019809	Transformed Regression R-Squared	0.1325
Durbin-Watson	1.9190	Total R-Squared	0.8130
		Observations	60

Exhibit 9.14 AR Model with Macroeconomic Variable

Parameter Estimates					
Variable	DF	Estimate	Standard Error	t Value	Approx Pr > |t|
Intercept	1	−2.1108	0.1567	−13.47	<.0001
gdp_time	1	−0.0378	0.0133	−2.83	0.0064
AR1	1	−0.5467	0.1375	−3.98	0.0002
AR2	1	−0.2830	0.1507	−1.88	0.0657
AR3	1	−0.0900	0.1409	−0.64	0.5255

Autoregressive Parameters Assumed Given					
Variable	DF	Estimate	Standard Error	t Value	Approx Pr > |t|
Intercept	1	−2.1108	0.1423	−14.83	<.0001
gdp_time	1	−0.0378	0.0130	−2.90	0.0054

Exhibit 9.14 (*Continued*)

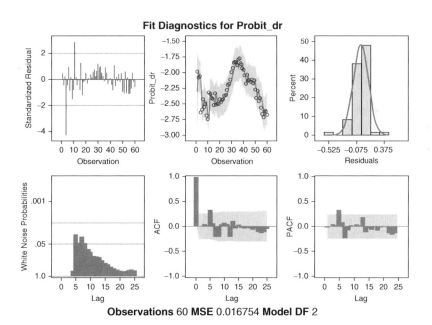

Observations 60 **MSE** 0.016754 **Model DF** 2

Exhibit 9.15 AR Model with Macroeconomic Variable

EXTENSIONS

Model Specifications Other Than Gaussian

The models in this chapter might seem rather restrictive at first sight because the basic framework introduced normally distributed variables. In risk management, however, particularly in market risk, the assumption of a normal distribution is often not reasonable. Asset returns usually have fatter tails than the normal distribution and exhibit asymmetry. The question then becomes how alternative distributional assumptions can be implemented in SAS and how they affect the shape of the loss distribution. In this subsection, we show how other distributions can be simulated. For exposition purposes, we compare the Gaussian model with a Clayton copula model and a simplified version of the CreditRisk+ (CR+) model. To compute the parameters for the non-Gaussian models, we use a moments-matching approach as in Gordy (2000) such that mean and variance of the distribution are the same. Given the PD and the asset correlation ρ in the Gaussian model, the variance is obtained as $Var = \Phi_2(c, c, \rho) - PD^2$ where $c = \Phi^{-1}(PD)$ and $\Phi_2(.)$ is the CDF of the bivarate normal distribution. The parameters for the Gamma distribution in CR+ are obtained as $\alpha = PD^2/Var$ and $\beta = 1/\alpha$. For the Clayton copula with dispersion parameter θ, the variance is $Var_C = \phi^{-1}(2\phi(PD)) - PD^2$ with $\phi(t) = t^{-\theta} - 1$ and $\phi^{-1}(s) = (1 + s)^{-1/\theta}$. From this θ can be backed out.

The Monte Carlo simulation for the Gaussian model is straightforward, as shown earlier. In the CR+ and the Clayton model, the systematic factor is gamma distributed. Given the systematic factor, the conditional PD is computed and defaults are binomial or Poisson distributed, respectively (see, e.g., Das and Geng 2003). The IML code generates 100,000 Monte Carlo simulation runs with 1,000 borrowers for each model. The output shows the three simulated loss distributions, and we see in Exhibit 9.16 that the differences between the distributions are almost negligible. Similar results have been obtained by other studies and other models; see, for example Hamerle and Rösch (2005) and Schloegl and O'Kane (2005) for comparisons of Gaussian and Student's t copula models.

```
/*Reparameterizing Gaussian, Clayton and CR+ Model and Simulation*/
PROC IML;

/*Set parameters*/
 Nsim = 100000;
 N = 1000;

/*Parameters for the Gaussian model*/
 pd_N = 0.0212;
 c = PROBIT(PD_N);
 rho_N = 0.055;
 ksi_N = SQRT(1-rho_N);
 Var_CPD = PROBBNRM(c,c,rho_N) - PD_N**2;
```

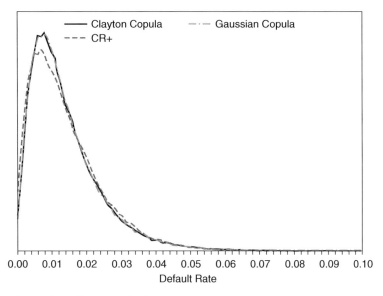

Exhibit 9.16 Comparison of Loss Distributions

```
/*Parameters for the CR+ model*/
pd_C = pd_N;
alpha_C = (PD_C**2)/Var_CPD;
beta_C = 1/alpha_C;

/*Parameters for the Clayton Copula model*/
pd_T = PD_N;
theta = 0.020401;

/*Generation of the default distribution for Gaussian model*/
x1_N = J(Nsim,1,0);
z_N = RANNOR(x1_N);
CPD_N = PROBNORM((PROBIT(pd_n)- SQRT(rho_N) * z_N)/ksi_N);
out_N = RANBIN(0,N,CPD_N)/N;

/*Generation of the default distribution for CR+ Model*/
x1_C = J(Nsim,1,0);
z_C = beta_C * RANGAM (x1_C,alpha_C);
CPD_C = N * PD_c * z_C ;
out_C = RANPOI(0,CPD_C)/N;

/*Generation of the default distribution for Clayton Copula Model*/
```

```
x1_T = J(Nsim,1,0);
z_T = RANGAM (x1_T,1/theta);
CPD_T = exp(-(PD_T**(-theta)-1)*z_T);
out_T = RANBIN(0,N,CPD_T)/N;

/*Export output data*/
CREATE Svsim_n FROM out_N;
APPEND FROM out_N;
CREATE  Svsim_T FROM out_T;
APPEND FROM out_T ;
CREATE  Svsim_CR FROM out_C;
APPEND FROM out_C ;
QUIT;

PROC UNIVARIATE DATA = svsim_t;
VAR COL1;
OUTPUT OUT=temp_pctl_t pctlpre=P_
pctlpts=50, 95, 99, 99.5, 99.9, 100;
HISTOGRAM / MIDPOINTS=0 TO 0.1 BY 0.001
OUTHISTOGRAM = temp_T NOPLOT;
RUN;
PROC UNIVARIATE DATA = svsim_n;
VAR COL1;
OUTPUT OUT=temp_pctl_g pctlpre=P_
pctlpts=50, 95, 99, 99.5, 99.9, 100;
HISTOGRAM / MIDPOINTS=0 TO 0.1 BY 0.001
OUTHISTOGRAM = temp_G NOPLOT;
RUN;
PROC UNIVARIATE DATA = svsim_CR;
VAR COL1;
OUTPUT OUT=temp_pctl_c pctlpre=P_
pctlpts=50, 95, 99, 99.5, 99.9, 100;
HISTOGRAM / MIDPOINTS=0 TO 0.1 BY 0.001
OUTHISTOGRAM = temp_C NOPLOT;
RUN;

DATA temp_t1;
SET temp_T (KEEP=_MIDPT_ _OBSPCT_
RENAME=(_MIDPT_=default_rate  _OBSPCT_=T)) ;
RUN;
DATA temp_g1;
```

```
SET temp_g (KEEP=_MIDPT_ _OBSPCT_
RENAME=(_MIDPT_=default_rate  _OBSPCT_=g)) ;
RUN;
DATA temp_c1;
SET temp_c (KEEP=_MIDPT_ _OBSPCT_
RENAME=(_MIDPT_=default_rate  _OBSPCT_=c)) ;
RUN;

DATA temp;
MERGE temp_T1 temp_G1 temp_C1;
BY default_rate;
ATTRIB default_Rate LABEL = 'Default Rate' T
LABEL = 'Clayton Copula' G LABEL = 'Gaussian Copula'
C LABEL = 'CR+';
RUN;
```

The loss distributions are then plotted using PROC GPLOT:

```
ODS GRAPHICS ON / WIDTH=10IN IMAGEMAP=ON;
GOPTIONS RESET=GLOBAL GUNIT=PCT NOBORDER CBACK=WHITE
COLORS=(BLACK BLUE GREEN RED)
FTITLE=SWISSB FTEXT=SWISS HTITLE=5 HTEXT=4.5;
SYMBOL1 COLOR=BLUE INTERPOL=SM LINE=1 WIDTH=3 HEIGHT=1;
SYMBOL2 FONT=MARKER VALUE=NONE COLOR=RED LINE=21 WIDTH=3
INTERPOL=SM HEIGHT=0;
SYMBOL3 FONT=MARKER COLOR=GREEN INTERPOL=SM LINE=21 WIDTH=3
HEIGHT=1;
AXIS1 ORDER=(0 TO 0.12 BY 0.02) OFFSET=(0,0) LABEL=('Default rate')
MAJOR=(HEIGHT=1) MINOR=(HEIGHT=1) WIDTH=3;
AXIS2 ORDER=(0 TO 6 BY 2) OFFSET=(0,0) LABEL=('Percent')
MAJOR=(HEIGHT=1) MINOR=NONE  WIDTH=3;
LEGEND1 LABEL=NONE SHAPE=SYMBOL(4,2)
POSITION=(TOP RIGHT INSIDE) MODE=SHARE;

PROC GPLOT DATA=temp;
PLOT T*default_rate G*default_rate  C*default_rate
 / OVERLAY LEGEND=LEGEND1
HAXIS=AXIS1
VAXIS=AXIS2;
RUN;
ODS GRAPHICS OFF;
```

Models with Idiosyncratic Effects

The earlier models for estimating correlations used aggregated data (default rates). This is sufficient if the portfolio or segment is large and idiosyncratic risk is diversified. For smaller segments, the models can be extended to include idiosyncratic effects. Then we actually obtain a nonlinear panel regression model with mixed effects; see Rösch and Scheule (2004), Rösch (2005), and Hamerle and Rösch (2006).

A general feature of these models, relative to the method of moments and the maximum-likelihood ASRF, is that the correlations are computed conditional on the covariates. Furthermore, the models include idiosyncratic as well as systematic information, whereas the probit-linear regression model only controls for systematic (i.e., macroeconomic) covariates. The effect of controlling for time-varying (systematic or idiosyncratic) information is that the resulting asset correlations (i.e., the residual systematic risk exposure as we have demonstrated for probit-linear regression models) are smaller than for unconditional models that do not control for such information. As a result, the loss distribution that is based on these PD and asset correlation measures becomes narrower and the tails are much lower.

The interpretation of these results is:

- Banks can lower their tail risk estimates and hence economic capital by providing for time-varying information that adds accuracy to their PD estimates.

- Banks that rely on unconditional models overestimate unexplained stochastic systematic risk, as they obtain spurious correlations that can be explained by macroeconomic risk factors.

- Asset correlation models that control for systematic information are more accurate with regard to the unknown data-generating process.

These approaches are quite advanced; they usually require programming the likelihood, solving multidimensional integrals, and using an efficient optimizer and are beyond the scope of this book. For further information, refer to the referenced literature (e.g., Hamerle and Rösch 2006).

Model and Estimation Risk

Usually, banks have yearly data available for estimation, and time series are hardly longer than 20 or 30 years. Thus, we have only about 20 to 30 observations for estimating correlations, which imposes sparse data and nonstationarity issues, as correlations are estimated using the time-series dimension rather than the cross-section dimension of the data. Even if we assume stationarity and no structural breaks, the standard errors of the correlation estimates might be quite high and asset correlation estimates might be downward biased; see Gordy and Heitfield (2010). As loss distributions and risk measures derived thereof react very sensitively to changes in correlations, it is very important to consider estimation errors when computing risk measures. The good news is that the model specification is not such a big issue (within certain limits), but the bad news is that measurement and estimation error can be a problem, as risk measures might be under- or overstated. An analysis of value-at-risk volatility is given in Hamerle and Rösch (2005) and in Rösch and Scheule (2013). Moreover, the models in this section could be extended to deal with time-varying correlations and structural breaks, which are beyond the scope of this book.

PRACTICE QUESTIONS

1. Compute loss distributions analytically and numerically for PDs of 1 percent, 2 percent, 3 percent, and 5 percent, and correlations of 0.01, 0.05, 0.1, and 0.3. Let the number of borrowers in the numerical solution vary between 10, 100, and 1,000. Interpret the results.

2. Generate the loss distribution via Monte Carlo simulation using the same parameter settings and compare the results. What are the advantages and the disadvantages of the Monte Carlo simulations?

3. Discuss how the inclusion of macroeconomic variables into a model for correlation estimation might affect the estimate for the correlation. Interpret the results in terms of the earlier discussion about point-in-time (PIT) versus through-the-cycle (TTC).

4. In the regulatory framework of Basel, the correlation is an important parameter for the internal ratings based approach (IRBA). Discuss how it affects regulatory capital.

5. Categorize the FICO score into three categories using PROC RANK. Compute and plot the default rates for the three categories using PROC GPLOT. Estimate the PD and asset correlation of the three classes using the method of moments. Use data set mortgage.

6. Estimate the PD and asset correlation of the three FICO classes from the previous question using maximum-likelihood ASRF and a probit linear regression approach. Use data set mortgage.

REFERENCES

Basel Committee on Banking Supervision. 2006. "International Convergence of Capital Measurement and Capital Standards: A Revised Framework, Comprehensive Version."

Basel Committee on Banking Supervision. 2011. "Basel III: A Global Regulatory Framework for More Resilient Banks and Banking Systems."

Box, G. 2015. *Time Series Analysis: Forecasting and Control*. Hoboken, NJ: John Wiley & Sons.

Das, S., and G. Geng. 2003. "Simulating Correlated Default Processes Using Copulas: A Criterion-Based Approach." Working paper, Santa Clara University.

Düellmann, Klaus, Trapp, and Monika. 2004. "Systemic Risk in Recovery Rates—An Empirical Analysis of US Corporate Credit Exposures." Deutsche Bundesbank Discussion Paper, Series 2: Banking and Financial Supervision, No 02/2004.

European Union. 2013. "Regulation (EU) no 575/2013 of the European Parliament and of the Council of 26 June 2013."

Gordy, M. 2000. "A Comparative Anatomy of Credit Risk Models." *Journal of Banking and Finance* 24: 119–149.

Gordy, M. 2003. "A Risk-Factor Model Foundation for Ratings-Based Bank Capital Rules." *Journal of Financial Intermediation* 12: 199–232.

Gordy, M., and E. Heitfield. 2010. "Small-Sample Estimation of Models of Portfolio Credit Risk." In *Recent Advances in Financial Engineering: Proceedings of the KIER-TMU International Workshop on Financial Engineering 2009*, edited by Masaaki Kijima et al. Singapore: World Scientific Publishing.

Hamerle, A., and D. Rösch. 2005. "Misspecified Copulas in Credit Risk Models: How Good Is Gaussian?" *Journal of Risk* 8: 41–58.

Hamerle, A., and D. Rösch. 2006. "Parameterizing Credit Risk Models." *Journal of Credit Risk* 3: 101–122.

Koyluoglu, H. U., and A. Hickman. 1998. "A Generalized Framework for Credit Risk Portfolio Models." Manuscript, Oliver Wyman & Company.

Rösch, D. 2005. "An Empirical Comparison of Default Risk Forecasts from Alternative Credit Rating Philosophies." *International Journal of Forecasting* 25(1): 37–51.

Rösch, D., and H. Scheule. 2004. "Forecasting Retail Portfolio Credit Risk." *Journal of Risk Finance* 5(2): 16–32.

Rösch, D., and H. Scheule. 2013. "Forecasting Mortgage Securitization Risk under Systematic Risk and Parameter Uncertainty." *Journal of Risk and Insurance* 81(3): 563–586.

SAS Institute Inc. 2015. *SAS/IML 14.1 User's Guide: Technical Report.* Cary, NC: SAS Institute.

Schloegl, E., and D. O'Kane. 2005. "A Note on the Large Homogeneous Portfolio Approximation with the Student-t Copula." *Finance and Stochastics* 9: 577–584.

Vasicek, O. 1987. "Probability of Loss on Loan Portfolio." Working paper, KMV Corporation.

Vasicek, O. 1991. "Limiting Loan Loss Probability Distribution." Working paper, KMV Corporation.

CHAPTER **10**

Loss Given Default (LGD) and Recovery Rates

INTRODUCTION

This chapter introduces models for loss given default (LGD) and recovery estimation. It is important to note that a loss arises only in the event of default and is conditional on the default event; hence it is called loss *given* default. Exhibit 10.1 shows that loss is conditional on the default events and that the loss given default is a continuous variable with density f.

LGDs are commonly expressed as a ratio and related to the outstanding amount or exposure at default (EAD). In other words, LGD is essentially a loss *rate* given default. The recovery rate is then $1 - LGD$.

Definition of Default

In order to unambiguously quantify the loss given default, you first need to have a well-framed definition of default. For a thorough discussion, see Van Gestel and Baesens (2009). For non-retail exposures, rating agencies such as Moody's, Standard & Poor's (S&P), and Fitch use definitions of default that, although to a large extent overlapping, are not identical. Hence, if you use different definitions of default, then of course you cannot compare the resulting default and loss rates. More specifically, there is a direct interrelation between the default definition, the default rates, and the loss or LGD values. Hence, when LGD rates are reported, it is always important to ask for the default definition adopted, to make sure you can correctly interpret and benchmark them.

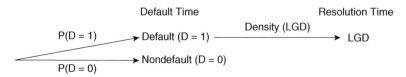

Exhibit 10.1 Conditionality of LGDs

Usually, a bank will distinguish among different types of defaults. An operational default is due to technical issues on the obligor side. For example, an obligor is accidentally late when making the payment. A technical default is a default due to an internal information system issue. For example, the payment was made on time, but on the wrong account. A real default is a default due to financial problems or insolvency. These are the defaults we are interested in when modeling LGD.

In case of default, various actions can take place. First, there can be a cure. This means a defaulter will pay back all outstanding debt and return to a performing or thus nondefaulter status with no accompanying loss. There could also be a restructuring or settlement, whereby the bank and the defaulter work out a recovery or repayment plan. The latter could, for example, result in an extension of the loan maturity to reduce the monthly installment amount. This usually comes with a medium loss. Finally, there could also be liquidation, repossession, or foreclosure, which implies that the bank takes full possession of the collateral asset, if available, and sells it by starting up a bankruptcy procedure. Depending upon the value of the collateral, this may come with a high loss.

When modeling LGD, it is of key importance that the default definition used is the same as for PD because PD and the LGD will be combined to calculate both expected and unexpected loss. Note that changing the default definition simultaneously impacts both the PD and the LGD. If you would, for example, relax the default definition from 90 days to 60 days in payment arrears, then the default rates and PD may increase, but the loss rates and LGD may decrease. Hence, the combined effect in terms of expected loss stays relatively constant.

Cures are those defaulters that become nondefaulters and return to performing by repaying all outstanding debt. The corresponding LGD will thus be zero, or close to zero. As already mentioned, note that this depends on the default definition. Relaxing the definition of a default, for example from 90 to 60 days, will typically increase the number of cures. In case of multiple defaults, you could opt to include only the last default event and also relate the PD and EAD to this.

Definition of LGD

The loss given default can now be defined as the ratio of the loss on an exposure due to the default of an obligor to the amount outstanding at default. As such, it is the complement of the recovery rate or, in other words, LGD equals 1 minus the recovery rate. Important to note here is that LGD focuses on economic loss, rather than accounting loss. Hence, all costs, but potentially also benefits, need to be properly taken into account when defining the LGD. Example costs are: the costs for realizing the collateral value, administrative costs incurred by sending collection letters or making telephone calls with the defaulted obligor, legal costs, and time delays in what is recovered. Also, benefits such as interest on arrears, penalties for delays, or other commissions can be considered.

LGD can be measured using various methods such as the workout method used for both corporate and retail exposures, the market approach used for corporate exposures, the implied historical LGD approach used for retail exposures, and the implied market approach used for corporate exposures. In what follows, we will discuss each of these in more detail.

The most popular method for defining LGD is the workout method, which is frequently adopted for both corporate and retail exposures. The idea here is to work out the collection process of a defaulted exposure and carefully inspect the incoming and outgoing cash flows. Both direct and indirect cash flows should be considered. Example indirect costs could be the operating costs of the workout department. These cash flows should then be discounted to the moment of default to calculate the loss. In Exhibit 10.2 you can see a simplified example.

Let us assume an exposure goes into default with an EAD of $100. Soon after default, the collection department will contact the defaulted obligor either by telephone or by sending a collection letter. Let us assume the cost for this equals $5. This is followed by the obligor paying back $20, which is clearly not enough to cover all outstanding debt. So, the collection department contacts the obligor again at a cost of $5. Let us say that the obligor does not react, so the bank decides to materialize the collateral and receives $70 for it. We can now discount all these cash flows back to the moment of default using a discount factor, which we leave unspecified for the moment. Let us say that the discounted amount equals $70. Note that this is smaller than the sum of the four numbers, which equals $80, because of the discounting that has been applied. In other words, this means that $70 has been recovered from the $100 EAD, hereby giving a recovery rate of 70 percent and an LGD of 30 percent.

Another way to measure the LGD is by using the market approach. The idea here is to look at firms that went bankrupt and have debt securities such as bonds or

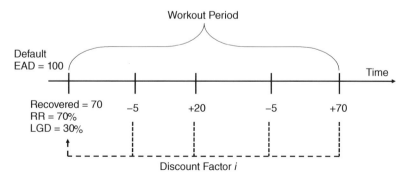

Exhibit 10.2 Workout LGDs

loans trading in the market. Once the bankruptcy event has occurred, the bonds will become junk bonds and investors will start trading them based on what they think they will recover from the bankrupt firm. To allow for some time for the market to stabilize and absorb all information, this approach looks at the market price (e.g., one month after the bankruptcy or default event). This market price is then used as a proxy for the recovery rate, which will then also allow a calculation of the LGD as 1 minus the recovery rate. Note that this approach works only for debt securities that trade in the market, and is thus not applicable for retail exposures. This approach was followed by Moody's in its LossCalc tool (see Gupton and Stein 2005). The implied historical LGD method works by using the PD estimates and the observed losses to derive the implied LGD. In other words, it calculates the expected loss first and then makes use of the expression $EL = PD \cdot LGD$. The LGD can then be computed as the expected loss divided by the PD.

Another way to measure the LGD is the implied market LGD approach. This is a very theoretical approach and we've rarely seen it used in the industry. It analyzes the market price of risky but not defaulted bonds using asset pricing models such as structural or reduced form models. It then finds the spread above the risk-free rate, which reflects the expected loss, and backs out the LGD from there. Some of the key concerns of this approach are that the market price is only partially determined by the credit risk and also includes risk aversion premiums.

Finally, according to the Basel Capital Accord, the definition of loss used in estimating LGD is economic loss. As already stated, this means that every cash flow or cost related to the default should be properly taken into account. In the foundation internal ratings based (IRB) approach, estimates of the LGD are prescribed in the Accord. For corporates, sovereigns, and banks, the following applies: Senior claims on corporates, sovereigns, and banks not secured by recognized collateral will be assigned a 45 percent LGD. All subordinated claims on corporates, sovereigns, and banks will be assigned a 75 percent LGD; see Basel Committee on Banking Supervision (2006).

Stage I: Computing Observed LGD

When computing observed LGDs from workout cash flow observations, various issues occur, such as:

- The data set should cover at least a complete business cycle.
- The workout or resolution period needs to be defined.
- Incomplete workouts need to be handled.
- The discount rate needs to be defined.
- LGDs outside the normal range should be handled.
- Indirect costs should be included.

In what follows, we will elaborate on each of these. Given all these ingredients, the LGD is then calculated as the exposure at default (EAD) minus the present value of

	Date of Default	Year 1	Year 2	Year 3
EAD	50,000			
Cash flows		20,000	10,000	10,000

Exhibit 10.3 Cash Flow Example

all cash flows, including internal costs:

$$LGD = \frac{EAD - \sum_{t=1}^{T}(CF_t/(1 + r_t)^t)}{EAD}$$

where CF_t is the cash flow and r_t is the discount rate for time t. As an example, consider an EAD of \$50,000 at time of default, and the stream of cash flows shown in Exhibit 10.3.

The LGD can then be computed once the workout process has finished (i.e., after year 3). If the bank uses a discount rate of, say, 5 percent per annum, the present value of recoveries at the date of default becomes $20,000/1.05 + 10,000/1.05^2 + 10,000/1.05^3 = 36,756$, and the LGD is $\frac{50,000-36,756}{50,000} = 26.5\%$.

Cash Flows

Recoveries

Cash recoveries refer to actual cash flows to be collected from defaulters during the workout period. Cash recoveries are easy to track since the details are typically recorded in one or more bank databases. Another form is noncash recoveries, including repossession of collateral or restructuring loans to support borrowers with their payments. Noncash recoveries are often treated case by case.

Recoveries can also be classified according to their source: product, collateral, guarantee, and residual (unsecured). Product recoveries relate to trade credit whereby the outstanding balance can be reduced if the underlying goods can be easily and quickly sold to buyers. Collateral recoveries include appraisal collateral values, carrying cost, and liquidation. Note that one collateral can be pledged for multiple facilities. In that case, collateral recovery should be reallocated specifically to each facility. Allocation approaches can be based on either pledge value or EAD of each facility. Guarantee recoveries involve a third party who is willing to pay (a part of) the outstanding balance owed in case of default. Note that guarantees can be either closely related or unrelated to the borrower. In case of a close relation (e.g., parent companies), guarantees may be treated as PD mitigants. Otherwise, if guarantees are unrelated to borrowers, they are considered LGD mitigants, meaning that they do not influence the default event, but provide support when default occurs. Unsecured recoveries include remaining parts of the assets that banks can claim after product, collateral, and guarantee recoveries.

Costs

We already mentioned that LGD represents economic loss. Hence, indirect costs should also be properly taken into account, as illustrated by the following quotes:
Committee of European Banking Supervisors (CEBS) (2005):

> Workout and collection costs should include the costs of running the institution's collection and workout department, the costs of outsourced services, and an appropriate percentage of other ongoing costs, such as corporate overhead.

Federal Register (2007):

> Cost data comprise the material direct and indirect costs associated with workouts and collections.

Federal Register (2007):

> Material indirect costs, costs of running the collection and workout department, costs of outsourced services, appropriate percentage of overhead, must be included.

The question now is how to take into account these indirect costs. Obviously, indirect costs are not tracked on a defaulter-by-defaulter basis; they need to be calculated on an aggregated level. Most banks conduct a small accounting exercise to calculate the indirect cost rate. In Exhibit 10.4 is an example.

Suppose we have four years of data, from 2010 to 2013. The second column represents the total exposure at default of files in workout measured at the end of the year. Note that because the workout period usually lasts longer than a year, most of these numbers include double counts. In other words, in the number 1,500 measured in 2011, there are some observations that were also already included in the 1,000 measured in 2010. The next column represents the amount recovered in each year. There are no double counts here. Finally, the last column represents the aggregated internal workout costs per year. This includes the costs of the workout department, the salaries of the people working in it, the electricity, the computer hardware and software, and so on.

Year	Total EAD of Files in Workout (End of Year)	Annual Recovered during Year	Internal Workout Costs per Year
2010	1,000	250	20
2011	1,500	500	28
2012	800	240	12
2013	1,250	350	27

Exhibit 10.4 Workout Costs

We can now calculate two cost rates. The first one uses the exposure at default as the denominator. The assumption here is that higher workout costs are incurred for higher exposures at default. The cost rate can now be calculated in a time-weighted or pooled way. The time-weighted cost rate is just the average for all years of the workout costs divided by the exposure at default. For our example, this becomes $1/4*(20/1{,}000 + 28/1{,}500 + 12/800 + 27/1{,}250)$ or 1.8 percent. The pooled cost rate divides the sum of all workout costs by the sum of all exposure values. In our case, this becomes $(20 + 28 + 12 + 27)/(1{,}000 + 1{,}500 + 800 + 1{,}250)$ or 1.91 percent. A disadvantage when using this cost rate is that it has to be multiplied by the number of years the workout lasted.

Another way of calculating the cost rate is by using the amount recovered as the denominator. The assumption here is that higher workout costs are incurred for higher recoveries. Again, the cost rate can be calculated in a time-weighted or pooled way. The time-weighted cost rate is the average for all years of the workout costs divided by the recovery amounts. For our example, this becomes $1/4*(20/250 + 28/500 + 12/240 + 27/350)$ or 6.5 percent. The pooled cost rate divides the sum of all workout costs by the sum of all recovered amounts. In our case, this becomes $(20 + 28 + 12 + 27)/(250 + 500 + 240 + 350)$ or 6.49 percent. The advantage of this approach is that it is independent of the length of the workout period because each amount was recovered during one year only. Hence, this is simpler to implement.

Discount Factor

We have already mentioned that LGD represents economic loss. Consequently, when quantifying the LGD, one should also take into account the time value of money. One dollar today is worth more than one dollar tomorrow. Hence, we should apply discounting. A key problem when applying discounting is setting the discount rate. The Basel Committee on Banking Supervision (2005a, 2005b) mandates that the discount rate includes the time value of money and a risk premium for undiversifiable risk:

> When recovery streams are uncertain and involve risk that cannot be diversified away, net present value calculations must reflect the time value of money and a risk premium appropriate to the undiversifiable risk. In establishing appropriate risk premiums for the estimation of LGDs consistent with economic downturn conditions, the bank should focus on the uncertainties in recovery cash flows associated with defaults that arise during the economic downturn conditions. When there is no uncertainty in recovery streams (e.g., recoveries derived from cash collateral), net present value calculations need only reflect the time value of money, and a risk free discount rate is appropriate.

A number of discount rate approaches have been proposed in the literature:

- Contract rate
- Weighted average cost of capital (WACC)
- Return on equity (ROE)

- ▨ Market return on defaulted bonds
- ▨ Equilibrium returns based on the capital asset pricing model (CAPM)

For a summary of some of these approaches, we refer to Maclachlan (2004) and Brady et al. (2006). Global Credit Data has recently undertaken a comparative study and found that the WACC and equilibrium approaches provide reasonable techniques to reflect the time value of money and systematic risk.

The contract rate is quite commonly used, although it has been criticized as it relates to the pricing at origination. Hence, it does not reflect the interest rate and price for systematic risk at the time of default and is not applicable to the distressed conditions to which recovery cash flows may be exposed.

Discount rates have recently been identified as a source of risk weight inconsistencies between financial institutions. This, and the fact that interest rates are at historic lows, means that some prudential regulators have considered imposing minimum floors. For example, the Prudential Regulation Authority of the United Kingdom stated the following (see Prudential Regulation Authority 2013):

> The PRA expects firms to ensure that no discount rate used to estimate LGD is less than 9%.

Whilst the controversy on discount rates continues, we see great merits in modeling risk-sensitive discount rates that are in line with the systematic risk that governs the realization of losses.

Workout Period

The length of the workout period can vary depending upon the type of credit, the workout policy of the financial institution, and the local regulation. Some regulators such as the Bank of International Settlements (BIS) and the Hong Kong Monetary Authority (HKMA) have provided further input on this. For example, the workout period can finish when the unrecovered value is less than 5 percent of the EAD, one year after default, at the time of repossession of the collateral, or at the time of selling off the debt to a collection agency. On average, many financial institutions have workout periods of two to three years. For a recent study and an international comparison on workout periods, see Betz, Kellner, and Rösch (2016).

Incomplete Workouts

We already briefly touched upon the issue of incomplete workouts. Incomplete workouts represent obligors that have gone into default status, and for which the workout process is still ongoing. Some regulatory authorities have provided further input about incomplete workouts. The Committee of European Banking Supervisors (CEBS), which is the predecessor of the European Banking Authority (EBA), initially mentioned in its regulation (see Committee of European Banking Supervisors (CEBS) 2005):

> Institutions should incorporate the results of incomplete workouts as data/information into their LGD estimates, unless they can demonstrate that the incomplete workouts are not relevant.

Part of this was copied by the Prudential Regulation Authority (PRA) of the United Kingdom as follows:

> In order to ensure that estimates of LGDs take into account the most up to date experience, we would expect firms to take account of data in respect of relevant incomplete workouts, i.e., defaulted exposures for which the recovery process is still in progress, with the result that the final realized losses in respect of those exposures are not yet certain.

See Prudential Regulation Authority (2013).

The most recent EU regulation does not mention anything further about incomplete workouts. Incomplete workouts can be treated in various ways. A first treatment option is to calculate the current LGD of an incomplete workout and use this as the final LGD value in the data set. This is a very conservative approach giving an upward bias to the LGDs. In other words, using this approach, the LGDs will be overestimated since additional future recoveries are likely. Note, however, that we have seen some banks systematically disregard recoveries after three or five years into their LGD calculations. Another option is to use expert or predictive models, which estimate the final LGD of an incomplete workout based on various characteristics such as date of default, percentage already collected, time of collection, and so on. The easiest method is simply to ignore incomplete workouts and include only complete workouts in the LGD modeling data set. This approach is quite commonly used in practice. Finally, you can also use survival analysis whereby the loss amount is considered as a censored variable. Note, however, that this is highly theoretical and not commonly applied in industry. For more information about this, we refer to the paper of Stoyanov (2009).

Business Cycle

The data set used for LGD modeling should cover at least a complete business cycle. The obvious question that follows is: What is a business cycle? Preferably, the data should include one or two downturn periods. This will be handy for the LGD calibration as we will discuss later. Note that you do not need to attach equal importance to each year of data. Hence, if you think data of five or seven years ago is less relevant today, you can attach a lower weight to it. Downturn periods are generally defined as periods with negative GDP growth. Hence the number of years of data required depends on the analyzed economy. For example, Japan has been in an extended economic downturn period since 1993 whereas Australia has not experienced an economic downturn since 1991.

LGDs Outside the Interval [0; 1]

Typically, any real-life LGD data set will contain negative LGDs and LGDs exceeding 100 percent. An obvious question is: Where do these extreme values come from and how should they be treated? A negative LGD is the same as a recovery rate exceeding 100 percent. There could be various reasons for this. One example is that the EAD was measured at the time of default, and the claim on the borrower increased after that because of fines or fees, and everything was recovered. In other words, the amount recovered was higher than the EAD, thereby giving a recovery rate of higher than 100 percent or a negative LGD. Another reason for a negative LGD could be a gain in collateral sales. Negative LGDs should be capped at zero. For example, the PRA expects firms to ensure that no LGD estimate is less than zero. Vice versa, LGDs exceeding 100 percent correspond to negative recovery rates. Also here, there could be various reasons for this, such as additional recovery costs were incurred and nothing was recovered. Alternatively, it could have been that additional drawings after default were considered as LGD, thereby seriously increasing the costs. Also here, it is recommended to cap such LGDs at 100 percent. The models that we will present later in this chapter provide ways of dealing with this sort of truncation and censoring.

Stage II: LGD Modeling

In a second stage, after the observed LGDs have been computed, a bank is generally interested in modeling the determinants of LGD (such as values of collaterals) and provide LGD forecasts *before* a default has happened, but also *after* a default. The remainder of this chapter details several variants of regression-type models that can be applied by a bank for modeling and forecasting LGD. The data set we use originates from a European bank and contains workout LGDs from mortgage loans that have been accordingly anonymized and preprocessed. The models can, however, also be applied to other LGD definitions, such as market LGDs.

Throughout the text we define LGD as a fraction and the recovery rate as (1 − LGD). Similar to PD models, the range of values for LGD requires specific models and considerations. First, LGD usually ranges between zero and one [0; 1], and values below zero or greater than one only rarely occur (or do not occur at all; see previous discussion). Second, special cases are values of exactly zero or exactly one, which indicate a zero loss or a total loss, respectively. A zero loss can occur when a default is fully cured. Third, LGDs by definition are conditional quantities and can be observed only if a default has happened. This imposes a sample selection problem when defaults and LGDs are dependent, which should be accounted for in order to avoid inconsistent parameter estimates.

Based on these considerations, this chapter starts with descriptive LGD statistics and some transformations thereof, which will be used in the empirical models. Next, marginal or stand-alone models for LGD are presented that are widely used in practice and research but do not account for the sample selection issue and LGD-PD dependence. Subsequently, the class of joint PD-LGD models that account for selection and censoring is illustrated, and differences between both are discussed. Finally, the chapter concludes with an outlook on advanced models that extend the models along several lines (e.g., random effects, downturn LGDs, and higher-order dependencies between defaults and LGDs). Exhibit 10.5 shows the different model classes.

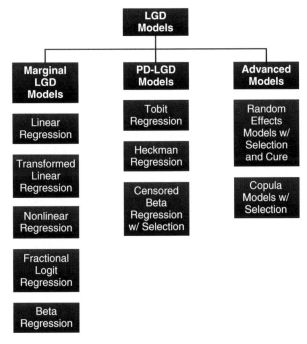

Exhibit 10.5 LGD Models in This Chapter

MARGINAL LGD MODELS

Standard models use data on LGDs for defaulted obligors only and do not consider those cases in which no default happened or treat cases with full recoveries in a special way; see Loterman et al. (2012). While this seems to be obvious at first sight and explains why these models are widely used in practice, as we will show later on this might impose inconsistency on the parameter estimates. Sometimes it is also the only way to develop models, as only LGD information is available and not information from nondefaulters. The simplest model uses LGDs as is and puts them into a linear regression. In addition, other standard models explicitly account in various ways for the fact that most LGDs are observed in the interval [0, 1] only.

Descriptive Statistics

The data was preprocessed in such a way that only values in the interval [0, 1] occur. Then, in order to show how models using transformed LGDs work, values of zero are set to 0.00001, and values of 1 are set to 0.99999. In practical applications one should carefully check all entries and should justify and report how they are treated. Given an LGD_i for each observation $i, i = 1,...,n$, we compute the three transformations:

$$y_i^{logistic} = \ln \frac{LGD_i}{1 - LGD_i}$$

$$y_i^{probit} = \Phi^{-1}(LGD_i)$$

$$lnrr_i = \ln(1 - LGD_i)$$

which will be used as dependent variables in the upcoming regressions.

The database has 2,545 entries for LGD. Besides LGD (labeled lgdtime), it has information about loan-to-value ratios (LTVs) and a dummy variable "purpose1," which is one if the purpose of the mortgage is to buy a house for investment purposes (rental) and zero otherwise. The following tables and figures (Exhibits 10.6 through 10.15) show the distributions for the LGDs, for their transformed values, and

The UNIVARIATE Procedure
Variable: lgd_time

Moments			
N	2545	Sum Weights	2545
Mean	0.22813007	Sum Observations	580.591017
Std Deviation	0.32910883	Variance	0.10831262
Skewness	1.30970595	Kurtosis	0.27943143
Uncorrected SS	407.99758	Corrected SS	275.547313
Coeff Variation	144.263682	Std Error Mean	0.00652372

Quantiles (Definition 5)	
Level	Quantile
100% Max	0.9999900
99%	0.9999900
95%	0.9999900
90%	0.8744005
75% Q3	0.3978541
50% Median	0.0320655
25% Q1	0.0000100
10%	0.0000100
5%	0.0000100
1%	0.0000100
0% Min	0.0000100

Exhibit 10.6 Descriptive Statistics

for LTVs. The LGD distribution is highly skewed with obvious clusters at the border values of 0.00001 and 0.99999.

We compute descriptive statistics and histograms for the LGDs and the three r=transformations using PROC UNIVARIATE:

```
ODS GRAPHICS ON;
PROC UNIVARIATE DATA = data.lgd;
VAR  lgd_time;
HISTOGRAM;
RUN;
ODS GRAPHICS OFF;
```

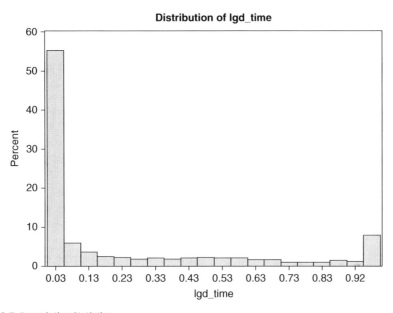

Exhibit 10.7 Descriptive Statistics

The UNIVARIATE Procedure
Variable: y_logistic

Moments			
N	2545	**Sum Weights**	2545
Mean	−3.9413426	**Sum Observations**	−10030.717
Std Deviation	6.07327988	**Variance**	36.8847286
Skewness	0.53155822	**Kurtosis**	0.2357088
Uncorrected SS	133369.241	**Corrected SS**	93834.7495
Coeff Variation	−154.09165	**Std Error Mean**	0.12038695

Exhibit 10.8 Descriptive Statistics

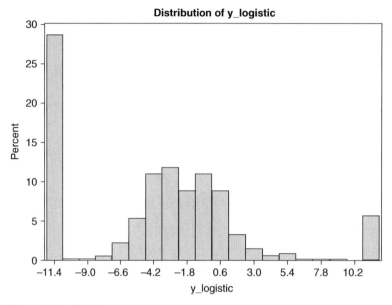

Exhibit 10.9 Descriptive Statistics

The UNIVARIATE Procedure

Variable: Y_probit

Moments			
N	2545	**Sum Weights**	2545
Mean	−1.6508126	**Sum Observations**	−4201.3182
Std Deviation	2.30412171	**Variance**	5.30897684
Skewness	0.79450046	**Kurtosis**	0.2987506
Uncorrected SS	20441.6263	**Corrected SS**	13506.0371
Coeff Variation	−139.575	**Std Error Mean**	0.04567321

Exhibit 10.10 Descriptive Statistics

Almost 30 percent of the data have an LGD at the border value. The average LGD is around 23 percent if these values are considered. The transformed variables exhibit similar clusters at the extremes:

```
ODS GRAPHICS ON;
PROC UNIVARIATE DATA = data.lgd;
VAR  y_logistic;
HISTOGRAM;
RUN;
ODS GRAPHICS OFF;
```

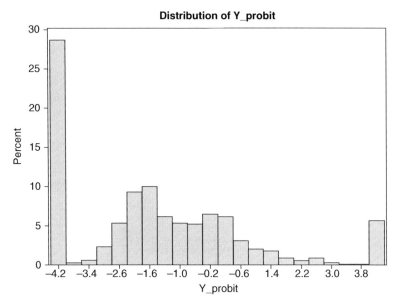

Exhibit 10.11 Descriptive Statistics

```
ODS GRAPHICS ON;
PROC UNIVARIATE DATA = data.lgd;
VAR  y_probit;
HISTOGRAM;
RUN;
ODS GRAPHICS OFF;

ODS GRAPHICS ON;
PROC UNIVARIATE DATA = data.lgd;
VAR  lnrr;
HISTOGRAM;
RUN;
ODS GRAPHICS OFF;
```

A key variable in our regression models is the loan-to-value ratio (LTV). We compute descriptive statistics for the LTV ratio and find that LTVs are more evenly distributed between almost zero and about 2 with a mean of 65 percent and only a smaller amount with ratios of more than 100 percent.

```
ODS GRAPHICS ON;
PROC UNIVARIATE DATA = data.lgd;
VAR  LTV;
HISTOGRAM;
RUN;
ODS GRAPHICS OFF;
```

The UNIVARIATE Procedure

Variable: lnrr

Moments			
N	2545	**Sum Weights**	2545
Mean	−0.9966471	**Sum Observations**	−2536.467
Std Deviation	2.69995967	**Variance**	7.28978221
Skewness	−3.3741473	**Kurtosis**	10.1240079
Uncorrected SS	21073.1685	**Corrected SS**	18545.2059
Coeff Variation	−270.90427	**Std Error Mean**	0.05351966

Exhibit 10.12 Descriptive Statistics

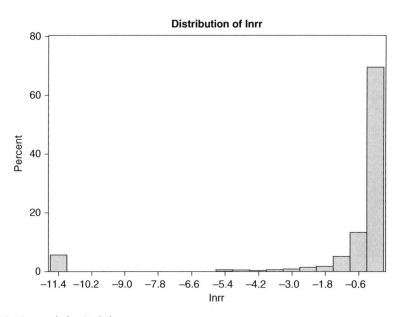

Exhibit 10.13 Descriptive Statistics

Linear Regression

The first standard model is the linear ordinary least squares (OLS) regression model, which is of the form

$$LGD_i = \boldsymbol{\beta}'\boldsymbol{x}_i + \epsilon_i \qquad i = 1, \dots, N \qquad (10.1)$$

where $\epsilon_i \sim N(0, \sigma^2)$, $\boldsymbol{x}_i$ is a vector of explanatory variables and $\boldsymbol{\beta}$ is a vector of unknown parameters to be estimated. We dropped the subscript "t" here, as there is no information about time in the data set. Thus, observations are treated on a

The UNIVARIATE Procedure
Variable: LTV

Moments			
N	2545	**Sum Weights**	2545
Mean	0.67655572	**Sum Observations**	1721.8343
Std Deviation	0.36412689	**Variance**	0.13258839
Skewness	0.47626178	**Kurtosis**	0.16150565
Uncorrected SS	1502.22171	**Corrected SS**	337.304876
Coeff Variation	53.820681	**Std Error Mean**	0.00721787

Quantiles (Definition 5)	
Level	**Quantile**
100% Max	1.98406494
99%	1.71272612
95%	1.29238796
90%	1.13542559
75% Q3	0.92354844
50% Median	0.65941731
25% Q1	0.39918053
10%	0.20919624
5%	0.12579613
1%	0.03580482
0% Min	0.00135864

Exhibit 10.14 Descriptive Statistics

cross-sectional basis. If time stamps are available, one can easily extend our models to time-varying covariates, such as macroeconomic variables.

We use PROC REG to estimate this linear regression model based on LTV and the dummy variable for renting purpose. As explained before, we set LGD values of zero to 0.00001 and values of one to 0.99999. Thus, the dependent variable has only values in [0, 1]. This allows transformations in the models that we show later. However, values ≤ 0 or ≥ 1 are sometimes also included in practical applications of the linear model.

```
ODS GRAPHICS ON;
PROC REG DATA=data.lgd
PLOTS(STATS= ALL)= DIAGNOSTICS;
```

```
MODEL lgd_time = LTV purpose1;
RUN;
ODS GRAPHICS OFF;
```

The R^2 and the fit diagnostics that are default output in PROC REG show the model fit. The explained variation (adjusted R^2) is about 19 percent for the model which uses two explanatory variables only (see Exhibits 10.16 and 10.17).

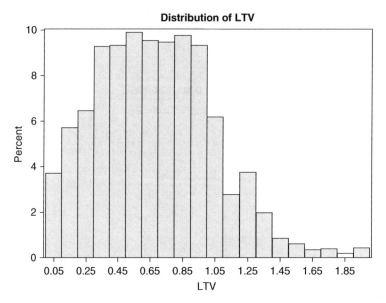

Exhibit 10.15 Descriptive Statistics

Parameter Estimates					
Variable	DF	Parameter Estimate	Standard Error	t Value	Pr > |t|
Intercept	1	−0.03786	0.01241	−3.05	0.0023
LTV	1	0.37761	0.01613	23.41	<.0001
purpose1	1	0.14470	0.02262	6.40	<.0001
Parameter Estimates					
Variable	DF	Parameter Estimate	Standard Error	t Value	Pr > |t|
Intercept	1	−0.03786	0.01241	−3.05	0.0023
LTV	1	0.37761	0.01613	23.41	<.0001
purpose1	1	0.14470	0.02262	6.40	<.0001

Exhibit 10.16 Linear Regression

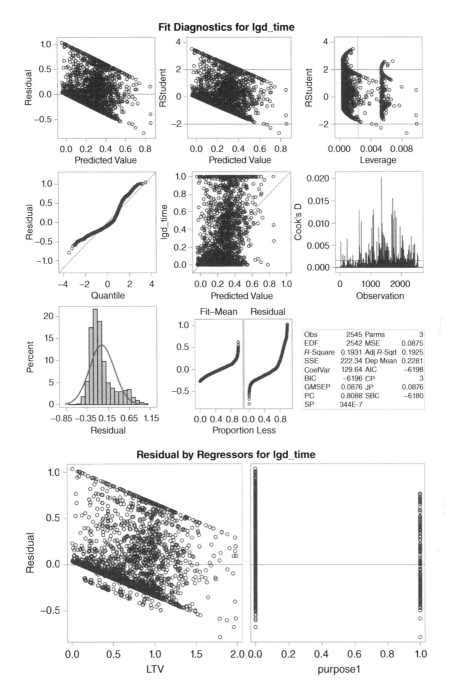

Exhibit 10.17 Linear Regression

The SAS output shows that the coefficients for LTV and for renting are positive and statistically different from zero. In other words, higher LTVs go with higher LGDs, and lower LTVs with lower LGDs, which is in line with economic intuition. An increase of LTV by 1 percentage point increases the LGD by about 0.38 percentage points. Buying a house for renting purposes increases LGDs by about 14 percent.

The plot of realized LGDs versus predicted LGDs shows a rather weak relationship. The model seems to fit the mean well but the idiosyncratic variation around the LGD, which is not explained by the model, is still somewhat huge, which can also be seen by the quantile plot. Moreover, one sees clusters for the borderline values at 0.00001 and 0.99999 and the respective residuals. While $R^2 = 0.19$ is not too bad for two explanatory variables only, the unexplained variation of 81 percent seems to be a widespread issue in practical applications, and a major challenge is to find the proper covariates that are able to explain a higher proportion of the variation. If you have a higher number of potential explanatory covariates available, you can make use of variable selection algorithms that are implemented in SAS PROC REG, such as a forward, backward, or stepwise selection, as discussed in the credit scoring chapter.

Transformed Linear Regression

A shortcoming of the linear regression model is the assumption of normally distributed residuals, because LGDs are usually between zero and one and are thus obviously not normal by definition. This shortcoming may be addressed by using a transformation of the LGD that computes values falling into the interval $(-\infty, +\infty)$, and applying a linear regression on the transformed values. Two frequently used transformations are the logistic $\ln \frac{LGD_i}{1-LGD_i}$, and the inverse normal (probit) transformation $\Phi^{-1}(LGD_i)$. The models look as follows:

$$\ln \frac{LGD_i}{1 - LGD_i} = \boldsymbol{\beta}' \boldsymbol{x}_i + \epsilon_i \qquad (10.2)$$

where $\epsilon_i \sim N(0, \sigma^2)$, and

$$\Phi^{-1}(LGD_i) = \boldsymbol{\beta}' \boldsymbol{x}_i + \epsilon_i$$

where $\epsilon_i \sim N(0, \sigma^2)$.

The regression codes using PROC REG and outputs (Exhibits 10.18 and 10.19) for the logistic-linear regression are:

```
ODS GRAPHICS ON;
PROC REG DATA=data.lgd
PLOTS( STATS= ALL)= DIAGNOSTICS;
MODEL y_logistic = LTV purpose1;
RUN;
ODS GRAPHICS OFF;
```

Both model results are basically similar to the linear regression in terms of economic and statistical significance of the parameter estimates and the model fit,

The REG Procedure
Model: MODEL1
Dependent Variable: y_logistic

Root MSE	5.49647	**R-Squared**	0.1816
Dependent Mean	−3.94134	**Adj R-Sq**	0.1809
Coeff Var	−139.45677		

Parameter Estimates					
Variable	**DF**	**Parameter Estimate**	**Standard Error**	**t Value**	**Pr > |t|**
Intercept	1	−8.68987	0.23070	−37.67	<.0001
LTV	1	6.72675	0.29978	22.44	<.0001
purpose1	1	2.71708	0.42035	6.46	<.0001

Exhibit 10.18 Logistic-Linear Regression

although particularly the probit transformation seems to capture the distribution characteristics of the residuals somewhat better. The reason is that the linear model assumes a normal distribution whereas the other models assume transformed normal distributions, which can sometimes be more appropriate for modeling the tails of a distribution. Both values for R^2 are basically similar to those of the linear regression model.

The regression codes using PROC REG and outputs (Exhibits 10.20 and 10.21) for the probit-linear regression are:

```
ODS GRAPHICS ON;
PROC REG DATA=data.lgd
PLOTS(STATS= ALL)= DIAGNOSTICS;
MODEL y_probit = LTV purpose1;
RUN;
ODS GRAPHICS OFF;
```

Nonlinear Regression

An alternative approach is to apply a nonlinear regression, which transforms the linear predictor of the explanatory variables rather than the left-hand side of the regression equation. An example model equation is:

$$LGD_i = \frac{1}{1 + \exp(-\boldsymbol{\beta}' \boldsymbol{x}_i)} + \epsilon_i \tag{10.3}$$

where a logit transformation for the predictor is used and $\epsilon_i \sim N(0, \sigma^2)$. Alternatively, another transformation, such as probit, could be used.

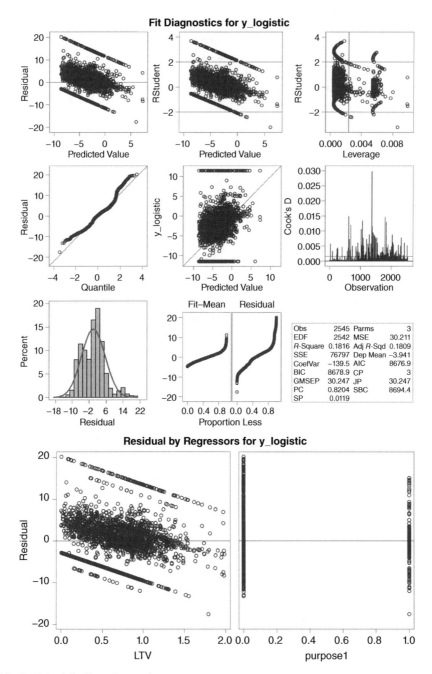

Exhibit 10.19 Logistic-Linear Regression

The REG Procedure
Model: MODEL1
Dependent Variable: Y_probit

Root MSE	2.06570	*R*-Squared	0.1969
Dependent Mean	−1.65081	Adj *R*-Sq	0.1962
Coeff Var	−125.13233		

Parameter Estimates					
Variable	DF	Parameter Estimate	Standard Error	*t* Value	Pr > |t|
Intercept	1	−3.52776	0.08670	−40.69	<.0001
LTV	1	2.66018	0.11266	23.61	<.0001
purpose1	1	1.06188	0.15798	6.72	<.0001

Exhibit 10.20 Probit-Linear Regression

The model can easily be estimated by maximum likelihood using PROC NLMIXED, as shown in the following code. The parameter estimates of the model exhibit similar economical and statistical significance as in the former models, although they now enter the model in a nonlinear way. The parameter σ denotes the (remaining) volatility of the residuals after controlling for the covariates.

PROC NLMIXED has a different structure to PROC REG as it supports programming statements (between the PARMS and the MODEL statements in the following code) that allow for a more complex specification of the likelihood via the MODEL statement. The linear predictor is coded by the statement "xb = b0 + b1 * LTV + b2 * purpose1." PROC NLMIXED estimates the parameters via the maximization of the likelihood. Furthermore, starting values for the parameters b0, b1, and b2 can be specified using the PARMS statement. (See Exhibit 10.22.) In the PROC NLMIXED line, one can include an option 'TECH=' which chooses the optimization algorithm. SAS offers several techniques here, and we choose trust region optimization as an example. Details can be found in the SAS manual; see SAS Institute Inc. (2015). The interested reader is encouraged to run the programs in this section using other techniques in order to check if and/or how they may affect the results.

```
ODS GRAPHICS ON;
PROC NLMIXED DATA = data.lgd TECH = TRUREG;
PARMS b0 = 0 b1 = 0 b2 = 0 sigma=1;
xb = b0 + b1 * LTV + b2 * purpose1 ;
mu = 1 / (1 + EXP(- xb));
lh = PDF('NORMAL', lgd_time, mu, sigma);
ll = LOG(lh);
RUN;
ODS GRAPHICS OFF;
```

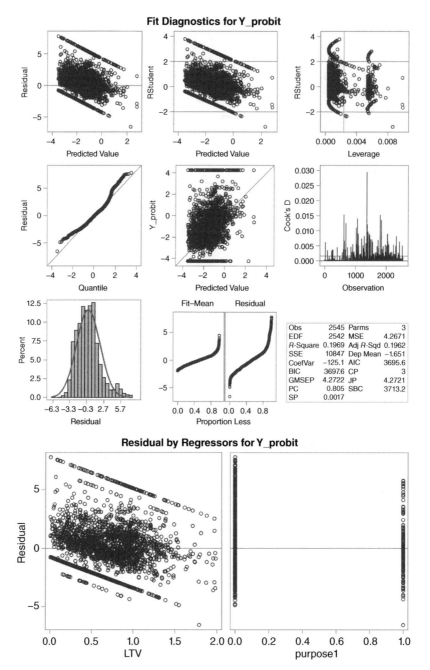

Exhibit 10.21 Probit-Linear Regression

The NLMIXED Procedure

Specifications	
Data Set	DATA.LGD
Dependent Variable	lgd_time
Distribution for Dependent Variable	General
Optimization Technique	Trust Region
Integration Method	None

Dimensions	
Observations Used	2545
Observations Not Used	0
Total Observations	2545
Parameters	4

Fit Statistics	
-2 Log-Likelihood	977.8
AIC (smaller is better)	985.8
AICC (smaller is better)	985.8
BIC (smaller is better)	1009.2

Parameter Estimates								
Parameter	Estimate	Standard Error	DF	t Value	Pr > |t|	95% Confidence Limits		Gradient
b0	−3.0603	0.1143	2545	−26.77	<.0001	−3.2844	−2.8361	6.568E−8
b1	2.3728	0.1204	2545	19.70	<.0001	2.1366	2.6090	3.82E−8
b2	0.7958	0.1122	2545	7.09	<.0001	0.5758	1.0159	4.022E−9
Sigma	0.2932	0.004110	2545	71.34	<.0001	0.2852	0.3013	2.127E−7

Exhibit 10.22 Nonlinear Regression

Fractional Logit Regression

The former models required specific assumptions for the residuals. A distribution-free alternative that uses quasi maximum likelihood is the fractional logit model. It requires only that the conditional mean $E(LGD_i|x_i)$ is correctly specified.

Given an assumption for the conditional mean, for example $E(LGD_i|x_i) = \frac{1}{1+\exp(-\beta'x_i)}$, the Bernoulli likelihood becomes:

$$L = \left(\frac{1}{1+\exp(-\beta'x_i)}\right)^{LGD_i} \left(1 - \frac{1}{1+\exp(-\beta'x_i)}\right)^{1-LGD_i}$$

Alternatively, another transformation, such as probit, could be used. This is similar to binary logistic regression, as we discussed earlier. The code and the output (Exhibit 10.23) are shown next. Because the model does not assume a distribution for the residuals, only the parameters for the regression equation need to be estimated. The outcomes are similar to those of the nonlinear regression model.

```
ODS GRAPHICS ON;
PROC NLMIXED DATA = data.lgd TECH = TRUREG;
PARMS b0 = 0 b1 = 0 b2 = 0 ;
xb = b0 + b1 * LTV + b2 *purpose1 ;
mu = 1 / (1 + exp(- xb));
lh = (mu ** lgd_time) * ((1 - mu) ** (1 - lgd_time));
ll = LOG(lh);
MODEL lgd_time ~ GENERAL(ll);
RUN;
ODS GRAPHICS OFF;
```

Beta Regression

The final standard model is the beta regression model. It is related to the beta distribution that is frequently used for modeling proportions and can deal with a variety of shapes. The beta distribution for the LGD has two parameters α and β and has the form:

$$f(lgd) = \frac{1}{B(\alpha,\beta)} lgd^{\alpha-1}(1-lgd)^{\beta-1}$$

where $B(\alpha,\beta)$ is the beta function

$$B(\alpha,\beta) = \int_0^1 lgd^{\alpha-1}(1-lgd)^{\beta-1} \, dlgd \quad \alpha,\beta > 0$$

The beta function is related to the gamma function by

$$B(\alpha,\beta) = \frac{\Gamma(\alpha)\Gamma(\beta)}{\Gamma(\alpha+\beta)}$$

We apply this relationship in the programming statements of PROC NLMIXED.

For the beta regression, both parameters are transformed into a location (mean) parameter μ and a shape parameter δ such that $\alpha = \mu * \delta$ and $\beta = (1 - \mu)\delta$, and the variance is obtained as $\sigma^2 = \frac{\mu(1-\mu)}{1+\delta}$.

The NLMIXED Procedure

Specifications	
Data Set	DATA.LGD
Dependent Variable	lgd_time
Distribution for Dependent Variable	General
Optimization Technique	Trust Region
Integration Method	None

Dimensions	
Observations Used	2545
Observations Not Used	0
Total Observations	2545
Parameters	3

Fit Statistics	
-2 Log-Likelihood	2430.4
AIC (smaller is better)	2436.4
AICC (smaller is better)	2436.4
BIC (smaller is better)	2453.9

Parameter Estimates								
Parameter	Estimate	Standard Error	DF	t Value	Pr > |t|	95% Confidence Limits		Gradient
b0	−2.9876	0.1307	2545	−22.86	<.0001	−3.2439	−2.7314	2.961E−9
b1	2.2713	0.1479	2545	15.35	<.0001	1.9812	2.5614	1.413E−9
b2	0.7879	0.1709	2545	4.61	<.0001	0.4528	1.1231	1.42E−10

Exhibit 10.23 Fractional Logit Regression

A regression model is then applied to the location and the shape parameter where usually the mean is transformed to stay in the interval $(0, 1)$ as in the former models, that is $\mu = \frac{1}{1+\exp(-\beta' x_i)}$, and the location parameter is transformed by the log function to ensure that it is strictly positive; that is, $\delta = \exp\{\beta'_\delta x_i\}$ where β_δ is a vector of parameters.

Generally, the parameters can be estimated using the method of moments (MM) or maximum likelihood (ML). The likelihood is given via the previous density. The following code shows the ML estimation using PROC NLMIXED and the resulting output (Exhibit 10.24). Note that we used the same set of covariates for both parameters (location and shape), resulting in six parameters (including two constants). We leave it up to the reader to estimate other models by applying different sets of covariates for each. In our case, the economic and statistical significance of the parameters for the mean are similar to the former models with the prime distinction that we are now able to explicitly model the dispersion parameter as a function of explanatory variables. For more information about beta regression in general, we refer to Ferrari and Cribari-Neto (2004).

```
ODS GRAPHICS ON;
PROC NLMIXED DATA=data.lgd TECH =TRUREG;
PARMS   b0 = 0 b1 = 0.001 b2 = 0.0001
c0 = 0 c1 = 0.001 c2 = 0.0001 ;

*Linear predictors;
Xb = b0 + b1 * LTV + b2 * purpose1 ;
Wc = c0 + c1 * LTV + c2 * purpose1 ;
mu = 1 / (1 + exp(-xb));
delta = EXP(Wc);

*transform to standard parameterization;
alpha = mu * delta;
beta = (1-mu) * delta;

*log-likelihood;
lh =  (GAMMA(alpha + beta) / (GAMMA(alpha) * GAMMA(beta))
    * (lgd_time ** (alpha - 1)) * ((1 - lgd_time) ** (beta - 1)));
ll = LOG(lh);

MODEL lgd_time ~ GENERAL(ll);
PREDICT mu OUT = out_mu;
PREDICT delta OUT = out_delta;
RUN;
ODS GRAPHICS OFF;
```

In order to check the predictions of the beta regression, you can use the predicted values for μ and produce a real-fit plot using PROC GPLOT of the realized LGDs versus the predicted values as done in Exhibit 10.25. Note that the same analysis may be performed for the nonlinear and the fractional logit regression. We limit our demonstration to beta regressions as they are more popular in practice.

The NLMIXED Procedure

Specifications	
Data Set	DATA.LGD
Dependent Variable	lgd_time
Distribution for Dependent Variable	General
Optimization Technique	Trust Region
Integration Method	None

Dimensions	
Observations Used	2545
Observations Not Used	0
Total Observations	2545
Parameters	6

Fit Statistics	
-2 Log-Likelihood	−13925
AIC (smaller is better)	−13913
AICC (smaller is better)	−13913
BIC (smaller is better)	−13878

Parameter Estimates								
Parameter	Estimate	Standard Error	DF	t Value	Pr > $|t|$	95% Confidence Limits		Gradient
b0	−1.9795	0.06634	2545	−29.84	<.0001	−2.1096	−1.8495	2.068E−7
b1	1.4917	0.07815	2545	19.09	<.0001	1.3385	1.6449	6.229E−8
b2	0.6131	0.1024	2545	5.99	<.0001	0.4123	0.8140	7.996E−9
c0	−0.2792	0.05874	2545	−4.75	<.0001	−0.3943	−0.1640	2.906E−7
c1	−0.2827	0.06714	2545	−4.21	<.0001	−0.4144	−0.1511	9.437E−8
c2	−0.1048	0.08190	2545	−1.28	0.2009	−0.2654	0.05583	2.321E−8

Exhibit 10.24 Beta Regression

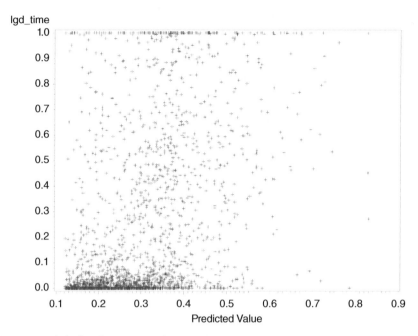

Exhibit 10.25 Real-Fit Plot of Beta Regression

Moreover, one can run a linear regression using PROC REG of realizations against predictions and compute the R^2. As shown in the output (Exhibit 10.26), the R^2 is around 20 percent, which is slightly better than the former regressions, but remember that the predictions are predictions of the mean values only and the standard deviations are modeled individually using covariates. Therefore, the realizations might be far off from the predicted means if the standard deviations are high (and the R^2 low). Modeling the individual standard deviation, however, is one advantage of

Root MSE	0.29402	*R*-Squared	0.2022
Dependent Mean	0.22813	Adj *R*-Sq	0.2019
Coeff Var	128.88377		

Parameter Estimates						
Variable	Label	DF	Parameter Estimate	Standard Error	*t* Value	Pr > |t|
Intercept	Intercept	1	−0.14287	0.01573	−9.08	<.0001
Pred	Predicted Value	1	1.25370	0.04939	25.38	<.0001

Exhibit 10.26 Real-Fit Regression of Beta Regression

the beta regression, besides modeling a more realistic distribution within $(0, 1)$ than the normal distribution. The regression also reveals that the intercept is statistically different from zero and the slope is statistically different from one (given that the value of one is more than two standard deviations away from the estimate).

```
ODS GRAPHICS ON;
PROC GPLOT DATA=out_mu;
PLOT lgd_time * PRED;
RUN;
PROC REG DATA = out_mu;
MODEL lgd_time = PRED;
RUN;
ODS GRAPHICS OFF;
```

PD-LGD MODELS

The former models use all LGDs that are observable in the sample and treat them in the same way. While widespread in academia and in practice, they exhibit the shortcoming of sample selection. Simply speaking, sample selection arises whenever an observable sample that is used for an analysis such as a regression model is the result of a selection mechanism that is not purely random and that is correlated with the variable of interest. In our data set, we have many cases where the recovery is (close to) one, which means that there is no economic loss for the bank. This could be because no default has happened or because the default has been cured. Both events create a selection mechanism for the recoveries or LGDs, and if there is some dependence between the event and the loss, the selection mechanism is not purely random. As a result from standard theory, estimators that ignore this kind of sample selection are inconsistent. In our data, all cures (i.e., observations with recoveries greater than 0.99999) and nondefaults are flagged by an event variable that is equal to zero (no default) and one otherwise (default).

Tobit Regression

A first model considered is the classic Tobit model; see Tobin (1958). It can be motivated using a classic Merton-type credit model (see Merton, 1974) as derived by Rösch and Scheule (2012). The model generally takes the form

$$\ln\ RR_i = \min\{Y_i^*, 0\} \tag{10.4}$$

where $RR_i = (1 - LGD_i)$ is the recovery rate and Y_i^* is a latent variable generated from the classic regression model

$$Y_i^* = \boldsymbol{\beta}'\boldsymbol{x}_i + \epsilon_i \tag{10.5}$$

The log transformation of the recovery rate is due to the analogy with the Merton model as shown in Rösch and Scheule (2012). Its descriptive statistics were computed and shown earlier in this chapter. In empirical applications, however, other transformations might also be used. Here, for easier comparison with the other approaches, we do not use any transformation at all; that is, we simply use LGD as the dependent variable 10. The lower bound is then censored to be 0.00001 and the equation becomes

$$LGD_i = \max\{0.00001, Y_i^*\}$$

The model acknowledges that recoveries (or LGDs, respectively) can only be observed if the underlying latent default-triggering variable crosses the threshold. The likelihood takes into account that observed values of the dependent variable are conditionally normally distributed and values on the boundary are censored values from the conditional normal distribution. In other words, in the histogram we saw earlier, the ln RR_i can be interpreted as the left tail of a normal distribution; see Rösch and Scheule (2012). The model can be evaluated with PROC NLMIXED and PROC QLIM, and we show that both alternatives obviously yield the same result. (See Exhibit 10.27.)

An example for a Tobit model using PROC NLMIXED is:

```
PROC NLMIXED DATA = data.lgd TECH = TRUREG;
PARMS b0 = 0 b1 = 0 b2 = 0  sigma = 1;
xb = b0 + b1 * LTV + b2 * purpose1;
IF event  = 1 THEN lh = pdf('NORMAL', lgd_time, xb, sigma);
ELSE IF event = 0 THEN lh = CDF ('NORMAL', 0, xb, sigma);
ll = LOG(lh);
MODEL lgd_time ~ GENERAL(ll);
RUN;
```

As previously, we include LTV and rental purpose as explanatory variables. Since we model the LGD as dependent variable, both coefficients have positive signs and are highly significant. While the results are economically similar to the results from the standard nonselection models, there can, however, arise situations where the significance of the coefficients is different and variables that are not significant in standard models might become significant if the selection mechanism is taken into account.

An example for a Tobit model using PROC QLIM is (see Exhibits 10.28 and 10.29):

```
PROC QLIM DATA=data.lgd  PLOTS=ALL ;
MODEL lgd_time =  LTV  purpose1;
ENDOGENOUS  lgd_time ~ CENSORED(LB=0.00001);
OUTPUT OUT = tobit1_out EXPECTED CONDITIONAL PROB RESIDUAL XBETA;
RUN;
```

The figures from PROC QLIM show the marginal profile likelihood functions, that is the likelihood values around the optimum, the marginal effects of the explanatory variables on the dependent variable, and the fitted expected recovery by regressor. The expression is given in Rösch and Scheule (2012) for the transformed model.

The NLMIXED Procedure

Specifications	
Data Set	DATA.LGD
Dependent Variable	lgd_time
Distribution for Dependent Variable	General
Optimization Technique	Trust Region
Integration Method	None

Dimensions	
Observations Used	2545
Observations Not Used	0
Total Observations	2545
Parameters	4

Fit Statistics	
-2 Log-Likelihood	2644.5
AIC (smaller is better)	2652.5
AICC (smaller is better)	2652.6
BIC (smaller is better)	2675.9

Parameter Estimates								
Parameter	Estimate	Standard Error	DF	t Value	Pr > |t|	95% Confidence Limits		Gradient
b0	−0.2134	0.01726	2545	−12.36	<.0001	−0.2473	−0.1796	4.605E−8
b1	0.5118	0.02148	2545	23.83	<.0001	0.4697	0.5539	3.071E−8
b2	0.1896	0.02898	2545	6.54	<.0001	0.1328	0.2465	2.69E−9
Sigma	0.3716	0.006400	2545	58.07	<.0001	0.3591	0.3842	2.318E−7

Exhibit 10.27 Tobit Regression with NL Mixed

For this model, it is also possible to provide a real-fit check and an R^2, similarly as in the case of the beta regression. (See Exhibits 10.30 and 10.31.) In PROC QLIM, one can compute the expected LGDs or the conditional expected LGDs, conditional on default. Both are computed in the program by the OUTPUT statement, and the latter are plotted against the realized values and used for computation of the R^2, which is almost 20 percent. When looking at the scatter plot, again remember that the predictions are for expected values, and the still rather low R^2 and the high estimate

The QLIM Procedure

Summary Statistics of Continuous Responses							
Variable	Mean	Standard Error	Type	Lower Bound	Upper Bound	*N* Obs Lower Bound	*N* Obs Upper Bound
lgd_time	0.22813	0.329109	Censored	0.00001		728	

Model Fit Summary	
Number of Endogenous Variables	1
Endogenous Variable	lgd_time
Number of Observations	2545
Log-Likelihood	−1322
Maximum Absolute Gradient	6.25233E−6
Number of Iterations	10
Optimization Method	Quasi-Newton
AIC	2653
Schwarz Criterion	2676

Parameter Estimates					
Parameter	DF	Estimate	Standard Error	*t* Value	Approx Pr > |*t*|
Intercept	1	−0.213414	0.017260	−12.36	<.0001
LTV	1	0.511773	0.021475	23.83	<.0001
purpose1	1	0.189627	0.028984	6.54	<.0001
_Sigma	1	0.371638	0.006400	58.07	<.0001

Exhibit 10.28 Tobit Regression with QLIM

for the volatility of about 0.37 indicate that the realizations are (randomly) far off the expectations. As the exercises in this chapter are for demonstration purposes only, it is recommended that practitioners look for other important explanatory variables.

```
ODS GRAPHICS ON;
PROC GPLOT DATA=Tobit1_out;
PLOT lgd_time * CExpct_lgd_time;
RUN;

PROC REG DATA = Tobit1_out;
MODEL lgd_time = CExpct_lgd_time;
RUN;
ODS GRAPHICS OFF;
```

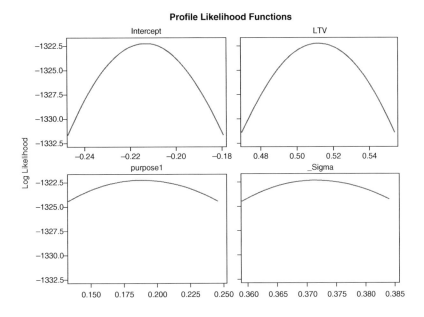

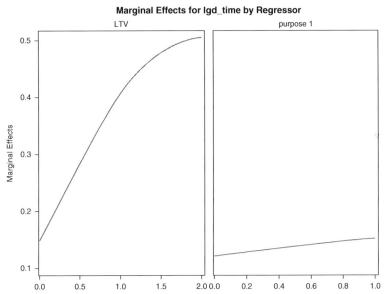

Exhibit 10.29 Tobit Regression with QLIM

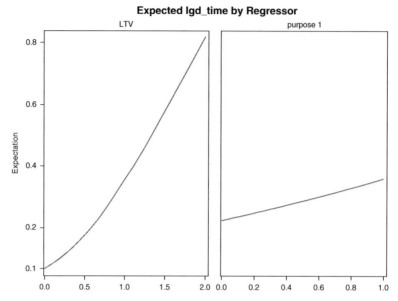

Exhibit 10.29 (*Continued*)

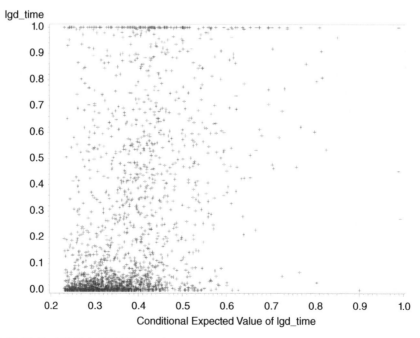

Exhibit 10.30 Real-Fit Plot of Tobit Regression

Root MSE	0.29485	R-Squared	0.1977
Dependent Mean	0.22813	Adj R-Sq	0.1974
Coeff Var	129.24525		

Parameter Estimates							
Variable	Label	DF	Parameter Estimate	Standard Error	t Value	Pr > |t|
Intercept	Intercept	1	−0.31220	0.02236	−13.96	<.0001
Cexpct_lgd_time	Conditional expected value of lgd_time	1	1.46066	0.05835	25.03	<.0001

Exhibit 10.31 Real-Fit Regression of Tobit Regression

Heckman Sample Selection Model

A generalization of the Tobit model is the Heckman model. Whereas the Tobit model uses the same mechanism for selection (i.e., a variable is observed if it crosses some threshold), the Heckman model uses two equations (see Bade, Rösch, & Scheule 2011 for an application). First, the selection process is given by the threshold model

$$D_i = \begin{cases} 1 & Z_i^* < 0 \\ 0 & Z_i^* \geq 0 \end{cases} \tag{10.6}$$

where

$$Z_i^* = \boldsymbol{\beta}' \boldsymbol{x}_i^z + \epsilon_i^z \tag{10.7}$$

and second, the recovery process is given as

$$\ln RR_i = \boldsymbol{\beta}' \boldsymbol{x}_i + \epsilon_i \quad \text{if} \quad D_i = 1 \tag{10.8}$$

where ϵ_i^z and ϵ_i are jointly normal with zero means, standard deviations of one and σ respectively, and correlation ρ. Selection is based on the variable D_i, and the recovery is observed when D_i has a value of 1. D_i is usually the default event; therefore recoveries or LGD are observed only in case of default. The correlation between the residuals is then the correlation between the LGD and the default-triggering process (e.g., asset value process). The code in PROC QLIM and the estimation output (Exhibit 10.32) are given next, where we again use LGD instead of ln RR as the dependent variable.

The intercept for the event process gives the selection probability (it could, however, also be modeled using explanatory variables). Both explanatory variables for the LGD process are again highly significant. The output also gives an estimate for the correlation ρ between both processes that is close to zero and not significant, showing that in this case, sample selection shouldn't be a big issue. You can now also

The QLIM Procedure

Summary Statistics of Continuous Responses								
Variable	N	Mean	Standard Error	Type	Lower Bound	Upper Bound	N Obs Lower Bound	N Obs Upper Bound
lgd_time	1,817	0.319529	0.350019	Censored	0.00001		0	

Model Fit Summary	
Number of Endogenous Variables	2
Endogenous Variable	event lgd_time
Number of Observations	2,545
Log-Likelihood	−2,042
Maximum Absolute Gradient	4.68009E−6
Number of Iterations	12
Optimization Method	Trust Region
AIC	4,096
Schwarz Criterion	4,131

Parameter Estimates					
Parameter	DF	Estimate	Standard Error	t Value	Approx Pr > |t|
lgd_time.Intercept	1	0.043047	1.325172	0.03	0.9741
lgd_time.LTV	1	0.355424	0.020469	17.36	<.0001
lgd_time.purpose1	1	0.126299	0.026590	4.75	<.0001
_Sigma.lgd_time	1	0.321905	0.005340	60.28	<.0001
event.Intercept	1	0.564958	0.026340	21.45	<.0001
_Rho	1	−0.000034660	8.641199	−0.00	1.0000

Exhibit 10.32 Heckman Regression with QLIM

use the computed output similarly to the Tobit model and compare realizations and predicted expectations.

```
PROC QLIM DATA=data.lgd PLOTS=ALL  METHOD = TRUREG;
MODEL event = / DISCRETE;
MODEL lgd_time = LTV purpose1/ SELECT(event=1) CENSORED(lb=0.00001);
OUTPUT OUT = heckman1_out EXPECTED CONDITIONAL PROB RESIDUAL XBETA;
RUN;
```

Censored Beta Regression

The final model with sample selection is a variant of the beta regression that takes selection and censoring explicitly into account. (See Exhibit 10.33.) As in the Tobit model, censored values for the LGD are explicitly taken into account and enter the likelihood; see Liu and Zhao (2013). The model then parameterizes the mean and the dispersion of the beta distribution as well as the censoring equation (the latter with a constant only). Again, while we used the same variables for both LGD parameters, it is not a requirement to do so and the reader is invited to check other combinations for the three equations. All coefficients are statistically and economically significant.

```
ODS GRAPHICS ON;
PROC NLMIXED DATA = data.lgd TECH = TRUREG;
PARMS  a0 = 0
b0 = 0 b1 = 0   b2=0
c0 = 1 c1 = 0   c2=0   ;
y = lgd_time;
xa = a0   ;
xb = b0 + b1 * LTV  + b2 * purpose1 ;
xc = c0 + c1 * LTV  + c2 * purpose1 ;
mu_xa = 1 / (1 + exp(-xa));
mu_xb = 1 / (1 + exp(-xb));
delta = EXP(xc);
alpha = mu_xb * delta;
beta = (1 - mu_xb) * delta;
IF  event=0 THEN lh = 1 - mu_xa;
ELSE lh = mu_xa * (GAMMA(alpha + beta) /
(GAMMA(alpha) * GAMMA(beta)) * (y ** (alpha - 1))
* ((1 - y) ** (beta - 1)));
ll = LOG(lh);
MODEL y ~ GENERAL(ll);
RUN;
ODS GRAPHICS OFF;
```

Which Model Should I Choose?

The final question is: Which model should I choose? While the results in this section didn't show a clear winner, some thoughts about the models presented are in order. First, it is a good idea not to limit oneself to one model only, but rather to estimate a variety of different models, to see whether the outcomes are robust with respect to the model specification. This is why we presented more models than necessary at first sight. You should take a closer look at the data and the reasons why a specific

The NLMIXED Procedure

Specifications	
Data Set	DATA.LGD
Dependent Variable	y
Distribution for Dependent Variable	General
Optimization Technique	Trust Region
Integration Method	None

Dimensions	
Observations Used	2545
Observations Not Used	0
Total Observations	2545
Parameters	7

Fit Statistics	
-2 Log-Likelihood	−148.5
AIC (smaller is better)	−134.5
AICC (smaller is better)	−134.5
BIC (smaller is better)	−93.6

Parameter Estimates								
Parameter	Estimate	Standard Error	DF	t Value	Pr > |t|	95% Confidence Limits		Gradient
a0	0.9146	0.04386	2545	20.85	<.0001	0.8286	1.0007	−114E−15
b0	−1.2322	0.07278	2545	−16.93	<.0001	−1.3749	−1.0895	3.209E−6
b1	1.1884	0.08523	2545	13.94	<.0001	1.0213	1.3556	1.12E−6
b2	0.4657	0.1086	2545	4.29	<.0001	0.2527	0.6787	6.558E−8
c0	−0.1449	0.06218	2545	−2.33	0.0199	−0.2668	−0.02294	8.126E−6
c1	−0.1470	0.07180	2545	−2.05	0.0408	−0.2877	−0.00618	3.422E−6
c2	−0.09619	0.08870	2545	−1.08	0.2783	−0.2701	0.07775	9.657E−7

Exhibit 10.33 Beta Regression with Censoring and Selection

model matches the data better than another model if the outcome of one model is completely different from another model (e.g., in terms of significances of parameters or prediction power). One plausible explanation may be that the assumptions of the model (e.g., distributional assumptions) provide for a better fit. Moreover, robustness checks across models are also important for regulatory purposes.

Second, while sample selection was not a big issue in our data set, it can be an issue for other data and can lead to biased and inconsistent parameter estimates. Therefore, a selection model should always be run in parallel.

Third, when choosing among different models, you should keep in mind complexity. Sometimes, a simpler model is easier to communicate within an institution and to supervisors if it yields results that are similar to those of a more advanced, complex model.

EXTENSIONS

This chapter has focused on the most fundamental methods for modeling and forecasting LGDs and recovery rates. Depending on the data that are available for a bank and depending on econometric skills, various extensions can be applied. In our data set, we used only two explanatory variables, which yielded R^2 values of about 20 percent. If more covariates are available, you could include more information in order to get a better picture about LGDs. Examples are loan- or borrower-specific data, such as seniority, collateral, income, and so on, or macroeconomic variables, such as interest rates, unemployment rate, or GDP. For applications, see for instance Rösch and Scheule (2004, 2005, 2009, 2012) or Bellotti and Crook (2012).

The models can also be extended by including nonobservable random effects that can be interpreted similarly to asset correlations for default events. By modeling LGDs via observable *and* unobservable components, it is also easy to do stress-testing (by stressing the observable, e.g., macroeconomic covariates to certain levels) or to provide downturn predictions for LGDs (by stressing observable and unobservable random components). For applications in this context see Rösch and Scheule (2010).

Other selection mechanisms and other dependence structures can also be implemented. For example, a selection mechanism for default and another for cure events can be included; see Wolter and Rösch (2014). An application of various copula dependencies between PD and LGD, including the generation of a term structure of LGDs over the lifetime of a loan, is given in Krüger et al. (2015).

Finally, besides the techniques we already discussed, more complex techniques such as neural networks or support vector machines (SVMs) can also be used for LGD modeling; see Loterman et al. (2012). Although these techniques benefit from a universal approximation property and are thus very powerful, they usually suffer from a loss of interpretability. The resulting models are very complex for the human decision maker to understand. Hence, it is not recommended to use these techniques for LGD modeling, particularly for supervisory purposes.

PRACTICE QUESTIONS

1. Explain why LTV should be a good explanatory variable for LGDs.

2. Categorize the current LTV ratio and include dummy variables in a regression model for the LGD. How do you interpret the parameter estimates for the LTV ratio, and what may be the advantages and disadvantages of including a metric variable in categories (relative to a stand-alone inclusion)? Use data set lgd.

3. In the PD chapter, we discussed point-in-time (PIT) versus through-the-cycle (TTC). Could this also be an issue for LGDs? How could macroeconomic variables (such as GDP) affect LGDs?

4. Include "LTV" and "purpose1" as explanatory variables in the probit transformed regression model, and estimate a stepwise regression using the option "stepwise" in PROC REG. Interpret the results. Use data set lgd.

5. Which other variables could be included in an LGD model and should be collected by banks?

6. Discuss the issue of sample selection for LGD models.

REFERENCES

Bade, B., D. Rösch, and H. Scheule. 2011. "Default and Recovery Risk Dependencies in a Simple Credit Risk Model." *European Financial Management* 17(1), 120–144.

Basel Committee on Banking Supervision. 2005a. "Guidance on Paragraph 468 of the Framework Document."

Basel Committee on Banking Supervision. 2005b. "The Joint Forum Credit Risk Transfer."

Basel Committee on Banking Supervision. 2006. "International Convergence of Capital Measurement and Capital Standards: A Revised Framework, Comprehensive Version."

Bellotti, T., and J. Crook. 2012. "Loss Given Default Models Incorporating Macroeconomic Variables for Credit Cards." *International Journal of Forecasting* 28(1): 171–182.

Betz, J., R. Kellner, and D. Rösch. 2016. "What Drives the Time to Resolution of Defaulted Bank Loans?" *Finance Research Letters* (April).

Brady, B., P. Chang, P., Miu, B. Ozdemir, and D. Schwartz. 2006. "Discount Rate for Workout Recoveries: An Empirical Study." Technical report, Working paper.

Committee of European Banking Supervisors (CEBS). 2005. "Guidelines on the Implementation, Validation and Assessment of Advanced Measurement (AMA) and Internal Ratings Based (IRB) Approaches." Technical report, CP10 consultation paper.

Federal Register. 2007. "Proposed Supervisory Guidance for Internal Ratings-Based Systems for Credit Risk, Advanced Measurement Approaches for Operational Risk, and the Supervisory Review Process (Pillar 2) Related to Basel II Implementation."

Ferrari, S., and F. Cribari-Neto. 2004. "Beta Regression for Modelling Rates and Proportions." *Journal of Applied Statistics* 31(7), 799–815.

Gupton, G., and R. Stein. 2005. "Losscalc v2: Dynamic Prediction of LGD Modeling Methodology." Moody's KMV Investors Services.

Krüger, S., T. Oehme, D. Rösch, and H. Scheule. 2015. "Expected Loss over Lifetime." Working paper, University of Regensburg and University of Technology, Sydney, Australia.

Liu, W., and K. Zhao. 2013. "Statistical Models for Proportional Outcomes." Working paper, MidWest SAS Users Group, FS-05-2013.

Loterman, G., I. Brown, D. Martens, C. Mues, and B. Baesens. 2012. "Benchmarking Regression Algorithms for Loss Given Default Modeling." *International Journal of Forecasting* 28: 161–170.

Maclachlan, I. 2004. "Choosing the Discount Factor for Estimating Economic LGD." In: Altman E, Resti A, Sironi A (Eds.): Recovery Risk, The Next Challenge in Credit Risk Management. Risk Books, London, 285–305.

Merton, R. C. 1974. "On the Pricing of Corporate Debt: The Risk Structure of Interest Rates." *Journal of Finance* 29: 449–470.

Prudential Regulation Authority. 2013. "Internal Ratings Based approaches." Working paper.

Rösch, D., and H. Scheule. 2004. "Forecasting Retail Portfolio Credit Risk." *Journal of Risk Finance* 5(2): 16–32.

Rösch, D., and H. Scheule. 2005. "A Multi-Factor Approach for Systematic Default and Recovery Risk." *Journal of Fixed Income* 15(2): 63–75.

Rösch, D., and H. Scheule. 2009. "Forecasting Downturn Credit Portfolio Risk." *Financial Markets, Institutions and Instruments* 18(1), 1–26.

Rösch, D., and H. Scheule. 2010. "Downturn Credit Portfolio Risk, Regulatory Capital and Prudential Incentives." *International Review of Finance* 10(2): 185–207.

Rösch, D., and H. Scheule. 2012. "Forecasting Probabilities of Default and Loss Rates Given Default in the Presence of Selection." *Journal of the Operational Research Society* 65(3): 393–407.

SAS Institute Inc. 2015. *SAS/STAT 14.1 User's Guide: Technical Report*. Cary, NC: SAS Institute.

Stoyanov, S. 2009. "Application LGD Model Development." *Credit Scoring and Credit Control XI Conference*.

Tobin, J. 1958. "Estimation of Relationships for Limited Dependent Variables." *Econometrica* 26.

Van Gestel, T., and B. Baesens. 2009. *Credit Risk Management: Basic Concepts: Financial Risk Components, Rating Analysis, Models, Economic and Regulatory Capital.* Oxford: Oxford University Press.

Wolter, M., and D. Rösch. 2014. "Cure Events in Default Prediction." *European Journal of Operational Research* 238: 846–857.

CHAPTER 11

Exposure at Default (EAD) and Adverse Selection

INTRODUCTION

In this chapter, you learn what exposure at default (EAD) modeling is, the Basel requirements for EAD, and the various methods for building EAD models. Remember, just as with LGD, EAD also has a linear impact on both the expected loss and the Basel capital. It is thus of key importance to model EAD as accurately as possible.

Let us first start by defining the concept of EAD modeling. For on-balance-sheet exposures, such as term loans, installment loans, and mortgages, the EAD is defined as the nominal outstanding balance, net of specific provisions. In other words, it represents the net outstanding debt.

Examples of studies on EAD include Jacobs (2011), who develops linear regression models for conversion measures for a corporate revolving credit facility with a number of determinants such as credit rating, utilization, tenor, industry, and macroeconomic factors. The significant finding is that utilization is the strongest factor influencing EAD. Barakova and Parthasarathy (2012) analyze syndicated corporate credit lines. The authors find that risk rating, line utilization, size, and sudden turns in the economic cycle have the most significant impact on EAD. Agarwal, Ambrose, and Liu (2006) use private bank data and analyze home equity lines of credit utilization. Tong et al. (2016) analyze EAD for credit card loans. We will describe this study in more detail later. Another example is Valvonis (2008), who discusses the estimation of exposure at default for regulatory capital.

Fixed versus Variable Outstanding

The EAD is deterministic for some loans (e.g., many corporate bonds) and variable for others. Within the loans with variable amount outstanding, two types may be distinguished: credit lines and loans with flexible payment schedules.

Credit lines (e.g., credit card loans) generally have a limit and a drawn amount. The borrower can draw on the line up to the limit. At the end of a period, the borrower is required to repay the drawn amount, after which it is set back to zero.

Loans with flexible payment schedules are often loans with a prepayment option and a redraw option. Amortizing loans (e.g., mortgage loans) generally require borrowers to make interest and principal payments prior to maturity, and the loan balance reduces with the principal amount that is repaid. A prepayment option allows the borrower to pay down more than the scheduled amount, whereas a redraw option allows the borrower to draw on prepayments and/or principal repayments.

It is common in some countries (e.g., Australia) to arrange for two connected accounts: a loan account (with a negative balance) and an offset account (with a positive balance). The outstanding loan amount is the net of the two balances, and borrowers can draw on the offset account at any time while principal repayments are credited to this account. This product in essence allows borrowers to redraw the prepayments. It is also common in other countries (e.g., United States) to arrange for a home equity line of credit next to a mortgage loan. The idea here is to redraw already-made principal payments on a separate account with the value of the house less the primary mortgage being used as collateral to determine the limit. Other home equity extraction contracts include reverse mortgages, which may also have redraw features.

Off-Balance-Sheet Exposures

As already mentioned, banks are exposed to off-balance-sheet exposures. Off-balance-sheet exposures include contingent credit exposures (e.g., credit guarantees and loan commitments) and counterparty credit risk in relation to over-the-counter (OTC), i.e., bilateral, derivative agreements on future deliveries. The exposure at default depends on the loss in relation to a guarantee or an adverse movement of an underlying measure in conjunction with the credit event of a counterparty in derivative contracts.

For off-balance-sheet exposures, you need to take into account what portion of the undrawn amount is likely to be converted into credit upon the default of a reference firm or person (in the case of a guarantee) or the counterparty (in the case of a derivative).

Conversion Measures

Exposures at default can be modeled directly by building a model for the exposure amount or a monotone transformation thereof. Alternatively, you may relate the EAD to a scaling variable and derive conversion measures. Yang and

Conversion Measure	Formula
Credit Conversion Factor (CCF)	$EAD = Drawn + CCF^*(Limit\text{-}Drawn)$
Credit Equivalent (CEQ)	$EAD = Drawn + CEQ^*Limit$
Limit Conversion Factor (LCF)/Loan Equivalent (LEQ)	$EAD = LCF^*Limit$
Used Amount Conversion Factor (UACF)	$EAD = UACF^*Drawn$

Exhibit 11.1 Conversion of Limits and Drawn Amounts to EAD for Off-Balance-Sheet Exposures

Tkachenko (2012) find that models for conversion measures are generally more robust than EAD models, as they scale all observations to a common denomination.

Exhibit 11.1 shows four conversion measures that are common. Other measures to convert drawn amounts and limits, as well as other quantities, may also be considered. Examples of such quantities include sales, number of staff, profitability, liquidity, or age.

The credit conversion factor (CCF) is defined as the portion of the undrawn amount that will be converted into credit. Note that the undrawn amount is equal to the limit minus the drawn amount. The EAD thus becomes the drawn amount plus the CCF times the limit minus the drawn amount. The credit equivalent (CEQ), is defined as the portion of the limit likely to be converted into credit. The EAD is then defined as the drawn amount plus the CEQ times the limit. The limit conversion factor (LCF), or loan equivalent (LEQ), is defined as a fraction of the limit representing the total exposure. The EAD is then defined as the LCF or LEQ times the limit. Finally, the used amount conversion factor (UACF) is defined using the drawn amount as the reference. Hence, the EAD is then computed as the UACF times the drawn amount.

Note that these measures need to be carefully chosen. For example, there is some controversy on the use of conversion measures as they may be too restrictive (compare Taplin, To, and Hee 2007) or volatile (compare Qi 2009).

REGULATORY PERSPECTIVE ON EAD

In the Basel Accord, generally the credit conversion factor (CCF) approach is used. The CCF ranges between zero and one, corresponding with an EAD equal to the drawn amount and limit, respectively. EAD modeling now comes down to estimating the CCF. Some financial institutions do not develop CCF models and use a conservative approach by consistently setting the CCF to one. In other words, they assume that the EAD will always be equal to the credit limit upon default of the exposure. In what follows, we will see what Basel says about EAD modeling. For corporates, sovereigns, and bank exposures, paragraph 310 of the Basel II Accord reads (see Basel Committee on Banking Supervision 2006):

> For off-balance sheet items, exposure is calculated as the committed but undrawn amount multiplied by a CCF. There are two approaches for the estimation of CCFs: a foundation approach and an advanced approach.

Remember, the IRB approach has two subapproaches, the foundation IRB approach and the advanced IRB approach. In the foundation IRB approach, banks can estimate the PD themselves, but rely on the Accord or local regulators for reference values of the LGD and EAD. In the advanced IRB approach, the bank can estimate all three risk parameters: the PD, LGD, and EAD. Also remember that the foundation IRB approach is not allowed for retail exposures. The reference values for EAD or thus CCF for corporate, sovereign, and bank exposures are provided for loan commitments in paragraph 83 of the Basel Committee on Banking Supervision 2006 as follows:

> Commitments with an original maturity up to one year and commitments with an original maturity over one year will receive a CCF of 20% and 50%, respectively. However, any commitments that are unconditionally cancelable at any time by the bank without prior notice will receive a 0% CCF.

For retail exposures, paragraph 334 of the Accord reads:

> Both on- and off-balance sheet retail exposures are measured gross of specific provisions or partial write-offs. The EAD on drawn amounts should not be less than the sum of (i) the amount by which a bank's regulatory capital would be reduced if the exposure were written-off fully, and (ii) any specific provisions and partial write-offs.

This paragraph is then followed by paragraph 335 as follows:

> For retail off-balance sheet items, banks must use their own estimates of CCFs.

Paragraph 336 then considers the issue of a consistent definition of both EAD and LGD as follows:

> For retail exposures with uncertain future drawdown such as credit cards, banks must take into account their history and/or expectation of additional drawings prior to default in their overall calibration of loss estimates. In particular, where a bank does not reflect conversion factors for undrawn lines in its EAD estimates, it must reflect in its LGD estimates the likelihood of additional drawings prior to default. Conversely, if the bank does not incorporate the possibility of additional drawings in its LGD estimates, it must do so in its EAD estimates.

To summarize, additional drawings prior to default can be included in either LGD or EAD. However, it is common practice to include those in the EAD definition by using credit conversion factors, as discussed earlier.

The EU and U.S. regulations also introduce the idea of a margin of conservatism and economic downturn EAD if it turns out that the EAD is volatile over the economic cycle. Note that this is actually very similar to LGD.

For OTC derivatives, the exposure is a combination of the current exposure and the potential future exposure. In the past, the EAD for OTC derivatives was the sum of the replacement cost (RC, also called current exposure) and the potential future exposure (PFE). PFE was determined by a multiplication of the notional amount and a look-up CCF (depending on the maturity and the underlying class). These rules will be updated in the standardized approach for measuring counterparty credit risk exposures (SA-CCR) (compare Basel Committee on Banking Supervision 2014). Under these rules, the exposure is calculated as follows:

$$EAD = 1.4(RC + PFE)$$

The replacement costs consider margining (i.e., provision of cash or collateral by the counterparty), and the potential future exposure considers a number of characteristics that describe the risk profile of the derivatives.

A practical problem with EAD models (regardless of whether they are modeling EAD, a transformation thereof, or a conversion measure) is that they could lead up to an estimate of the EAD that is lower than the current outstanding or drawn amount. Hence, a flooring operation is generally applied for determining EAD for regulatory purposes. EAD is always at least the drawn amount, or, in other words, the EAD equals the maximum of the drawn amount and the LCF times the limit. This was also confirmed by the PRA as follows:

> The PRA expects that EAD estimates should not be less than current drawings.

In terms of CCF, a negative value may occur when the obligor has paid back a portion of the debt prior to default. For estimation purposes, it is, however, recommended to floor a negative CCF to zero.

The CCF can also exceed one. This can be due to credit limit changes or off-line transactions that allow borrowers to exceptionally exceed the credit limit. In other words, the limit communicated to the customer is a soft limit that the customer can occasionally exceed. If the CCF is above one, then the exposure decreases as the drawn balance increases.

Let us illustrate this with a brief example. Suppose that the credit limit is 2,500 and the CCF equals 110%. If the drawn balance is 1,000, then the EAD becomes 2,650. However, if the drawn balance equals 1,500, then the exposure decreases to 2,600. It is recommended to always have the CCF limited between zero and one. One way to ensure it is always below one is to work with a hard credit limit that absolutely cannot be exceeded. This hard credit limit can be set based on historical data or by using a confidence level, if needed.

EAD MODELING

Models for EAD and conversion measures can be created using similar techniques as the ones presented in our LGD chapter. Since EAD modeling is also exposed to default selection, models like the Tobit model and the Heckman selection model may provide interesting approaches.

Data Preprocessing

Let's now have a look at how we can create the development sample for EAD. For defaulted exposures, the EAD at the moment of default can be determined. We now need to consider a period δ_t before the time of default to determine the risk factors and drawn amount. The risk factors are the variables that will be used as predictors in the CCF model. Once the drawn amount is known, the CCF can be calculated as the ratio of the EAD minus the drawn amount, and the limit minus the drawn amount.

A key problem is the determination of the time lag between the observed exposure amount at default and the observed drawn amount and limit. The Prudential Regulation Authority (PRA) in the United Kingdom says the following about this:

> The PRA expects firms to use a time horizon of one year for EAD estimates; unless they can demonstrate that another period would be more conservative.

Various methods to determine this time horizon exist, and their impact on the composition of the development sample will be discussed in the following.

Cohort Method

A first way is the cohort approach. This approach groups defaulted facilities into discrete calendar periods, for example, 12 months unless another time period would be more conservative and appropriate. It collects information about the risk factors and drawn/undrawn amounts at the beginning of the calendar period and the drawn amount at the date of default. Data of different calendar periods can then be pooled for estimation.

For example, if the calendar period is defined as the 1st of November 2015 to the 31st of October 2016, then information about the risk factors and drawn/undrawn amounts is collected on November 1, 2015, and the drawn amounts of the defaulted facilities upon default. Facilities can then go into default in January 2016, February 2016, March 2016, until October 2016. In other words, the time lag between the risk factors and the EAD is different for each defaulter depending upon the time of default. This is also what will happen as we will start using our model for predicting the EAD. Some exposures may default in the next three months, four months, five months, and so on.

Fixed Time Horizon Method

The fixed horizon method starts by defining a fixed time horizon, usually 12 months, unless another time period would be more conservative and appropriate. It then collects information about the risk factors and drawn/undrawn amounts 12 months prior to the date of default, and the drawn amount on the date of default, regardless of the actual calendar date on which the default occurred. For example, if a default occurred on July 15, 2016, then information about the risk factors and the drawn/undrawn amounts of the defaulted facility on July 16, 2015, is used. Hence, the time frame between measuring the risk factors and the CCF is always 12 months. When we use the model to predict EAD, it generally assumes that if default occurs, it will occur exactly 12 months from now. About the cohort and fixed time horizon approach, the Prudential Regulation Authority says the following:

> EAD estimates can be undertaken on the basis that default occurs at any time during the time horizon (the cohort approach), or at the end of the time horizon (the fixed horizon approach). The PRA considers that either approach is acceptable in principle.

Variable Time Horizon Method

The variable time horizon approach is a variant of the fixed time horizon approach whereby several reference times within a chosen time horizon are used to determine the drawn/undrawn amounts and risk factors. For example, the drawn amount upon default is compared to the drawn/undrawn amounts and risk factors one, two, three, or more months before default.

We now showcase the data preparation for our mortgage data set. Note that these are loan exposures with flexible payment schedules and that low-risk mortgage borrowers often make prepayments, while high-risk borrowers usually do not, even if contractually allowed.

In a first step, we set up the data by computing the lagged exposure amounts (variable balance_time) for mortgage borrowers as a measure for the drawn amount at the beginning of the reference period. Consistent with the variable time horizon method, we consider one to four lags under the assumption that one period equals one quarter (i.e., a lag of four periods is equal to one year).

The ARRAY command in SAS allows us to set the first observations for which no lagged value is available (and otherwise would be taken from the previous borrower) to a missing value for multiple lags. The data are first sorted by the BY variable "id." We prefer to apply the calculations on all observations and not on default observations only, as we will later estimate regression models that control for the selecting default event.

```
PROC SORT DATA=data.mortgage;
BY id;
RUN;

DATA mortgage(drop=i count);
 SET data.mortgage;
 BY id;
```

```
/* Create lagged variables*/
ARRAY x(*) lag1-lag4;
lag1=LAG1(balance_time);
lag2=LAG2(balance_time);
lag3=LAG3(balance_time);
lag4=LAG4(balance_time);

/* Reset count at the start of each new BY-Group */
IF FIRST.id THEN COUNT=1;

/* assign missing values to first observation/s of a BY group*/
DO i=count TO DIM(x);
 x(i)=.;
END;
count + 1;
RUN;
```

A selection of variables of the resulting data set is shown in Exhibit 11.2.

Next, we generate the dependent variable based on the four concepts: CCF, CEQ, LCF, and UACF. (See Exhibit 11.3.) We derive theoretical limits for mortgages that allow prepayments and redraws prior to principal repayments, and suggest transformation functions that may be used as dependent variables in later regression models. The transformations ensure that the predicted conversion measures and hence EAD are within our expectations (i.e., do not exceed the limit or become negative).

We define the limit as the outstanding loan amount at origination (variable "balance_orig_time"). The drawn amount is the outstanding loan amount prior to the observation period. We will focus on the four-period lag (variable "lag4"), which is equal to one year if one period equals a quarter. The exposure amount is the outstanding loan amount in the observation period (variable "balance_time").

Furthermore, we cap the variables' exposure and drawn amount by the credit limit. CCF is set to zero if the drawn amount is equal to the limit. As we are interested in economic EAD and mortgages are exposed to prepayments, we do not impose

id	time	default_ time	balance_ orig_ time	balance_ time	lag1	lag2	lag3	lag4
46	25	0	88000	86884.83	.	.	.	.
46	26	0	88000	86718.33	86884.83	.	.	.
46	27	0	88000	86379.71	86718.33	86884.83	.	.
46	28	0	88000	86207.57	86379.71	86718.33	86884.83	.
46	29	1	88000	86033.51	86207.57	86379.71	86718.33	86884.83
47	25	0	132000	130286.14	.	.	.	.
47	26	0	132000	129925.24	130286.14	.	.	.
47	27	0	132000	129558.06	129925.24	130286.14	.	.

Exhibit 11.2 Panel Data

Measure	Formula	Lower Bound	Upper Bound	Transformation
CCF	(EAD-Drawn)/(Limit-Drawn)	$-\infty$	1	$-\ln(1\text{-CCF})$
CEQ	(EAD-Drawn)/Limit	-1	1	$\ln((1\text{+CEQ})/(1\text{-CEQ}))$
LCF	EAD/Limit	0	1	$\ln(\text{LCF}/(1\text{-LCF}))$
UACF	EAD/Drawn	0	∞	$\ln(\text{UACF})$

Exhibit 11.3 Definitions, Boundaries, and Transformations for Credit Conversion Measures

the regulatory floor of the exposure by the drawn amount. Note that the latter assumption is required by the Basel Committee on Banking Supervision for regulatory EAD and may be implemented by an additional line (IF exposure<drawn THEN exposure=drawn;). We compute the transformations as highlighted in Exhibit 11.3. We add one restriction (IF drawn=limit THEN CCF=0;) as the data has observations where the limit is completely drawn.

```
DATA mortgage1(WHERE=(drawn NE . AND limit NE . AND exposure NE .
AND exposure NE 0));
SET mortgage;

/*Definitions*/
drawn=lag4;
limit=balance_orig_time;
exposure=balance_time;

/*Caps for exposure and draw*/
if exposure>limit then exposure=limit;
if drawn>limit then drawn=limit;

/*Conversion measures*/
CCF=(exposure-drawn)/(limit-drawn);
if drawn=limit then CCF=0;

CEQ=(exposure-drawn)/limit;
LCF=exposure/limit;
UACF=exposure/drawn;
RUN;
```

We compute the 5th and 95th percentiles of the conversion measures (see Exhibit 11.4):

```
PROC MEANS DATA=mortgage1 P1 P99;
VAR CCF CEQ LCF UACF;
RUN;
```

The MEANS Procedure

Variable	1st Pctl	99th Pctl
CCF	−18.0502849	1.0000000
CEQ	−0.1297378	0.0102912
LCF	0.3724166	1.0000000
UACF	0.7492269	1.0105358

Exhibit 11.4 Percentiles for Conversion Measures

The MEANS Procedure

Variable	N	Mean	Std Dev	Minimum	Maximum
CCF	11673	−0.6358660	2.0406573	−18.0502849	0.9999999
CEQ	11673	−0.0044892	0.0095413	−0.1297378	0.0102912
LCF	11673	0.9781223	0.0505083	0.3724166	0.9999999
UACF	11673	0.9949136	0.0146982	0.7492269	1.0105358
CCF_t	11673	0.1218104	2.6773378	−2.9470821	16.1180957
CEQ_t	11673	−0.0089835	0.0191379	−0.2609463	0.0205831
LCF_t	11673	8.1114383	5.5361960	−0.5218635	16.1180956
UACF_t	11673	−0.0052234	0.0162798	−0.2887134	0.0104807

Exhibit 11.5 Percentiles for Conversion Measures

We winsorize the conversion measures by the 1st and 99th percentile (i.e., floor the measures at their 1st percentile and cap the measures at their 99th percentile). We further confirm that the boundary values are not hit, as the numerator and the natural logarithm are not defined for zero. As a result, for CCF and LCF, we substitute an observation of one with 0.9999999.

We then transform the variables CCF, CEQ, LCF, and UACF by using the following transformation functions to match the range of normally distributed residuals in our regressions (see Exhibit 11.5):

```
DATA mortgage2;
SET mortgage1;

/*Floors*/
IF CCF<=-18.0502849 THEN CCF=-18.0502849;
IF CEQ<=-0.1297378 THEN CEQ=-0.1297378;
IF LCF<=0.3724166 THEN LCF=0.3724166;
IF UACF<=0.7492269 THEN UACF=0.7492269;
```

```
/*Caps*/
IF CCF>=0.9999999 THEN CCF=0.9999999;
IF CEQ>=0.0102912 THEN CEQ=0.0102912;
IF LCF>=0.9999999 THEN LCF=0.9999999;
IF UACF>=1.0105358 THEN UACF=1.0105358;


/*Transformations*/
CCF_t=-LOG(1-CCF);
CEQ_t=LOG((1+CEQ)/(1-CEQ));
LCF_t=LOG(LCF/(1-LCF));
UACF_t=LOG(UACF);


RUN;
```

We generate moments of the four dependent variables for the complete data set using PROC MEANS for CCF, CEQ, LCF, and UACF, as well as their transforms for all observations and by the default indicator:

```
PROC MEANS DATA=mortgage2(where=(default_time=1));
VAR CCF CEQ LCF UACF CCF_t CEQ_t LCF_t UACF_t;
RUN;
```

Furthermore, we generate the histograms using PROC UNIVARIATE for CCF, CEQ, LCF, and UACF, as well as their transforms (see Exhibits 11.6 through 11.13):

```
ODS GRAPHICS ON;
PROC UNIVARIATE DATA=mortgage2(where=(default_time=1));
VAR CCF CEQ LCF UACF CCF_t CEQ_t LCF_t UACF_t;
HISTOGRAM;
RUN;
ODS GRAPHICS OFF;
```

Credit Line Models

A number of risk factors can generally be considered in EAD models:

- Facility-specific: covenant protection, utilization, or LTV
- Borrower-specific: industry, geographical region, PD, credit rating, recent new loans/payoff, change in frequency of payment, or prepayment
- Time density: time to default, time since origination
- Macroeconomic variables

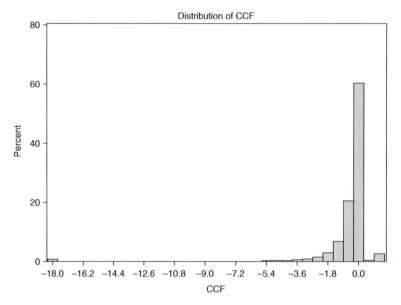

Exhibit 11.6 Histogram Credit Conversion Factor (CCF)

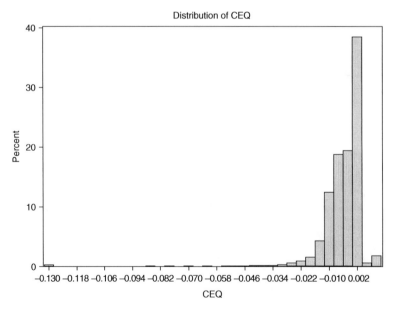

Exhibit 11.7 Histogram Credit Equivalent (CEQ)

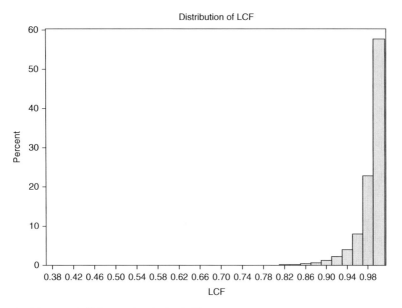

Exhibit 11.8 Histogram Limit Conversion Factor (LCF)

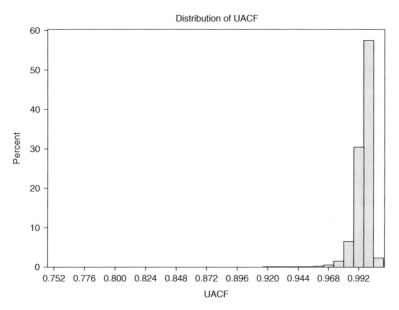

Exhibit 11.9 Histogram Used Amount Conversion Factor (UACF)

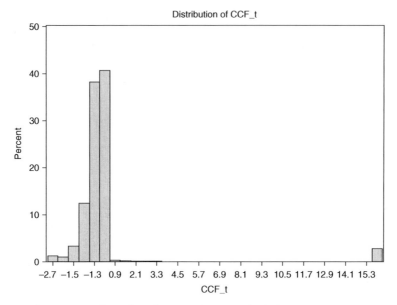

Exhibit 11.10 Histogram Transformed Credit Conversion Factor (CCF_t)

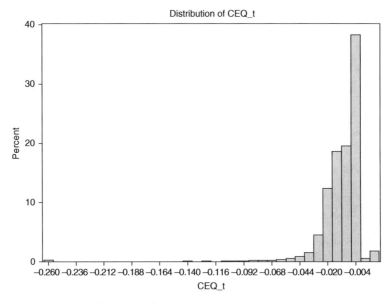

Exhibit 11.11 Histogram Transformed Credit Equivalent (CEQ_t)

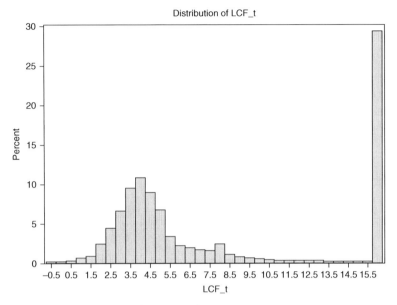

Exhibit 11.12 Histogram Transformed Limit Conversion Factor (LCF_t)

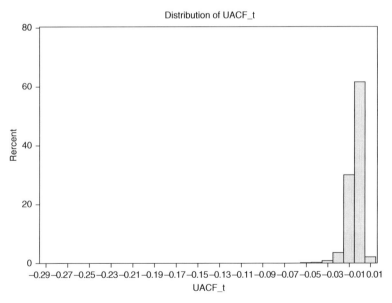

Exhibit 11.13 Histogram Transformed Used Amount Conversion Factor (UACF_t)

Furthermore, Moral (2011) recommends using the following risk factors:

- The committed amount, which is the advised credit limit at the start of the cohort
- The drawn amount, which is the exposure at the start of the cohort
- The undrawn amount, which is the advised limit minus the exposure at the start of the cohort
- The credit percentage usage, which is the exposure at the start of the cohort divided by the advised credit limit at the start of the cohort
- The time to default, which is the number of months between the start of the cohort and the default date
- The rating class, which is the behavioral score at the start of the cohort, binned into four categories

Let us now have a look at the risk factors that can be used to model CCF for credit lines. Exposure modeling for credit card loans has been the focus in the existing literature. For example, Tong et al. (2016) find a bimodal distribution for the CCF with a peak at zero and one, similar to LGDs. The authors include the following variables next to the variables from Moral (2011):

- The average number of days delinquent during the previous 3, 6, 9, and 12 months prior to the start of the cohort
- The increase in committed amount, which is a binary variable indicating whether there has been an increase in the committed amount since 12 months prior to the start of the cohort
- The undrawn percentage, which is the undrawn amount at the start of the cohort divided by the advised credit limit at the start of the cohort
- The relative change in drawn, undrawn, and committed amounts
- The absolute change in drawn, undrawn, and committed amounts

Tong et al. (2016) find the following significant variables: the credit percentage usage, the committed amount, the undrawn amount, the time-to-default, the rating class, and the average number of days delinquent in the past six months. Of the additional variables tested, only the average number of days delinquent in the past six months turned out to be significant. Note that the maximum performance in terms of R-squared equals about 0.10, which is rather low but in line with LGD modeling.

Loans with Flexible Payment Schedules

Linear Regression

To showcase regression models for the conversion measures, we estimate a linear regression model for each transform of CCF, CEQ, LCF, and UACF. We include LTV_time as the sole covariate and encourage the reader to go beyond this specification and enhance the model's accuracy:

```
   ODS GRAPHICS ON;
PROC REG DATA=mortgage2(WHERE=(default_time=1))
PLOTS(MAXPOINTS=20000 STATS= ALL)= DIAGNOSTICS;
   MODEL CCF = LTV_time;
   RUN;
   ODS GRAPHICS OFF;

   ODS GRAPHICS ON;
PROC REG DATA=mortgage2(WHERE=(default_time=1))
PLOTS(MAXPOINTS=20000 STATS= ALL)= DIAGNOSTICS;
   MODEL CEQ = LTV_time;
   RUN;
   ODS GRAPHICS OFF;

   ODS GRAPHICS ON;
PROC REG DATA=mortgage2(WHERE=(default_time=1))
PLOTS(MAXPOINTS=20000 STATS= ALL)= DIAGNOSTICS;
   MODEL LCF = LTV_time;
   RUN;
   ODS GRAPHICS OFF;

   ODS GRAPHICS ON;
PROC REG DATA=mortgage2(WHERE=(default_time=1))
PLOTS(MAXPOINTS=20000 STATS= ALL)= DIAGNOSTICS;
   MODEL UACF = LTV_time;
   RUN;
   ODS GRAPHICS OFF;
```

Exhibits 11.14 through 11.17 show that the R-squared is highest for LCF.

The fit diagnostics and residual plots for a linear model for the best-fitting (with regard to R-squared) measure LCF are shown in Exhibit 11.18.

The comparison of the fitted normal distribution and the histogram of the residuals shows that the fit is not that good. Thus, we try the transformations of the conversion measures as a next step.

Transformed Linear Regression

We regress our transformed conversion measures on the covariate LTV_time.

```
   ODS GRAPHICS ON;
PROC REG DATA=mortgage2(WHERE=(default_time=1))
PLOTS(MAXPOINTS=20000 STATS= ALL)= DIAGNOSTICS;
   MODEL CCF_t = LTV_time;
   RUN;
   ODS GRAPHICS OFF;
```

The REG Procedure

Model: MODEL1

Dependent Variable: CCF

Root MSE	2.03501	*R*-Squared	0.0056
Dependent Mean	−0.63587	Adj *R*-Sq	0.0055
Coeff Var	−320.03702		

Parameter Estimates					
Variable	DF	Parameter Estimate	Standard Error	*t* Value	Pr > |*t*|
Intercept	1	−1.35217	0.09022	−14.99	<.0001
LTV_time	1	0.00710	0.00087437	8.12	<.0001

Exhibit 11.14 Linear Regression Fit for CCF

The REG Procedure

Model: MODEL1

Dependent Variable: CEQ

Root MSE	0.00906	*R*-Squared	0.0983
Dependent Mean	−0.00449	Adj *R*-Sq	0.0982
Coeff Var	−201.83151		

Parameter Estimates					
Variable	DF	Parameter Estimate	Standard Error	*t* Value	Pr > |*t*|
Intercept	1	−0.01850	0.00040169	−46.06	<.0001
LTV_time	1	0.00013886	0.00000389	35.67	<.0001

Exhibit 11.15 Linear Regression Fit for CEQ

```
    ODS GRAPHICS ON;
 PROC REG DATA=mortgage2(WHERE=(default_time=1))
 PLOTS(MAXPOINTS=20000 STATS= ALL)= DIAGNOSTICS;
    MODEL CEQ_T = LTV_time;
    RUN;
    ODS GRAPHICS OFF;

    ODS GRAPHICS ON;
 PROC REG DATA=mortgage2(WHERE=(default_time=1))
 PLOTS(MAXPOINTS=20000 STATS= ALL)= DIAGNOSTICS;
```

The REG Procedure
Model: MODEL1
Dependent Variable: LCF

Root MSE	0.04605	R-Squared	0.1688
Dependent Mean	0.97812	Adj R-Sq	0.1687
Coeff Var	4.70817		

Parameter Estimates					
Variable	DF	Parameter Estimate	Standard Error	t Value	Pr > |t|
Intercept	1	0.88093	0.00204	431.48	<.0001
LTV_time	1	0.00096316	0.00001979	48.68	<.0001

Exhibit 11.16 Linear Regression Fit for LCF

The REG Procedure
Model: MODEL1
Dependent Variable: UACF

Root MSE	0.01411	R-Squared	0.0781
Dependent Mean	0.99491	Adj R-Sq	0.0780
Coeff Var	1.41856		

Parameter Estimates					
Variable	DF	Parameter Estimate	Standard Error	t Value	Pr > |t|
Intercept	1	0.97568	0.00062570	1559.34	<.0001
LTV_time	1	0.00019063	0.00000606	31.44	<.0001

Exhibit 11.17 Linear Regression Fit for UACF

```
    MODEL LCF_t = LTV_time;
    RUN;
    ODS GRAPHICS OFF;

    ODS GRAPHICS ON;
PROC REG DATA=mortgage2(WHERE=(default_time=1))
PLOTS(MAXPOINTS=20000 STATS= ALL)= DIAGNOSTICS;
    MODEL UACF_t = LTV_time;
    RUN;
    ODS GRAPHICS OFF;
```

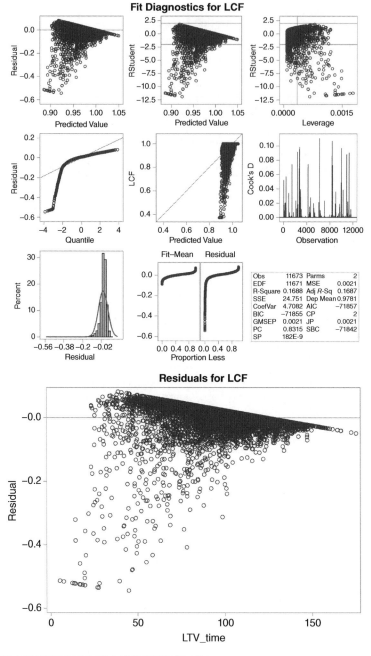

Exhibit 11.18 Linear Regression Fit and Residuals for LCF

The REG Procedure
Model: MODEL1
Dependent Variable: CCF_t

Root MSE	2.65749	*R*-Squared	0.0149
Dependent Mean	0.12181	Adj *R*-Sq	0.0148
Coeff Var	2181.66187		

Parameter Estimates					
Variable	DF	Parameter Estimate	Standard Error	*t* Value	Pr > |*t*|
Intercept	1	−1.40669	0.11782	−11.94	<.0001
LTV_time	1	0.01515	0.00114	13.27	<.0001

Exhibit 11.19 Transformed Linear Regression Fit for CCF_t

The REG Procedure
Model: MODEL1
Dependent Variable: CEQ_t

Root MSE	0.01818	*R*-Squared	0.0979
Dependent Mean	−0.00898	Adj *R*-Sq	0.0979
Coeff Var	−202.34252		

Parameter Estimates					
Variable	DF	Parameter Estimate	Standard Error	*t* Value	Pr > |*t*|
Intercept	1	−0.03704	0.00080587	−45.96	<.0001
LTV_time	1	0.00027803	0.00000781	35.60	<.0001

Exhibit 11.20 Transformed Linear Regression Fit for CEQ_t

Exhibits 11.19 through 11.22 show that the *R*-squared is highest for the transformed LCF.

Generally speaking, our transformation models have a poorer fit, and we continue by estimating a beta regression model for the currently dominating model for LCF, as this might provide a better fit of the empirical distribution of the residuals.

Beta Regression

We now apply a beta regression for LCF as we suspect that, similar to LGD, this may also be an interesting approach for EAD modeling. Next to a better model fit, LCF has the benefit of the same range of values as LGD and does not require a further

The REG Procedure

Model: MODEL1

Dependent Variable: LCF_t

Root MSE	5.21231	R-Squared	0.1137
Dependent Mean	8.11144	Adj R-Sq	0.1136
Coeff Var	64.25870		

Parameter Estimates					
Variable	DF	Parameter Estimate	Standard Error	t Value	Pr > |t|
Intercept	1	−0.63130	0.23108	−2.73	0.0063
LTV_time	1	0.08664	0.00224	38.69	<.0001

Exhibit 11.21 Transformed Linear Regression Fit for LCF_t

The REG Procedure

Model: MODEL1

Dependent Variable: UACF_t

Root MSE	0.01570	R-Squared	0.0706
Dependent Mean	−0.00522	Adj R-Sq	0.0705
Coeff Var	−300.48693		

Parameter Estimates					
Variable	DF	Parameter Estimate	Standard Error	t Value	Pr > |t|
Intercept	1	−0.02548	0.00069584	−36.62	<.0001
LTV_time	1	0.00020073	0.00000674	29.77	<.0001

Exhibit 11.22 Transformed Linear Regression Fit for UACF_t

transformation to the range of zero to one. We encourage the reader to explore other conversion measures, covariates, and other regression models such as nonlinear regressions, fractional logit regression, and a beta regression from the previous LGD chapter. Furthermore, an application of the LGD-PD model may be able to control for the bias of the selecting default event (see Exhibit 11.23).

```
ODS GRAPHICS ON;
PROC NLMIXED DATA=mortgage2(WHERE=(default_time=1)) TECH =TRUREG;
PARMS   b0 = 0 b1 = 0.001
c0 = 0 c1 = 0.001 ;
```

The NLMIXED Procedure

Specifications	
Data Set	WORK.MORTGAGE2
Dependent Variable	LCF
Distribution for Dependent Variable	General
Optimization Technique	Trust Region
Integration Method	None

Dimensions	
Observations Used	11673
Observations Not Used	0
Total Observations	11673
Parameters	4

Fit Statistics	
-2 Log-Likelihood	−124E3
AIC (smaller is better)	−124E3
AICC (smaller is better)	−124E3
BIC (smaller is better)	−124E3

Parameter Estimates								
Parameter	Estimate	Standard Error	DF	t Value	Pr > |t|	95% Confidence Limits		Gradient
b0	0.8062	0.07272	12E3	11.09	<.0001	0.6637	0.9487	0.000013
b1	0.03272	0.000757	12E3	43.22	<.0001	0.03123	0.03420	0.001216
c0	0.6939	0.08126	12E3	8.54	<.0001	0.5346	0.8531	−0.00001
c1	0.01769	0.000833	12E3	21.22	<.0001	0.01605	0.01932	−0.00160

Exhibit 11.23 Beta Regression for LCF

```
*Linear predictors;
Xb = b0 + b1 * LTV_time ;
Wc = c0 + c1 * LTV_time ;
mu = 1 / (1 + exp(-xb));
delta = EXP(Wc);
```

```
*transform to standard parameterization;
alpha = mu * delta;
beta = (1-mu) * delta;

*log-likelihood;
lh = (GAMMA(alpha + beta) / (GAMMA(alpha) * GAMMA(beta))
* (LCF ** (alpha - 1)) * ((1 - LCF) ** (beta - 1)));
ll = LOG(lh);

MODEL LCF ~ GENERAL(ll);
PREDICT mu OUT = out_mu;
PREDICT delta OUT = out_delta;
RUN;
ODS GRAPHICS OFF;
```

As for modeling LGDs, we use the predicted values for μ and produce a real-fit plot using PROC GPLOT of the realized LGDs versus the predicted values as illustrated next. We also run a linear regression using PROC REG of the realizations against the predictions and compute the R^2. The regression reveals that the intercept is statistically different from zero and the slope is statistically different from one. (See Exhibits 11.24 and 11.25.)

```
ODS GRAPHICS ON;
PROC GPLOT DATA=out_mu;
PLOT LCF * PRED;
RUN;
PROC REG DATA = out_mu;
MODEL LCF = PRED;
RUN;
ODS GRAPHICS OFF;
```

Interestingly, the R-squared is now much higher than in the case of linear regression and transformed linear regression models.

Controlling for Adverse Selection in PD Models

Interaction of PD and EAD

Generally speaking, low-risk borrowers are more likely to reduce the loan balance below the expected or scheduled balance, while high-risk borrowers are more likely to increase the loan balance above the expected balance. Consider, for example, a revolving credit line or credit card. If the financial distress worsens, the obligor might try to draw down as much as possible on his or her existing unutilized credit lines in order to avoid default, thereby significantly increasing the EAD risk.

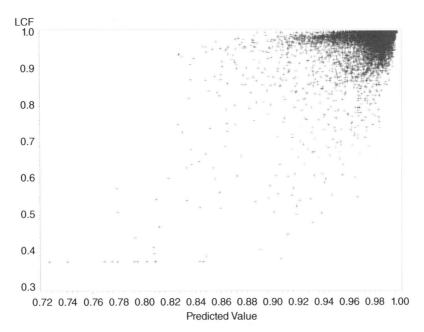

Exhibit 11.24 Real-Fit Plot of Beta Regression for LCF

Root MSE	0.04250	*R*-Squared	0.2922
Dependent Mean	0.97812	Adj *R*-Sq	0.2921
Coeff Var	4.34461		

Parameter Estimates						
Variable	Label	DF	Parameter Estimate	Standard Error Error	*t* Value	Pr > |*t*|
Intercept	Intercept	1	−0.32001	0.01871	−17.11	<.0001
Pred	Predicted Value	1	1.32615	0.01911	69.41	<.0001

Exhibit 11.25 Real-Fit Regression of Beta Regression for LCF

In other words, exposures generally increase in the case of default. Another important aspect for mortgage lending is that borrowers typically have a prepayment option, which they generally exercise if they are low risk and have excess cash to repay the mortgage loan. A prepayment has a limited impact and can be controlled for by a separate risk factor. However, after the complete mortgage has been paid off, low-risk borrowers leave the observed population, while high-risk mortgage borrowers remain. It is common in such situations to model the competing states default, payoff, and nondefault/nonpayoff by the following status variable:

$$S_{it} = \begin{cases} 1 & \text{borrower } i \text{ defaults at time } t \\ 2 & \text{borrower } i \text{ pays loan off at time } t \\ 0 & \text{otherwise} \end{cases}$$

To account for this, you may consider a discrete-time hazard model such as the multinomial logit or probit model, or a continuous-time hazard model (compare Deng, Quigley, and Van Order 2000).

Discrete Time Hazard Models

The first option is a multinomial logit (or probit) model that is a representative of the class of discrete-time hazard models as follows:

$$P(S_{it} = s|x_{it-1}) = \frac{exp\ (\boldsymbol{\beta}'_s x_{it-1})}{1 + \sum_{s=1}^{2} exp\ (\boldsymbol{\beta}'_s x_{it-1})}$$

We can estimate a multinomial logit model in SAS using PROC LOGISTIC (see Exhibit 11.26):

```
PROC LOGISTIC DATA=data.mortgage;
CLASS status_time (REF='0');
MODEL status_time = FICO_orig_time LTV_time gdp_time/ LINK=GLOGIT RSQUARE;
OUTPUT OUT=probabilities PREDICTED=p;
RUN;
```

We obtain two parameter estimates for every covariate. FICO decreases the probabilities of default and payoff. LTV increases the probability of default but decreases the probability of payoff. GDP growth decreases the probability of default and increases the probability of payoff.

To compute performance measures, we generally include the estimated default (payoff) probabilities in a discrete-time hazard model with the default (payoff) indicator as the dependent variable, and obtain the standard pseudo-R-squared, AUROC, and accuracy ratio measures. For details, refer to the chapter on discrete-time hazard models.

Estimation of Default Probabilities

The probabilities of default can be estimated with the OUTPUT statement, which has evaluated the model equation and estimated parameters (indicated by a hat) as follows:

$$\hat{P}(S_{it} = 1|x_{it-1}) = \frac{\exp\ (\hat{\boldsymbol{\beta}}'_1 x_{it-1})}{1 + \exp\ (\hat{\boldsymbol{\beta}}'_1 x_{it-1}) + \exp\ (\hat{\boldsymbol{\beta}}'_2 x_{it-1})}$$

with

$$\hat{\boldsymbol{\beta}}'_1 x_{it-1} = \hat{\beta}_{0,1} + \hat{\beta}_{1,1} * \text{FICO\_orig\_time} + \hat{\beta}_{2,1} * \text{LTV\_time} + \hat{\beta}_{3,1} * \text{gdp\_time}$$
$$\hat{\boldsymbol{\beta}}'_2 x_{it-1} = \hat{\beta}_{0,2} + \hat{\beta}_{1,2} * \text{FICO\_orig\_time} + \hat{\beta}_{2,2} * \text{LTV\_time} + \hat{\beta}_{3,2} * \text{gdp\_time}$$

The LOGISTIC Procedure

Model Information	
Data Set	DATA.MORTGAGE
Response Variable	status_time
Number of Response Levels	3
Model	Generalized logit
Optimization Technique	Newton-Raphson

Number of Observations Read	622489
Number of Observations Used	622219

Response Profile		
Ordered Value	status_time	Total Frequency
1	0	580484
2	1	15153
3	2	26582

Note	Logits modeled use status_time=0 as the reference category.

Model Convergence Status
Convergence criterion (GCONV=1E−8) satisfied.

Model Fit Statistics		
Criterion	Intercept Only	Intercept and Covariates
AIC	360828.66	346768.56
SC	360851.35	346859.28
-2 Log L	360824.66	346752.56

R-Squared	0.0224	Max-Rescaled *R*-Squared	0.0508

Testing Global Null Hypothesis: Beta = 0			
Test	Chi-Square	DF	Pr > ChiSq
Likelihood Ratio	14072.1083	6	<.0001
Score	14159.6297	6	<.0001
Wald	13072.9694	6	<.0001

Exhibit 11.26 Multinomial Logit Model

Analysis of Maximum Likelihood Estimates						
Parameter	status_time	DF	Estimate	Standard Error	Wald Chi-Square	Pr > ChiSq
Intercept	1	1	−1.5286	0.0833	337.0219	<.0001
Intercept	2	1	−1.2835	0.0607	447.4465	<.0001
FICO_orig_time	1	1	−0.00545	0.000116	2195.5817	<.0001
FICO_orig_time	2	1	−0.00122	0.000084	208.9571	<.0001
LTV_time	1	1	0.0178	0.000373	2281.1240	<.0001
LTV_time	2	1	−0.0159	0.000271	3444.4963	<.0001
gdp_time	1	1	−0.1059	0.00375	797.6120	<.0001
gdp_time	2	1	0.1460	0.00452	1042.9821	<.0001

Exhibit 11.26 (Continued)

The MEANS Procedure			
Variable	Mean	Variable	Mean
default_time	0.0243506	p	0.0243532

Exhibit 11.27 Calibration of Multinomial Logit Models: Comparison of Default Indicators and Estimated Default Probabilities

with $\hat{\beta}_{0,1}$ to $\hat{\beta}_{3,2}$ being the estimated default parameters. A PROC MEANS calculates the mean for the default indicators and the estimated PDs (see Exhibit 11.27).

```
PROC MEANS DATA=probabilities(WHERE=(_LEVEL_=1)) MEAN NOLABELS;
VAR default_time p;
RUN;
```

The calibration is clear, as the mean of the default event almost matches the mean of the estimated PDs. The minor difference that we observe is due to the estimation algorithm that iteratively maximizes the likelihood and stops if a target function indicates a low model improvement.

We now compute the default rates and average estimated default probabilities by time:

```
PROC SORT DATA=probabilities;
BY time;
RUN;


PROC MEANS DATA=probabilities(WHERE=(_LEVEL_=1));
BY time;
OUTPUT OUT=means MEAN(default_time p)=default_time p;
RUN;
```

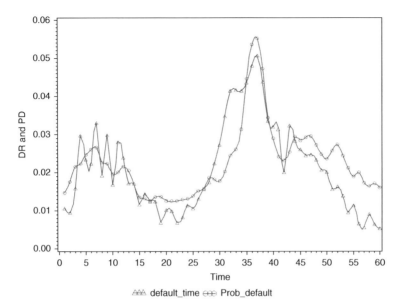

Exhibit 11.28 Real-Fit Diagram for the Default Probabilities

The chart in Exhibit 11.28 compares the observed default rate (DR) and the average of the estimated default probabilities (PD):

```
DATA means;
SET means;
LABEL p="Prob_default";
RUN;


ODS GRAPHICS ON;
AXIS1 ORDER=(0 to 60 by 5) LABEL=('Time');
AXIS2 order=(0 to 0.06 by 0.01) LABEL=('DR and PD');
SYMBOL1 INTERPOL=SPLINE WIDTH=2 VALUE=TRIANGLE C=BLUE;
SYMBOL2 INTERPOL=SPLINE WIDTH=2 VALUE=CIRCLE C=RED;
LEGEND1 LABEL=NONE SHAPE=SYMBOL(4,2) POSITION=(bottom outside);

PROC GPLOT DATA=means;
PLOT (default_time p)*time
/ OVERLAY HAXIS=AXIS1 VAXIS=AXIS2 LEGEND=LEGEND1;
RUN;
ODS GRAPHICS OFF;
```

The MEANS Procedure

Variable	Mean	Variable	Mean
payoff_time	0.0427140	p	0.0427213

Exhibit 11.29 Calibration of Multinomial Logit Models: Comparison of Payoff Indicators and Estimated Payoff Probabilities

Estimation of Payoff Probabilities

Similarly, the probabilities of payoff can be estimated with the OUTPUT statement, which has evaluated the model equation and estimated parameters (indicated by a hat) as follows:

$$\hat{P}(S_{it} = 2 | x_{it-1}) = \frac{\exp(\hat{\beta}_2' x_{it-1})}{1 + \exp(\hat{\beta}_1' x_{it-1}) + \exp(\hat{\beta}_2' x_{it-1})}$$

with

$$\hat{\beta}_1' x_{it-1} = \hat{\beta}_{0,1} + \hat{\beta}_{1,1} * \text{FICO\_orig\_time} + \hat{\beta}_{2,1} * \text{LTV\_time} + \hat{\beta}_{3,1} * \text{gdp\_time}$$

$$\hat{\beta}_2' x_{it-1} = \hat{\beta}_{0,2} + \hat{\beta}_{1,2} * \text{FICO\_orig\_time} + \hat{\beta}_{2,2} * \text{LTV\_time} + \hat{\beta}_{3,2} * \text{gdp\_time}$$

with $\hat{\beta}_{0,1}$ to $\hat{\beta}_{3,2}$ being the estimated payoff parameters. A PROC MEANS calculates the mean for the payoff indicators and the estimated payoff probabilities (see Exhibit 11.29).

```
PROC MEANS DATA=probabilities(WHERE=(_LEVEL_=2)) MEAN NOLABELS;
VAR payoff_time p;
RUN;
```

The calibration is clear, as the mean of the payoff event almost matches the mean of the estimated payoff probabilities.

We now compute the payoff rates and average estimated payoff probabilities by time:

```
PROC SORT DATA=probabilities;
BY time;
RUN;


PROC MEANS DATA=probabilities(WHERE=(_LEVEL_=2));
BY time;
OUTPUT OUT=means MEAN(payoff_time p)=default_time p;
RUN;
```

The chart in Exhibit 11.30 compares the observed payoff rate (PR) and the average of the estimated payoff probabilities (PP):

```
DATA means;
SET means;
LABEL p="Prob_payoff";
RUN;

ODS GRAPHICS ON;
AXIS1 ORDER=(0 to 60 by 5) LABEL=('Time');
AXIS2 order=(0 to 0.14 by 0.02) LABEL=('PR and PP');
SYMBOL1 INTERPOL=SPLINE WIDTH=2 VALUE=TRIANGLE C=BLUE;
SYMBOL2 INTERPOL=SPLINE WIDTH=2 VALUE=CIRCLE C=RED;
LEGEND1 LABEL=NONE SHAPE=SYMBOL(4,2) POSITION=(bottom outside);

PROC GPLOT DATA=means;
PLOT (default_time p)*time
/ OVERLAY HAXIS=AXIS1 VAXIS=AXIS2 LEGEND=LEGEND1;
RUN;
ODS GRAPHICS OFF;
```

Generally speaking, default rates and payoff rates move in opposite directions, which explains the opposite signs of the covariates, in particular the macroeconomic factors.

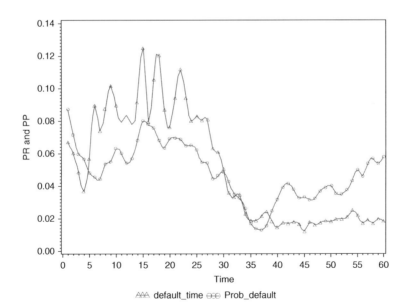

Exhibit 11.30 Real-Fit Diagram for the Payoff Probabilities

Continuous-Time Hazard Models

Reshaping the Data

We first replicate the data steps from our chapter on continuous-time hazard models as follows:

```
PROC SORT DATA=data.mortgage;
BY id;
RUN;

DATA lifetest_temp1;
SET data.mortgage;
time2 = time-first_time+1;
BY id;
RETAIN id;
IF LAST.id THEN indicator=1;
RUN;

DATA lifetest_temp2;
SET lifetest_temp1;
IF indicator = 1 OR status_time =1 OR status_time =2;
RUN;

DATA lifetest;
SET lifetest_temp2;
BY id;
RETAIN id;
IF FIRST.id THEN output;
RUN;
```

Exhibit 11.31 shows three borrower observations as an example. The time stamp time2 shows the time to default since the first observation period. This is contrary to the panel data set applied for discrete-time hazard models, where the time indicates the absolute time and loans were generally originated at different times. The first mortgage results in a default event, the second mortgage in a payoff event, and

id	first_ time	time2	default_ time	payoff_ time	status_ time
46	25	5	1	0	1
47	25	3	0	1	2
56	25	36	0	0	0

Exhibit 11.31 Cross-Sectional Data

the third mortgage in neither. The second and third mortgages are considered to be censored.

A competing risk analysis is also available for continuous-time hazard models. One way to compute such a model in SAS is by using PROC PHREG:

```
PROC PHREG data=lifetest;
MODEL time2*status_time(0,2)=FICO_orig_time LTV_orig_time / TIES=EFRON;
RUN;
```

The structure of PROC PHREG is very similar to PROC LOGISTIC. The dependent variable in the model is the (survival) observation time and an indicator variable, which indicates default (coded by one), or whether the borrower is no longer observed (i.e., censored, coded by zero and two). The censoring state is specified between parentheses and the two variables connected by "*".

The model output is presented in Exhibit 11.32.

The computation of default and payoff probabilities is beyond the scope of this book. However, note that the cumulative incidence for the subcategories can be modeled by a methodology proposed by Fine and Gray (1999) with a slight variation of the MODEL statement.

The PHREG Procedure

Model Information	
Data Set	WORK.LIFETEST
Dependent Variable	time2
Censoring Variable	status_time
Censoring Value(s)	0 2
Ties Handling	EFRON

Number of Observations Read	50000	Number of Observations Used	50000

Convergence Status
Convergence criterion (GCONV=1E−8) satisfied.

Model Fit Statistics		
Criterion	Without Covariates	With Covariates
-2 LOG L	303232.75	301068.64
AIC	303232.75	301072.64
SBC	303232.75	301087.89

Exhibit 11.32 CPH Model

Testing Global Null Hypothesis: BETA=0			
Test	Chi-Square	DF	Pr > ChiSq
Likelihood Ratio	2164.1072	2	<.0001
Score	2198.7891	2	<.0001
Wald	2183.5710	2	<.0001

Analysis of Maximum Likelihood Estimates						
Parameter	DF	Parameter Estimate	Standard Error	Chi-Square	Pr > ChiSq	Hazard Ratio
FICO_orig_time	1	−0.00442	0.0001114	1571.3114	<.0001	0.996
LTV_orig_time	1	0.01554	0.0008019	375.6040	<.0001	1.016

Exhibit 11.32 *(Continued)*

Extensions

Other ways to control for adverse selection include bivariate probit models, estimation of the inverse Mills ratio in a first-stage probit model for the payoff event and control for the inverse Mills ratio in a second-stage probit model for the default event, and the continued observation of paid-off borrowers (although this might be an impossible or very costly solution). For the last option, we refer to our discussion on reject inference in the credit scoring chapter.

PRACTICE QUESTIONS

1. Identify two credit exposures that have uncertain exposures at default. Identify the most suitable conversion measure for each exposure class, and justify your choice. It has been argued that regression models for conversion measures dominate models for EAD. Can you explain the reasoning for this argument?

2. Compute the conversion measures CCF, CEQ, LCF, and UACF based on the drawn loan amount one period prior to the observation of default events. Estimate a linear regression model for default events, and compute the EAD for all observations of the data set. Choose the dependent variable and covariates so that the R-squared is maximized. Use data set mortgage.

3. Compute the conversion measure LCF and estimate a Tobit model. Choose LTV_time and time to maturity (which you would have to compute using a DATA step) as covariates. Use data set mortgage.

4. Estimate a multinomial logit model for the default probability, and payoff probability, and interpret the parameters with regard to both probabilities.

Include the following risk factors: FICO_orig_time, LTV_time, RE-type_CO_orig_time, REtype_PU_orig_time, and REtype_SF_orig_time. Stratify the data into a training sample and a validation sample with approximately an equal amount of observations. Compute the realized default and payoff rates and average estimated default and payoff probabilities for the validation sample by time and plot using PROC GPLOT. Use data set mortgage.

REFERENCES

Agarwal, S., B. W. Ambrose, and C. Liu. 2006. "Credit Lines and Credit Utilization." *Journal of Money, Credit and Banking*, 1–22.

Barakova, I., and H. Parthasarathy. 2012. "How Committed Are Bank Corporate Line Commitments?" Manuscript, Washington, DC: Office of the Comptroller of the Currency.

Basel Committee on Banking Supervision. 2006. "International Convergence of Capital Measurement and Capital Standards: A Revised Framework, Comprehensive Version."

Basel Committee on Banking Supervision. 2014. "The Standardised Approach for Measuring Counterparty Credit Risk Exposures."

Deng, Y., J. M. Quigley, and R. Van Order. 2000. "Mortgage Terminations, Heterogeneity and the Exercise of Mortgage Options." *Econometrica* 68 (2): 275–307.

Fine, J. P., and R. J. Gray. 1999. "Proportional Hazards Model for the Subdistribution of a Competing Risk." *Journal of the American Statistical Association* 94 (446): 496–509.

Jacobs, M. 2011. "An Empirical Study of Exposure at Default." *Journal of Advanced Studies in Finance* 1: 31–59.

Moral, G. 2011. "EAD Estimates for Facilities with Explicit Limits." In *The Basel II Risk Parameters*, edited by Bernd Engelmann and Robert Rauhmeier, 201–246. *Springer Science+Business Media*.

Qi, M. 2009. *Exposure at Default of Unsecured Credit Cards*. Washington, DC: Office of the Comptroller of the Currency.

Taplin, R., H. To, and J. Hee. 2007. "Modeling Exposure at Default, Credit Conversion Factors and the Basel II Accord." *Journal of Credit Risk* 3: 75–84.

Tong, E. N., C. Mues, I. Brown, and L. C. Thomas. 2016. "Exposure at Default Models with and without the Credit Conversion Factor." *European Journal of Operational Research* 252 (3): 910–920.

Valvonis, V. 2008. "Estimating EAD for Retail Exposures for Basel II Purposes." *Journal of Credit Risk* 4 (1): 79–110.

Yang, B. H., and M. Tkachenko. 2012. "Modeling Exposure at Default and Loss Given Default: Empirical Approaches and Technical Implementation," *Journal of Credit Risk* 8 (2): 81.

CHAPTER 12

Bayesian Methods for Credit Risk Modeling

INTRODUCTION

Bayesian statistics is an alternative perspective of statistics compared to the classical frequentist approach. A good introduction on Bayesian statistics is given in Greenberg (2014). Simply speaking, the frequentist or classical statistician interprets probabilities as limits of empirical frequencies of realizations of random events when the number of repetitions of the random experiment goes to infinity. Hence, probabilities are objective. Model estimation is performed by maximizing the likelihood using sample information. In contrast, the Bayesian approach makes use of subjective probabilities in addition to information from the likelihood. The subjective probabilities make up the prior distribution of the events under consideration. In other words, information from the sample data is complemented by prior (subjective) information and assumptions. It can be shown that the estimation results using the Bayesian approach become more and more similar to the estimates from the classical approach when larger information is available. On the other hand, when only little information from the data is available, the prior approach is more dominant. Bayesian statistics can provide powerful tools, particularly for sparse data such as short time series or credit portfolios with small numbers of defaults. However, the prior assumptions have to be chosen wisely, as these may dominate the posterior outcome.

As an example, consider data y from a number of n random coin tosses. The frequentist approach treats the parameter (i.e., the probability π of "head") as an unknown parameter (i.e., a fixed, but unknown number) that can be estimated from the sample data. In contrast, the Bayesian approach considers this parameter to be unknown *and* a random variable itself and assigns a prior distribution $f(\pi), 0 \leq \pi \leq 1$ to it. It then links the prior distribution with observable data from the realized coin tosses and generates a posterior distribution $f(\pi|y)$, that is, the conditional distribution of π, given the data y. The goal is then to learn about the parameter from the data and update the prior distribution. The Bayesian view is therefore different from the frequentist approach in many perspectives. Parameter estimators are derived under the frequentist approach claiming criteria such as unbiasedness or consistency. The Bayesian approach obtains point estimates for parameters as minima of specific loss functions. The frequentist approach constructs confidence intervals and computes p-values, while the Bayesian method computes credibility intervals directly from the posterior distribution and compares different models (similar to hypotheses) via marginal likelihoods. The following table contrasts the main differences between the frequentist and the Bayesian approach.

	Frequentist	*Bayesian*
Probability view	Objective	Subjective
Data	Data are a repeatable random sample	Data are observed from a realized sample
Parameters	Parameters are unknown but fixed	Parameters are unknown but random
Estimation criterion	Unbiasedness, consistency	Minimizing a loss function
Parameter estimate	Point estimate from estimation approach	Location measure (e.g., mean) of posterior distribution
Interval	Confidence interval	Credibility interval from posterior distribution
Hypothesis testing	Via p-value	Via marginal likelihoods of various models

THE BAYESIAN APPROACH TO STATISTICS

To understand the Bayesian approach more formally, we start with Bayes' theorem. Consider two random events A and B. Bayes' theorem states that the conditional probability of A given B is

$$P(A \mid B) = \frac{P(B \mid A)P(A)}{P(B)}$$

Now, if we consider random data Y (e.g., coin tosses) and a parameter θ (e.g., the probability of a head occurring), Bayes' theorem gives the posterior distribution

$$f(\theta \mid y) = \frac{f(y \mid \theta)f(\theta)}{f(y)}$$

where $f(y) = \int f(y \mid \theta)f(\theta)\,d\theta$ is the unconditional distribution of the data and $f(y \mid \theta)$ is the likelihood function. This basically indicates that the conditional (posterior) distribution of the parameter θ given some realized data y is the ratio of the product of the likelihood and the prior distribution $f(\theta)$ of the parameter divided by the unconditional distribution of the data. The prior distribution may consist of further parameters (such as expectation and variance of the normal distribution), which are called hyper parameters and can also be modeled as random variables with hyper prior distributions and so forth.

The likelihood function is given by a model and the data as in the frequentist approach. The prior distribution is prespecified by the Bayesian statistician according to her or his beliefs and prior experiences or from other data sources. Unless we assume special cases for the likelihood and the prior, the posterior distribution cannot be evaluated analytically. Rather, the evaluation can be performed via a special Monte Carlo technique, the Markov chain–Monte Carlo (MCMC) method, which generates a large number of simulation trials via special sampling algorithms in order to approximate the posterior. In SAS, this is implemented in PROC MCMC.

Once the posterior distribution is generated, analogously to the frequentist approach, estimates of the moments of the posterior and so-called *credibility intervals* can be derived. However, instead of claiming specific properties for the estimators such as unbiasedness and consistency, the Bayesian criterion for creating an estimator is the minimization of a "loss function." Consider a loss function $L(\hat{\theta}, \theta)$, which specifies the loss incurred by using estimate $\hat{\theta}$ instead of the true θ. Examples are

▨ Absolute value loss function:

$$L_1(\hat{\theta}, \theta) = |\hat{\theta} - \theta|$$

▨ Quadratic loss function:

$$L_2(\hat{\theta}, \theta) = (\hat{\theta} - \theta)^2$$

▨ Bilinear loss function:

$$L_3(\hat{\theta}, \theta) = \begin{cases} a\,|\hat{\theta} - \theta| & \text{for } \theta > \hat{\theta} \\ b\,|\hat{\theta} - \theta| & \text{for } \theta \leq \hat{\theta} \end{cases}$$

where $a, b > 0$

The *Bayes estimator* for θ is the value $\hat{\theta}$ that minimizes the expected value of the loss, where expectation is taken over the posterior distribution; that is, $\hat{\theta}$ is chosen to minimize

$$E\left[L(\hat{\theta}, \theta)\right] = \int L(\hat{\theta}, \theta) f(\theta \mid y)\, d\theta$$

For example, under quadratic loss we minimize

$$E\left[L(\hat{\theta}, \theta)\right] = \int (\hat{\theta} - \theta)^2 f(\theta \mid y)\, d\theta$$

We then differentiate with respect to $\hat{\theta}$ and set the result equal to zero:

$$2 \int (\hat{\theta} - \theta) f(\theta \mid y) \, d\theta = 0$$

$$\hat{\theta} = \int \theta f(\theta \mid y) \, d\theta$$

Hence, under the quadratic loss function the Bayes estimator is $\hat{\theta} = E(\theta \mid y)$ (i.e., the expectation of the posterior distribution). For computing credibility intervals, the Bayesian approach reports an interval estimate of the form

$$P(\theta_L \leq \theta \leq \theta_U) = 0.95$$

In other words, it requires that the probability of the parameter θ being between a lower bound θ_L and an upper bound θ_U equals some (high) probability (e.g., 95% or 99%).

Given the posterior distribution, forecasts for out-of-sample (e.g., future) observations can be derived. Let y_f be some forecast, then its density, given the observed data y and the posterior distribution is given by

$$f(y_f \mid y) = \int f(y_f \mid \theta, y) f(\theta \mid y) \, d\theta$$

This implies that one computes the probability or density of y given the data and given some parameter value, and mixes over the (posterior) density of all potential parameter values.

PD ESTIMATION WITH BAYESIAN STATISTICS

Probit Analysis

We start introducing the Bayesian approach with PD estimation and compare it to the classical approach using a probit model. As the Bayesian approach generally requires evaluating the posterior distribution by MCMC, it might have a longer running time. For illustration purposes, we therefore draw a random sample from the entire data set of size 1 percent and the reader is encouraged to evaluate the estimation for the entire data set or larger subsamples. The sample is drawn using only those observations for which a randomly drawn uniformly distributed random variable is lower than 0.01. The probit model is then estimated as in the former chapter on PD estimation using three covariates.

Following our chapter on continuous-time hazard models, we prepare the data and draw a 1 percent random sample (see Exhibit 12.1):

```
/*Data preprocessing and selection of 1 percent random sample*/
DATA sample;
SET data.mortgage;
```

The LOGISTIC Procedure

Analysis of Maximum Likelihood Estimates					
Parameter	DF	Estimate	Standard Error	Wald Chi-Square	Pr > ChiSq
Intercept	1	−1.4138	0.4730	8.9331	0.0028
FICO_orig_time	1	−0.00224	0.000504	19.7709	<.0001
LTV_orig_time	1	0.0119	0.00360	10.9189	0.0010
gdp_time	1	−0.0676	0.0163	17.1275	<.0001

Exhibit 12.1 Probit Model with PROC LOGISTIC

```
time1 = time-first_time;
time2 = time-first_time+1;
IF RANUNI(12345) < 0.01;
RUN;
/*Probit Model with PROC LOGISTIC*/
ODS GRAPHICS ON;
PROC LOGISTIC DATA=sample DESCENDING;
MODEL default_time = FICO_orig_time
LTV_orig_time gdp_time
 / OUTROC=roc_logistic RSQUARE LINK=Probit;
RUN;
ODS GRAPHICS OFF;
```

Next, we estimate the Bayesian model using PROC MCMC with the following code. As usual in this book, for computational details of this procedure we refer the reader to the SAS manual; see SAS Institute Inc. (2015). The options after the PROC MCMC statement refer, among others, to the number of MCMC simulation steps (NMC). The model has four parameters $(\beta_0, \beta_1, \beta_2, \beta_3)$ for which a normal distribution each with mean zero and variance of 1,000 is assumed. As the variance is very high compared to the parameters, this prior reflects only diffuse information and is therefore called a diffuse or uninformative prior. The model is specified in a similar way as in PROC LOGISTIC. However, the PD as a function of the covariates and the distribution of defaults is explicitly given. Note that the parameters are scaled by factors 10 and 100, respectively, for numerical reasons.

```
/*Probit Model with MCMC*/
ODS LISTING CLOSE;
ODS LATEX;
ODS GRAPHICS ON / IMAGEFMT=PDF  IMAGENAME='bayesprobit';
PROC MCMC DATA = sample Statistics=ALL Diagnostics=ALL
SCALE=5 MINTUNE=5 NBI=1000 NMC=10000 THIN=2 PROPCOV=QUANEW SEED=12345;
```

```
PARMS beta0 beta1 beta2 beta3;
PRIOR beta0 beta1 beta2 beta3 ~ normal(0, var = 1000);
pd = PROBNORM(beta0 + beta1 / 10 * FICO_orig_time +
beta2 / 100 * LTV_orig_time + beta3 /100 * gdp_time);
MODEL default_time ~ binomial(1,pd);
RUN;

ODS GRAPHICS OFF;
```

The first table (Exhibit 12.2) shows the number of observations and the prior assumptions about the parameters.

The next table (Exhibit 12.3) gives the summaries for the simulated posterior distributions of the parameters. Especially the means of the posteriors, the standard deviations, and some percentiles are of interest. Here, the means have the expected signs and their values are very similar to those of the frequentist model (after scaling is taken into account). Also note that the standard deviations are similar to the standard errors of PROC LOGISTIC.

In contrast to the frequentist approach, the Bayesian approach computed credibility intervals directly from the posterior distribution, which are shown in the next

The MCMC Procedure

Number of Observations Read	6333	Number of Observations Used	6333

Parameters				
Block	Parameter	Sampling Method	Initial Value	Prior Distribution
1	beta0	N–Metropolis	0	normal(0, var = 1000)
	beta1		0	normal(0, var = 1000)
	beta2		0	normal(0, var = 1000)
	beta3		0	normal(0, var = 1000)

Exhibit 12.2 MCMC Parameter Information for Probit Model

The MCMC Procedure

Posterior Summaries						
Parameter	N	Mean	Standard Deviation	Percentiles		
				25	50	75
beta0	5000	−1.4239	0.4820	−1.7587	−1.4253	−1.0884
beta1	5000	−0.0226	0.00510	−0.0262	−0.0225	−0.0191
beta2	5000	1.2069	0.3746	0.9513	1.2011	1.4690
beta3	5000	−6.7046	1.6374	−7.7341	−6.6887	−5.5764

Exhibit 12.3 MCMC Parameter Summaries for Probit Model

Posterior Intervals					
Parameter	Alpha	Equal-Tail Interval		HPD Interval	
beta0	0.050	−2.3432	−0.4655	−2.3373	−0.4625
beta1	0.050	−0.0323	−0.0124	−0.0325	−0.0128
beta2	0.050	0.4878	1.9404	0.4827	1.9224
beta3	0.050	−9.9586	−3.6301	−9.8259	−3.5376

Exhibit 12.4 MCMC Procedure Output for Probit Model

Posterior Correlation Matrix				
Parameter	beta0	beta1	beta2	beta3
beta0	1.0000	−0.7772	−0.7161	−0.0939
beta1	−0.7772	1.0000	0.1248	0.1045
beta2	−0.7161	0.1248	1.0000	−0.0138
beta3	−0.0939	0.1045	−0.0138	1.0000

Exhibit 12.5 MCMC Procedure Output for Probit Model

Posterior Autocorrelations				
Parameter	Lag 1	Lag 5	Lag 10	Lag 50
beta0	0.7380	0.1887	0.0316	−0.0246
beta1	0.7528	0.2400	0.0749	−0.0196
beta2	0.7235	0.1796	0.0012	−0.0512
beta3	0.7639	0.2724	0.0555	0.0005

Exhibit 12.6 MCMC Procedure Output for Probit Model

table (Exhibit 12.4). If one computes equal-tail and highest posterior density (HPD) 95 percent posterior credibility intervals as in the output, it can be seen that the value of zero is outside the interval for FICO and GDP, which is analogous to their significance in the frequentist approach.

Next, the correlation matrix of the parameters is given in Exhibit 12.5. Except for the constant, it shows only small correlations, which means that there is no issue with correlated samples.

In order to check convergence of the simulation, autocorrelations are important and are shown in the next table (Exhibit 12.6). High correlations between long lags indicate poor mixing. As can be seen, the autocorrelation is high for small lags and decreases sharply for longer lags, which is the desired property.

Geweke Diagnostics		
Parameter	z	Pr > |z|
beta0	0.1421	0.8870
beta1	−1.1085	0.2676
beta2	0.9280	0.3534
beta3	0.3963	0.6919

Exhibit 12.7 MCMC Diagnostics

For a closer check of convergence, some diagnostics are computed, named Geweke, Raftery-Lewis, and Heidelberger-Welch diagnostics, with accompanying tests as reported in the next table (Exhibit 12.7). The Geweke diagnostics test whether the mean estimates have converged by comparing the means from the early and latter part of the Markov chain. It comes with a two-sided test based on a z-score statistic. Large absolute z values indicate rejection. In our example the convergence is obviously satisfactory.

The Raftery-Lewis diagnostics evaluate the accuracy of the estimated (desired) percentiles by reporting the number of samples needed to reach the desired accuracy of the percentiles. Failure could indicate that a longer Markov chain is needed. If the total samples needed are fewer than the Markov chain sample, this indicates rejection. Here, the total sample is larger and therefore the accuracy should be satisfactory.

The Heidelberger-Welch diagnostics are divided into a stationarity test and a half-width test. The former tests whether the Markov chain is a covariance (or weakly) stationary process. Failure could indicate that a longer Markov chain is needed. It is a one-sided test based on a Cramer–von Mises statistic. Small p-values indicate rejection. In Exhibit 12.8 the p-values are large (with the exception for β_0) and therefore, the chain can be considered as covariance stationary. SAS automatically returns the information whether the test is passed or not. The half-width test

Raftery-Lewis Diagnostics				
Quantile = 0.025 Accuracy = +/−0.005 Probability = 0.95 Epsilon = 0.001				
Parameter	Number of Samples			Dependence Factor
	Burn-In	Total	Minimum	
beta0	11	11486	3746	3.0662
beta1	18	21054	3746	5.6204
beta2	11	11311	3746	3.0195
beta3	11	12287	3746	3.2800

Exhibit 12.8 MCMC Diagnostics

Heidelberger-Welch Diagnostics								
Parameter	Stationarity Test				Half-Width Test			
	Cramer–von Mises Stat	p-Value	Test Outcome	Iterations Discarded	Half-Width	Mean	Relative Half-Width	Test Outcome
beta0	0.0750	0.7216	Passed	0	0.0378	−1.4239	−0.0265	Passed
beta1	0.0803	0.6900	Passed	0	0.000480	−0.0226	−0.0213	Passed
beta2	0.1276	0.4656	Passed	0	0.0233	1.2069	0.0193	Passed
beta3	0.0738	0.7286	Passed	0	0.1212	−6.7046	−0.0181	Passed

Exhibit 12.9 MCMC Diagnostics

Effective Sample Sizes			
Parameter	ESS	Autocorrelation Time	Efficiency
beta0	776.4	6.4399	0.1553
beta1	565.6	8.8397	0.1131
beta2	899.4	5.5594	0.1799
beta3	689.5	7.2520	0.1379

Exhibit 12.10 MCMC Diagnostics

reports whether the sample size is adequate to meet the required accuracy for the mean estimate. Failure could indicate that a longer Markov chain is needed. If a relative half-width statistic is greater than a predetermined accuracy measure, this indicates rejection. In Exhibit 12.9, the tests signal that the length of the Markov chain should be sufficient.

Finally, the effective sample size is computed (see Exhibit 12.10). It relates to autocorrelation and measures the mixing of the Markov chain. A large discrepancy between the effective sample size and the simulation sample size indicates poor mixing.

In addition to the statistics, PROC MCMC also shows some diagnostic plots (see Exhibits 12.11 through 12.14). For each parameter, the simulation history is shown in the upper plot. If it looks like a "white-noise" process without drift (as is the case for our four parameters), it indicates good convergence. In the lower left, the auto-correlations are shown for lags up to 50. As in the table, the autocorrelations are high for short lags and close to zero for longer lags, which is the desired property. Finally, in the lower right the simulated posterior distribution is given for each parameter from which the point estimates (i.e., the means) and the credibility intervals are computed.

In this example, the MCMC results lead to similar conclusions about the parameters as in the classical approach. So, what is the difference between the two approaches, or, in other words, when is it really helpful to use Bayesian statistics?

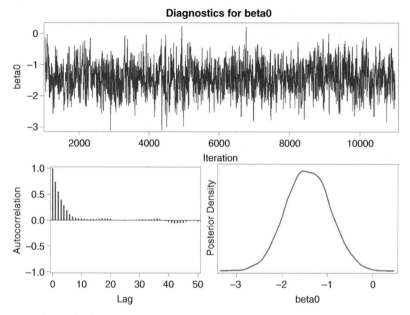

Exhibit 12.11 Diagnostic Plots

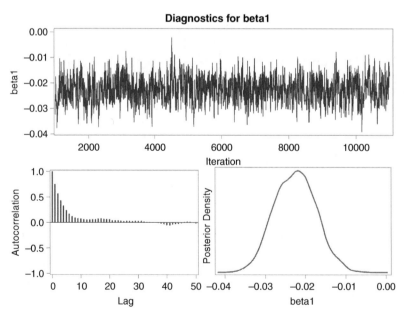

Exhibit 12.12 Diagnostic Plots

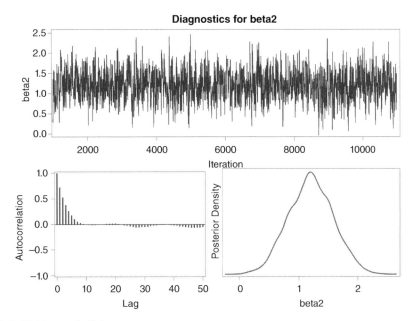

Exhibit 12.13 Diagnostic Plots

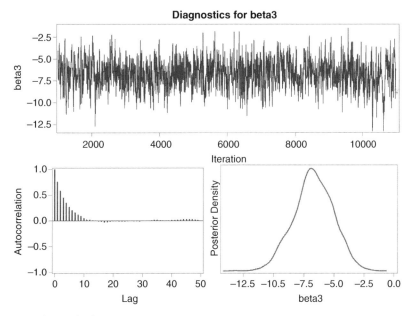

Exhibit 12.14 Diagnostic Plots

One important instance is the availability of useful prior information. Suppose there is an expert on mortgages who has the strong opinion that it is very important to consider loan-to-value (LTV) information and he or she insists that the coefficient should be a lot higher than the output of the classical approach suggests. The expert also remembers an earlier study where the coefficient was "around 3 or so." This can now be included as prior information. Instead of using a diffuse prior with mean 0 and variance of 1,000, one may now specify a normal prior with mean 3 and variance 0.5 as shown in the following code.

```
/*Probit Model with MCMC*/
ODS LISTING CLOSE;
ODS LATEX;
ODS GRAPHICS ON / IMAGEFMT=PDF  IMAGENAME='bayes2probit';
PROC MCMC DATA = sample STATISTICS=ALL DIAGNOSTICS=ALL
SCALE=5 MINTUNE=5 NBI=1000 NMC=10000 THIN=2 PROPCOV=QUANEW SEED=12345;
PARMS beta0 beta1 beta2 beta3;
PRIOR beta0 beta1 beta3 ~ normal(0, var = 1000);
PRIOR beta2 ~ normal (3, var = 0.5);
pd = PROBNORM(beta0 + beta1 / 10 * FICO_orig_time +
beta2 / 100 * LTV_orig_time + beta3 /100 * gdp_time);
MODEL default_time ~ BINOMIAL(1,pd);
RUN;
ODS GRAPHICS OFF;
```

As can be seen from the output (Exhibits 12.15 through 12.19), the mean coefficient for LTV has now shifted upward as a result of mixing data information with the expert's prior opinions (and the constant has moved in the opposite direction). The means and intervals for the other parameters are similar to what they were before and the simulations have converged well. This demonstrates the importance and usefulness of expert information, but also that one should include expert information wisely as it may impose restrictions on the parameters. The reader is encouraged to use other specifications of the priors and other options for PROC MCMC to become more familiar with its features and outputs. For example, an informative prior could be used with low variance and other mean values in order to gauge how the prior information changes the posterior.

Survival Analysis

Next, we show how a simple survival model can be analyzed with Bayesian statistics. (See Exhibits 12.20 through 12.23.) As in the earlier section, we specify a Cox proportional hazards model. Under the Bayesian approach, we use a diffuse prior. SAS offers the possibility to estimate a Bayesian CPH model with PROC PHREG as a very convenient alternative to PROC MCMC; see SAS Institute Inc. (2015). The code is

The MCMC Procedure

Number of Observations Read	6,333	Number of Observations Used	6,333

Parameters				
Block	Parameter	Sampling Method	Initial Value	Prior Distribution
1	beta0	N–Metropolis	0	normal(0, var = 1000)
	beta1		0	normal(0, var = 1000)
	beta2		3.0000	normal(3, var = 0.5)
	beta3		0	normal(0, var = 1000)

The MCMC Procedure

Posterior Summaries						
Parameter	N	Mean	Standard Deviation	Percentiles		
				25	50	75
beta0	5000	−1.7798	0.4526	−2.0959	−1.7869	−1.4780
beta1	5000	−0.0216	0.00519	−0.0252	−0.0215	−0.0181
beta2	5000	1.5697	0.3242	1.3546	1.5684	1.7869
beta3	5000	−6.7201	1.7121	−7.9134	−6.6850	−5.5423

Posterior Intervals					
Parameter	Alpha	Equal-Tail Interval		HPD Interval	
beta0	0.050	−2.6565	−0.8580	−2.7087	−0.9374
beta1	0.050	−0.0319	−0.0115	−0.0319	−0.0115
beta2	0.050	0.9207	2.1885	0.9647	2.2171
beta3	0.050	−9.9649	−3.3740	−9.8994	−3.3423

Posterior Autocorrelations				
Parameter	Lag 1	Lag 5	Lag 10	Lag 50
beta0	0.7300	0.2033	0.0151	−0.0104
beta1	0.7443	0.2444	0.0402	−0.0341
beta2	0.7418	0.2175	0.0294	−0.0201
beta3	0.7416	0.2036	0.0624	−0.0443

Heidelberger-Welch Diagnostics								
Parameter	Stationarity Test				Half-Width Test			
	Cramer–von Mises Stat	p-Value	Test Outcome	Iterations Discarded	Half-Width	Mean	Relative Half-Width	Test Outcome
beta0	0.0766	0.7118	Passed	0	0.0290	−1.7798	−0.0163	Passed
beta1	0.1445	0.4068	Passed	0	0.000399	−0.0216	−0.0185	Passed
beta2	0.2136	0.2426	Passed	0	0.0231	1.5697	0.0147	Passed
beta3	0.1492	0.3920	Passed	0	0.1301	−6.7201	−0.0194	Passed

Exhibit 12.15 Summary Statistics

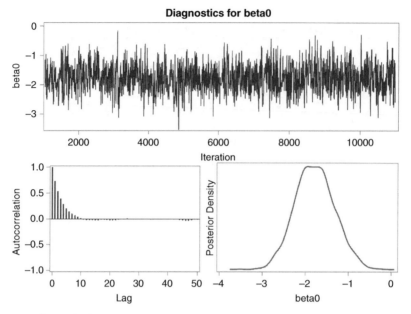

Exhibit 12.16 Diagnostic Plots

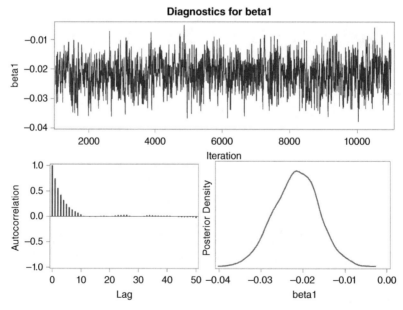

Exhibit 12.17 Diagnostic Plots

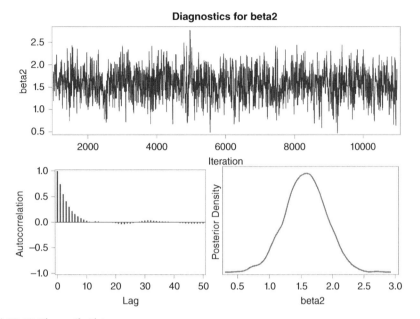

Exhibit 12.18 Diagnostic Plots

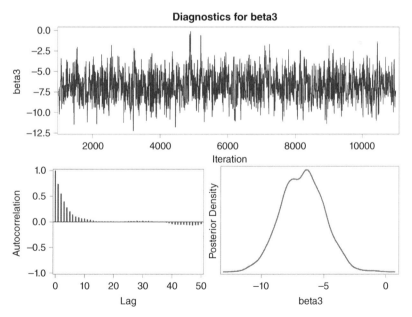

Exhibit 12.19 Diagnostic Plots

The PHREG Procedure

Bayesian Analysis

Model Information	
Data Set	WORK.SAMPLE
Dependent Variable	time1
Dependent Variable	time2
Censoring Variable	default_time
Censoring Value(s)	0
Model	Cox
Ties Handling	BRESLOW
Sampling Algorithm	ARMS
Burn-In Size	2000
MC Sample Size	5000
Thinning	1

Number of Observations Read	6333	Number of Observations Used	6333

Maximum Likelihood Estimates					
Parameter	DF	Estimate	Standard Error	95% Confidence Limits	
FICO_orig_time	1	−0.00468	0.00119	−0.00701	−0.00236
LTV_orig_time	1	0.0270	0.00838	0.0106	0.0435
gdp_time	1	−0.0899	0.0419	−0.1720	−0.00776

Independent Normal Prior for Regression Coefficients		
Parameter	Mean	Precision
FICO_orig_time	0	1E−6
LTV_orig_time	0	1E−6
gdp_time	0	1E−6

Fit Statistics	
DIC (smaller is better)	1463.113
pD (Effective Number of Parameters)	3.018

The PHREG Procedure

Bayesian Analysis

Posterior Summaries						
Parameter	N	Mean	Standard Deviation	Percentiles		
				25%	50%	75%
FICO_orig_time	5000	−0.00469	0.00118	−0.00547	−0.00469	−0.00390
LTV_orig_time	5000	0.0267	0.00837	0.0212	0.0268	0.0323
gdp_time	5000	−0.0892	0.0425	−0.1188	−0.0899	−0.0594

Exhibit 12.20 Summary Statistics

Posterior Intervals

Parameter	Alpha	Equal-Tail Interval		HPD Interval	
FICO_orig_time	0.050	−0.00701	−0.00239	−0.00697	−0.00236
LTV_orig_time	0.050	0.0101	0.0428	0.00943	0.0420
gdp_time	0.050	−0.1718	−0.00558	−0.1747	−0.00991

Posterior Correlation Matrix

Parameter	FICO_orig_time	LTV_orig_time	gdp_time
FICO_orig_time	1.0000	0.1745	0.0131
LTV_orig_time	0.1745	1.0000	−.0306
gdp_time	0.0131	−.0306	1.0000

The PHREG Procedure

Bayesian Analysis

Posterior Autocorrelations

Parameter	Lag 1	Lag 5	Lag 10	Lag 50
FICO_orig_time	0.0251	−0.0007	0.0022	0.0114
LTV_orig_time	0.0349	0.0059	0.0118	−0.0038
gdp_time	−0.0039	−0.0014	−0.0087	−0.0114

Geweke Diagnostics

Parameter	z	Pr > |z|
FICO_orig_time	−0.6374	0.5239
LTV_orig_time	−3.4405	0.0006
gdp_time	0.3633	0.7164

Raftery-Lewis Diagnostics

Quantile = 0.025 Accuracy = +/−0.005 Probability = 0.95 Epsilon = 0.001

Parameter	Number of Samples			Dependence Factor
	Burn-In	Total	Minimum	
FICO_orig_time	2	3742	3746	0.9989
LTV_orig_time	2	3681	3746	0.9826
gdp_time	2	3655	3746	0.9757

Heidelberger-Welch Diagnostics

Parameter	Stationarity Test				Half-Width Test			
	Cramer–von Mises Stat	p-Value	Test Outcome	Iterations Discarded	Half-Width	Mean	Relative Half-Width	Test Outcome
FICO_orig_time	0.0956	0.6067	Passed	0	0.000032	−0.00469	−0.00691	Passed
LTV_orig_time	0.2301	0.2161	Passed	0	0.000320	0.0267	0.0120	Passed
gdp_time	0.1904	0.2868	Passed	0	0.00123	−0.0892	−0.0138	Passed

Effective Sample Sizes

Parameter	ESS	Autocorrelation Time	Efficiency
FICO_orig_time	4760.9	1.0502	0.9522
LTV_orig_time	4479.9	1.1161	0.8960
gdp_time	5000.0	1.0000	1.0000

Exhibit 12.20 (*Continued*)

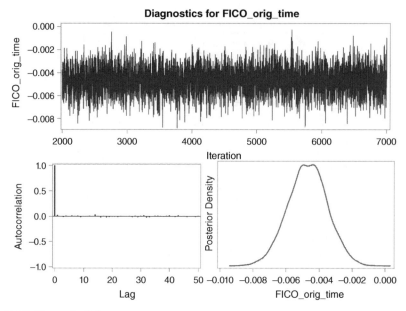

Exhibit 12.21 Diagnostic Plots

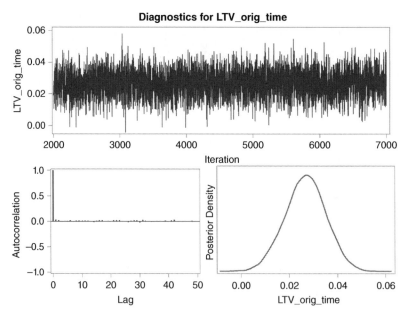

Exhibit 12.22 Diagnostic Plots

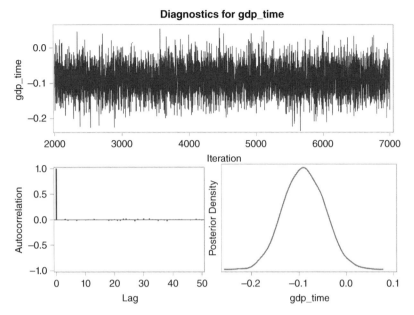

Exhibit 12.23 Diagnostic Plots

analogous to the earlier PHREG and MCMC code. The command line starting with
BAYES requires a Bayesian model to be estimated.

```
/*Survival Model using PROC PHREG with Bayesian approach*/
ODS GRAPHICS ON / IMAGEFMT=PDF IMAGENAME='bayessurvival';
PROC PHREG DATA=sample PLOTS=CUMHAZ PLOTS(OVERLAY)=SURVIVAL;
MODEL (Time1,Time2)*default_time(0)=FICO_orig_time
    LTV_orig_time gdp_time;
BAYES SEED=1 COEFFPRIOR=NORMAL STATISTICS=ALL NMC=5000
DIAGNOSTICS=ALL PLOTS=ALL;
ID ID Time default_time;
STORE out=score_phreg;
RUN;
ODS GRAPHICS OFF;
```

Similarly to PROC MCMC, the output starts with some general model information
and returns the results of the ML estimates as comparison. There is no need to run a
separate ML model. The Bayesian output is actually very similar to the MCMC output
and shows the same information. Due to the diffuse prior and availability of rich data,
the posterior means for the parameters are very close to those from the ML estimation
and the model has converged well. As in the PD estimation, Bayesian statistics are
particularly useful if only sparse sample data were available. This will be shown in a
later section.

CORRELATION ESTIMATION WITH BAYESIAN STATISTICS

Asset correlations can also be estimated using the Bayesian approach, as will be shown in this section. We use the same simple aggregated model and the same data as in the chapter on correlations. So, we regress $\Phi^{-1}(dr_t)$ on a constant. The extension to covariates is left to the reader for training purposes. In other words, we have two parameters, namely a constant coded as β_0 and the residual standard variance. These can be transformed into the PD and the asset correlation as discussed earlier. For both, we use noninformative, diffuse priors. β_0 is assumed to be normally distributed with mean 0 and variance 10,000 whereas σ^2 is assumed uniformly distributed between 0 and 1. Then, $\Phi^{-1}(dr_t)$ is modeled as $N(\beta_0, \sigma^2)$.

```
/*Probit-Linear Regression without Covariates with MCMC*/
ODS LISTING CLOSE;
ODS LATEX;
ODS GRAPHICS ON / IMAGEFMT=PDF  IMAGENAME='bayescorr';
PROC MCMC DATA = data.tmp2 Statistics=ALL Diagnostics=ALL
SCALE=5 MINTUNE=5 NBI=1000 NMC=10000 THIN=2 PROPCOV=QUANEW SEED=12345;
PARMS beta0 0 sigma2 0.1;
PRIOR beta0  ~ normal(0, var = 10000);
PRIOR sigma2 ~ Uniform(0,1);
mu = beta0;
MODEL probit_dr ~ n(mu, var = sigma2);
RUN;
ODS GRAPHICS OFF;
```

The output (see Exhibits 12.24 through 12.26) shows good convergence and low autocorrelation for both coefficients. The means of the posterior distributions are very similar to those from the classical approach, which can be attributed to good sample information and the diffuse priors. Now consider that an expert strongly argues that the variance or the correlation should be a lot higher. As an example, we use a lognormal prior for σ with mean 0.1 and variance 0.1 in the next program code. It can be seen that the mean value for σ^2 is now more than twice as high. If this value is transformed into the asset correlation, one obtains approximately $\rho = \frac{\sigma^2}{1+\sigma^2} = 0.17$. In other words, the expert's prior information is linked with the data and leads to more conservative estimates (see Exhibits 12.27 through 12.29).

```
/*Probit-Linear Regression without Covariates with MCMC*/
ODS LISTING CLOSE;
ODS GRAPHICS ON / IMAGEFMT=PDF  IMAGENAME='bayes2corr';
PROC MCMC DATA = data.tmp2 Statistics=ALL Diagnostics=ALL Scale=5
MINTUNE=5 NBI=1000 NMC=10000 THIN=2 PROPCOV=QUANEW SEED=12345;
PARMS beta0 0 sigma2 0.1;
PRIOR beta0  ~ normal(0, var = 10000);
PRIOR sigma2 ~ lognormal(0.1, var = 0.1);
```

The MCMC Procedure

Number of Observations Read	60	Number of Observations Used	60

Parameters				
Block	Parameter	Sampling Method	Initial Value	Prior Distribution
1	beta0	N–Metropolis	0	normal(0, var = 10000)
	sigma2		0.1000	uniform(0,1)

The MCMC Procedure

Posterior Summaries						
Parameter	N	Mean	Standard Deviation	Percentiles		
				25	50	75
beta0	5000	−2.2772	0.0358	−2.3013	−2.2761	−2.2528
sigma2	5000	0.0793	0.0154	0.0686	0.0773	0.0880

Posterior Intervals					
Parameter	Alpha	Equal-Tail Interval		HPD Interval	
beta0	0.050	−2.3484	−2.2084	−2.3533	−2.2143
sigma2	0.050	0.0545	0.1149	0.0523	0.1105

Posterior Correlation Matrix		
Parameter	beta0	sigma2
beta0	1.0000	−0.0099
sigma2	−0.0099	1.0000

Posterior Autocorrelations				
Parameter	Lag 1	Lag 5	Lag 10	Lag 50
beta0	0.5959	0.0601	−0.0180	0.0055
sigma2	0.6112	0.0809	−0.0215	−0.0144

Geweke Diagnostics		
Parameter	z	Pr > |z|
beta0	0.5783	0.5631
sigma2	0.2690	0.7880

Raftery-Lewis Diagnostics				
Quantile = 0.025 Accuracy = +/−0.005 Probability = 0.95 Epsilon = 0.001				
Parameter	Number of Samples			Dependence Factor
	Burn-In	Total	Minimum	
beta0	10	10534	3746	2.8121
sigma2	11	12172	3746	3.2493

Exhibit 12.24 Summary Statistics

Heidelberger-Welch Diagnostics								
Parameter	Stationarity Test				Half-Width Test			
	Cramer–von Mises Stat	*p*-Value	Test Outcome	Iterations Discarded	Half-Width	Mean	Relative Half-Width	Test Outcome
beta0	0.1014	0.5782	Passed	0	0.00179	−2.2772	−0.00079	Passed
sigma2	0.1666	0.3426	Passed	0	0.000798	0.0793	0.0101	Passed

Effective Sample Sizes			
Parameter	ESS	Autocorrelation Time	Efficiency
beta0	1321.6	3.7834	0.2643
sigma2	1249.2	4.0026	0.2498

Exhibit 12.24 *(Continued)*

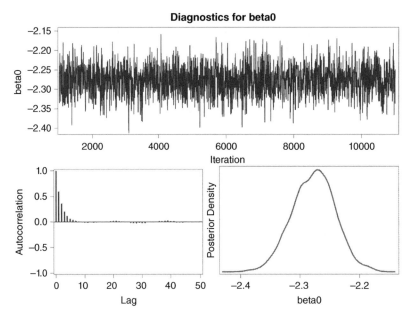

Exhibit 12.25 Diagnostic Plots

```
mu = beta0;
MODEL probit_dr ~ n(mu, var = sigma2);
RUN;
ODS GRAPHICS OFF;
```

PD ESTIMATION FOR LOW DEFAULT PORTFOLIOS

An interesting and helpful application of Bayesian statistics is in the case where only sparse data are available, such as low default portfolios (LDPs). The approaches

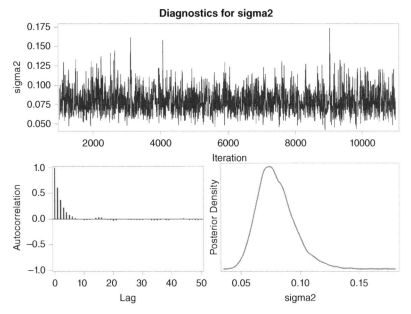

Exhibit 12.26 Diagnostic Plots

already presented in the chapter on LDPs can be augmented by Bayesian approaches. Early work on this has been done by Kiefer (2009), from whom we use an illustration of the approach before we apply it to real data. Consider a portfolio of $n = 100$ loans and $d = 0$ defaults. Assume further that all loans have the same PD π and are uncorrelated. Hence, the number of defaults is binomially distributed. The likelihood function for the parameter π is then given by the binomial distribution and is plotted in Exhibit 12.30. The maximum is at value $\pi = 0$, which yields the maximum-likelihood estimator. Similarly, if there were $d \in \{1, 2, 5\}$ defaults, the ML estimate would be at the peak of the likelihood with 1 percent, 2 percent, and 5 percent, respectively. Using 0 percent as an estimate for the PD of a segment of a loan portfolio obviously does not make much sense.

We can now mix the sample information with prior information. Suppose there is an expert who specifies a prior of the PD as a beta distribution, for example with parameters $\alpha = 1$ and $\beta = 200$ yielding the black solid distribution in Exhibit 12.31.[1] We can then compute the posterior distributions for various numbers of defaults.[2] For example, for $d = 0$ the maximum of the posterior distribution would be zero. However, in Bayesian statistics we would rather use the mean of the distribution as an estimate for the parameter, which is now about 0.5 percent. Similarly, if $d = 5$ the estimate for the PD would no longer be 5 percent but rather somewhere around 2 percent. Hence, the Bayesian estimate for LDP pulls the likelihood toward the prior distribution.

Let us now apply this to our data set. Before we do so, we construct a sample that actually exhibits LDP properties. We simply pick out those mortgages that have

The MCMC Procedure

Number of Observations Read	60	Number of Observations Used	60

Parameters				
Block	Parameter	Sampling Method	Initial Value	Prior Distribution
1	beta0	N–Metropolis	0	normal(0, var = 10000)
	sigma2		0.1000	lognormal(0.1, var = 0.1)

The MCMC Procedure

Posterior Summaries						
Parameter	N	Mean	Standard Deviation	Percentiles		
				25	50	75
beta0	5000	−2.2784	0.0574	−2.3164	−2.2792	−2.2409
sigma2	5000	0.1919	0.0415	0.1620	0.1873	0.2164

Posterior Intervals					
Parameter	Alpha	Equal-Tail Interval		HPD Interval	
beta0	0.050	−2.3941	−2.1647	−2.3994	−2.1720
sigma2	0.050	0.1253	0.2844	0.1223	0.2803

Posterior Autocorrelations				
Parameter	Lag 1	Lag 5	Lag 10	Lag 50
beta0	0.6043	0.0785	0.0281	−0.0017
sigma2	0.5857	0.1188	−0.0234	−0.0319

Geweke Diagnostics		
Parameter	z	Pr > |z|
beta0	0.3971	0.6913
sigma2	1.4173	0.1564

Raftery-Lewis Diagnostics				
Quantile = 0.025 Accuracy = +/−0.005 Probability = 0.95 Epsilon = 0.001				
Parameter	Number of Samples			Dependence Factor
	Burn-In	Total	Minimum	
beta0	11	11744	3746	3.1351
sigma2	10	10668	3746	2.8478

Heidelberger-Welch Diagnostics								
Parameter	Stationarity Test				Half-Width Test			
	Cramer–von Mises Stat	p-Value	Test Outcome	Iterations Discarded	Half-Width	Mean	Relative Half-Width	Test Outcome
beta0	0.1595	0.3618	Passed	0	0.00341	−2.2784	−0.00150	Passed
sigma2	0.2558	0.1811	Passed	0	0.00193	0.1919	0.0101	Passed

Exhibit 12.27 Summary Statistics

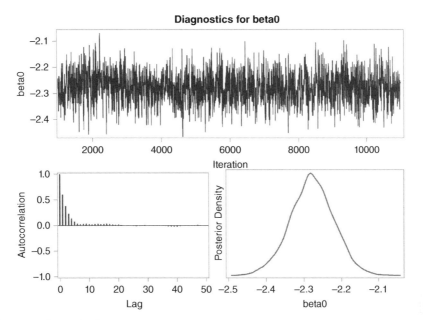

Exhibit 12.28 Diagnostic Plots

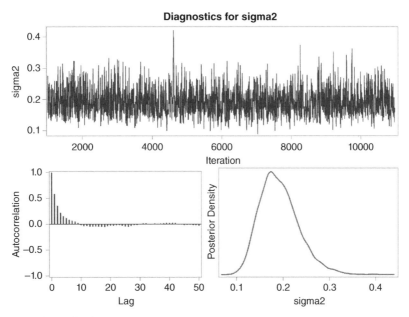

Exhibit 12.29 Diagnostic Plots

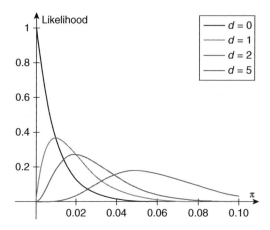

Exhibit 12.30 Various Likelihoods

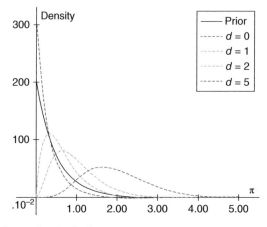

Exhibit 12.31 Prior and Posterior Distributions

a FICO score higher than 810, resulting in only 0 or very small fractions of defaults per time. The average default rate is about 0.27 percent. We then use PROC MCMC to specify a binomial distribution for the number of defaults per time, given the number of observations per time. For the PD parameter of the binomial distribution, we specify a *beta*(1, 1) prior distribution, which is actually a uniform distribution and reflects uninformativeness. PROC MCMC shows good convergence of the simulations, and the mean of the posterior distribution is about 0.4 percent with a 95 percent equal tail credibility interval ranging from 0.16 percent to 0.73 percent. Hence, the uninformative prior pulls the estimate away from the low average default rate. (See Exhibits 12.32 and 12.33.)

The MCMC Procedure

Number of Observations Read	47	Number of Observations Used	47

Parameters				
Block	Parameter	Sampling Method	Initial Value	Prior Distribution
1	pd	Conjugate	0.5000	beta(1,1)

The MCMC Procedure

Posterior Summaries						
Parameter	N	Mean	Standard Deviation	Percentiles		
				25	50	75
pd	10000	0.00393	0.00148	0.00284	0.00374	0.00482

Posterior Intervals					
Parameter	Alpha	Equal-Tail Interval		HPD Interval	
pd	0.050	0.00160	0.00730	0.00140	0.00691

Posterior Autocorrelations				
Parameter	Lag 1	Lag 5	Lag 10	Lag 50
pd	0.0080	−0.0049	−0.0079	−0.0062

Geweke Diagnostics		
Parameter	z	Pr > |z|
pd	−2.0005	0.0454

Raftery-Lewis Diagnostics			
Quantile = 0.025 Accuracy = +/−0.005 Probability = 0.95 Epsilon = 0.001			
Parameter	Number of Samples		Dependence Factor
	Burn-In	Total	Minimum
pd	2	3741	3746	0.9987

Heidelberger-Welch Diagnostics								
Parameter	Stationarity Test				Half-Width Test			
	Cramer–von Mises Stat	p-Value	Test Outcome	Iterations Discarded	Half-Width	Mean	Relative Half-Width	Test Outcome
pd	0.1329	0.4460	Passed	0	0.000031	0.00393	0.00786	Passed

Exhibit 12.32 Summary Statistics

```
DATA tmp;
SET data.mortgage;
IF FICO_orig_time > 810;
RUN;
```

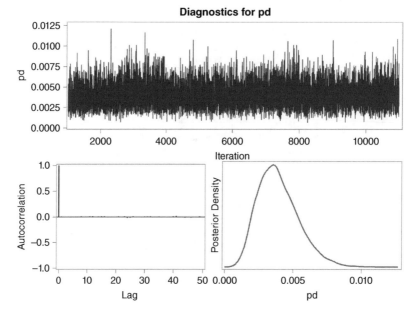

Exhibit 12.33 Diagnostic Plots

```
PROC SORT DATA = tmp;
BY time;
RUN;

PROC MEANS data = tmp;
VAR default_time;
BY time;
OUTPUT OUT = means;
RUN;

DATA tmp_ldp;
SET means;
IF _STAT_ = "MEAN";
n_default = default_time * _FREQ_;
default_time_1 = LAG(default_time);
RUN;

/*Independence model*/
ODS GRAPHICS ON;
PROC MCMC DATA = tmp_ldp STATISTICS=ALL DIAGNOSTICS=ALL
    NMC=10000 SEED=12345;
```

```
PARMS pd;
PRIOR pd ~ beta(1,1);
MODEL n_default ~ BINOMIAL(_FREQ_,pd);
RUN;
ODS GRAPHICS OFF;
```

One can also extend the Bayesian LDP approach to a more advanced parametric model, such as a probit model for individual data with a sample of 1,940 low default observations. (See Exhibits 12.34 through 12.38.) First, we estimate a classical probit model with PROC LOGISTIC with LTV and GDP as covariates. Neither of them is statistically significant at the 5 percent level. For the Bayes model, we use uninformative priors with normal distributions with a very high variance of 10,000. The output of the classical analysis returns estimates for LTV of 0.0815 and for GDP of 0.1062, whereas the means in the Bayesian model are lower. Hence, the means of the posterior distributions are quite different from the classical estimates. Also check whether the value of 0 lies within an equal—tail 95 percent credibility interval for GDP and LTV, which would signal low significance. We could now continue the analysis by specifying a more informative prior if there is valuable information about the parameters.

```
ODS GRAPHICS ON;
PROC LOGISTIC DATA=tmp DESCENDING;
MODEL default_time =
LTV_orig_time gdp_time
/ OUTROC=roc_logistic RSQUARE;
STORE OUT=model_logistic;
RUN;
ODS GRAPHICS OFF;

ODS GRAPHICS ON;
ODS LISTING CLOSE;
ODS LATEX;
ODS GRAPHICS ON / IMAGEFMT=PDF  IMAGENAME='bayesldp';
PROC MCMC DATA = tmp STATISTICS=ALL DIAGNOSTICS=ALL
NMC=10000 SEED=12345;
PARMS beta0 beta1 beta2;
PRIOR beta0 beta1 beta2 ~ normal(0, var = 10000);
pd = PROBNORM(beta0 +
beta1 * LTV_orig_time + beta2* gdp_time);
MODEL default_time ~ binomial(1,pd);
RUN;
ODS GRAPHICS OFF;
```

The LOGISTIC Procedure

Model Information	
Data Set	WORK.TMP
Response Variable	default_time
Number of Response Levels	2
Model	Binary logit
Optimization Technique	Fisher's scoring

Number of Observations Read	1780
Number of Observations Used	1780

Response Profile		
Ordered Value	default_time	Total Frequency
1	1	6
2	0	1774

Note	Probability modeled is default_time=1.

Model Convergence Status
Convergence criterion (GCONV=1E−8) satisfied.

Model Fit Statistics		
Criterion	Intercept Only	Intercept and Covariates
AIC	82.291	82.441
SC	87.775	98.894
−2 Log L	80.291	76.441

R-Squared	0.0022	Max-Rescaled R-Squared	0.0490

Analysis of Maximum Likelihood Estimates					
Parameter	DF	Estimate	Standard Error	Wald Chi-Square	Pr > ChiSq
Intercept	1	−12.0679	3.6221	11.1006	0.0009
LTV_orig_time	1	0.0815	0.0454	3.2266	0.0725
gdp_time	1	0.1062	0.2397	0.1963	0.6578

Association of Predicted Probabilities and Observed Responses			
Percent Concordant	67.4	Somers' D	0.353
Percent Discordant	32.1	Gamma	0.355
Percent Tied	0.6	Tau-a	0.002
Pairs	10644	c	0.676

Exhibit 12.34 Probit Model

The MCMC Procedure

Number of Observations Read	1780	Number of Observations Used	1780

Parameters				
Block	Parameter	Sampling Method	Initial Value	Prior Distribution
1	beta0	N–Metropolis	0	normal(0, var = 10000)
	beta1		0	normal(0, var = 10000)
	beta2		0	normal(0, var = 10000)

The MCMC Procedure

Posterior Summaries						
Parameter	N	Mean	Standard Deviation	Percentiles		
				25	50	75
beta0	10000	−5.1413	1.2773	−5.9951	−5.0784	−4.2407
beta1	10000	0.0300	0.0160	0.0188	0.0294	0.0408
beta2	10000	0.0556	0.0837	−0.00266	0.0486	0.1059

Posterior Intervals					
Parameter	Alpha	Equal-Tail Interval		HPD Interval	
beta0	0.050	−7.7185	−2.8015	−7.6983	−2.7956
beta1	0.050	0.000467	0.0618	0.000811	0.0621
beta2	0.050	−0.0882	0.2382	−0.1007	0.2142

Posterior Autocorrelations				
Parameter	Lag 1	Lag 5	Lag 10	Lag 50
beta0	0.8732	0.5026	0.2620	0.0038
beta1	0.8690	0.4912	0.2518	−0.0027
beta2	0.8415	0.4597	0.2413	0.0009

Geweke Diagnostics		
Parameter	z	Pr > |z|
beta0	−1.9757	0.0482
beta1	1.8469	0.0648
beta2	1.0318	0.3022

Exhibit 12.35 Summary Statistics

Raftery-Lewis Diagnostics				
Quantile = 0.025 Accuracy = +/–0.005 Probability = 0.95 Epsilon = 0.001				
Parameter	Number of Samples			Dependence Factor
	Burn-In	Total	Minimum	
beta0	23	24192	3746	6.4581
beta1	20	21310	3746	5.6887
beta2	18	19686	3746	5.2552

Heidelberger-Welch Diagnostics								
Parameter	Stationarity Test				Half-Width Test			
	Cramer–von Mises Stat	p-Value	Test Outcome	Iterations Discarded	Half-Width	Mean	Relative Half-Width	Test Outcome
beta0	0.2758	0.1584	Passed	0	0.0969	–5.1413	–0.0188	Passed
beta1	0.1905	0.2867	Passed	0	0.00119	0.0300	0.0395	Passed
beta2	.	.	Failed	.	.	.	.	.

Exhibit 12.35 (*Continued*)

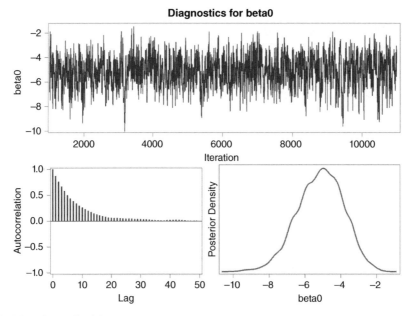

Exhibit 12.36 Diagnostic Plots

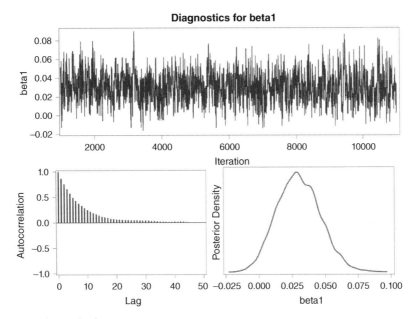

Exhibit 12.37 Diagnostic Plots

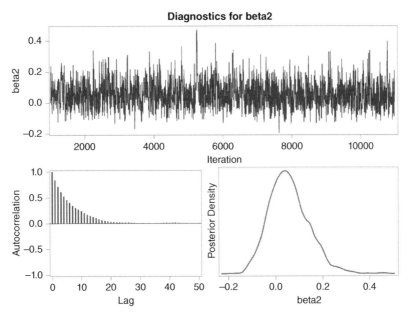

Exhibit 12.38 Diagnostic Plots

PRACTICE QUESTIONS

1. Describe the differences between the Bayesian approach and the classical frequentist approach.

2. Consider the first example in this chapter. Evaluate the Bayesian model with more informative priors for FICO and GDP in addition to LTV.

3. Run a Bayesian regression model for estimating asset correlation with inclusion of the lagged default rate, and interpret the results.

4. Run a Bayesian probit model for the low default portfolio using more informative priors where the mean of the GDP coefficient is 0.3 and the mean of the FICO coefficient is 0.02. Interpret and discuss the results.

NOTES

1. Kiefer (2009) actually proposes a generalized 4-parameter beta distribution and obtains the prior from a real-world expert.

2. It is well known in Bayesian statistics that a binomial likelihood and a beta prior result in a posterior that is also a beta distribution; see Greenberg (2014). Thus, the beta distribution is the *conjugate* prior for the binomial distribution.

REFERENCES

Greenberg, E. 2014. *Introduction to Bayesian Econometrics*. 2nd ed. Cambridge: Cambridge University Press.

Kiefer, N. 2009. "Default Estimation for Low-Default Portfolios." *Journal of Empirical Finance* 16: 164–173.

SAS Institute Inc. 2015. *SAS/STAT 14.1 User's Guide: Technical Report*. Cary, NC: SAS Institute.

CHAPTER 13

Model Validation

INTRODUCTION

Let us now assume that our probability of default (PD), loss given default (LGD), and exposure at default (EAD) models have been built. The next step is to then put them into production and start monitoring or validating them. Validation stems from the Latin word *validus* and refers to being effective, strong, or firm. It appears in many scientific disciplines, particularly in engineering, where it means a confirmation that a service or product meets the operator's requirements. Very similarly, in statistics, validation is a process of deciding whether the numerical results for quantification of hypotheses are proper descriptions of the data and is implemented, for example, via goodness-of-fit tests, residual analyses (as partly already discussed in earlier chapters), or backtesting of prediction power. In this chapter, we discuss various ways of validating credit risk models. The Basel Committee Validation Subgroup defines it in the following way:

> [T]he term validation encompasses a range of processes and activities
> that contribute to an assessment of whether ratings adequately
> differentiate risk, and whether estimates of risk components (such as PD,
> LGD, or EAD) appropriately characterize the relevant aspects of risk.
> (Basel Committee on Banking Supervision 2005b)

In what follows, you will first gain more insight into the regulatory aspects of validation, as well as learn key terms and principles. Next, you will learn about the characteristics of quantitative and qualitative validation.

REGULATORY PERSPECTIVE

We first start by discussing the regulatory perspective on validation. The Basel Committee on Banking Supervision stipulates various paragraphs on validation.

We cannot state all of them, but rather we select several that are important for understanding the core concept of the regulatory perspective on model validation. Generally, a bank that uses models for the risk parameters is required

> to satisfy its supervisor that a model or procedure has good predictive power and that regulatory capital requirements will not be distorted as a result of its use. The variables that are input to the model must form a reasonable set of predictors. The model must be accurate on average across the range of borrowers or facilities to which the bank is exposed and there must be no known material biases. (Basel Committee on Banking Supervision 2006, §417)

In the same paragraph, it states:

> The bank must have a regular cycle of model validation that includes monitoring of model performance and stability; review of model relationships; and testing of model outputs against outcomes.

Banks therefore conduct validation on a regular basis. This usually occurs on a monthly basis and sometimes even more frequently. Obviously, the more frequently it's undertaken, the more quickly performance deviations or other critical issues can be detected. All this has to be accompanied by a proper documentation; see Basel Committee on Banking Supervision (2006, §418). The paragraphs §500 to §505 describe more details:

- §500: *Banks must have a robust system in place to validate the accuracy and consistency of rating systems, processes, and the estimation of all relevant risk components. A bank must demonstrate to its supervisor that the internal validation process enables it to assess the performance of internal rating and risk estimation systems consistently and meaningfully.*

- §501: *Banks must regularly compare realised default rates with estimated PDs for each grade and be able to demonstrate that the realised default rates are within the expected range for that grade. Banks using the advanced IRB approach must complete such analysis for their estimates of LGDs and EADs. Such comparisons must make use of historical data that are over as long a period as possible. The methods and data used in such comparisons by the bank must be clearly documented by the bank. This analysis and documentation must be updated at least annually.*

- §502: *Banks must also use other quantitative validation tools and comparisons with relevant external data sources. The analysis must be based on data that are appropriate to the portfolio, are updated regularly, and cover a relevant observation period. Banks' internal assessments of the performance of their own rating systems must be based on long data histories, covering a range of economic conditions, and ideally one or more complete business cycles.*

- §503: *Banks must demonstrate that quantitative testing methods and other validation methods do not vary systematically with the economic cycle. Changes in methods and data (both data sources and periods covered) must be clearly and thoroughly documented.*

- §504: *Banks must have well-articulated internal standards for situations where deviations in realised PDs, LGDs and EADs from expectations become significant enough to call the validity of the estimates into question. These standards must take account of business cycles and similar systematic variability in default experiences. Where realised values continue to be higher than expected values, banks must revise estimates upward to reflect their default and loss experience.*

- §505: *Where banks rely on supervisory, rather than internal, estimates of risk parameters, they are encouraged to compare realised LGDs and EADs to those set by the supervisors. The information on realised LGDs and EADs should form part of the bank's assessment of economic capital.*

§500 takes a very broad view on validation. A key point to remember here is that it is not only about the estimation of all relevant risk parameters, which constitutes a narrow view on validation, but also about the accuracy and consistency of the rating systems and processes as a whole, which is a much broader perspective on validation. In §501, comparing realized default rates with estimated PDs refers to the quantitative validation activity of *backtesting*. Also important here is that this must be done at least annually, although, as already indicated, banks will typically do this more often. §502 and §505 refer to the idea of *benchmarking*, another key quantitative validation activity. The purpose here is to compare internal models and/or estimates with an external reference model and/or estimates. The aim of benchmarking is to find model deficiencies and identify opportunities for improvement. §503 refers to *model stability*, which requires that the outputs of models and the validation results should not systematically change over time. §504 is basically stating that validation encompasses two activities. First, a validation framework provides a diagnosis; it should tell us if the rating system is robust or not. Second, once a diagnosis has been obtained, the validation framework should also foresee action plans. For example, if the diagnosis is that the rating system is not robust and that the PDs are systematically underestimated, then an action plan is needed to remedy this situation.

A general overview introduced by the BIS 14 Working Paper is given in Exhibit 13.1; see Basel Committee on Banking Supervision (2005a).

The supervisor is the person who will evaluate the internal validation conducted by the bank. Usually, a bank will have both a modeling team and a validation or audit team. The purpose of the latter is to closely inspect and validate all PD, LGD, and EAD models, both quantitatively and qualitatively. Many banks adopt the principle of a Chinese wall separation between the modeling and validation teams to enforce an independent, unbiased, and fair evaluation. Validation encompasses both the validation of the rating system as well as the validation of the rating process. In terms of the rating system, a first activity concerns the validation of the model design. This refers to the definition of the model, its perimeter and scope. Another key task is the validation of the risk components, which include both the backtesting and benchmarking of the PD, LGD, and EAD estimates. In terms of the rating process, a first validation

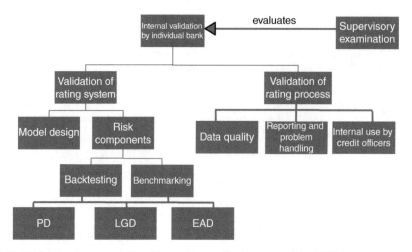

Exhibit 13.1 Validation Framework (Basel Committee on Banking Supervision 2005a)

activity concerns the issue of data quality. As said earlier, data is the key ingredient of an analytical PD, LGD, or EAD model, and data quality should thus be optimally safeguarded. A next activity concerns the reporting and problem handling. This basically relates to the reports and documentation available about the various steps and results of the rating process. Finally, it is of key importance that the analytical PD, LGD, and EAD models are used not only for Basel capital calculation purposes, but also for other activities and business purposes. This is the so-called use test, which we clarify in the following.

BASIC CONCEPTS OF VALIDATION

Defining Validation

Let us briefly refresh two key activities of quantitative validation: backtesting and benchmarking. Backtesting refers to comparing ex ante made estimates to ex post realized numbers. In Exhibit 13.2 you can see an example of this.

Rating Category	Estimated PD	Number of Observations	Number of Observed Defaults
A	2%	1000	17
B	3%	500	20
C	7%	400	35
D	20%	100	50

Exhibit 13.2 Example of Validation

Suppose we have four ratings with corresponding PD estimates: 2 percent, 3 percent, 7 percent, and 20 percent. Each rating has a number of observations assigned to it and a number of observed defaults, both of which allow us to calculate the default rate. Backtesting refers to comparing this default rate to the estimated PD. For example, for rating D, backtesting will conduct a statistical test whether the observed default rate of 50 percent is significantly different from the predicted PD of 20 percent. Benchmarking is another key quantitative validation activity, the primary concept here being to compare internal models and or estimates with a reference model and/or estimates. Note that validation is more than just backtesting and benchmarking. In this chapter, we will discuss both quantitative and qualitative validation. In terms of quantitative validation, we will take a closer look at backtesting and benchmarking. In terms of qualitative validation, we will discuss data quality, use test, model design, documentation, corporate governance, and management oversight.

Common Validation Issues

Before we continue the discussion, let us offer some initial observations. Banks employ a wide range of techniques to validate internal ratings, and the techniques used to assess corporate and retail ratings are substantially different. One of the reasons behind this is that, contrary to retail portfolios, in many corporate portfolios data availability is paramount. If there is a data shortage, credit risk model development will be altered, as will validation, an example of which is an expert-based qualitative credit risk model.

Ratings validation is not an exact science. Absolute performance measures are considered counterproductive by some institutions. It is challenging to derive minimum performance benchmarks that PD, LGD, or EAD models need to achieve in order to be considered satisfactory. This typically depends on the data characteristics, portfolio composition, and strategy of the financial institution. Hence, any performance metric reported should be interpreted in terms of its own specific context.

Expert judgment is critical. Data scarcity makes it almost impossible to develop statistically based internal ratings models in some asset classes. This refers to our earlier point concerning the lack of data, which can be observed in low default portfolios (LDPs): An insufficient number of defaulters ultimately prevents construction of a meaningful statistical model. Consult Chapter 8 for further information on LDPs. Thus, the role of credit experts and qualitative valuation becomes important.

Data issues center around both quantity and quality. Default data, in particular, is insufficient to produce robust statistical estimates for some asset classes. For PD modeling, the quality of the data is usually satisfactory, though sometimes the issue of quantity, in terms of number of defaulters, complicates the development of statistical models, as discussed previously. For LGD and EAD modeling, data quality is often a key concern. This is one of the major reasons why LGD and EAD models typically have a low predictive performance.

General Validation Principles

Here, you can see some General Validation Principles put forward by the Basel Committee Validation Subgroup; see Basel Committee on Banking Supervision (2005b).

- *Principle 1: Validation is fundamentally about assessing the predictive ability of a bank's risk estimates and the use of ratings in credit processes.*
  This refers to the ideas of backtesting and use testing.

- *Principle 2: The bank has the primary responsibility for validation;*
  The supervisor does not perform the validation; the bank has this responsibility. The supervisor reviews the validation only.

- *Principle 3: Validation is an iterative process.*
  Validation is not a single-shot, sequential activity. On the contrary, it is a continuous, iterative process, and sometimes quite ad hoc.

- *Principle 4: There is no single validation method.*
  Validation is context dependent. This can refer to the type of portfolio, the strategy of the firm, the quality of the data, and so on.

- *Principle 5: Validation should encompass both quantitative and qualitative elements.*
  Quantitative validation refers to backtesting and benchmarking. Qualitative validation refers to data quality, use test, model design, documentation, and corporate governance and management oversight.

- *Principle 6: Validation processes and outcomes should be subject to independent review.*
  This refers to the supervisor reviewing the validation of the bank. Actually, validation is a very difficult activity to optimally organize from an organizational perspective. When adopting a strict split between the modeling and the validation team, where the latter is conceived as the watchdog of the former, then friction may arise between both teams. To be successful it's vital that validation is constructive and focuses on constructive feedback about the developed credit risk models. Validation does not provide a fixed decision but rather a suggestion for further action and study. Hence, both model diagnostic frameworks as well as action plans need to be developed. Finally, validation methods are not allowed to change with the economic cycle unless this is clearly and thoroughly documented.

Developing a Validation Framework

When implementing a validation framework, various things need to be considered. First, the validation needs must be unambiguously diagnosed. What credit risk models must be validated in which portfolios? Then the various validation activities need to be worked out in detail. All of this should be put into a timetable, specifying what validation activity should be conducted by when. Also the various statistical tests and analyses must be clearly defined. Obviously, this will highly depend upon the type of credit risk parameter, for example, PD, LGD, or EAD, to be validated. Finally, the actions must be defined in response to the potential findings. Suppose the validation exercise tells us that the LGD is systematically underestimated. To remedy this, an action plan must be defined. To summarize, the validation policy should clearly specify the why, what, who, how, and when of the whole validation exercise.

QUANTITATIVE VALIDATION

Introduction

In this section, we look closely at quantitative validation. The goal here is to verify how well the various ratings predict default (PD), loss (LGD), exposure, or credit conversion factor (CCF). As mentioned in the Basel II Accord, the burden is on the bank to satisfy its supervisor that a model or procedure has good predictive power and that regulatory capital requirements will not be distorted as a result of its use. Actually, the whole idea of quantitative validation boils down to comparing realized numbers to predicted numbers. It speaks for itself that those numbers will seldom be identical. Hence, various appropriate performance metrics and test statistics must be specified to assist in this comparison. When using these, appropriate cutoffs such as significance levels must be set. The severity of each cutoff will then determine the severity of the whole validation exercise. A more severe cutoff will result in a more conservative validation which will more readily detect a performance difference. Also, when performing validation, you should think carefully about the split-up of the data. In other words, on what data are you going to calculate the various validation performance metrics and statistics? Let us look closely at this next.

Data Set Split-Up

Exhibit 13.3 displays the various ways of splitting up your data for performing validation.

A first option to consider is out-of-sample validation. This works by splitting up a data set observed during a particular time frame into a training set and a test set.

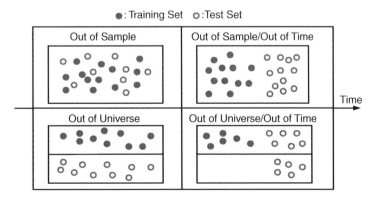

Exhibit 13.3 Data Set Split-Up

Remember, the training set is used to develop the model, whereas the test set is used to calculate its performance in an independent way. In this method, the training and test sets overlap in time. This is the most commonly used method of doing validation during the development of PD, LGD, and EAD models. In out-of-sample/out-of-time validation, there is a strict time difference between the test set and the training set. In other words, the test set comes from a subsequent time period. This is typically the type of validation that you will do during model usage, or after the models have been deployed and put into production. Out-of-universe validation entails the validation of a model in another population than that on which it was developed. As an example, think of a PD model developed on U.S. small and medium-sized enterprises (SMEs) being validated on a set of Canadian SMEs. Out-of-Universe validation directly relates to the model perimeter since it tells us how well a model generalizes beyond its original scope. This is very important given the many mergers and acquisitions seen in the financial industry lately, wherein banks suddenly have multiple credit risk models for similar types of portfolios. Finally, the most ambitious validation setup is out-of-universe and out-of-time validation, where a credit risk model is validated on data from another population and subsequent time frame.

Challenges

Various challenges arise when doing quantitative validation. One concerns the sources of variation you are being confronted with. For example, the difference between the predicted PDs and observed default rates can have at least three different causes. A first one concerns random sample variability. This is the variability due to the fact that the predicted PDs have been calculated using a limited sample of observations. A subsequent consideration is external effects, as macroeconomic up- or downturns will have an impact on default rates. Finally, there are internal or endogenous effects due to a change in portfolio composition, strategy shift, or a merger or acquisition, for example. Suppose now that you focus only on sample variation and you know that the PD for a rating grade with independent obligors is 100 basis points. Let us now say that you want to be 95 percent confident that the realized default rate is not more than 20 basis points off from the estimate. When modeling this using a binomial confidence interval, the number of obligors you would need equals or, in other words, Should be 9,500 obligors.

$$n = \left(\frac{1.96\sqrt{PD \cdot (1-PD)}}{0.002} \right)^2 \tag{13.1}$$

For n independent obligors with identical PD, the default rate is approximately normally distributed with mean PD and variance $PD(1 - PD)/n$. Thus, a two-sided 95 percent confidence interval for the default rate is given by $PD \pm z(97.5) \cdot \sqrt{PD(1 - PD)/n}$, where $z(97.5)$ is the 97.5th percentile of the standard normal distribution, which is 1.96. Hence, if $PD = 0.01$ and the default rate should not be more than 0.002 off from the PD, it follows that $0.002 = 1.96 \cdot \sqrt{PD(1 - PD)/n}$. Rearranging yields equation (13.1). In retail portfolios, this is usually no problem. However, in corporate portfolios, the number of obligors may be substantially less, thereby increasing the confidence bounds and thus the uncertainty around the PD estimates.

Another complication is the statistical independence assumption that is typically assumed when building credit risk models, which is often untrue in reality. Think about the correlation between defaults and the correlation between PD, LGD, and EAD, for example. Hence, this further complicates the validation exercise. Finally, data availability can also be a general concern, especially in corporate portfolios.

Backtesting PD Models

In this section we discuss backtesting PD models. An overview on backtesting and benchmarking is given in Castermans et al. (2010). We adopt a multilevel perspective on a PD model. (See Exhibit 13.4.) At level 0, we start by checking the data stability. In other words, we measure to what extent the population that was used to construct the PD rating system is similar to the population that is currently being observed. At level 1, we measure how well the PD rating system provides an ordinal ranking of the risk measure considered. Finally, at level 2, the mapping of the rating to a quantitative risk measure (PD) is evaluated. A rating system is considered well-calibrated if the (ex ante) estimated risk measures deviate only marginally from what has been observed ex post.

In the context of PD models, at level 0 the stability of the internal, external, and expert judgment data needs to be backtested. At level 1, the application and behavioral scorecard is evaluated. Both will typically have been constructed using logistic regression models. At level 2, the risk ratings and PD calibration are backtested.

When backtesting PD models, it is common to adopt a traffic light indicator approach to encode the outcomes of the various performance metrics or test statistics. (See Exhibit 13.5.) A green traffic light means that everything is okay and thus the model predicts well and no changes are needed. A yellow light indicates a decreasing performance and early warning that a potential problem may soon arise. An orange light is a more severe warning that a problem is very likely to occur and should be more closely monitored. A red light then indicates a severe problem that needs immediate attention and action. Depending upon the implementation, more or fewer traffic lights can be adopted. Note that within the context of PD modeling,

Calibration	Mapping of a rating to a quantitative risk measure. A rating system is considered well-calibrated if the (ex ante) estimated risk measures deviate only marginally from what has been observed ex post.
Discrimination	Measures how well the rating system provides an ordinal ranking of the risk measure considered.
Stability	Measures to what extent the population that was used to construct the rating system is similar to the population that is currently being observed.

Exhibit 13.4 Backtesting

dark green can also be used to refer to the fact that the risk measure is becoming too conservative. The traffic lights can be related to the *p*-values of a statistical test, for example, as follows:

- A *p*-value less than 0.01 corresponds to a red light.
- A *p*-value between 0.01 and 0.05 corresponds to an orange light.
- A *p*-value between 0.05 and 0.10 corresponds to a yellow light.
- A *p*-value higher than 0.10 corresponds to a green light.

In Exhibit 13.5 you can see an example of a traffic light indicator approach applied to backtesting PD models at the calibration level, where through years 1993 until 2002 a statistical test (see later) has been run for several rating grades. Note that green corresponds to normal type, yellow to italic, orange to bold, and red to underlined bold. It can be easily seen that from 2001 onwards the calibration is no longer satisfactory, because of the many red lights.

Backtesting PD at Level 0

When validating data stability at level 0, you should check whether internal or external environmental changes will impact the PD classification model. Examples of external environmental changes are new developments in the economic, political,

PD	Baa1	Baa2	Baa3	Ba1	Ba2	Ba3	B1	B2	B3	Caa-C	Av.
	0.26%	0.17%	0.42%	0.53%	0.54%	1.36%	2.46%	5.76%	8.76%	20.89%	3.05%
DR	Baa1	Baa2	Baa3	Ba1	Ba2	Ba3	B1	B2	B3	Caa-C	Av.
1993	0.00%	0.00%	0.00%	*0.83%*	0.00%	0.76%	3.24%	5.04%	**11.29%**	28.57%	*3.24%*
1994	0.00%	0.00%	0.00%	0.00%	0.00%	0.59%	1.88%	3.75%	7.95%	5.13%	1.88%
1995	0.00%	0.00%	0.00%	0.00%	0.00%	*1.76%*	**4.35%**	*6.42%*	4.06%	11.57%	2.51%
1996	0.00%	0.00%	0.00%	0.00%	0.00%	0.00%	1.17%	0.00%	3.28%	13.99%	0.78%
1997	0.00%	0.00%	0.00%	0.00%	0.00%	0.47%	0.00%	1.54%	7.22%	14.67%	1.41%
1998	0.00%	*0.31%*	0.00%	0.00%	*0.62%*	1.12%	2.11%	**7.55%**	5.52%	15.09%	2.83%
1999	0.00%	0.00%	0.34%	0.47%	0.00%	*2.00%*	**3.28%**	**6.91%**	*9.63%*	20.44%	**3.35%**
2000	*0.28%*	0.00%	**0.97%**	**0.94%**	*0.63%*	1.04%	**3.24%**	4.10%	**10.88%**	19.65%	3.01%
2001	*0.27%*	*0.27%*	0.00%	0.51%	**1.38%**	2.93%	3.19%	**11.07%**	**16.38%**	34.45%	5.48%
2002	**1.26%**	**0.72%**	**1.78%**	**1.58%**	**1.41%**	*1.58%*	2.00%	**6.81%**	6.86%	**29.45%**	**3.70%**
Av.	0.26%	0.17%	0.42%	0.53%	0.54%	1.36%	2.46%	5.76%	8.76%	20.90%	3.05%

Exhibit 13.5 Traffic Lights Approach

or legal environment; changes in commercial law; or new bankruptcy procedures. Examples of internal environmental changes are alterations of business strategy, exploration of new market segments, or changes in organizational structure.

A two-step approach is suggested as follows:

Step 1: Check whether the population on which the model is currently being used is similar to the population that was used to develop it.

Step 2: If differences occur in step 1, verify the stability of the individual variables.

For step 1, a population stability index (PSI) or system stability index (SSI) can be calculated. This is also called a deviation index in SAS. It is calculated by contrasting the expected or training e_k and observed or actual population percentages a_k across the various score ranges $k, k = 1, \ldots, K$. In other words, it is calculated as:

$$PSI = \sum_{k=1}^{K}(a_k - e_k) \cdot (\ln(a_k) - \ln(e_k))$$

The following example shows how the PSI can be computed via SAS/IML. After reading the data with score grades from 1 to 10 and expected/training as well as actual/observed percentages, IML computes the PSI columnwise and then sums up these values. Running the code and printing out the values shows that $PSI = 0.059$.

```
DATA data.psi1;
INPUT score expected actual;
DATALINES;
1 0.06 0.07
2 0.1 0.08
3 0.09 0.07
4 0.12 0.09
5 0.12 0.11
6 0.08 0.11
7 0.07 0.1
8 0.08 0.12
9 0.12 0.11
10 0.16 0.15
;

PROC IML;
USE data.psi1;
READ ALL VAR _NUM_ INTO DATA;
PSI_row = (data[,3]-data[,2])
# (LOG(data[,3])- LOG(data[,2]));
PSI = PSI_row[+];
PRINT PSI_row PSI;
QUIT;
```

Important to note is that the percentages reported in the data set are the percentages of the population and thus not default rates. In other words, they add up to 100 percent. Also observe that the PSI is defined in a similar way as the information value, which we discussed in the chapter on data preprocessing. A rule of thumb can then be defined as follows:

- PSI < 0.10: no significant shift (green traffic light)
- $0.10 \leq$ PSI < 0.25: moderate shift (yellow traffic light)
- PSI $\geq$ 0.25: significant shift (red traffic light)

It is also recommended to monitor the system stability index through time as illustrated in the next example where another column is added with actual/observed values at a later date, $t + 1$. Then expected versus actual in the same period are compared as well as actual in t versus actual in $t + 1$.

```
DATA data.psi2;
INPUT score expected actual_t actual_t1;
DATALINES;
1 0.06 0.07 0.06
2 0.1 0.08 0.07
3 0.09 0.07 0.1
4 0.12 0.09 0.11
5 0.12 0.11 0.1
6 0.08 0.11 0.09
7 0.07 0.1 0.11
8 0.08 0.12 0.11
9 0.12 0.11 0.1
10 0.16 0.15 0.15
;

PROC IML;
USE data.psi2;
READ ALL VAR _NUM_ INTO DATA;
PSI_row_e0 = (data[,3]-data[,2])
# (LOG(data[,3])- LOG(data[,2]));
PSI_row_e1 = (data[,4]-data[,2])
# (LOG(data[,4])- LOG(data[,2]));
PSI_row_t = (data[,4]-data[,3])
# (LOG(data[,4])- LOG(data[,3]));
PSI_e0 = PSI_row_e0[+];
PRINT PSI_row_e0 PSI_e0;
PSI_e1 = PSI_row_e1[+];
PRINT PSI_row_e1 PSI_e1;
PSI_t = PSI_row_t[+];
PRINT PSI_row_t PSI_t;
QUIT;
```

	Range	Expected (Training)%	Observed (Actual) at t	Observed (Actual) at $t + 1$
Income	0–1,000	16%	18%	10%
	1,001–2,000	23%	25%	12%
	2,001–3,000	22%	20%	20%
	3,001–4,000	19%	17%	25%
	4,001–4,000	15%	12%	20%
	5000+	5%	8%	13%
	S SI reference		0,029	0,208
	SSI $t - 1$			0,238
Years client	Unknown Client	15%	10%	5%
	0–2 years	20%	25%	15%
	2–5 years	25%	30%	40%
	5–10 years	30%	30%	20%
	10+ years	10%	5%	20%
	S SI reference		0,075	0,304
	SSI $t - 1$			0,362

Exhibit 13.6 PSI for Two Variables across Time

The first two values compare the observed or actual population with the expected or training population for two periods. The third one then compares the observed or actual population at time $t + 1$ with the population at time t. This allows us to see the evolution of the PSI through time and detect when important changes occur. The same traffic light coding can be used as discussed previously. In the context of credit ratings and scores over time, the composition of the rating grades over time might change not only due to structural changes in the ratings but also simply due to the macroeconomy. In a point-in-time (PIT) rating system, obligors will ceteris paribus be upgraded in an economic upswing and therefore obligors will move into the upper rating grades, whereas the opposite might happen in a downswing. Thus, you have to be careful in diagnosing the reasons for instabilities.

When population instability has been diagnosed, you can then verify the stability of the individual variables. Again, a system stability index can be calculated at the variable level as illustrated in Exhibit 13.6 for the variables income and years client. The reader is encouraged to program this example by herself as an exercise. Note that also histograms and/or t-tests can be handy tools to diagnose variable instability. These are discussed in the chapter on exploratory data analysis.

Another way of testing stability of a PD model is to include dummy variables for the in-sample and out-of-sample (or out-of-time) periods in a logistic regression model and test whether the dummies and time interactions are statistically significant. In the following example, we use the mortgage data set and define a dummy that is 1 if time < 60 and a dummy that is 2 if time is 60. We then estimate a probit regression using FICO scores, LTVs, and gross domestic product (GDP) as explanatory variables, as well as the time dummies and interactions between the dummies, and the explanatory variables LTV and FICO.

```
DATA tmp_pdstab;
SET data.mortgage;
time_dummy  = 0;
IF time < 60 THEN time_dummy =1;
IF time > 59 THEN time_dummy =2;
RUN;

PROC LOGISTIC DATA=tmp_pdstab DESCENDING ;
CLASS time_dummy (ref='1')/ PARAM = REF ;
MODEL default_time = FICO_orig_time
```

```
LTV_orig_time gdp_time time_dummy time_dummy*FICO_orig_time
    time_dummy*LTV_orig_time
/ LINK=Probit ;
STORE OUT=stab1;
RUN;
```

The output (Exhibit 13.7) shows that the time intercept as well as the interactions are not significant. This means that the model is stable across time periods 1–59 and 60. Moreover, the marginal coefficients for FICO and LTV can now be interpreted on a stand-alone basis and are highly significant.

Backtesting PD at Level 1

We now climb up one level in the credit risk model architecture and validate the discriminatory power of a scorecard or a PD model. It is recommended to first have a look at the scorecard and the model itself. For example, what was the logic behind the model used? Were there any assumptions made such as independence or normality? Also important is to verify the sign of the regression coefficients. Are the signs as anticipated? Are there any unexpected signs? Suppose that your scorecard or your PD model tells you that a higher debt ratio corresponds to a better credit score or a lower PD. This is clearly counterintuitive and needs to be further investigated since no one will be prepared to use a scorecard with this pattern. It is important to inspect all the *p*-values and the model significance. Also, the input selection procedure adopted and any remaining multicollinearity issues need to be clarified. Finally, the various data preprocessing activities such as missing values, outlier handling, and coarse classification need to be verified.

Next, the *discrimination performance* should be considered at level 1. Two key performance metrics here are the *receiver operating characteristic (ROC)* curve and the *area underneath (area under ROC, or AUROC, or AUC)*, together with the *cumulative accuracy profile (CAP)* and the *accuracy ratio (AR)*. They can be derived in various ways. One way is to order the predicted scores from the riskiest score to the least risky. For the validation data set (in-sample, or better, out-of-sample / out-of-time), you then compute cumulative percentages of defaulters for the ordered scores. If this function is plotted in a diagram, it is called the CAP curve or Gini curve (as it is similar to a Gini coefficient in terms of computation).

As a metric measure, you can compute the AR. For this, you first compute the so-called ideal CAP curve, which is obtained if all defaulters are clustered in the riskiest scores. The AR then becomes the ratio of the area between the real CAP curve and the diagonal and the ideal CAP curve and the diagonal; that is,

$$AR = \frac{\text{Area between real CAP curve and diagonal}}{\text{Area between ideal CAP curve and diagonal}}$$

This gives a theoretical range of the AR between zero and one. The higher the value, the closer the real curve is to the ideal curve. The basic idea is that the better the discriminatory power of the score for the defaulters and nondefaulters, the

The LOGISTIC Procedure

Model Information	
Data Set	WORK.TMP_PDSTAB
Response Variable	default_time
Number of Response Levels	2
Model	Binary probit
Optimization Technique	Fisher's scoring

Number of Observations Read	622489
Number of Observations Used	622489

Model Fit Statistics		
Criterion	Intercept Only	Intercept and Covariates
AIC	142575.79	137588.22
SC	142587.13	137667.61
-2 Log L	142573.79	137574.22

Analysis of Maximum Likelihood Estimates						
Parameter		DF	Estimate	Standard Error	Wald Chi-Square	Pr > ChiSq
Intercept		1	−1.0883	0.0455	571.5166	<.0001
FICO_orig_time		1	−0.00209	0.000049	1836.5919	<.0001
LTV_orig_time		1	0.00738	0.000352	439.1122	<.0001
gdp_time		1	−0.0805	0.00152	2795.0299	<.0001
time_dummy	2	1	−0.3047	0.6650	0.2100	0.6468
FICO_orig*time_dummy	2	1	0.000081	0.000728	0.0122	0.9119
LTV_orig_*time_dummy	2	1	−0.00250	0.00521	0.2304	0.6312

Association of Predicted Probabilities and Observed Responses			
Percent Concordant	66.9	Somers' D	0.338
Percent Discordant	33.1	Gamma	0.338
Percent Tied	0.0	Tau-a	0.016
Pairs	9205923298	c	0.669

Exhibit 13.7 Stability Test with Interactions

more defaulters should cluster at the risky scores and the fewer should be in the less risky scores.

The ROC is computed in the following way. First, the scores are also ordered according to their riskiness. You then move along the scores and compute:

- The proportion of correctly classified defaulters among all defaulters (the so-called hit rate or sensitivity), and

- The proportion of incorrectly classified nondefaulters (the so-called false alarm rate or "1 − specificity").

A plot of these values yields the ROC. The area under the ROC gives the metric measure AUROC. It is important to know that AUROC is actually a transformation of AR and can be computed by the relation

$$AR = 2(AUROC - 0.5)$$

Both measures give the same information. However, AUROC has a minimum value of 0.5 (instead of 0 for AR) and therefore usually looks more optimistic. In SAS, the ROC curve, AUROC, and AR can be computed via PROC LOGISTIC using the option ROC as shown in the following example with the mortgage data set. We first divide the data set into an estimation data set (using time up to 59) and an (out-of-time) validation data set (using time 60). We then estimate three probit models: one with LTV only, one with LTV and FICO scores, and one with LTV, FICO scores, and GDP. Using the OUTMODEL option in the PROC LOGISTIC statement, the model output is stored. After estimating each model, this output is called into PROC LOGISTIC and the validation data set is scored using the SCORE command. Using the OUTROC option, the values required for the ROC analysis are stored. Next, the predicted PDs of the three models are merged and transformed into scores. Using these three sets of scores, three probit models are estimated for the validation data set, and the ROCs are compared. (See Exhibits 13.8 and 13.9.)

```
DATA tmp_pdvali1;
SET data.mortgage;
IF time < 60;
RUN;
DATA tmp_pdvali2;
SET data.mortgage;
IF time > 59;
RUN;

PROC SORT data = tmp_pdvali1;
BY id time;
RUN;

PROC SORT data = tmp_pdvali2;
BY id time;
RUN;
```

The LOGISTIC Procedure

ROC Model: model1

Model Fit Statistics		
Criterion	Intercept Only	Intercept and Covariates
AIC	537.247	537.468
SC	544.235	551.444
-2 Log L	535.247	533.468

ROC Association Statistics							
ROC Model	Mann-Whitney				Somers' D	Gamma	Tau-a
	Area	Standard Error	95% Wald Confidence Limits				
model1	0.5718	0.0484	0.4770	0.6667	0.1437	0.1584	0.00154
model2	0.6362	0.0403	0.5572	0.7152	0.2724	0.2725	0.00291
model3	0.6366	0.0402	0.5579	0.7153	0.2732	0.2733	0.00292

ROC Contrast Coefficients		
ROC Model	Row1	Row2
model1	−1	−1
model2	1	0
model3	0	1

ROC Contrast Test Results			
Contrast	DF	Chi-Square	Pr > ChiSq
Reference = model1	2	6.5944	0.0370

ROC Contrast Estimation and Testing Results by Row						
Contrast	Estimate	Standard Error	95% Wald Confidence Limits		Chi-Square	Pr > ChiSq
model2 - model1	0.0644	0.0373	−0.00875	0.1375	2.9773	0.0844
model3 - model1	0.0648	0.0381	−0.00979	0.1394	2.8992	0.0886

Exhibit 13.8 Out-of-Sample Association Statistics

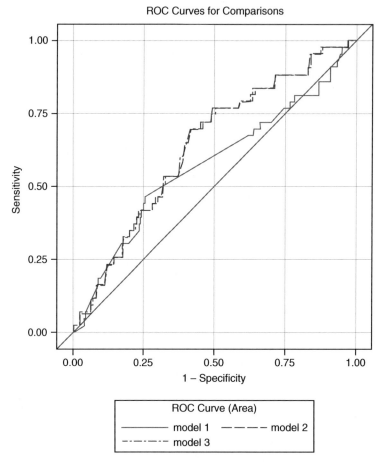

Exhibit 13.9 Out-of-Time ROC Curves

```
PROC LOGISTIC DATA=tmp_pdvali1 DESCENDING  OUTMODEL=model1;
MODEL default_time = /*FICO_orig_time */
LTV_orig_time  /*gdp_time*/
/ LINK=Probit ;
RUN;

PROC LOGISTIC /*DATA=model*/ DESCENDING  INMODEL=model1;
*MODEL default_time = FICO_orig_time
/*LTV_orig_time  gdp_time*/
/ LINK=Probit ;
SCORE DATA = tmp_pdvali2 OUT= pred1 OUTROC=outroc1;
RUN;
```

```
PROC LOGISTIC DATA=tmp_pdvali1 DESCENDING  OUTMODEL=model2;
MODEL default_time = FICO_orig_time
LTV_orig_time /* gdp_time*/
/ LINK=Probit ;
RUN;

PROC LOGISTIC /*DATA=model*/ DESCENDING  INMODEL=model2;
*MODEL default_time = FICO_orig_time
/*LTV_orig_time  gdp_time*/
/ LINK=Probit ;
SCORE DATA = tmp_pdvali2 OUT= pred2 OUTROC=outroc2;
RUN;

PROC LOGISTIC DATA=tmp_pdvali1 DESCENDING  OUTMODEL=model3;
MODEL default_time = FICO_orig_time
LTV_orig_time gdp_time
/ LINK=Probit ;
OUTPUT OUT=inpred3 predicted=Predicted3 Xbeta=xbeta3;
RUN;

PROC LOGISTIC /*DATA=model*/ DESCENDING  INMODEL=model3;
*MODEL default_time = FICO_orig_time
/*LTV_orig_time  gdp_time*/
/ LINK=Probit ;
SCORE DATA = tmp_pdvali2 OUT= pred3 OUTROC=outroc3;
RUN;

DATA pred2 ;
SET pred2 (RENAME = (P_1=P_2));
RUN;

DATA pred3 ;
SET pred3 (RENAME = (P_1=P_3));
RUN;

DATA pred;
MERGE pred1 pred2 pred3;
BY id time;
xbeta1 = PROBIT(P_1);
xbeta2 = PROBIT(P_2);
xbeta3 = PROBIT(P_3);
RUN;
```

```
ODS GRAPHICS ON;
PROC LOGISTIC DATA=PRED PLOTS=ROC(ID=id);
MODEL default_time(EVENT='1') = xbeta1 xbeta2 xbeta3 / NOFIT;
ROC 'model1' xbeta1;
ROC 'model2' xbeta2;
ROC 'model3' xbeta3;
ROCCONTRAST REFERENCE('model1') / ESTIMATE E;
STORE OUT=roc1;
RUN;
ODS GRAPHICS OFF;
```

SAS computes the AUROCs for the three models, including standard errors and confidence intervals (for the formulas we refer to the SAS manual; see SAS Institute Inc. (2015)). The AR measure is given as Somers' D, which has actually been a very popular measure used by statisticians for a long time; see Agresti (1984). You can see that the discriminatory performance increases with more included variables; in particular FICO adds much power. Moreover, the table computes statistical tests for a cross-wise AUROC comparison; see the SAS manual (SAS Institute Inc. 2015). While the AUROCs of model 2 and model 3 are significantly different from that of model 1, those of model 3 and 2 are not significantly different from each other. Similarly, the ROC curves show that models 2 and 3 are considerably better in terms of discrimination than model 1.

When exploring discriminatory power, you should keep a few caveats in mind. First, as the defaults are random events, the outcomes of the discriminatory power measures are random variables as well. Hence, comparisons should be done using statistical tests and confidence intervals, as shown previously. Second, it can be shown that the measures are *portfolio dependent*; see Hamerle, Rauhmeier, and Rösch (2003) and Blochwitz et al. (2005). This means that the outcomes depend on the PDs of the portfolio under consideration. When you compare portfolios with different PDs (and most portfolios *will* have different PDs unless they are exactly identical), the expectations of the measures will be different, and therefore also the outcomes, just because the portfolios are different. Similarly, when comparing AR values for a portfolio over time, the values *will* be different just because the PDs of the portfolio have changed. Therefore, it only makes sense to compare values for the same portfolio for the same time across different models. Moreover, as the values depend on the portfolio, requiring minimum levels, such as "AR should be at least 0.5," or threshold levels at which the performance is good and alike, does not make sense. Third, the distributions of the measures are typically derived under the assumption of independence. For correlated defaults, it might be more difficult to conduct statistical tests. This, however, is not part of this book and is left for future research.

The importance of both the AR and the AUROC has been stressed by the Basel committee, as you can see in this quote from the BIS 14 working paper (see Basel Committee on Banking Supervision 2005a, 32):

> The group has found that the Accuracy Ratio (AR) and the ROC measure appear to be more meaningful than the other above-mentioned indices because of their statistical properties.

The BIS 14 paper then also provides a benchmark range as follows:

> Practical experience shows that the Accuracy Ratio has tendency to take values in the range 50% and 80%. However, such observations should be interpreted with care as they seem to strongly depend on the composition of the portfolio and the numbers of defaulters in the sample.

The paper therefore acknowledges the previous caveat of portfolio dependence. It is important to be aware that a benchmark is always relative and depends on the characteristics of the portfolio, application, and data quality.

Backtesting PD at Level 2

Let us now move to level 2 of our credit risk model architecture, which is the level of the calibration (see Exhibit 13.4). This is probably the most important level, as this gives us the PDs that we use to calculate the capital requirements. Key questions that should be answered here are:

- Do the ratings properly reflect the obligor's default risk?
- Are the credit characteristics of obligors in the same rating sufficiently homogeneous?
- Are there enough ratings to allow for an accurate and consistent estimation of default risk per rating?
- Are the assigned/estimated PDs in line with ex post observed default rates?

When backtesting PD at level 2, you should investigate whether the ratings provide a correct ordinal ranking of risk, and a correct cardinal measure of risk. In terms of the former, it should be verified whether the default rates (DRs) are properly ranked through the ratings. In other words, $DR(A) < DR(B) < DR(C)$. In terms of cardinal measure of risk, the calibrated PD should be as close as possible to the realized default rates. Various test statistics can be used to compare the estimated PDs to the realized default rates. The most popular are the binomial test, the Hosmer-Lemeshow test, the Vasicek (ASRF) one-factor model, and the normal test. All these tests suffer from a couple of complications such as an insufficient number of defaults, the fact that defaults are typically correlated, and the issue of choosing an appropriate significance level. Since each statistical test has its shortcomings, they are typically used as early warning indicators. Note that the impact of the rating philosophy, point-in-time (PIT) or through-the-cycle (TTC), is also important to consider.

Brier Score

We start by defining a performance measure at level 2, the Brier score, which is defined as

$$BS = \frac{1}{n} \sum_{i}^{n} (\hat{\pi}_i - d_i)^2$$

where $\hat{\pi}_i$ is the estimated PD and d_i is the observed default ($d_i = 1$) or nondefault ($d_i = 0$) for obligor i. Obviously, the Brier score is always bounded between 0 and 1, and lower values are to be preferred. A higher discrimination in terms of higher

brier_1
0.0057251

brier_2
0.0057741

brier_3
0.0055243

Exhibit 13.10 Brier Scores

granularity of rating grades and/or PD estimates might help to decrease the value if obligors are not homogeneous within a grade. Also, better calibration in terms of getting the right PDs will decrease the value. Note, however, that this score is only occasionally used in the industry. The following PROC IML code uses the out-of-time predicted PDs from the previous example and calculates the squared differences between the defaults and the predictions for each model, and then computes the average of each. (See Exhibit 13.10.)

```
ODS GRAPHICS ON;
DATA brier;
SET pred (KEEP=default_time P_1 P_2 P_3);
RUN;
QUIT;
PROC IML;
USE brier;
READ ALL VAR _NUM_ INTO data;
brier_row_1 = (data[,2]-data[,1])##2;
brier_row_2 = (data[,3]-data[,1])##2;
brier_row_3 = (data[,4]-data[,1])##2;
brier_1 = brier_row_1[+]/NROW(data);
brier_2 = brier_row_2[+]/NROW(data);
brier_3 = brier_row_3[+]/NROW(data);
PRINT brier_1, brier_2, brier_3;
QUIT;
ODS GRAPHICS OFF;
```

As the values show, the best model fit is given by model 3 (which includes the GDP), which seems to be better calibrated than the other models using LTV and FICO only.

Binomial Test

Another (very popular) test for backtesting PD calibration is the binomial test. Three key assumptions of a binomial experiment are:

1. It should be an experiment with only two outcomes, success or failure.

2. It should be repeated multiple times with the same outcome probabilities.

3. There should be independence between the outcomes of the individual experiments.

Usually, when dealing with rating grades, two of these requirements are fulfilled, as we have only two outcomes, default or nondefault, and multiple obligors are considered with the assumption of identical PDs within a rating grade. Due to the correlation with the default behavior, the independence assumption is often not fulfilled. Hence, the binomial test will be used as a heuristic or early-warning indicator only and deliver results that are too conservative. The null hypothesis, H_0, states that the PD of a rating grade, call it π_0, is correct. The alternative hypothesis can be two-sided or one-sided. From a regulatory perspective, it is important that capital is not underestimated, so let us make the alternative hypothesis, H_1, the PD of the rating is underestimated. As already explained, to use the binomial test, we are assuming that the default events are uncorrelated. Given a confidence level α (for example, 99 percent), the null hypothesis H_0 is rejected if the number of defaulters $d = \sum_{i=1}^{n} d_i$ in the rating is greater than or equal to k^*, which is obtained as follows: It is the minimum k such that the cumulative probability, as quantified using the binomial distribution, of observing between k and d defaulters is less than or equal to one minus α. The probability distribution function (PDF) of the binomial distribution is given by

$$P\left(\sum_{i=1}^{n} D_i = d | n, \pi_0\right) = P(d|n, \pi_0) = \binom{n}{d} \pi_0^d (1 - \pi_0)^{n-d}, \quad d = 0, \ldots, n$$

Therefore,

$$k^* = \min\left\{ k \left| \sum_{j=k}^{n} \binom{n}{j} \pi_0^j (1 - \pi_0)^{n-j} \leq 1 - \alpha \right.\right\}$$

The central limit theorem can now be used for large n, and when $n\pi_0 > 5$ and $n(1 - \pi_0) > 5\%$. The number of defaulters D can then be modeled as a normal distribution with expected value $n\pi_0$ and variance $n\pi_0(1 - \pi_0)$ under H_0. We can now look for the k^* value such that the probability that D is less than or equal to k^* equals α. Hence, we have

$$P\left(Z \leq \frac{k^* - n\pi_0}{\sqrt{n\pi_0(1 - \pi_0)}}\right) = \alpha$$

with Z following a standard normal distribution. The critical value k^* can then be obtained as

$$k^* = \Phi^{-1}(\alpha)\sqrt{n\pi_0(1 - \pi_0)} + n\pi_0$$

where Φ^{-1} is the inverse of the standard normal cumulative distribution function (CDF). In terms of a maximum observed default rate p^*, we simply divide k^* by n and have

$$p^* = \Phi^{-1}(\alpha)\sqrt{\frac{\pi_0(1 - \pi_0)}{n}} + \pi_0$$

To summarize, we can reject H_0 at significance level α if the observed default rate is higher than p^*.

We apply the binomial test to a simple exercise using the mortgage data and the FICO score as a predictor. In the estimation and the validation data set, we create three rating grades with similar numbers of observations as follows:

- Grade 1: FICO $\geq$ 713

- Grade 2: 648 $\geq$ FICO < 713

- Grade 3: FICO < 648

using the following code:

```
DATA fico_class1;
SET tmp_pdvali1;
fico_class = 0 ;
IF FICO_orig_time >= 713        THEN  fico_class = 1;
IF 713 > FICO_orig_time >= 648  THEN  fico_class = 2;
IF 648 > FICO_orig_time         THEN  fico_class = 3;
RUN;


DATA fico_class2;
SET tmp_pdvali2;
fico_class = 0 ;
IF FICO_orig_time >= 713        THEN  fico_class = 1;
IF 713 > FICO_orig_time >= 648  THEN  fico_class = 2;
IF 648 > FICO_orig_time         THEN  fico_class = 3;
RUN;
```

Using PROC FREQ, we then compute for the estimation sample the in-sample default rates for each of the FICO grades and for each grade the respective out-of-sample default rate. Out-of-sample confidence intervals are also computed and a binomial test is requested. The confidence intervals are computed using the exact binomial test and the normal approximation.

```
ODS GRAPHICS ON;
PROC FREQ DATA = fico_class1;
TABLES fico_class * default_time / NOCOL NOPERCENT NOCUM;
RUN;
ODS GRAPHICS OFF;
```

The FREQ Procedure

fico_class	default_time		
	0	1	Total
1	193938	2694	196632
	98.63	1.37	
2	199243	5189	204432
	97.46	2.54	
3	206189	7232	213421
	96.61	3.39	
Total	599370	15115	614485

Table of fico_class by default_time

Exhibit 13.11 In-Sample Default Rates

The in-sample default rates are 1.37 percent, 2.54 percent, and 2.39 percent, respectively, as shown in Exhibit 13.11, computed from a total number of 614,485 observations and the three rating grades with roughly equal size. We set as H_0 for the out-of-sample test a value of 1 percent. The tables in Exhibit 13.12 show the output for each rating grade separately.

```
PROC SORT DATA = fico_class2;
BY fico_class;
RUN;


ODS GRAPHICS ON;
PROC FREQ DATA = fico_class2;
BY fico_class;
TABLES default_time
/ BINOMIAL (LEVEL='1' P=0.01) ALPHA=.05;
RUN;
ODS GRAPHICS OFF;
```

The realized default rates are given as the proportions 0.0028, 0.0039, and 0.0089. These values are considerably lower than those for the estimation sample. This is due to the upswing of the economic cycle in the final observation period, as already shown in the chapter on PD models. Whether this difference is just random or systematic can be checked using the confidence intervals or the binomial test. For grade 1 (where the in-sample default rate was about 1 percent), the 95 percent confidence limits are 0.0011 and 0.0058 (note also the slight difference between the exact and the asymptotic limits), which does not include 0.01 (or 1 percent). Thus, the test $H_0 = 0.01$ is rejected with one-sided and two-sided p-values < 0.001. Note, however, that the realized default rates are *lower* than the PD under H_0. That is, from a statistical perspective,

The FREQ Procedure

fico_class=1

Binomial Proportion	
default_time = 1	
Proportion	0.0028
ASE	0.0011
95% Lower Conf Limit	0.0007
95% Upper Conf Limit	0.0049
Exact Conf Limits	
95% Lower Conf Limit	0.0011
95% Upper Conf Limit	0.0058

fico_class=1

Test of H_0: Proportion = 0.01	
ASE under H_0	0.0020
Z	−3.5936
One-sided Pr < Z	0.0002
Two-sided Pr > |Z|	0.0003

fico_class=2

Binomial Proportion	
default_time = 1	
Proportion	0.0039
ASE	0.0012
95% Lower Conf Limit	0.0015
95% Upper Conf Limit	0.0062
Exact Conf Limits	
95% Lower Conf Limit	0.0019
95% Upper Conf Limit	0.0071

Exhibit 13.12 Out-of-Time Default Rates and Tests

fico_class=2

Test of H_0: Proportion = 0.01	
ASE under H_0	0.0020
Z	−3.1427
One-sided Pr < Z	0.0008
Two-sided Pr > |Z|	0.0017

fico_class=3

Binomial Proportion	
default_time = 1	
Proportion	0.0089
ASE	0.0017
95% Lower Conf Limit	0.0055
95% Upper Conf Limit	0.0123
Exact Conf Limits	
95% Lower Conf Limit	0.0058
95% Upper Conf Limit	0.0130

fico_class=3

Test of H_0: Proportion = 0.01	
ASE under H_0	0.0018
Z	−0.6145
One-sided Pr < Z	0.2695
Two-sided Pr > |Z|	0.5389

Exhibit 13.12 (*Continued*)

H_0 is rejected. From a regulatory perspective, the value under H_0 might seem to be rather conservative and therefore the *upper* one-sided hypothesis would not be rejected. The results are quite similar for the second grade (for testing a different grade specific PD estimates in H_0 you should repeat the test with other values in the P = option in PROC FREQ). For grade 3, the null hypothesis is not rejected, although it seems that the PD estimates based on the FICO score alone are miscalibrated (compared to their historical PD estimate) and additional time-varying (macroeconomic) variables should be included, in order to provide better out-of-time forecasts.

Hosmer-Lemeshow Statistic

As the binomial backtests are usually done on a grade-by-grade basis, another test can be applied that tests all rating grades simultaneously. This is called the *Hosmer-Lemeshow statistic*; see Hosmer and Lemeshow (2000). It compares defaults and predictions for ordered groups. First, the observations are sorted in increasing order of their estimated default probability. The observations are then divided into approximately 10 groups according to a specific scheme. For technical details, we refer to the SAS manual; see SAS Institute Inc. (2015). Next, the following statistic is computed:

$$\chi_{HL}^2 = \sum_{g=1}^{G} \frac{(O_g - n_g\hat{\pi}_g)^2}{n_g\hat{\pi}_g(1 - \hat{\pi}_g)}$$

where G is the number of groups (or rating grades in our case), O_g is the observed total frequency of defaults in group g, n_g is the total number of observations in group g, and $\hat{\pi}_g$ is the average estimated predicted probability of default for the gth group. The statistic is χ^2 distributed with $g - 2$ degrees of freedom. Large values of χ_{HL}^2 (and corresponding small p-values) indicate a lack of fit of the model. It can be computed using the LACKFIT option in PROC LOGISTIC as shown in the following code.

```
ODS GRAPHICS ON;
ODS OUTPUT LackFitPartition = LackFitPartition ;
PROC LOGISTIC DATA=pred ;
MODEL default_time(EVENT='1') = xbeta3 /LACKFIT RSQUARE;
EFFECTPLOT /NOOBS;
RUN;
ODS GRAPHICS OFF;
```

We compute the statistic for model 3 from the earlier ROC comparison example. The output (Exhibit 13.13) shows the 10-group partition for the test with the computed expected and observed frequencies from which the final statistic is evaluated. It is not significant at the 10 percent level, which shows that the model fit is okay. As you can see from the observed and expected numbers in the table, the fractions of defaults divided by the total numbers increase only slightly through the groups.

You can also check calibration graphically, as is done in the following code. (See Exhibit 13.14.) The ODS OUTPUT statement in PROC LOGISTIC in the preceding code creates the Partition Table with Expected and Observed Frequencies as a SAS data set. We then compute the relative frequencies and plot them against each other in order to see how well the 10 classes are calibrated. Ideally, they should all lie close to the diagonal. Here again the fit is rather moderate. The graphical analysis also helps to discover those PD regions with better and poorer fit.

```
DATA Calibration;
SET LackFitPartition;
Obs_freq = EventsObserved/ Total;
Exp_freq = EventsExpected/ Total;
RUN;
```

The LOGISTIC Procedure

Partition for the Hosmer and Lemeshow Test					
Group	Total	default_time = 1		default_time = 0	
		Observed	Expected	Observed	Expected
1	800	1	1.87	799	798.13
2	804	4	2.39	800	801.61
3	801	2	2.78	799	798.22
4	809	2	3.21	807	805.79
5	798	2	3.59	796	794.41
6	800	4	4.07	796	795.93
7	800	8	4.63	792	795.37
8	801	6	5.39	795	795.61
9	801	7	6.47	794	794.53
10	790	7	8.61	783	781.39

Hosmer and Lemeshow Goodness-of-Fit Test		
Chi-Square	DF	Pr > ChiSq
5.7581	8	0.6743

Exhibit 13.13 Hosmer-Lemeshow Statistics

```
ODS GRAPHICS ON;
SYMBOL1 INTERPOL=NONE
VALUE=CIRCLE
CV=BLUE
WIDTH=4 HEIGHT=4;
PROC GPLOT DATA = Calibration;
PLOT Exp_freq * Obs_freq
/HAXIS=0 TO 0.01 BY 0.002 VAXIS = 0 TO 0.01 BY 0.002;
RUN;
ODS GRAPHICS OFF;
```

Similarly, if we plot the predicted PDs, produced by the LACKFIT option in the MODEL statement of PROC LOGISTIC, against the linear predictor (the score, named xbeta3) as shown in Exhibit 13.15, we see that there is only a moderate increase when moving up the linear predictor. Additional variables might be needed to develop a better model that might deliver better forecasting results.

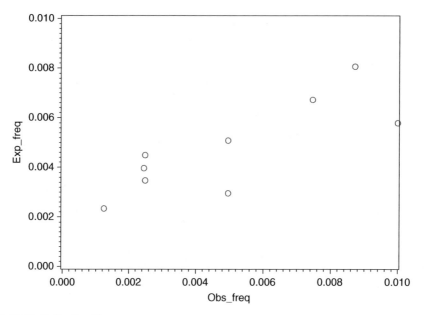

Exhibit 13.14 Calibration Diagram

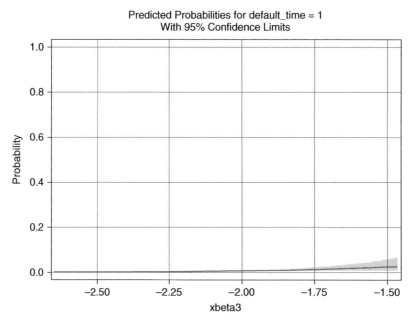

Exhibit 13.15 Out-of-Sample PD Predictions

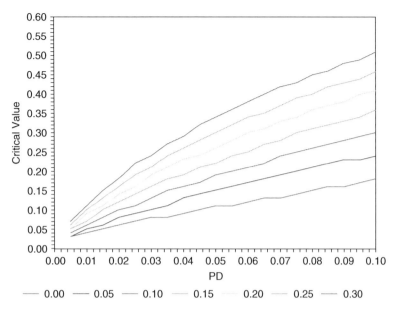

Exhibit 13.16 Critical Values under Extended Binomial Model with Various Correlations

Binomial Test with Correlation

The previous tests assume uncorrelated defaults. As we know from the chapter about default correlations, the distribution of defaults becomes wider when defaults are correlated. As a correlation model, it is convenient to use the Basel one-factor model from the earlier chapter. The unconditional probability distribution for the number of defaults is given as:

$$P(D = d) = \int_{-\infty}^{\infty} \binom{n}{d} CPD(x)^d (1 - CPD(x))^{n-d} \phi(x)dx, d = 0, \ldots, n$$

where:

$$CPD(X) = \Phi\left(\frac{c - \sqrt{\rho}X}{\sqrt{1 - \rho}}\right)$$

and $c = \Phi^{-1}(PD)$. The critical value for $PD = \pi_0$ is then given by the respective quantile against which the observed default rate is compared. If the observed default rate is higher, H_0 is rejected (one-sided). The following code computes and plots the critical values for $\alpha = 0.99$ and 100 obligors as a function of the PD and the correlation ρ. As can be seen, the critical values sharply increase with the correlation. (See Exhibit 13.16.)

```
ODS GRAPHICS ON;
PROC IML SYMSIZE=10000000 WORKSIZE = 10000000;
/*Number of Obligors*/
N            = 100;
```

```
/*Vary Asset Correlation*/
DO rho = 0 TO 0.3 BY 0.05;

/*Vary PD*/
DO  p = 0.005 TO 0.1 BY 0.005;

START fun(x) GLOBAL(k,p,N,rho);
pi = CONSTANT('PI');

/*Compute the Integral*/
CPD = PROBNORM((1/SQRT(1-rho)) * (PROBIT(p)-SQRT(rho)*x));
v   = PROBBNML(CPD,n,k) * (exp(-(x*x)/2))/(SQRT(2*pi));
RETURN(v);
FINISH fun;
k=0;

/*Increase k up to desired Quantile*/
DO UNTIL(z>0.99);
/*Call QUADRATURE */
a    = {.M .P};
eps = 1.34E-15;
CALL QUAD(z,"fun",a,eps);
quantile=k;
default_rate= quantile/N;
k=k+1;
prob=z;
END;
out = out//(N||rho||p||quantile||default_rate||z||prob);
END;
END;
CREATE  crit_reg FROM out;
APPEND FROM out;
QUIT;

GOPTIONS RESET=GLOBAL GUNIT=PCT NOBORDER CBACK=WHITE
COLORS=(BLACK BLUE GREEN RED)
FTITLE=SWISSB FTEXT=SWISS HTITLE=3 HTEXT=3;
SYMBOL1 COLOR=RED    INTERPOL=JOIN
WIDTH=3 VALUE=NONE   HEIGHT=0;
SYMBOL2 FONT=MARKER VALUE=NONE
COLOR=BLUE   INTERPOL=JOIN
```

```
WIDTH=3 HEIGHT=0;
SYMBOL3 COLOR=GREEN INTERPOL=JOIN
VALUE=NONE WIDTH=3  HEIGHT=0;
SYMBOL4 COLOR=ORANGE INTERPOL=JOIN
WIDTH=3 VALUE=NONE  HEIGHT=0;
SYMBOL5 COLOR=YELLOW INTERPOL=JOIN
WIDTH=3 VALUE=NONE  HEIGHT=0;
SYMBOL6 COLOR=VIOLET INTERPOL=JOIN
WIDTH=3 VALUE=NONE  HEIGHT=0;
SYMBOL7 COLOR=BROWN INTERPOL=JOIN
WIDTH=3 VALUE=NONE  HEIGHT=0;
AXIS1 ORDER=(0 TO 0.1 BY 0.01) OFFSET=(0,0)
LABEL=('PD')
MAJOR=(height=1) MINOR=(height=1)
WIDTH=3;
AXIS2 ORDER=(0 TO 0.6 BY 0.05) OFFSET=(0,0)
LABEL=('critical value')
MAJOR=(HEIGHT=1) MINOR=(HEIGHT=1)
WIDTH=3;
LEGEND1 LABEL=NONE;

ODS GRAPHICS ON;
PROC GPLOT DATA=crit_reg;
PLOT COL5*COL3 = COL2/ OVERLAY LEGEND=LEGEND1
HAXIS=AXIS1
VAXIS=AXIS2;
RUN;
QUIT;
ODS GRAPHICS OFF;
```

The binomial test under correlation can also be approximated by the ASRF formula (Vasicek model). (See Exhibit 13.17.) The critical value p^* is then given as the α-quantile of the ASRF model:

$$p^* = \Phi\left(\frac{\Phi^{-1}(\pi_0) + \sqrt{\rho}\Phi^{-1}(\alpha)}{\sqrt{1-\rho}}\right)$$

The following code computes the respective critical values for $\alpha = 0.99$.

```
ODS GRAPHICS ON;
/*ASRF model*/
DATA ASRF_crit;
DO PD = 0.005 TO 0.1 BY 0.005;
DO rho = 0 TO 0.3 BY 0.05;
```

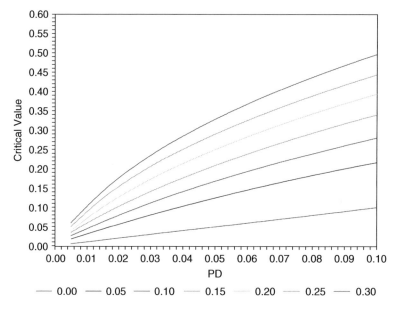

Exhibit 13.17 Critical Values under ASRF Model with Various Correlations

```
p_crit = PROBNORM((PROBIT(PD)+SQRT(rho)*PROBIT(0.99))/SQRT(1-rho));
OUTPUT;
END;
END;
RUN;

ODS GRAPHICS ON;
PROC GPLOT DATA=ASRF_crit;
PLOT p_crit*PD = rho/ OVERLAY LEGEND=LEGEND1
HAXIS=AXIS1
VAXIS=AXIS2;
RUN;
QUIT;
ODS GRAPHICS OFF;
```

Other Important Issues

Confidence Level, α- versus β-Error

Whenever you conduct a statistical test, the question about the error probability of the test decision arises. Given a null hypothesis H_0 and an alternative hypothesis H_1, you can differentiate between the true but unknown states of the world (either H_0

or H_1 is true), and the decision based on the statistical test (either rejection of H_0 or no rejection of H_0). Thus, four scenarios can arise:

1. H_0 is true and the test decision is *not* to reject H_0 → This is a correct decision.
2. H_0 is true but the test decision is to (erroneously) reject H_0 → This is a wrong decision.
3. H_0 is not true (and H_1 is true instead) and the test decision is to reject H_0 → This is a correct decision.
4. H_0 is not true (and H_1 is true instead) but the test decision is *not* to reject H_0 → This is a wrong decision.

Situations 1 and 3 are not problematic; situations 2 and 4 might hold, as you make a wrong decision. Situation 2, however, is under control, because the probability for a wrong decision when H_0 is true is given by the confidence level α. Therefore, a general question concerns the confidence level to be chosen, as it can be set by the decision maker who controls the α-error (or type 1 error) probability per test construction. The Hong Kong Monetary Authority (HKMA) has given some further recommendations about confidence levels to be adopted for the binomial test. More specifically, it states:

> For example, if a Binomial test is used, authorized institutions (AIs) can set tolerance limits at confidence levels of 95% and 99.9%. Deviations of the forecast PD from the realized default rates below a confidence level of 95% should not be regarded as significant and remedial actions may not be needed. Deviations at a confidence level higher than 99.9% should be regarded as significant and the PD must be revised upward immediately. Deviations which are significant at confidence levels between 95% and 99.9% should be put on a watch list, and upward revisions to the PD should be made if the deviations persist. (Hong Kong Monetary Authority (HKMA) 2006)

Situation 4, however, is somewhat problematic. Here, the test does not signal that H_0 is untrue, although H_1 holds in reality. The issue is that the probability for this type of error (the β- or type 2 error) depends on the parameter under H_1, which is unfortunately unknown (otherwise you would not need a statistical test). The way out here is to conduct a "what-if" analysis and check how the error would be under specific scenarios for the parameters (PD).

Let P be the random default rate (i.e., $P = D/n$), π_0 be the PD under H_0, and π be the true PD where $\pi_0 \neq \pi$. The β-error in the normal approximation of the simple binomial test (without correlation) can then be computed as

$$Prob_\beta = P(P < p^* | \pi, \pi_0 \neq \pi) = P(P \leq \pi_0 + \Phi^{-1}(\alpha)\sqrt{\pi_0(1 - \pi_0/n)} | \pi, \pi_0 \neq \pi)$$

$$= \Phi\left(\frac{\pi_0 - \pi + \Phi^{-1}(\alpha)\sqrt{\pi_0(1 - \pi_0/n)}}{\sqrt{\pi(1 - \pi/n)}}\right)$$

and returns the probability that the default rate P does not exceed the critical value p^*, as a function of the true parameter π. As can be seen from the formula, the closer the true value π is to π_0, the higher the type 2 error becomes, ceteris paribus. The following code computes the β-error for various values of π_0 and π, for $\alpha = 0.99$ and $n = 1,000$ obligors. The four curves are computed such that π is $\pi_0 + h$ where $h \in \{0.005, 0.01, 0.025, 0.05\}$.

```
/*Beta error under simple Binomial Test*/
DATA Binomial_simple_beta_error;
ALPHA = 0.99;
N=1000;
DO PD0 = 0.005 TO 0.1 BY 0.005;
PD1 = PD0 + 0.005;
PD2 = PD0 + 0.01;
PD3 = PD0 + 0.025;
PD4 = PD0 + 0.05;
P_beta_005 = PROBNORM( (PD0-PD1 + PROBIT(alpha)*SQRT(PD0*(1-PD0)/n))
/ (SQRT(PD1*(1-PD1)/n)) );
P_beta_01 = PROBNORM( (PD0-PD2 + PROBIT(alpha)*SQRT(PD0*(1-PD0)/n))
/ (SQRT(PD2*(1-PD2)/n)) );
P_beta_025 = PROBNORM( (PD0-PD3 + PROBIT(alpha)*SQRT(PD0*(1-PD0)/n))
/ (SQRT(PD3*(1-PD3)/n)) );
P_beta_05 = PROBNORM( (PD0-PD4 + PROBIT(alpha)*SQRT(PD0*(1-PD0)/n))
/ (SQRT(PD4*(1-PD4)/n)) );
OUTPUT;
END;
RUN;
QUIT;


ODS GRAPHICS ON;
PROC GPLOT DATA=Binomial_simple_beta_error;
PLOT P_beta_005*PD0  P_beta_01*PD0 P_beta_025*PD0 P_beta_05*PD0
/ OVERLAY LEGEND=LEGEND1
HAXIS=0 TO 0.1 BY 0.02
VAXIS=0 TO 1 BY 0.2;
RUN;
QUIT;
ODS GRAPHICS OFF;
```

As can be seen in Exhibit 13.18, the type 2 error decreases with the difference between π_0 and π rising. It should also be noted that the α- and β-error are related. The higher the confidence level α (that is, the lower the type 1 error probability), the higher the type 2 error probability will be, ceteris paribus. Therefore, there is a

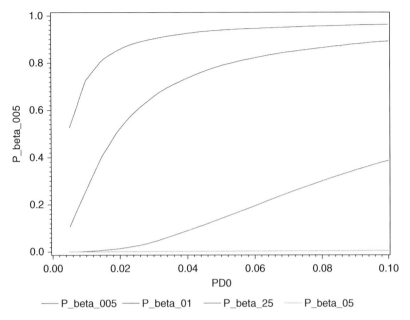

Exhibit 13.18 Beta Error for Simple Binomial Test

trade-off between the two error probabilities. We leave it as an exercise to the reader to check this for our example.

Unfortunately, the type 2 error probability becomes larger (all other parameters fixed) when defaults are correlated, that is, when we apply the extended binomial test under correlation. To see this, we look at the ASRF model with the critical value p^*. The type 2 error probability is then given as the probability that $P < p^*$ given that π is the true value rather than π_0. In the correlation chapter, we have seen that this probability is the CDF of the ASRF model, evaluated at π, and thus,

$$Prob_\beta = P(P < p^* | \pi, \pi_0 \neq \pi)$$
$$= \Phi\left(\frac{\sqrt{1 - \rho} \cdot \Phi^{-1}(p^*) - \Phi^{-1}(\pi)}{\sqrt{\rho}} \right)$$

for a given correlation ρ. The following code computes and plots these critical values under the assumption that $\pi = \pi_0 + 0.05$ for various values of $\rho \in \{0.01, 0.05, 0.1, 0.2, 0.3\}$.

```
/*Beta error under correlated Binomial Test*/
DATA Binomial_corr_beta_error;
ALPHA = 0.99;
DO PD0 = 0.005 TO 0.1 BY 0.005;
PD1     = PD0 + 0.05;
rho1    = 0.01;
rho2    = 0.05;
```

```
rho3    = 0.1;
rho4    = 0.2;
rho5    = 0.3;
p_crit_rho01
= PROBNORM( (PROBIT(PD0)+SQRT(rho1)*PROBIT(alpha))/ SQRT(1-rho1));
p_beta_rho01
= PROBNORM( (SQRT(1-rho1)*PROBIT(p_crit_rho01) -PROBIT(PD1) )
/ SQRT(rho1) );
p_crit_rho05
= PROBNORM( (PROBIT(PD0)+SQRT(rho2)*PROBIT(alpha))/ SQRT(1-rho2));
p_beta_rho05
= PROBNORM( (SQRT(1-rho2)*PROBIT(p_crit_rho05) -PROBIT(PD1) )
/ SQRT(rho2) );
p_crit_rho10
= PROBNORM( (PROBIT(PD0)+SQRT(rho3)*PROBIT(alpha))/ SQRT(1-rho3));
p_beta_rho10
= PROBNORM( (SQRT(1-rho3)*PROBIT(p_crit_rho10) -PROBIT(PD1) )
/ SQRT(rho3) );
p_crit_rho20
= PROBNORM( (PROBIT(PD0)+SQRT(rho4)*PROBIT(alpha))/ SQRT(1-rho4));
p_beta_rho20
= PROBNORM( (SQRT(1-rho4)*PROBIT(p_crit_rho20) -PROBIT(PD1) )
/ SQRT(rho4) );
p_crit_rho30
= PROBNORM( (PROBIT(PD0)+SQRT(rho5)*PROBIT(alpha))/ SQRT(1-rho5));
p_beta_rho30
= PROBNORM( (SQRT(1-rho5)*PROBIT(p_crit_rho30) -PROBIT(PD1) )
/ SQRT(rho5) );
OUTPUT;
END;
RUN;
QUIT;


ODS GRAPHICS ON;
PROC GPLOT DATA=Binomial_corr_beta_error;
PLOT P_beta_rho01*PD0 P_beta_rho05*PD0  P_beta_rho10*PD0
P_beta_rho20*PD0  P_beta_rho30*PD0  / OVERLAY LEGEND=LEGEND1
HAXIS=0 TO 0.1 BY 0.02
VAXIS=0 TO 1 BY 0.2;
RUN;
QUIT;
ODS GRAPHICS OFF;
```

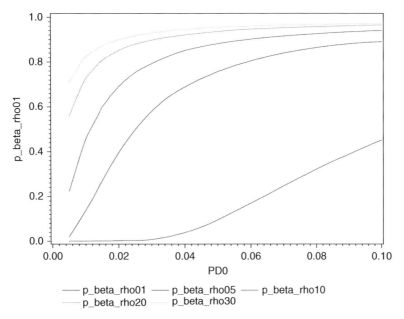

Exhibit 13.19 Beta Error for Extended Binomial Test under Correlations

As can be seen in Exhibit 13.19, the β error probability rapidly increases toward 1 if the correlation is increased. Note that this is even the case for small values of π_0 where the difference between π_0 and π is huge (in relative terms). Such an analysis of type 2 errors should accompany any kind of PD backtesting procedure.

Data Aggregation

Data aggregation can be interesting to consider during backtesting. Let's assume we have a portfolio with n obligors and G ratings. This implies that there are approximately n/G observations per rating. Hence, more ratings makes backtesting more difficult, since there will be fewer observations per rating, which will increase the standard errors and consequently the critical values. To improve the significance of the backtesting, data aggregation can be considered. One example would be to merge ratings with a low number of observations, for example, AA+, AA, and AA− into one overall rating AA. The aggregation can then also be considered for important segments or even at the overall portfolio level.

Risk Philosophy

The risk philosophy should also be taken into account during backtesting. In our chapter on time-discrete hazard models, we introduced the PIT and TTC rating philosophies. PIT ratings take into account both cyclical and noncyclical information.

Hence, the backtesting should find that the realized default rates are close to the forecast PD, or, in other words, the PIT PDs should be validated against the 12-month default rates. TTC ratings consider only noncyclical information and are thus more stable. Hence, backtesting should find that the realized default rates vary around the forecast PD, rising in downturns and falling in upturns, or, the TTC PDs should be validated against cycle average default rates; see also Rösch (2005) for an analysis.

Setting up a Traffic Light Indicator Dashboard for PD Backtesting

Up until now, we have discussed various backtesting performance metrics and statistics to backtest PD models at levels 0, 1, and 2 of the credit risk model architecture. It is important that all these backtesting statistics are now combined in a traffic light indicator dashboard. In Exhibit 13.20, you can see an example of this starting at level 2.

You can see that both quantitative tests as well as qualitative tests are included. The binomial, Hosmer-Lemeshow, Vasicek, and normal tests are the quantitative tests, possibly accompanied by an analysis of α- and β-errors. Qualitative tests are more subjective and are based on expert evaluation. Here, we include an inspection of the portfolio distribution, the overall difference between the estimated and realized default rates, and an evaluation of the portfolio stability. The result of each of these tests has been encoded using three traffic lights.

Level 2: Calibration	Quantitative	Binomial	Not significant at 95% level	Significant at 95% but not at 99% level	Significant at 99% level
		Hosmer-Lemeshow	Not significant at 95% level	Significant at 95% but not at 99% level	Significant at 99% level
		Vasicek	Not significant at 95% level	Significant at 95% but not at 99% level	Significant at 99% level
		Normal	Not significant at 95% level	Significant at 95% but not at 99% level	Significant at 99% level
	Qualitative	Portfolio distribution	Minor shift	Moderate shift	Major shift
		Difference	Correct	Over-estimation	Under-estimation
		Portfolio stability	Minor migrations	Moderate migrations	Major migrations

Exhibit 13.20 Backtesting PD at Level 2

This can then be continued at level 1. In Exhibit 13.21, you can see quantitative tests based on the accuracy ratio, the area under the ROC curve (both are related), and the overall model significance. Qualitative checks inspect the data preprocessing activities conducted, the coefficient signs of the scorecard, the number of overrides, and the model documentation available. Again, the outcome of each of these tests is represented as a traffic light.

Finally, as depicted in Exhibit 13.22 for level 0, the quantitative tests include the system stability index at the population level and the attribute level, and a t-test at

Level 1: Discrimination					
	Quantitative	AR difference with reference model	<5%	Between 5% and 10%	>10%
		AUC difference with reference model	<2,5%	Between 2.5% and 5%	>5%
		Model significance	p-value < 0.01	p-value between 0.01 and 0.10	p-value > 0.10
	Qualitative	Preprocessing (missing values, outliers)	Considered	Partially considered	Ignored
		Coefficient signs	All as expected	Minor exceptions	Major exceptions
		Number of overrides	Minor	Moderate	Major
		Documentation	Sufficient	Minor issues	Major issues

Exhibit 13.21 Backtesting PD at Level 1

Level 0: Data					
	Quantitative	SSI (current versus training sample)	SSI < 0.10	0.10 < SSk 0.25	SSI > 0.25
		SSI attribute level	SSI < 0.10	0.10 < SSk 0.25	SSI > 0.25
		t-test attribute level	p-value > 0.10	p-value between 0.10 and 0.01	p-value < 0.01
	Qualitative	Characteristic analysis	No change	Moderate change	Major change
		Attribute histogram	No shift	Moderate shift	Major shift

Exhibit 13.22 Backtesting PD at Level 0

the attribute level (not discussed in this chapter). It can be accompanied by a test of model stability. Qualitative checks include characteristics analysis and histogram inspection.

Action Plan

Based on all these tests, a decision needs to be made as to whether the PD model is performing well. Remember, if there are issues with the PD model, a backtesting action plan should be available to remedy the situation. This plan will specify what to do in response to the findings of the PD backtesting exercise.

In Exhibit 13.23, you can see an example of an action scheme for PD backtesting. If the model calibration is okay, you can continue to use the PD model, since the capital is appropriately calculated and there is no problem. If the model calibration is not okay, you need to verify the model discrimination or ranking at level 1. If this is OK, then the solution might be to simply recalibrate the probabilities upward or downward using a scaling factor. If not, the next step is to check the data and model stability at level 0. If the stability is still okay, you may consider tweaking the model to see if you can remedy the situation. This is not always straightforward and will often involve completely reestimating the PD model, as is the case when the stability is not okay.

Backtesting LGD and EAD

In what follows, we discuss backtesting LGD and EAD models. An empirical study on LGD model comparison is given by Loterman et al. (2012). Remember, both models are typically developed using similar methodologies. Hence, the backtesting

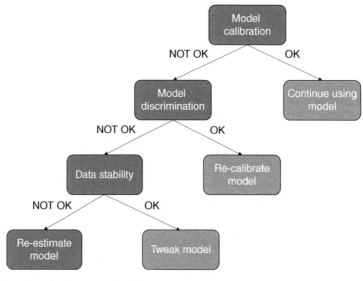

Exhibit 13.23 Action Plan for PD Backtesting

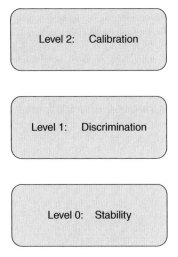

Exhibit 13.24 Backtesting LGD and EAD

procedures will also be similar. We illustrate the techniques using LGDs only, but application to EADs is straightforward using the same codes. As with PD backtesting, we also make use of the multilevel model architecture. At level 0, we backtest the stability of the data. At level 1, we verify the discrimination and at level 2 the calibration (see Exhibit 13.24).

For backtesting the stability of the data, a system stability index can be used, just as with PD. This SSI will then contrast the distribution of the actual population with that of the training population across the various LGD ranges. Similarly, a test on model stability can be conducted using time dummies.

Backtesting at Level 1

At level 1, the discrimination can be verified using ROC plots and corresponding AUROCs and ARs. However, defaults are binary variables whereas LGDs and EADs are metric variables. Therefore, some adjustments have to be made. To provide insight into the implementation in SAS, we divide the data that we used in the chapter on LGDs into a training and an out-of-sample validation data set (named lgd_is and lgd_os). For ease of exposition, we show our examples with the linear models. The following code estimates the LGD for the in-sample training data with PROC REG and scores the validation sample using PROC PLM; that is, it computes the out-of-sample predicted values.

```
ODS GRAPHICS ON;
PROC REG DATA=data.lgd_is OUTEST=Reg1Out;
MODEL lgd_time= LTV purpose1/  DETAILS=ALL;
STORE OUT=model1;
RUN;
QUIT;
```

```
PROC PLM SOURCE=model1;
SCORE DATA = data.lgd_os OUT = lgd_os1;
RUN;
ODS GRAPHICS OFF;
```

We then compare the predictions in the validation sample with the actual LGDs. We first use PROC UNIVARIATE and PROC BOXPLOT in order to compare the distributions of actual and predicted values (see Exhibits 13.25 and 13.26).

```
ODS GRAPHICS ON;
PROC UNIVARIATE data = lgd_os1;
HISTOGRAM lgd_time predicted / KERNEL(c = 0.25 0.50 0.75 1.00
l = 1 20 2 34
NOPRINT);
RUN;
ODS GRAPHICS OFF;

ODS GRAPHICS ON;
PROC BOXPLOT data = lgd_os1;
PLOT lgd_time*group; INSET MIN MEAN MAX STDDEV ;
PLOT predicted*group; INSET MIN MEAN MAX STDDEV ;
RUN;
ODS GRAPHICS OFF;
```

The histograms (Overlaid by kernel densities) show serious deviations between actual and predicted values. This is particularly attributable to the nonnormal shape of the LGD distribution, which cannot be properly fitted by the OLS regression model with only two explanatory variables. Similarly, the different distributions can be seen in the box plots. The means (the diamond in the plot) are quite similar but the medians (the line in the box), the 25 percent and the 75 percent percentiles (the frames of the boxes), and the maximum and minimum values are quite different.

Next, we analyze the ROC curve. Here you must keep in mind that LGD is a continuous variable whereas for PD we had a binary outcome. Therefore, we follow the suggestion in Gupton and Stein (2005) and transform the observed LGDs into a binary variable using

$$d(\text{LGD}_i) = \begin{cases} 1 & \text{LGD}_i \geq \overline{\text{LGD}} \\ 0 & \text{LGD}_i < \overline{\text{LGD}} \end{cases}$$

where $\overline{\text{LGD}}$ is the mean observed LGD. As can be seen from the box plot, the mean of the LGDs is about 0.2311. The transformation is given by the following code.

```
DATA lgd_os2;
SET lgd_os1;
D_LGD = 0;
IF lgd_time > 0.2312 THEN D_LGD = 1;
RUN;
```

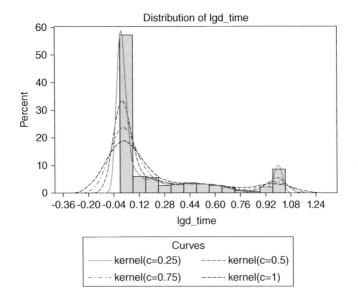

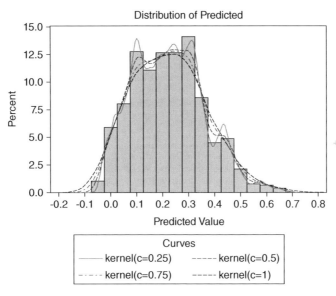

Exhibit 13.25 Histograms of Actual and Predicted LGDs

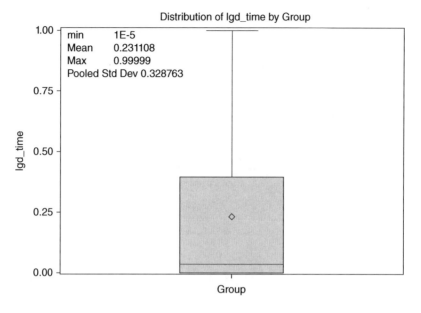

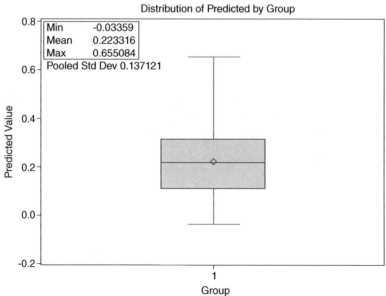

Exhibit 13.26 Box Plots of Actual and Predicted LGDs

Next, PROC LOGISTIC is used to plot the ROC curve and compute association statistics of the model which regresses the dummy against the predicted values. (See Exhibit 13.27.)

```
ODS GRAPHICS ON;
PROC LOGISTIC data = lgd_os2 PLOTS(ONLY)=ROC;
CLASS D_LGD;
MODEL D_LGD = predicted;
RUN;
QUIT;
ODS GRAPHICS OFF;
```

The discriminatory power of high (above-mean) versus low (below-mean) LGDs can be seen from the plot and from the AUROC measure, which is 0.7784. As for

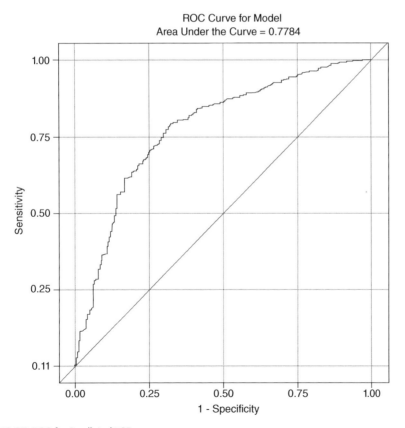

Exhibit 13.27 ROC for Predicted LGDs

PDs, the measure and the curve depend on the portfolio composition, and in order to make an assessment about the quality of the discrimination, the ROC should ideally be compared relative to a benchmark model.

Finally, we can compute correlation coefficients for measuring the association between the predicted and the observed LGDs. The linear *Bravais-Pearson* correlation should be obvious from the chapter on exploratory data analysis and therefore a formula is not provided. The nonparametric *Spearman* rank correlation is given by:

$$\theta = \frac{\sum_i((R_i - \overline{R})(S_i - \overline{S}))}{\sqrt{\sum_i(R_i - \overline{R})^2 \ \sum(S_i - \overline{S})^2}}$$

where R_i is the rank of LG D_i^{obs}, S_i is the rank of LGD_i^{pred}, $\overline{R}$ is the mean of the R_i values, and $\overline{S}$ is the mean of the S_i values.

Another popular nonparametric measure for association is *Kendall's* τ-b, which is given by:

$$\tau = \frac{\sum_{i<j}(sgn(LGD_i^{obs} - LGD_j^{obs})sgn(LGD_i^{pred} - LGD_j^{pred}))}{\sqrt{(T_0 - T_1)(T_0 - T_2)}}$$

where $T_0 = n(n-1)/2$, $T_1 = \sum_k t_k(t_k - 1)/2$, and $T_2 = \sum_l u_l(u_l - 1)/2$. t_k is the number of tied LGD^{obs} values in the kth group of tied LGD^{obs} values, u_l is the number of tied LGD^{pred} values in the lth group of tied LGD^{pred} values, n is the number of observations, and $sgn(z)$ is defined as

$$sgn(z) = \begin{cases} 1 & \textit{if } z > 0 \\ 0 & \textit{if } z = 0 \\ -1 & \textit{if } z < 0 \end{cases}$$

All measures (and some more) can be computed via PROC CORR as shown in the following code (see Exhibit 13.28).

```
ODS GRAPHICS ON;
PROC CORR DATA = lgd_os2 Pearson Spearman Kendall;
VAR lgd_time predicted ;
RUN;
QUIT;
ODS GRAPHICS OFF;
```

The linear correlation is about 0.43, which shows a medium size association (remember that the correlation ranges between −1 and +1). Similarly, the Spearman measure, which is 0.48, and Kendall's τ, which is 0.33, show moderate positive association.

The CORR Procedure

Pearson Correlation Coefficients, *N* = 760 Prob > |r| under *H0*: Rho = 0		lgd_time	Predicted	Plgd_time	PPredicted
lgd_time		1.00000	0.43601		<.0001
Predicted	Predicted Value	0.43601	1.00000	<.0001	

Spearman Correlation Coefficients, *N* = 760 Prob > |r| under *H0*: Rho = 0		lgd_time	Predicted	Plgd_time	PPredicted
lgd_time		1.00000	0.47656		<.0001
Predicted	Predicted Value	0.47656	1.00000	<.0001	

Kendall's Tau b Correlation Coefficients, *N* = 760 Prob > |tau| under *H0*: Tau = 0		lgd_time	Predicted	Plgd_time	PPredicted
lgd_time		1.00000	0.33440		<.0001
Predicted	Predicted Value	0.33440	1.00000	<.0001	

Exhibit 13.28 Measures for Correlation and Association

Backtesting at Level 2

Next, we check the calibration at level 2. We analyze several measures that can be obtained by running a regression of actual versus predicted values as illustrated in the following code (see Exhibits 13.29 and 13.30).

```
ODS GRAPHICS ON;
PROC REG DATA=lgd_os1
     PLOTS(MAXPOINTS= 10000 STATS= ALL)= (CRITERIA QQ);
MODEL lgd_time= predicted  ;
RUN;
QUIT;
ODS GRAPHICS OFF;
```

The intercept is close to zero and the slope close to one, which shows good calibration for the mean. However, the model returns an adjusted $R^2 = 0.19$ only and a root MSE of 0.30. In other words, the average deviation of the LGDs is 0.3. As can also be seen from the plots, the different shape of the distributions translates into a very moderate fit. Again, such figures would call for better covariates to be included.

We extend the preceding analysis from an individual level to a bucket-wise level. The following code uses PROC RANK (which you already know from the PD chapter)

The REG Procedure
Model: MODEL1
Dependent Variable: lgd_time

Root MSE	0.29606	*R*-Squared	0.1901
Dependent Mean	0.23111	Adj *R*-Sq	0.1890
Coeff Var	128.10582		

Parameter Estimates						
Variable	Label	DF	Parameter Estimate	Standard Error	*t* Value	Pr > |*t*|
Intercept	Intercept	1	−0.00234	0.02053	−0.11	0.9092
Predicted	Predicted Value	1	1.04538	0.07837	13.34	<.0001

Exhibit 13.29 Real-Fit Diagnostics

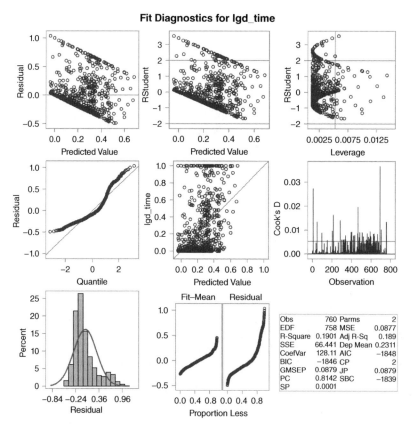

Exhibit 13.30 Linear Regression

to create five groups of LGD buckets according to the observed LGDs. In a next step, the data are sorted according to their ranks, and mean LGDs are computed for the predictions and the observations for each bucket.

```
PROC RANK DATA=lgd_os1 OUT=LGD_ranks GROUPS=5;
VAR lgd_time;
RANKS lgd_time_ranks;
RUN;

PROC SORT DATA = lgd_ranks;
BY lgd_time_ranks;
RUN;

PROC MEANS DATA = lgd_ranks;
VAR lgd_time predicted;
BY lgd_time_ranks;
OUTPUT OUT = means1 MEAN(lgd_time predicted)=lgd_time predicted;
RUN;
```

Next, we compute box plots for each bucket in order to learn about the groupwise distribution (see Exhibit 13.31).

```
ODS GRAPHICS ON;
PROC BOXPLOT data = lgd_ranks;
PLOT lgd_time*lgd_time_ranks; inset min mean max stddev ;
PLOT predicted*lgd_time_ranks; inset min mean max stddev ;
RUN;
ODS GRAPHICS OFF;
```

As the box plots reveal, we find increasing predicted LGD distributions for each bucket, which is desired. However, the distributions of the observed LGDs steeply increase from low to high buckets. Similarly, in the next step, you can plot the mean actual LGDs versus the mean predicted LGDs.

```
ODS GRAPHICS ON;
SYMBOL1 INTERPOL=NONE
VALUE=CIRCLE
CV=BLUE
WIDTH=4 HEIGHT=4;
PROC GPLOT DATA = means1;
PLOT lgd_time * predicted / HAXIS=0 TO 1 BY 0.2
VAXIS=0 TO 1 BY 0.2;
RUN;
ODS GRAPHICS OFF;
```

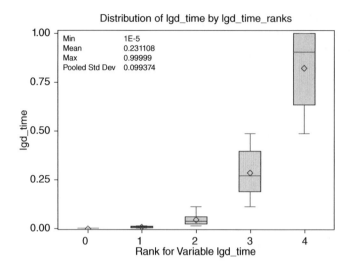

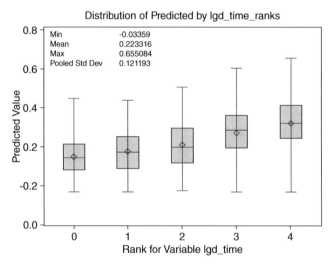

Exhibit 13.31 Box Plots of Actual and Predicted LGDs

The scatter plot (Exhibit 13.32) supports the former analyses and shows that for the lower LGD buckets the predicted values are too high whereas they are too low for the higher LGD buckets. The next steps would now be to apply some of the other LGD modeling methods discussed in the LGD chapter and/or include better explanatory variables.

We conclude with references to more backtesting techniques. First, more discrimination measures can be computed, as shown in Fischer and Pfeuffer (2014). Second, statistical tests can be applied for the variances of the LGD distributions, or a bootstrap procedure can be used for conducting a test for R^2 or MSE (see Loterman et al. 2012).

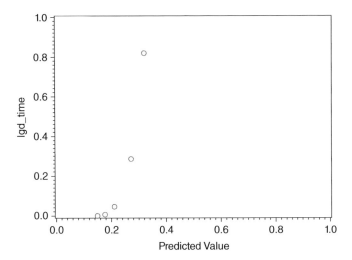

Exhibit 13.32 Scatter Plot of Actual and Predicted LGDs

Benchmarking

Benchmarking is another important quantitative validation activity. The idea here is to compare the output and performance of the analytical PD, LGD, or EAD model with a reference model or benchmark. This is recommended as an extra validity check to make sure that the current credit risk model is the optimal one to be used. Various credit risk measurements can be benchmarked, for example credit scores, ratings, calibrated risk measurements such as PDs, LGDs, CCFs, or even migration matrices. Various benchmarking partners can be considered. Examples are credit bureaus, rating agencies, data poolers, and even internal experts. As an example of a simple benchmarking exercise, consider benchmarking an application score against a FICO score.

The benchmark can be externally or internally developed. Various problems arise when performing external benchmarking. Firstly, there is no guarantee that external ratings are necessarily of good quality. Think about what happened during the credit crisis, when many rating agencies were criticized because their ratings turned out to be overly optimistic. Next, the external partner might also have a different portfolio composition and adopt different model development methodologies and/or processes, making a comparison less straightforward. Also, different rating philosophies might be used, where the benchmark rating system is either more point-in-time or through-the-cycle. The default and loss definitions might differ, and different LGD weighting schemes can be adopted, along with different discount factors or collection policies. External benchmarking might also be complicated because of legal constraints where information cannot be exchanged due to banking secrecy regulation. Credit risk is typically also an endogenous phenomenon, which is highly dependent upon the internal credit culture and/or process. There is also a risk of cherry-picking where a close-match external benchmark is selected without further critical evaluation.

Given these complications with external benchmarking, the idea of internal benchmarking has been advocated. It was first introduced by the Hong Kong Monetary Authority (HKMA), as illustrated by this quote:

> Where a relevant external benchmark is not available (e.g., PD for SME and retail exposures, LGD, and EAD), an authorized institution (AI) should develop an internal benchmark. For example, to benchmark against a model-based rating system, an AI might employ internal rating reviewers to re-rate a sample of credit on an expert-judgment basis. (Hong Kong Monetary Authority (HKMA) 2006)

The internal benchmark can be a statistical or an expert-based benchmark. Consider, for example, a PD model built using a plain-vanilla logistic regression model. You can then consider building a neural network benchmark where the performance of both the logistic regression and the neural network can then be contrasted. Although the neural network is clearly a black box model, and thus cannot be used as the final credit risk model, the result of this benchmarking exercise will tell whether there are any nonlinear effects in the data. If it turns out that the neural network performs better than the logistic regression, you can then start looking for nonlinear effects or interactions and try to add them to your logistic regression model to further boost its performance. The benchmark can also be expert based. Remember, an expert-based benchmark is a qualitative model based on expert experience and/or common sense. An example of this could be an expert committee ranking a set of small and medium-sized enterprises (SMEs) in terms of default risk by merely inspecting their balance sheet and financial statement information in an expert-based, subjective way. The ranking obtained by an expert-based rating system can then be compared to the ranking obtained by the logistic regression.

A champion challenger approach can be used when benchmarking. The current model is the champion that is challenged by the benchmark. If the benchmark beats the champion in performance, then it can become the new champion. This way, models are continuously challenged and further improved.

As tools for comparison, the previously discussed techniques that were used for backtesting can be applied, (e.g., correlation and measures of association).

QUALITATIVE VALIDATION

To conclude this chapter, we touch on qualitative validation and consider these topics:

- Use testing
- Data quality
- Model design
- Documentation
- Corporate governance and management oversight

Use Testing

The idea of use testing is to use the IRB models and estimates not only for Basel capital calculation, but also for other business activities such as credit pricing, credit approval, and economic capital calculations. This can be illustrated with the following regulatory articles:

- *"Internal ratings and default and loss estimates must play an essential role in the credit approval, risk management, internal capital allocations, and corporate governance functions of banks using the IRB approach"* (§444, Basel Committee on Banking Supervision 2006).

- *"The systems and processes used by a bank for risk-based capital purposes must be consistent with the bank's internal risk management processes and management information reporting systems"* (Federal Register 2007).

- *"When institutions use different estimates for the calculation of risk weights and for internal purposes, it shall be documented and be reasonable"* (Art. 179, European Union 2013).

So to summarize, the IRB estimates must play an essential role in other business activities. This, however, does not mean an exclusive role. Earlier, the Financial Services Authority (FSA) put forward three conditions that should be satisfied in order to meet the use test requirement.

1. Consistency: The information the IRB estimates, PD, LGD, and EAD, are based on should be consistent with internal lending standards and policies.

2. Use of all relevant information: Any relevant information used in internal lending standards and policies must also be used in calculating the IRB estimates.

3. Disclosure: If differences exist between the calculation of the IRB estimates and those used for internal purposes, then they must be documented and the reasonableness demonstrated.

Some examples of use test issues are as follows. For application scoring, many firms use a time window of 18 months. Remember, however, that for PD, Basel requires a time window of only 12 months. Also, the Basel default definition is 90 days, whereas some financial institutions like to use their own definitions. Most regulators will tolerate these differences, as long as they are properly documented and the reasonableness thereof is demonstrated.

Another issue concerns the use of downturn LGD for other business activities. This is often perceived to be too conservative for other applications. FSA has indicated:

> Firms can use different LGDs for business purposes to those used for regulation and not fail the use test, provided that the rationale for their use and differences/transformation to capital numbers is understood.

Hence, average LGD values can be used for economic capital calculation, IFRS provisions, and other accounting applications.

Data Quality

Data is the key ingredient to any credit risk model, be it a PD, LGD, or EAD model. It speaks for itself that to have good models, data should be of high quality. About this, the regulators said:

- *"The institution shall have in place a process for vetting data inputs into the model, which includes an assessment of the accuracy, completeness and appropriateness of the data"* (Art. 173, European Union 2013).

- *"The data used to build the model shall be representative of the population of the institution's actual obligors or exposures"* (Art. 173, European Union 2013).

- *"The PRA expects a firm to set standards for data quality, aim to improve them over time and measure its performance against those standards"* (Section 10, Prudential Regulation Authority 2013).

Data quality can be measured in various ways. A first important dimension is accuracy. The aim here is to verify if the inputs measure what they are supposed to measure. The FSA introduced the data accuracy scorecard to measure this. Bad data accuracy can be caused by data entry errors, measurement errors, and outliers.

Another important dimension is data completeness. Observations with missing values can be removed only if sound justifications can be given. About this, the CEBS mentioned:

> While missing data for some fields or records may be inevitable, institutions should attempt to minimize their occurrence and aim to reduce them over time. (Committee of European Banking Supervisors (CEBS) 2005)

Data timeliness refers to the recency of the data. Data should be updated at least annually, although higher updating frequencies are recommended for the riskier obligors. Data should also be appropriate in the sense that there should be no biases or unjustified data truncation. Furthermore, data should be unambiguously defined. As an example, consider the definition of a ratio variable, commonly used in corporate credit risk models: Ratios are defined as a numerator divided by a denominator, and both should be clearly defined. It should also be mentioned what happens to the ratio when the denominator equals zero; missing values should also be defined in an unambiguous way and not coded as zero, as is often the case.

To summarize, it is very important that financial institutions set up master data management and data governance initiatives. This applies not only to internally collected but also to externally obtained data. Moges et al. (2013) conducted a worldwide survey with more than 50 banks on the topic of data quality. Note that the focus of the survey was on credit risk analytics. The main findings were:

- Most banks indicated that between 10 to 20 percent of their data suffers from data quality problems.

- Manual data entry is one of the key problems, together with the diversity of data sources and the consistency of corporate-wide data representation.

- Regulatory compliance is the key motive to improve data quality, rather than strategic or competitive advantage, for example.

Model Design

A next qualitative validation activity relates to model design. Some example questions that need to be answered here are:

- When was the model designed and by whom?

- What is the perimeter of the model in terms of counterparty types, geographical region, industry sectors? For example, was the model developed using Belgian SMEs active in the agricultural sector?

- What are the strengths and weaknesses of the model?

- What data was used to build the model? How was the sample constructed? What is the time horizon of the sample? Which default definition was adopted?

- Is human judgment used, and if so, how?

Being able to adequately answer all these questions is very important for correctly using the model and for facilitating model maintenance. It is also essential that all this is properly documented.

Documentation

All steps of the credit risk model development and monitoring process should be adequately documented. This can be illustrated by means of the following regulatory quotes:

- *"All material elements of the internal models and the modeling process and validation shall be documented"* (Art. 188, European Union 2013).

- *"Documentation should be transparent and comprehensive"* (Federal Register 2007).

- *"Documentation should encompass, but is not limited to, the internal risk rating and segmentation systems, risk parameter quantification processes, data collection and maintenance processes, and model design, assumptions, and validation results"* (Federal Register 2007).

Documentation is needed both for internally developed as well as for externally purchased models. It is advisable to use document management systems with appropriate versioning facilities to keep track of all document versions. An ambitious goal here is to aim for a documentation test that verifies whether a newly hired analytical team could use the existing documentation to continue development or production of the existing analytical PD, LGD, and EAD models.

Corporate Governance and Management Oversight

A final qualitative validation activity concerns corporate governance and management oversight. The idea here is to pursue active involvement of the board of directors and senior management in the implementation and validation process of the various credit risk models. About this, the EU regulation mentioned:

> All material aspects of the rating and estimation processes shall be approved by the institution's management body or a designated committee thereof and senior management. These parties shall possess a general understanding of the rating systems of the institution and detailed comprehension of its associated management reports. (Art. 189, European Union 2013)

Senior management should demonstrate active involvement on an ongoing basis, assign clear responsibilities, and put into place organizational procedures and policies that will allow the proper and sound implementation and validation of the IRB systems. The outcome of the validation exercise must also be communicated to senior management and, if needed, accompanied by an appropriate response.

PRACTICE QUESTIONS

1. Discuss the most important validation issues and validation principles.
2. Compute the PSI/SSI for the example in Exhibit 13.6 with the variables income and years client.
3. Estimate logistic regression PD models with LTV only and FICO only, and compare the ROC curves. Use data set mortgage.
4. Why are discrimination measures portfolio dependent? Research the literature and provide examples.
5. Conduct the binomial test for the example using the PD estimates of the other two rating grades in the Quantitative Valuation section, and interpret the results.
6. Show via the examples of type 1 and type 2 errors that there is a trade-off between both error probabilities.

REFERENCES

Agresti, A. 1984. *Analysis of Ordinal Categorical Data*. New York: John Wiley & Sons.

Basel Committee on Banking Supervision. 2005a. "Studies on the Validation of Internal Rating Systems (Revised)."

Basel Committee on Banking Supervision. 2005b. "Update on Work of the Accord Implementation Group Related to Validation under the Basel II Framework."

Basel Committee on Banking Supervision. 2006. "International Convergence of Capital Measurement and Capital Standards: A Revised Framework, Comprehensive Version."

Blochwitz, S., A. Hamerle, S. Hohl, R. Rauhmeier, and D. Rösch. 2005. "Myth and Reality of Discriminatory Power for Rating Systems." *Wilmott Magazine*, 2–6.

Castermans, G., D. Martens, T. Van Gestel, B. Hamers, and B. Baesens. 2010. "An Overview and Framework for PD Backtesting and Benchmarking." *Journal of the Operational Research Society, Special Issue on Consumer Credit Risk Modeling* 61: 359–373.

Committee of European Banking Supervisors (CEBS). 2005. "Guidelines on the Implementation, Validation and Assessment of Advanced Measurement (AMA) and Internal Ratings Based (IRB) Approaches." Technical report, CP10 consultation paper.

European Union. 2013. "Regulation (EU) no 575/2013 of the European Parliament and of the Council of 26 June 2013."

Federal Register. 2007. "Proposed Supervisory Guidance for Internal Ratings-Based Systems for Credit Risk, Advanced Measurement Approaches for Operational Risk, and the Supervisory Review Process (Pillar 2) Related to Basel II Implementation."

Fischer, M., and M. Pfeuffer. 2014. "A Statistical Repertoire for Quantitative Loss Given Default Validation: Overview, Illustration, Pitfalls and Extensions." *Journal of Risk Model Validation* 8: 3–29.

Gupton, G., and R. Stein. 2005. "Losscalc v2: Dynamic Prediction of LGD, Moody's KMV Company, Modeling Methodology."

Hamerle, A., R. Rauhmeier, and D. Rösch. 2003. "Uses and Misuses of Measures for Credit Rating Accuracy." Available at SSRN 2354877.

Hong Kong Monetary Authority (HKMA). 2006. "Validating Risk Rating Systems under the IRB Approaches."

Hosmer, D. W., and S. Lemeshow. 2000. *Applied Logistic Regression.* 2nd ed. New York: John Wiley & Sons.

Loterman, G., T. Brown, D. Martens, C. Mues, and B. Baesens. 2012. "Benchmarking Regression Algorithms for Loss Given Default Modeling." *International Journal of Forecasting* 28: 161–170.

Moges, H., K. Dejaeger, W. Lemahieu, and B. Baesens. 2013. "A Multidimensional Analysis of Data Quality for Credit Risk Management: New Insights and Challenges." *Information and Management* 50: 43–58.

Prudential Regulation Authority. 2013. "Internal Ratings Based Approaches." Working paper.

Rösch, D. 2005. "An Empirical Comparison of Default Risk Forecasts from Alternative Credit Rating Philosophies." *International Journal of Forecasting* 25(1), 37–51.

SAS Institute Inc. 2015. *SAS/STAT 14.1 User's Guide: Technical Report.* Cary, NC: SAS Institute.

CHAPTER **14**

Stress Testing

INTRODUCTION

In this chapter, we will zoom in on stress testing. Stress testing is an activity that is done once the PD, LGD, and EAD models have been built. Its purpose is to analyze how credit risk models behave under adverse internal or external circumstances. We will discuss various ways of doing stress testing such as sensitivity-based stress testing, historical scenario–based stress testing, and hypothetical scenario–based stress testing.

Purpose of Stress Testing

An obvious question is: "Why do we need stress testing?" An answer you will often get is because it is required by regulators. However, besides regulatory value, stress testing is also valuable from a business perspective. First, it can be used to help set pricing and product features. The output of a stress testing exercise can be helpful to determine the spread above the risk-free rate when pricing loans. It also allows for the capture of the impact of exceptional but plausible loss events. Value-at-risk (VaR) models, as discussed earlier, typically reflect everyday market behavior. Stress testing looks into the tail of the loss distribution to study the impact of abnormal markets. It also allows for a clearer picture of the risk profile of the firm. It is especially important here to comprehensively aggregate the risks across various credit and noncredit portfolios.

Types of Stress Tests

In Exhibit 14.1 you can see a taxonomy of stress testing approaches, as introduced by the Monetary Authority of Singapore in 2002.

A high-level distinction can be made between scenario-based and sensitivity-based stress testing. A single-factor sensitivity test analyzes the impact of varying a single variable. A multifactor sensitivity test varies multiple variables simultaneously,

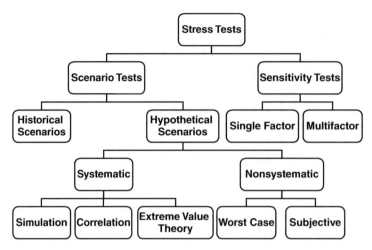

Exhibit 14.1 Types of Stress Tests

ideally by taking into account the correlation between them. A scenario test can be historical, whereby the impact of a historical adverse event is reenacted. It can also be hypothetical when a new scenario is devised. This can be done in a systematical way using correlation, simulation, and extreme value theory. It can also be done in a nonsystematical way by assuming a worst-case scenario or by using expert-based input.

Sensitivity-Based Stress Testing

The idea of sensitivity-based stress testing is to gauge the impact of changing variables. This is a static approach that does not take into account external effects, such as macroeconomic information. Single-factor sensitivity tests have proven to be very popular for market risk. Some examples are a yield curve shift by 100 basis points or a decrease in the GBP/USD exchange rate of 5 percent.

In credit risk, a single-factor sensitivity stress test can be conducted at each of the levels of the credit risk model architecture, as we discussed earlier. At level 0, the data can be stressed. For example, an income drop of 10 percent, an increase in the loan-to-value ratio of 20 percent, a rise in unemployment of 5 percent, and so on. At level 1, the scores can be stressed. For example, assume all application and behavioral scores drop by 5 percent. At level 2, the ratings and PD can be stressed. For example, downgrade every obligor one notch, such that an AAA-rated obligor becomes an AA-rated obligor, an AA-rated obligor an A-rated obligor, and so on. Also, the PD can be multiplied with a stress factor.

The advantage of sensitivity-based stress tests is that they are very easy to understand. They are also typically used in the starting phase of a stress testing exercise. Their key shortcoming is that it is difficult to defend the connection with changes in economic conditions. A multifactor stress test analyzes multiple variables simultaneously. When conducted appropriately, it takes into account the correlation between the selected variables such that it will quickly become a scenario test.

Scenario-Based Stress Testing

The next approach to stress testing is scenario-based testing. The idea here is to work out an adverse shock event and gauge the impact on the various parameters. Typically, the source of the shock and the parameters affected are well defined. Scenarios can be defined in several ways, such as portfolio driven versus event driven, or historical versus hypothetical. Defining a scenario usually involves a trade-off between realism and comprehensibility.

Portfolio-Driven versus Event-Driven Scenario Stress Testing

Portfolio-Driven Stress Testing

In the portfolio-driven approach, you can start from portfolio characteristics. To start, it is crucial to ask what the risk parameter changes that result in a portfolio loss are. This question should be decomposed across the various levels of the credit risk model architecture. For example, at level 2 a key parameter is the PD, at level 1 you can think of application and behavioral scores, and at level 0 you can then further consider data characteristics such as debt ratio, income, unemployment, and credit bureau score. A next step is then to define events or scenarios that bring about adverse changes in any of these data variables.

Event-Driven Scenario (Reverse) Stress Testing

An event-driven approach works the other way around. It starts from identifying an event or a risk source that causes adverse changes in financial markets. From there onward, how these changes affect the risk parameters and corresponding portfolio loss are studied. This is also referred to as bottom-up or reverse stress testing.

Historical versus Hypothetical Scenario Stress Testing

Historical Scenario Stress Testing

In historical scenario stress testing, historical stress scenarios are analyzed and reenacted in the current portfolio. Since you can rely on actual past events, fewer qualitative judgments are needed by the business experts. Note, however, that the future does not always resemble the past; thus this approach might be less suited to the current situation due to changes in either portfolio or strategy, or both.

Historical recession scenarios are sometimes also referred to as black swan events. Europeans thought black swans did not exist until they were discovered in Australia. Like black swans, economic downturns that came as a surprise include:

- European sovereign crisis, 2010/2011
- Subprime and U.S. credit crisis, 2008/2009
- Enron/WorldCom, 2002

- September 11, 2001
- Dot-com bubble burst, 2000
- Russian credit crisis, August 1998
- Asian currency crisis, summer 1997

Hypothetical Scenario Stress Testing

When no historical scenario is appropriate, hypothetical scenario stress testing might be considered. The idea here is to model a scenario that has not yet happened. In contrast to historical stress testing, the scenario should be forward looking and focus on the vulnerabilities of the portfolio and/or firm. Since you have no historical events to rely on, this will require more qualitative judgment from the business expert. Historical data can be useful to analyze relationships and correlations, which can then be extrapolated in the hypothetical scenario. Ideally, the scenario should also include dynamic projections of firm revenue, income/losses, and other balance sheet figures. Note that these scenarios are more labor intensive but also likely to be relevant. They should also be defined in a comprehensive way by taking into account corporate banker behavior toward stress events. Examples here are adjusting the underwriting standards or marketing programs, cutting dividends, or raising capital.

When defining hypothetical scenarios, you should first thoroughly analyze the various factors that may cause stress. A first example is a macroeconomic downturn, such as successive periods of gross domestic product (GDP) contraction. Other examples are deterioration in reputation, an adverse change in competitive position, failure of a market counterparty, or illiquidity conditions.

Various types of hypothetical scenarios can be considered. First is the worst-off scenario. The idea is to look at the most adverse movement in each risk factor. Obviously, this is a very conservative scenario and not that plausible since it ignores the correlations between the various risk factors. Note that it is commonly applied.

Second is a subjective scenario. Here, expert-based input is used to qualitatively define the stress scenario. The quality of the scenario will then depend on the experience of the expert. Also, simulations can be used to analyze the behavior of the loss distribution under stressed conditions.

Ideally, the simulations should be backed by appropriate correlation analysis. The idea here is to stress some factors and use the correlation matrix to simulate values of the rest. A popular example concerns the correlation between PD and LGD, or default and loss rates. It is important to understand that correlations are time varying and may be different during stress and nonstress periods. Expert input may come in handy to adjust the empirically observed correlations. Also, the asset correlation values as reported in the Basel Accords can be useful.

Finally, extreme value theory can also be used for stress testing. Typically, the loss distribution is assumed normal or lognormal. It has been shown in earlier research that under extreme stress, the tail of the distribution is fatter than normal. The theory of stochastic processes then allows for identification of suitably extreme distributions for stress testing.

Post-GFC Stress Testing

Since the global financial crisis (GFC), prudential regulators have mandated that stress tests must be conducted by banks to gauge their capital resilience against central bank–prescribed macroeconomic scenarios. For example, in the United States the Federal Reserve Bank requires the following stress tests:

- Dodd-Frank Act supervisory stress test (DFAST)
- Comprehensive Capital Analysis and Review (CCAR) stress test

In Europe, the European Banking Authority (EBA) has conducted several European Union–wide stress tests for the largest banking institutions. In addition, various national regulators have conducted tests for their countries (e.g., the Financial Services Authority and the Bank of England in the United Kingdom). Similar examples exist for Australasian economies with prominent examples in Australia (Australian Prudential Regulation Authority), Singapore (Monetary Authority of Singapore), and China (China Banking Regulatory Commission).

Exhibit 14.2 shows a number of U.S. domestic macroeconomic scenarios for some of the key variables describing the economic activity under the DFAST "baseline," "adverse," and "severely adverse" scenarios for 2015 (Federal Reserve System 2015).

These stress scenarios ("adverse" and "severely adverse") are generally based on initial economic shocks that revert to (and in some instances exceed) the "baseline" scenarios in later periods.

These stress tests require banks to demonstrate that the ultimate parent companies (bank holding companies) have adequate capital to sustain the various stress-test scenarios and that capital distributions (i.e., dividends and share repurchases) do not put the banks at substantial risk. While the analysis is performed in both qualitative and quantitative ways, the assessment of credit risk losses is a key consideration and the conditioning of bank PD, LGD, and EAD models on these macroeconomic stress tests is an important undertaking.

Not meeting minimum compliance standards has major business implications such as restrictions on remuneration of stakeholders and increased regulation. A major component of stress testing is the analysis of the impact of macroeconomic stress scenarios on the performance of the lending book. In this chapter, we discuss approaches to implementing stress tests in line with current requirements. In addition, we analyze the impact of risk realizations that exceed current requirements but may be of interest for economic consideration, for example, in order to meet bank investor expectations.

Challenges in Stress Testing

Various challenges arise when undertaking stress testing. An initial challenge relates to the various regulatory authorities that impose stress testing. A key concern is the often-observed discrepancies in terms of severity of the imposed stress tests. A more homogeneous and consistent definition of stress testing would be much welcomed.

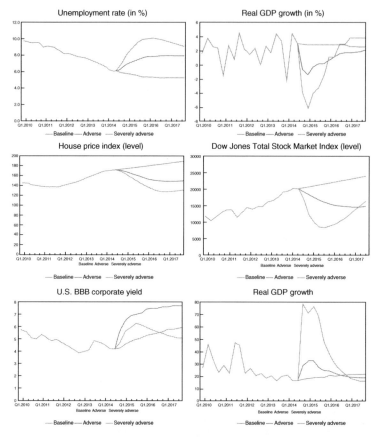

Exhibit 14.2 DFAST "Baseline," "Adverse," and "Severely Adverse" Scenario

Stress testing is also more developed for market risk than for credit risk. Market risk stress testing is typically conducted on a daily basis, whereas credit risk stress testing usually occurs less frequently. Ideally, to generate a corporate-wide view on the impact of a stress testing scenario, both market risk and credit risk should be integrated. Unfortunately, this is still far away for most financial institutions. One of the key difficulties here concerns the time horizon and confidence levels adopted, which are typically not identical. Hence, both market and credit risk stress testing scenarios are typically difficult or even impossible to integrate.

Given its strategic impact, it is of key importance to also actively engage senior management in defining and interpreting the stress tests conducted. In credit risk, many institutions are increasing the frequency of stress testing from annually to quarterly. There appears to be a greater consensus in the industry that a stress event corresponds to a once-in-25-years event.

Stress Testing Governance

From a governance perspective, it is important to appropriately and unambiguously define the following items:

- The scope and aim of the stress tests, such as business versus regulatory
- The ownership of the stress test
- The various contributors, reporting lines, frequency of tests, and committees

Once finalized, the stress testing results should also be presented to senior management and the board of directors, who should ensure that the necessary training and coaching are available. Also, accompanying strategies and actions should be foreseen, if necessary. Finally, the outcome of the stress testing exercise should be publicly disclosed and documented.

INTEGRATION WITH THE BASEL RISK MODEL

Financial institutions often provide a capital buffer in excess of regulatory capital. The capital buffer is based on the assessment of risks that are not included in the Basel capital calculations (e.g., risks other than credit risk, market risk, and operational risk) and other assessment techniques that complement a portfolio's risk model such as stress testing (e.g., risk measurements in excess of Basel requirements).

The Basel Committee on Banking Supervision (2006) has formulated the following stress testing requirements for financial institutions:

> A bank must have in place sound stress testing processes for use in the assessment of capital adequacy. These stress measures must be compared against the measure of expected positive exposure and considered by the bank as part of its internal capital adequacy assessment process. Stress testing must also involve identifying possible events or future changes in economic conditions that could have unfavorable effects on a firm's credit exposures and assessment of the firm's ability to withstand such changes. Examples of scenarios that could be used are:

1. Economic or industry downturns,
2. Market-place events, or
3. Decreased liquidity conditions.

Berkowitz (2000) and others have questioned the use of stress tests as they should be part of the loss distribution and provide no further informational value. Hence, stress testing has to be interpreted in conjunction with the portfolio risk model and related level of conservatism as capital is assigned to higher percentiles of the portfolio loss distribution.

Furthermore, recent stress testing requirements are based on very precisely defined macroeconomic scenarios and include soft (not measurable) and hard (measurable) information. As such, the level of detail placed in this single evaluation exceeds the efforts for scenarios in a portfolio loss distribution and may provide information that is not part of the risk model. The capital that banks hold then becomes:

Minimum capital = max(regulatory capital, stress test capital, economic capital)

In what follows, we discuss the capital allocation under the Basel regulation and stress testing. Economic capital considerations are generally institution-specific. For example, some banks may target a minimum credit rating to limit their interbank funding costs. There are many, often offsetting, underlying considerations, which are beyond the scope of this book, and we do not provide further guidance on these matters.

Risk Model under Basel Regulations

The Basel Committee on Banking Supervision (2006) expects financial institutions to provide sufficient Tier I and Tier II capital to cover future worst-case credit portfolio losses. These worst-case losses are based on conservative assumptions for a set of parameters such as the probability of default (PD), asset correlation ρ, loss given default (LGD), and exposure at default (EAD):

- Stress of PDs: PDs are based on a one-factor nonlinear model where the factor equals the 99.9th percentile of a systematic standard normally distributed variable and the sensitivity is based on the so-called asset correlation.

- Stress of asset correlations: Asset correlations can be interpreted as a measure of the sensitivity of PDs to the business cycle and therefore have a major impact on the stress of the PDs. The Basel Committee on Banking Supervision has provided conservative estimates (sometimes in dependence with PD) for these parameters.

- Stress of EADs and LGDs: EADs and LGDs are modeled based on an economic downturn condition.

Exhibit 14.3 shows a typical credit portfolio loss distribution. The expected loss is covered by loan loss provisions that are already deducted from the capital account. The unexpected loss (in excess of the expected loss) is covered by regulatory capital. The stressed loss (in excess of the unexpected loss) is covered by the capital buffer.

The Basel Accord introduces different types of capital regulations, which can be categorized into standardized (ratings-based) and internal ratings based approaches:

- Standardized approach: In this approach credit risk exposures are categorized into risk buckets, and risk weights are assigned. Risk buckets are generated by ratings provided from certified credit rating agencies (CRAs). Outstanding asset exposures are multiplied by risk weights, and the risk-weighted assets are computed. Off-balance-sheet exposures are converted into the asset equivalents, which are then risk weighted.

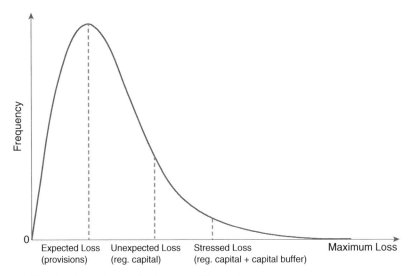

Exhibit 14.3 Expected Loss, Unexpected Loss, and Stressed Loss

- Internal ratings based (IRB) approach: The capital requirement is computed using a portfolio model based on risk parameters assuming an infinitely granular credit portfolio and independence between the risk parameters. The risk parameters are default probabilities (PDs), asset correlations, loss rates given default (LGDs), exposures given default (EADs), and the maturity for loans and together with some other characteristics for securitizations (for details, we refer to Rösch and Scheule 2012a). The risk parameters are stressed conditional on economic downturns. As mentioned previously, the conditioning on economic downturns is explicitly formulated in the case of EAD and LGD and implied in the case of PDs and asset correlations by the formulation of a worst-case default rate and provision of conservative asset correlation values.

Furthermore, risk mitigation by guarantees, collateral, and netting is considered. For the rest of this section, we focus on the risk model implied by the IRB approach. Here, regulatory capital is calculated as follows:

$$\text{Regulatory capital} = (\text{WCDR} - \text{PD}) * \text{DEAD} * \text{DLGD} * \text{MA}$$

with the worst-case default rate (WCDR) and the maturity adjustment (MA) for corporate exposures. No maturity adjustment is applied for retail loans. DEAD is the downturn exposure at default, and DLGD is the downturn loss rate given default.

We do not discuss the maturity adjustment further, as it applies only to corporate loans and is a function of the PD and the maturity of a loan. The intention is to allocate a slightly higher capital amount for longer-maturity corporate financial instruments.

The difference between WCDR and PD implies that regulatory capital is based on unexpected losses, that is, losses that exceed their expected level based on the default probability. Basel follows this approach, as expected losses are deducted from the capital base via loan loss provisioning and hence the remaining capital is required for covering unexpected losses.

Note that the regulatory capital for credit risk is converted to risk weights by multiplication of $1/cr$ with capital ratio cr to aggregate the risk-weighted assets for credit risk with those for market risk and operational risk:

$$\text{RWA}_{\text{credit, market, operational}} = \text{RWA}_{\text{credit}} + \text{RWA}_{\text{market}} + \text{RWA}_{\text{operational}}$$

$$= \frac{\text{capital}_{\text{credit}}}{cr} + \frac{\text{capital}_{\text{market}}}{cr} + \frac{\text{capital}_{\text{operational}}}{cr}$$

The capital and risk-weighted assets (RWA) for market risk and operational risk are subject to other models and required computations. Given a capital ratio underlying these computations of 8 percent, the multiplier $1/cr$ is 12.5 or 1,250 percent for the conversion of risk-based capital into risk-weighted assets.

Asset Correlations and Worst-Case Default Rate

The worst-case default rate (WCDR) is a central element in the Basel risk model and an example of a stress test for the default probability. We refer to the default models presented in our credit portfolio risk chapter. The asset return A_{it} of borrower i ($i = 1,...,I$) in time period t ($t = 1,...,T$) is a latent process of a systematic risk factor F_t that is specific to the time period under consideration, and an idiosyncratic factor ϵ_{it}. Both are random and independent from each other and over time.

$$R_{it} = -\sqrt{\rho}X_t + \sqrt{1-\rho}\epsilon_{it}$$

The sensitivity to the systematic factor is $\sqrt{\rho}$. We chose a negative sign for consistency with the Basel formula but this is irrelevant as X_t follows the standard normal distribution. The sensitivity to the idiosyncratic factor is $\sqrt{1-\rho}$. A default event occurs if the asset return R_{it} falls below a threshold c_{it}. The probability of default (PD) given a standard normal distribution of the random variables is:

$$PD_{it} = P(D_{it} = 1) = P(R_{it} < c_{it}) = \Phi(c_{it})$$

Φ is the cumulative density function of the standard normal distribution. This probability corresponded to an unconditional default probability with regard to the unobserved systematic risk factor X_t and is estimated with discrete-time or continuous-time approaches as discussed in the default probability chapters. The default probability conditional on the realization of the systematic risk factor is:

$$WCDR = P(D_{it} = 1|x_t) = P(R_{it} < c_{it|X_t}) = \Phi\left(\frac{c_{it} + \sqrt{\rho}X_t}{\sqrt{1-\rho}}\right)$$

with $c_{it} = \Phi^{-1}(PD_{it})$. The Basel Committee specifies the asset correlation ρ and the realization x_t of X_t as the worst in 1,000 economic scenarios (i.e., as X_t is standard normal: $x_t = \Phi^{-1}(0.999)$). The following well-known equation results for the worst-case default rate under the IRB approach:

$$WCDR = P(D_{it} = 1|x_t) = P(R_{it} < c_{it}|x_t) = \Phi\left(\frac{\Phi^{-1}(PD_{it}) + \sqrt{\rho}\Phi^{-1}(0.999)}{\sqrt{1-\rho}}\right)$$

We have discussed in the default correlations and credit portfolio risk chapter how to estimate default and asset correlations. In the Basel regulations, prudential regulators currently do not allow banks to estimate this parameter. Instead, they specify the asset correlation as a constant value (15 percent for mortgages and 4 percent for revolving loans) or as a function of the default probability for corporate and other retail loans. The asset correlation for standard corporate loans is computed as follows:

$$\rho = 0.12\frac{1 - exp(-50PD)}{1 - exp(-50)} + 0.24\left(1 - \frac{1 - exp(-50PD)}{1 - exp(-50)}\right) \approx 0.12(1 + exp(-50PD))$$

and for other retail exposures:

$$\rho = 0.03\frac{1 - exp(-35PD)}{1 - exp(-35)} + 0.16\left(1 - \frac{1 - exp(-35PD)}{1 - exp(-35)}\right) \approx 0.03(1 + exp(-35PD))$$

The rather complicated smoothing function implies that the asset correlation is a declining function in terms of the default probability from 24 percent (PD of zero) to 12 percent (PD of one) for corporate loans and a declining function in terms of the default probability from 16 percent (PD of zero) to 3 percent (PD of one) for other retail loans. The thinking behind this is that high-PD companies are primarily exposed to idiosyncratic risk and to a lesser degree systematic risk. Researchers have found mixed empirical evidence on both the levels of asset correlations and their link to PDs. The following program computes and plots the asset correlations in relation to the PDs:

```
DATA graph;
DO PD=0 to 0.1 by 0.001;
ac_corporate=0.12 *(1-EXP(-50*PD))/(1-EXP(-50))
+ 0.24*(1-(1-EXP(-50*PD)/(1-EXP(-50))));
ac_mortgage=0.15;
ac_revolving=0.04;
ac_retail=0.13 *(1-EXP(-35*PD))/(1-EXP(-35))
+ 0.16*(1-(1-EXP(-35*PD)/(1-EXP(-35))));
OUTPUT;
END;
RUN;


ODS GRAPHICS ON;
AXIS1 ORDER=(0 to 0.1 BY 0.02) LABEL=('PD');
AXIS2 ORDER=(0 to 0.25 BY 0.05) LABEL=('Asset correlation');
SYMBOL1 INTERPOL=SPLINE WIDTH=2 VALUE=TRIANGLE C=BLUE;
SYMBOL2 INTERPOL=SPLINE WIDTH=2 VALUE=CIRCLE C=RED;
SYMBOL3 INTERPOL=SPLINE WIDTH=2 VALUE=CIRCLE C=GREEN;
SYMBOL4 INTERPOL=SPLINE WIDTH=2 VALUE=SQUARE C=BLACK;
LEGEND1 LABEL=NONE SHAPE=SYMBOL(4,2) POSITION=(BOTTOM OUTSIDE);
```

```
PROC GPLOT DATA=graph;
PLOT ac_corporate*PD ac_mortgage*PD ac_revolving*PD ac_retail*PD
/ OVERLAY LEGEND=legend1 HAXIS=AXIS1 VAXIS=AXIS2;
RUN;
ODS GRAPHICS OFF;
```

Exhibit 14.4 is the resulting figure produced by PROC GPLOT,

High sensitivities to the systematic risk imply high worst-case default probabilities (i.e., conditional PDs conditional on a 1 in 1,000 economic scenario) and eventually high capital requirements. The following code computes worst-case default rates in relation to the input PD and plots this relationship:

```
DATA graph;
SET graph;
wcdr_corporate=PROBNORM((PROBIT(PD)+SQRT(ac_corporate))
/SQRT(1-ac_corporate));
wcdr_mortgage=PROBNORM((PROBIT(PD)+SQRT(ac_mortgage))
/SQRT(1-ac_mortgage));
wcdr_revolving=PROBNORM((PROBIT(PD)+SQRT(ac_revolving))
```

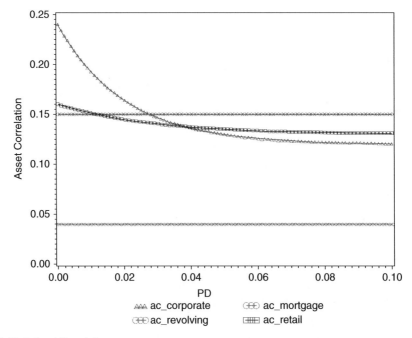

Exhibit 14.4 Asset Correlations

```
/SQRT(1-ac_revolving));
wcdr_retail=PROBNORM((PROBIT(PD)+SQRT(ac_retail))
/SQRT(1-ac_retail));
RUN;

ODS GRAPHICS ON;
AXIS1 ORDER=(0 to 0.1 BY 0.02) LABEL=('PD');
AXIS2 ORDER=(0 to 0.2 BY 0.05) LABEL=('WCDR');
SYMBOL1 INTERPOL=SPLINE WIDTH=2 VALUE=TRIANGLE C=BLUE;
SYMBOL2 INTERPOL=SPLINE WIDTH=2 VALUE=CIRCLE C=RED;
SYMBOL3 INTERPOL=SPLINE WIDTH=2 VALUE=CIRCLE C=GREEN;
SYMBOL4 INTERPOL=SPLINE WIDTH=2 VALUE=SQUARE C=BLACK;
LEGEND1 LABEL=NONE SHAPE=SYMBOL(4,2) POSITION=(BOTTOM OUTSIDE);
PROC GPLOT DATA=graph;
PLOT wcdr_corporate*PD wcdr_mortgage*PD wcdr_revolving*PD wcdr_retail*PD
/ OVERLAY LEGEND=legend1 HAXIS=AXIS1 VAXIS=AXIS2;
RUN;
ODS GRAPHICS OFF;
```

Exhibit 14.5 is the resulting figure produced by PROC GPLOT.

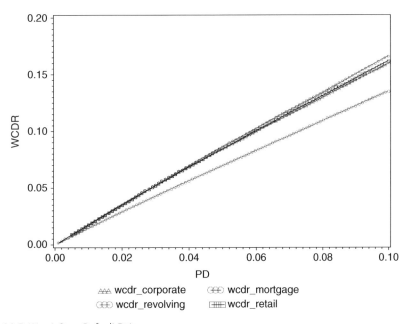

Exhibit 14.5 Worst-Case Default Rate

The following code computes the resulting unexpected losses and hence capital (based on an EAD of one, an LGD of one, and a maturity adjustment of one) and plots this relationship:

```
DATA graph;
SET graph;
DEAD=1;
DLGD=1;
MA=1;

capital_corporate=(wcdr_corporate-PD)*DEAD*DLGD*MA;
capital_mortgage=(wcdr_mortgage-PD)*DEAD*DLGD;
capital_revolving=(wcdr_revolving-PD)*DEAD*DLGD;
capital_retail=(wcdr_retail-PD)*DEAD*DLGD;
RUN;

ODS GRAPHICS ON;
AXIS1 ORDER=(0 to 0.1 BY 0.02) LABEL=('PD');
AXIS2 ORDER=(0 to 0.08 BY 0.02) LABEL=('Capital');
SYMBOL1 INTERPOL=SPLINE WIDTH=2 VALUE=TRIANGLE C=BLUE;
SYMBOL2 INTERPOL=SPLINE WIDTH=2 VALUE=CIRCLE C=RED;
SYMBOL3 INTERPOL=SPLINE WIDTH=2 VALUE=CIRCLE C=GREEN;
SYMBOL4 INTERPOL=SPLINE WIDTH=2 VALUE=SQUARE C=BLACK;
LEGEND1 LABEL=NONE SHAPE=SYMBOL(4,2) POSITION=(BOTTOM OUTSIDE);
PROC GPLOT DATA=graph;
PLOT capital_corporate*PD capital_mortgage*PD capital_revolving*PD
capital_retail*PD
/ OVERLAY LEGEND=legend1 HAXIS=AXIS1 VAXIS=AXIS2;
RUN;
ODS GRAPHICS OFF;
```

Exhibit 14.6 is the resulting figure produced by PROC GPLOT.

Downturn LGD

The Basel Committee on Banking Supervision (2006) requires a downturn loss rate given default (downturn LGD) as an input for LGD in the regulatory capital computations:

> A bank must estimate a LGD for each facility that aims to reflect economic downturn conditions where necessary to capture the relevant

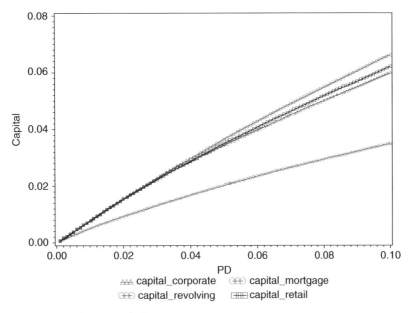

Exhibit 14.6 Unexpected Loss (Capital)

risks. This LGD cannot be less than the long-run default-weighted average loss rate given default calculated based on the average economic loss of all observed defaults within the data source for that type of facility. In addition, a bank must take into account the potential for the LGD of the facility to be higher than the default-weighted average during a period when credit losses are substantially higher than average.

In short, there are two key ideas presented here: The LGD should be higher than the long-run default-weighted average loss rate given default, and it should be an economic downturn LGD. We will discuss both in more detail in what follows.

Averaging LGD

There are various ways of calculating an average LGD. A time-weighted LGD first calculates the LGD for the individual years of observation and then averages those. A default-weighted LGD is calculated by dividing the total losses by the total number of defaults. An exposure-weighted LGD weighs each default by its EAD, whereas a default count LGD assigns an equal weight to each default. Based on this, an average LGD can be computed in four possible ways. In Exhibit 14.7 you can see the four possible average LGDs.

	Default Count Averaging	**Exposure-Weighted Averaging**
Default-Weighted Averaging	**Option 1:** Each default has equal weighting. Defaults from all years are grouped into a single cohort.	**Option 2:** The weighting of each default is determined by the exposure at default. Defaults from all years are grouped into a single cohort.
Time-Weighted Averaging	**Option 3:** Each default has equal weighting within the annual cohort average. The average is calculated as the average of annual averages.	**Option 4:** The weighting of each default within the annual cohort average is determined by the exposure at default. The average is calculated as the average of annual averages.

Exhibit 14.7 Options for Averaging LGD

Economic Downturn LGD

Various approaches to specify the downturn LGD are common in industry:

- Basel foundation approach: The Basel Committee on Banking Supervision (2006) specifies within the internal ratings based (IRB) approach a benchmark loss rate given default as follows:

$$DLGD = \begin{cases} 75\% & \text{for all subordinated claims} \\ 45\% & \text{for corporate senior unsecured loans} \\ 10\% & \text{for real estate secured loans} \end{cases}$$

- Office of the Comptroller of the Currency (OCC) proposal: The U.S. Department of the Treasury, Federal Reserve System, and Federal Deposit Insurance Corporation (2006) proposed a linear relationship between the downturn LGD and the expected LGD (ELGD). The formula implies a floor of 8 percent and a cap of 100 percent:

$$DLGD = 0.08 + 0.92 \times ELGD$$

- Historical approach: Financial institutions may apply the expected loss rate given default of selected historical downturn periods.

Historical Approach

The expected LGD may be computed for a risk segment as the average LGD over time. The correct computation is often controversial. In particular, the second and third approaches lead to different outcomes for financial institutions in different economies. Economies that have experienced a severe economic downturn in recent history are likely to have a higher downturn LGD than economies that have not.

Rösch and Scheule (2010, 2012b) show how to estimate downturn LGD based on two econometric techniques. In the first approach, downturn LGD is estimated by restricting the LGD data to downturn periods (i.e., periods where the loss rate is below the median). In the second approach, downturn LGD is estimated based on the Basel worst in 1,000 economic scenarios and the estimated correlation between the default and recovery processes. Similar principles apply to downturn EAD.

Here, we show two simple examples to determine downturn LGD. In the first example, a bank may allocate the maximum average LGD observed in its history to a risk segment j:

$$DLGD_j = \max_t(LGD_{jt})$$

In the second example, downturn LGD is computed by constructing a table as depicted in Exhibit 14.8.

Let us assume we have K LGD ratings or segments. Assume period 1 is the year with the highest default rate, period 2 is the two years with the highest default rate, and so on. We can then calculate the average LGD for each of the cells in the table. If the averages reported within each of the columns are relatively similar, then it can be concluded that there is no PD-LGD correlation and no downturn calibration is needed. However, if the averages do vary substantially, then a correlation is present, and a downturn LGD can be obtained by only including the first one, two, or more rows.

	Segment 1	Segment 2			Segment K	
Period 1: (year with highest DR)	AVG LGD (period 1, segment 1)	AVG LGD (period 1, segment 2)	...	...	AVG LGD (period 1, segment K)	
Period 2: (2 years with highest DR)	AVG LGD (period 2, segment 1)	AVG LGD (period 2, segment 2)	...	...	AVG LGD (period 2, segment K)	Periods with Decreasing Default Rates
...						
...						
...						
Period $n-1$: (all years except with lowest DR)	AVG LGD (period $n-1$, segment 1)	AVG LGD (period $n-1$, segment 2)	...	...	AVG LGD (period $n-1$, segment K)	
Period n: (all years)	AVG LGD (period n, segment 1)	AVG LGD (period n, segment 2)	...	...	AVG LGD (period n, segment K)	
Reference	**Calibrated LGD1**	**Calibrated LGD2**			**Calibrated LGDK**	

Exhibit 14.8 Example for Computing the Downturn LGD

STRESS TESTING APPLICATIONS IN SAS

Rösch and Scheule (2007, 2008) show that the following uncertainties may be considered by a bank in its stress testing analysis:

- Scenario stress testing
- Parameter uncertainty

In light of the presence of a risk model and the Berkowitz critiques, stress testing results in capital increases only if a stress test produces a more severe outcome than the risk model. Examples that will increase the required capital are:

- A stress test of the PD that exceeds the worst-case default
- A stress test of the asset correlations that exceeds the Basel asset correlations
- A stress test of the LGD that exceeds the downturn LGD
- A stress test of the EAD that exceeds the downturn EAD

Scenario-Based Stress Testing

We start off with the DFAST "severely adverse" scenario for GDP (gdp_time) and unemployment rate (uer_time). We include these macroeconomic variables in a probit model for the PD next to the idiosyncratic FICO score and the idiosyncratic and time-varying current LTV ratio:

```
PROC LOGISTIC DATA=data.mortgage DESCENDING;
MODEL default_time = FICO_orig_time
LTV_time GDP_time uer_time/ LINK=PROBIT;
STORE OUT=model_probit;
RUN;
```

The parameter estimates show that the GDP growth rate reduces the credit risk (PD) whereas the unemployment rate increases the risk (see Exhibit 14.9).

We will now estimate the PDs for all loans in time period 60 for the baseline scenario by generating a data set that includes only observations for this period and scoring the data set using PROC PLM:

```
DATA mortgage_base;
SET data.mortgage;
WHERE time=60;
KEEP FICO_orig_time LTV_time gdp_time uer_time;
run;

PROC PLM SOURCE=model_probit;
SCORE DATA= mortgage_base out= probabilities;
RUN;
```

The LOGISTIC Procedure

Analysis of Maximum Likelihood Estimates					
Parameter	DF	Estimate	Standard Error	Wald Chi-Square	Pr > ChiSq
Intercept	1	−0.9135	0.0363	633.3864	<.0001
FICO_orig_time	1	−0.00239	0.000050	2,288.8365	<.0001
LTV_time	1	0.00851	0.000179	2,269.6179	<.0001
gdp_time	1	−0.0546	0.00173	996.4997	<.0001
uer_time	1	−0.0260	0.00218	142.3360	<.0001

Exhibit 14.9 Probit Model

We then convert the predicted scores into baseline PDs (PD_time_base) and Basel worst-case default rates. Next, we overwrite the baseline economic scenarios by the DFAST severely adverse scenarios in the first quarter in 2015: GDP growth of −6.1 percent and an unemployment rate of 8 percent. Note that the actual values for the period included a GDP growth of 2.84 percent and an unemployment rate of 5.7 percent.

```
DATA probabilities;
set probabilities;
PD_time_base=PROBNORM(predicted);
PD_time_wcdr=PROBNORM((PROBIT(PD_time_base)+SQRT(0.15))/SQRT(1-0.15));
gdp_time=-6.1;
uer_time=8;
run;
```

We then compute the cumulative frequencies for the resulting baseline PDs and worst-case default rate:

```
proc sort data=probabilities;
  by PD_time_base;
run;

data probabilities;
set probabilities nobs=totalobs;
PD_time_base_pcs = _n_ / totalobs;
PD_time_wcdr_pcs = _n_ / totalobs;
run;
```

We estimate the PDs for all loans in time period 60 for the severely adverse economic scenario by generating a data set that includes only observations for this period and scoring the data set using PROC PLM:

```
PROC PLM SOURCE=model_probit;
SCORE DATA= probabilities out= probabilities2;
RUN;
```

We then convert the predicted scores into stressed PDs (PD_time_stress) and compute the cumulative frequencies for the resulting stressed PDs:

```
DATA probabilities2;
SET probabilities2;
PD_time_stress=PROBNORM(predicted2);
RUN;


PROC SORT DATA=probabilities2;
  BY PD_time_stress;
RUN;


DATA probabilities2;
SET probabilities2 NOBS=totalobs;
PD_time_stress_pcs = _N_ / totalobs;
RUN;
```

We use PROC GPLOT to plot the cumulative distribution functions for the baseline PDs, worst-case default rates, and stressed PDs. We see that the worst-case default rates are substantially higher than the baseline PDs and that the stressed PDs are substantially higher than the worst-case default rates.

```
ODS GRAPHICS ON;
AXIS1 ORDER=(0 to 0.1 BY 0.02) LABEL=('PD');
AXIS2 ORDER=(0 to 1 BY 0.25) LABEL=('Frequency');
SYMBOL1 interpol=SPLINE WIDTH=2 VALUE=TRIANGLE C=BLUE;
SYMBOL2 interpol=SPLINE WIDTH=2 VALUE=CIRCLE C=RED;
SYMBOL3 INTERPOL=SPLINE WIDTH=2 VALUE=SQUARE C=BLACK;
LEGEND1 LABEL=NONE SHAPE=SYMBOL(4,2) POSITION=(BOTTOM OUTSIDE);
PROC GPLOT DATA=probabilities2;
PLOT PD_time_base_pcs*PD_time_base PD_time_wcdr_pcs*PD_time_wcdr
PD_time_stress_pcs*PD_time_stress /
OVERLAY LEGEND=legend1 HAXIS=axis1 VAXIS=axis2;
RUN;
ODS GRAPHICS OFF;
```

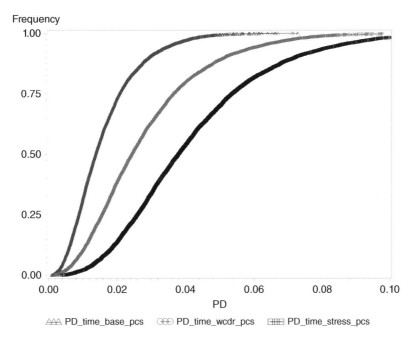

Exhibit 14.10 Cumulative Distribution Function for Baseline PDs, Basel Worst-Case Default Rates, and Stressed PDs

In Exhibit 14.10, a stress is more pronounced the farther the cumulative distribution function moves to the right. A bank performs similar analyses for a large number of macroeconomic stress scenarios covering multiple future periods for the various credit risk parameters. Similarly to stressing PDs, other risk parameters such as asset correlations, LGDs, and EADs can also be stressed. All stressed parameters will be aggregated into cumulative losses. The cumulative losses from the loan portfolios will be aggregated with the bank risk exposures (e.g., the trading book and operational risk exposure). The aggregated loss will then be compared with existing loss levels. Alternatively, a bank may compute the capital level that is required to sustain such a severely adverse economic scenario.

Stress Testing and Parameter Uncertainty

Another important aspect is the consideration of model risk. Examples in the literature include Rösch and Scheule (2007), Tarashev and Zhu (2008), and Lee, Rösch, and Scheule (2016).

Most risk models rely on the estimation of parameters β that in a linear combination $\beta'x$ with covariates characterize the risk measure PD, EAD, or LGD. A similar concept may apply to asset correlations, but we do not discuss this further due to time-series data limitations. The parameter estimates are random, and it is common to assume a multivariate (if there are two or more parameters) normal distribution, which can also be justified by maximum-likelihood theory:

$$\beta \sim N(\hat{\beta}, \Sigma)$$

with the parameter estimates being the mean and the estimated covariance matrix. The variances on the diagonal are equal to the squared standard errors that are reported in addition to the parameter estimates in SAS.

Next, we work out an example based on the probit model from our PD chapter (including the macroeconomic variable GDP growth rate) where we add the COVB in the MODEL statement to show the estimated parameter estimates and covariance matrix. We export both into the SAS data sets ParameterEstimates and covb:

```
PROC LOGISTIC DATA=data.mortgage DESCENDING;
MODEL default_time = FICO_orig_time
LTV_time GDP_time/ LINK=probit COVB;
STORE OUT=model_probit;
ODS OUTPUT ParameterEstimates=ParameterEstimates COVB=covb;
RUN;
```

The parameter estimates and estimated covariance matrix are presented in Exhibit 14.11.

The LOGISTIC Procedure

Analysis of Maximum Likelihood Estimates					
Parameter	DF	Estimate	Standard Error	Wald Chi-Square	Pr > ChiSq
Intercept	1	−1.0091	0.0354	814.0574	<.0001
FICO_orig_time	1	−0.00242	0.000050	2366.9776	<.0001
LTV_time	1	0.00781	0.000158	2447.5807	<.0001
gdp_time	1	−0.0496	0.00167	883.8005	<.0001

Estimated Covariance Matrix				
Parameter	Intercept	FICO_orig_time	LTV_time	gdp_time
Intercept	0.001251	−1.58E−6	−2.08E−6	−0.00001
FICO_orig_time	−1.58E−6	2.473E−9	−443E−12	4.097E−9
LTV_time	−2.08E−6	−443E−12	2.492E−8	9.593E−8
gdp_time	−0.00001	4.097E−9	9.593E−8	2.789E−6

Exhibit 14.11 Probit Model

Note that the parameter estimates are different from those of the probit model in the previous section, as this model does not include the unemployment rate.

Basic Stress Testing of Parameter Uncertainty

We may be interested in computing the probabilities of default under consideration of the upper percentile (e.g., the 99th percentile) for all parameters. To do this, we proceed as follows:

In a first step, we compute the stressed PDs by computing the stressed parameters. We take the upper or lower percentile for the parameter distribution that produces the highest default probability in a stress test. For covariates that are positive throughout (e.g., FICO_orig_time and LTV_time), we take the upper percentile, and for covariates that are negative and positive (GDP_time), we take the lower percentile. For example, the parameters for both the FICO score and GDP growth are negative and the stressed PD will be higher if the stressed parameter for FICO score is higher (as FICO is always positive) and the stressed parameter for GDP growth is lower (as GDP growth is generally positive in economic upturns and negative during economic downturns).

```
DATA ParameterEstimates(KEEP=variable estimate estimate_stress);
SET ParameterEstimates;
estimate_stress=estimate+StdErr*PROBIT(0.99);
IF variable= 'gdp_time' THEN estimate_stress=estimate-StdErr*PROBIT(0.99);
RUN;
```

In a second step, we transpose the parameter estimates:

```
PROC TRANSPOSE DATA=ParameterEstimates OUT=ParameterEstimates2(DROP=_NAME_)
SUFFIX=_base;
VAR estimate;
ID variable;
RUN;
```

```
PROC TRANSPOSE DATA=ParameterEstimates OUT=ParameterEstimates3(DROP=_NAME_)
SUFFIX=_stress;
VAR estimate_stress;
ID variable;
RUN;
```

In a third step, we merge the resulting data set with the covariate data set for the time period 60. The match merge is by joint variable "one," which is one for all observations. We do this as we require the base and stressed parameter estimates for all covariate observations to compute the base and stressed default probabilities:

```
DATA ParameterEstimates2;
set ParameterEstimates2;
one=1;
RUN:

DATA ParameterEstimates3;
set ParameterEstimates3;
one=1;
RUN:

DATA mortgage;
SET data.mortgage;
WHERE time=60;
one=1;
KEEP FICO_orig_time LTV_time one gdp_time;
run;

DATA mortgage_parameters;
MERGE mortgage ParameterEstimates2 ParameterEstimates3;
BY one;
RUN;
```

In a fourth step, we compute the base PDs using the base parameter estimates and covariates and the stressed PDs using the stressed parameters and covariates:

```
DATA mortgage_parameters;
SET mortgage_parameters;
PD_time_base=probnorm(
intercept_base+FICO_orig_time_base*FICO_orig_time+LTV_time_base*LTV_time
+GDP_time_base*GDP_time);
PD_time_stress=probnorm(
intercept_stress+FICO_orig_time_stress*FICO_orig_time+LTV_time_stress*LTV_time
+GDP_time_stress*GDP_time);
RUN;
```

The cumulative distribution functions for the base and stressed PDs are computed using the same methodology as in the previous section with the PLOT statement PLOT PD_time_base_pcs * PD_time_base PD_time_stress_pcs * PD_time_stress in

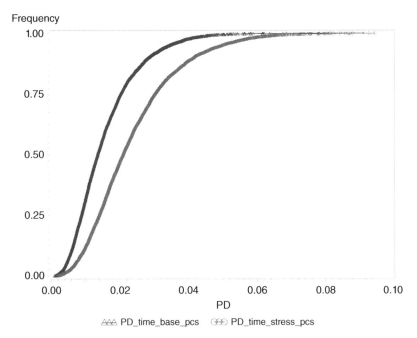

Frequency

△△△ PD_time_base_pcs   ⊕⊕⊕ PD_time_stress_pcs

Exhibit 14.12 Cumulative Distribution Function for Baseline and Stressed PDs under Consideration of Model Risk (Basic Stress Test)

PROC GPLOT. The resulting figure (Exhibit 14.12) shows that the stressed default probability is greater than the base default probability.

Multivariate Stress Testing of Parameter Uncertainty

In the basic stress test of the previous section, we assigned an error likelihood of 1 percent to all stressed parameters. In other words, we assume that every stressed parameter estimate is set to the 99th percentile. As we have multiple covariates and parameters, a more sophisticated stress test would be to construct joint, simultaneous (e.g., Bonferroni) confidence intervals instead of separate intervals for each parameter.

In order to compute this stressed PD, we need to consider the covariance matrix and apply Monte Carlo simulation analysis, which can be implemented in PROC IML. We have shown earlier examples in the context of the simulation of portfolio loss distributions in our default correlations and credit portfolio risk chapter.

In terms of data preprocessing, we continue with the data set from the basic stress test of model risk, which already contains the base PD and stressed PD from the basic parameter stress test. Care must be taken to ensure that the variables are in the order of the covariates specified in PROC LOGISTIC as we will import the parameter estimates, estimated covariance matrix, and covariates into PROC IML, which numbers but does not name columns and rows. In other words, the first (second, and so on) row in the parameter estimates and covariance data must match the first (second, and so on) column in the covariate data set.

```
DATA mortgage_parameters;
RETAIN FICO_orig_time LTV_time GDP_time;
SET mortgage_parameters;
RUN;
```

We now import the three SAS data sets ParameterEstimates and covb as well as the data set from the previous section mortgage_parameters that includes base and stressed PDs (basic stress test) into PROC IML. We add comments in the code as indicated by /*[...]*/. We then run 1,000 simulations with 1,000 stressed parameter values and compute a PD for every borrower and iteration.

```
PROC IML;

/*import data*/
USE ParameterEstimates;
READ ALL VAR _ALL_ INTO ParameterEstimates;

USE covb;
READ ALL VAR _ALL_ INTO cov;

USE mortgage_parameters;
READ ALL VAR _ALL_ INTO mortgage_parameters;

/*limit data sets*/
mean=ParameterEstimates[,1];
mortgage_parameters=mortgage_parameters[,1:2];

/*start simulation - multiple iterations*/
DO k=1 TO 1000;

/*draw random correlated normals*/
param_sim= RANDNORMAL(1, mean, cov);

/*compute stress PD*/
linear_predictor=param_sim[,1]+param_sim[,2]*mortgage_parameters[,1]
+param_sim[,3]*mortgage_parameters[,2];
PD_time_stress=PROBNORM(linear_predictor);

print PD_time_stress;
```

```
/*collect all PD vectors*/
IF k=1 THEN DO;
PD_time_stress2=PD_time_stress;
END;
IF k>1 THEN DO;
PD_time_stress2=PD_time_stress2||PD_time_stress;
END;

END;

/*export to Base SAS*/
CREATE PD_time_stress2 FROM PD_time_stress2;
APPEND FROM PD_time_stress2;
QUIT;
```

The result is a data set that has 1,000 columns (for every iteration one column) and I_{60} rows with I_{60} being the number of borrowers at time period 60 (here: 8,004). We can then compute the 99th percentile for every borrower by using PROC TRANSPOSE and PROC MEANS:

```
PROC TRANSPOSE DATA=PD_time_stress2 OUT=PD_time_stress3;
RUN;

PROC MEANS DATA=PD_time_stress3;
OUTPUT OUT=PD_time_stress4 P99(COL1-COL8004)=COL1-COL8004;
RUN;
```

We then transpose the resulting data set with the stressed PDs and append it to the data set mortgage_parameters:

```
PROC TRANSPOSE DATA=PD_time_stress4 OUT=PD_time_stress5;
RUN;

data PD_time_stress5;
SET PD_time_stress5;
IF _NAME_='_TYPE_' or _NAME_='_FREQ_' THEN DELETE;
RENAME COL1=PD_time_stress2;
RUN;

DATA mortgage_parameters2;
SET mortgage_parameters;
SET PD_time_stress5;
RUN;
```

We can now again plot the base PD, stressed PD (basic stress test), and stressed PD (multivariate stress test) using PROC GPLOT with PLOT statement:

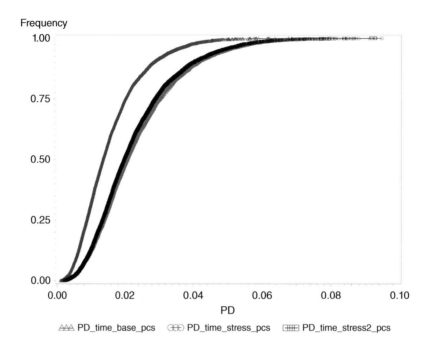

Exhibit 14.13 Cumulative Distribution Function for Baseline and Stressed PDs under Consideration of Model Risk (Basic Stress Test and Multivariate Stress Test)

PLOT PD_time_base_pcs * PD_time_base PD_time_stress_pcs * PD_time_stress
PD_time_stress2_pcs * PD_time_stress2. (See Exhibit 14.13.)

```
proc sort data=mortgage_parameters2;
  by PD_time_stress2;
run;

data mortgage_parameters2;
set mortgage_parameters2 nobs=totalobs;
PD_time_stress2_pcs = _n_ / totalobs;
run;

ODS GRAPHICS ON;
AXIS1 ORDER=(0 to 0.1 BY 0.02) LABEL=('PD');
AXIS2 ORDER=(0 to 1 BY 0.25) LABEL=('Frequency');
SYMBOL1 interpol=SPLINE WIDTH=2 VALUE=TRIANGLE C=BLUE;
SYMBOL2 interpol=SPLINE WIDTH=2 VALUE=CIRCLE C=RED;
SYMBOL3 INTERPOL=SPLINE WIDTH=2 VALUE=SQUARE C=BLACK;
LEGEND1 LABEL=NONE SHAPE=SYMBOL(4,2) POSITION=(BOTTOM OUTSIDE);
PROC GPLOT DATA=mortgage_parameters2;
```

```
PLOT PD_time_base_pcs*PD_time_base PD_time_stress_pcs*PD_time_stress
PD_time_stress2_pcs*PD_time_stress2 /
OVERLAY LEGEND=legend1 HAXIS=axis1 VAXIS=axis2;
RUN;
ODS GRAPHICS OFF;
```

The multivariate stress test is less pronounced than the basic stress test, as the 99th percentile of the simulated default probabilities is only slightly higher than the base default probabilities.

As an extension, correlations between the risk model (via extended PD, LGD, and EAD models, which include random effects) and model risk may be included by applying the same methodology.

PRACTICE QUESTIONS

1. Explain the Berkowitz critique and show how stress testing and bank capital are related.

2. Estimate a logit model for PDs based on the FICO score and LTV ratio at origination. Stress the resulting PDs using the Basel worst-case default rate. Categorize the LTV ratio at origination and compute the maximum average current LTV per time for every bucket: Use this value to compute a second stressed PD. Compare and interpret the two stress definitions. Use data set mortgage.

3. Estimate a cloglog model for PDs based on the FICO score and LTV ratio at origination. Compute the expected PD, worst-case default rate, and stressed PD. Compute the loan loss provisions, regulatory capital, and minimum capital buffer assuming an EAD of $1 million and an LGD of 20 percent. Assume that Basel and stressed EAD/LGD are equal to the expected EAD/LGD. Use data set mortgage.

4. Estimate the expected and stressed LGD based on the LTV ratio using the OCC and a historical approach. Use data set lgd.

5. Estimate a stressed PD based on parameter uncertainty for a probit model based on the FICO score and LTV ratio at origination. Apply a one-sided error likelihood of 5 percent to all parameters. Use data set mortgage.

6. Parameter uncertainty is one source of model risk. Can you think of other sources of model risk?

REFERENCES

Basel Committee on Banking Supervision. 2006. "International Convergence of Capital Measurement and Capital Standards: A Revised Framework, Comprehensive Version."

Berkowitz, J. 2000. "A Coherent Framework for Stress-Testing." *Journal of Risk* 2: 1–11.

Department of the Treasury, Federal Reserve System, and Federal Deposit Insurance Corporation. 2006. "Basel 2 Capital Accord—Notice of Proposed Rulemaking."

Federal Reserve System. 2015. "Dodd-Frank: A Stress Test 2015: Supervisory Stress Test Methodology and Results." Board of Governors of the Federal Reserve System, Washington, DC (March).

Lee, Y., D. Rösch, and H. Scheule. 2016. "Accuracy of Mortgage Portfolio Risk Forecasts during Financial Crises." *European Journal of Operational Research* 249 (2): 440–456.

Rösch, D., and H. Scheule. 2007. "A Consistent Framework for Stressing Credit Risk Parameters." *Journal of Risk Model Validation* 1 (1): 55–76.

Rösch, D., and H. Scheule. 2008. *Integrating Stress-Testing Frameworks*. London: Risk Books.

Rösch, D., and H. Scheule. 2010. "Downturn Credit Portfolio Risk, Regulatory Capital and Prudential Incentives." *International Review of Finance* 10 (2): 185–207.

Rösch, D., and H. Scheule. 2012a. "Capital Incentives and Adequacy for Securitizations." *Journal of Banking & Finance* 36 (3): 733–748.

Rösch, D., and H. Scheule. 2012b. "Forecasting Probabilities of Default and Loss Rates Given Default in the Presence of Selection." *Journal of the Operational Research Society* 65 (3): 393–407.

Tarashev, N., and H. Zhu. 2008. "Specification and Calibration Errors in Measures of Portfolio Credit Risk: The Case of the ASRF Model." *International Journal of Central Banking*, 129–173.

CHAPTER 15

Concluding Remarks

OTHER CREDIT RISK EXPOSURES

In this book, we have focused on credit risk exposures for loans and loan portfolios. Other sources of credit risk exist, and, as mentioned in the introductory chapter, they include fixed income securities (e.g., bank, corporate, and sovereign bonds), securitization investments, contingent credit exposures (loan commitments and guarantees), credit derivatives, and over-the-counter (OTC) derivatives.

Securitization credit risk models often build on credit portfolio loss distributions where simulated credit portfolio losses are tranched. The risk profile of the credit portfolio is driven by all credit risk parameters: probabilities of default (PDs), exposures at default (EADs), losses given default (LGDs), and asset correlations. The risk of a tranche is determined by the rules that specify the allocation of free cash flows from the underlying collateral portfolio to the tranche investors. Important elements are the credit enhancement (attachment level, subordination) and thickness of a tranche. Banks often sell these tranches to nonbank investors but may retain the equity tranche (i.e., the most subordinate tranche) and invest in more senior tranches for liquidity reasons (i.e., to maintain the liquidity coverage ratio and the net stable funding ratio above 100 percent). Example contributions in the literature that focus on the risk measurement of securitizations include Das and Stein (2011) and Rösch and Scheule (2016a).

The Basel Committee on Banking Supervision computes the capital for retained and invested tranches by offering a Ratings Based Approach (RBA) (i.e., a lookup table that allocates risk weights to the ratings provided by credit rating agencies) and a Supervisory Formula Approach (SFA). The Supervisory Formula Approach is the equivalent of the Internal Ratings Based approach for loans and includes the required capital for the underlying credit portfolio, as well as the credit enhancement and thickness of a tranche as additional risk characteristics. For details, we refer to Rösch and Scheule (2012) for the SFA, and Lützenkirchen, Rösch, and Scheule (2013) for the RBA.

Generally speaking, credit guarantees and loan commitments are comparable to standard loans and loan portfolios from a modeling perspective. The challenge for loan commitments lies mainly on the determination of drawdown rates of credit lines, and these details were discussed in our EAD chapter (Chapter 11).

Credit derivatives expose financial institutions to the credit risk of large financial institutions and other corporates. Credit derivative instruments include credit default swaps (CDSs), CDS portfolios, and CDS portfolios tranches. For example, common CDS portfolios are the CDX.NA.IG, which includes 125 North American corporate CDSs, and the iTraxx Europe index, which includes 125 European corporate CDSs. Different maturities are available and generally lie between 3 and 10 years. Tranche prices are quoted for some credit portfolio indexes: for example, 0–3, 3–7, 7–15, 15–100 (all in percentage of the underlying CDS portfolio) for CDX.NA.IG and 0–3, 3–6, 6–9, 9–12, 12–22, 22–100 (all in percentage of the underlying CDS portfolio) for the iTraxx Europe index. The risk is generally modeled by explaining the market prices for these instruments. For details, we refer to Löhr et al. (2013) and Jobst et al. (2015). The credit risk of CDS derivatives is modeled by trading book value at risk (VaR) models, which are based on a 99 percent confidence level and a time reference period of 10 days.

The credit risk in relation to OTC derivatives is computed like standard credit facilities with the distinction that the exposure is the sum of the current exposure (the amount by which a derivative is in-the-money; i.e., an actual credit exposure exists) and the potential future exposure that results from the application of credit conversion factors (see the EAD chapter for more details).

LIMITATIONS OF CREDIT RISK ANALYTICS

Consistency

The product-modularized risk architecture in banking and banking supervision led to credit risk analytics that match this modularity, which is one of the many reasons for model inconsistencies within a bank and across banks. The European Banking Authority (2015) has surveyed 43 banks in 14 countries and found that risk weights and hence risk models differ across financial institutions. The sources of risk weight variations have been identified as follows:

a) definition of default;
b) application of regulatory floors (e.g., minimum 10% LGD floor for exposures secured by real estates);
c) mapping into regulatory portfolio categories (SMEs, Corporate versus Retail, Retail secured by real estate versus Housing loans);
d) differences in reporting and LGD calibration for exposures only partially secured;
e) heterogeneity in the margin of conservatism, data sources, length of the time series and approaches used for the calibration of PD models;

f) different practices in the frequency and triggers for the re-development and re-estimation of internal models;
g) use of global IRBA models for exposures located in different countries; LGD estimation (defaulted and non-defaulted);
h) different practices in the estimation of the LGD parameter on defaulted and non-defaulted assets (inclusion of incomplete workout positions, level of discount rates and legal and administrative costs, internal hair-cuts estimates, repossession likelihood and use/definition of cure rates);
i) banks try to capture downturn conditions in the LGD computation using broadly similar approaches but with different final outcomes;
j) a wide range of practices followed by banks in the treatment of defaulted assets (varying interpretation and use of different approaches for the computation of the best estimate LGD and RWA on defaulted assets) and in the calculations of the IRB shortfall.

Parallel to this, the Institute of International Finance (2015) and the Basel Committee on Banking Supervision (2013) have conducted similar studies and find considerable variation in risk weights. A big industry effort in the upcoming years is needed to standardize credit risk and other risk models.

Another related issue is the link between the risk parameters (PD, LGD, EAD, and asset correlations), which are often modeled independently. Dependence is sometimes considered by means of conditioning on economic downturns (as in the case of worst-case default rates, downturn LGD, and downturn EAD), or by modeling correlated default events by asset correlations and other dependence parameters. However, many economic dependencies remain unconsidered in contemporary risk models. This is an area where integration models are important. One interesting approach for integration models is offered by random effect modeling. For example, it has been observed that the PD and LGD parameters are positively correlated. One way to account for this correlation may be to include random effects in both measurement equations and estimate the empirical correlations between these processes after controlling for covariates (see Rösch and Scheule 2005). Similar integration models may be provided for other dependencies.

Accuracy

Complementary Models

In various applications we have found that in empirical credit risk analytics strategic concepts matter more than the actual implementation framework. For example, logit and probit models forecast very similar default probabilities. Likewise, life cycle time variation can be addressed by continuous time models or by strategic use of time stamps as covariates in discrete time models. Hence, the consideration of risk drivers such as origination, macroeconomic, and maturity profiles in the models is important. Very often, it is better to have a simple model that is robust and easily understood by the managers than a complex model that is not.

Statistical versus Economic Significance

Generally speaking, economic intuition is essential, in particular in situations where the dependent variables are constrained. Every statistical analysis should be accompanied by an economic impact analysis in which realistic variations in the covariates are compared with the model-implied variation of the dependent variables. For example, unobserved variations can be modeled by fixed and random effects that are clustered with reference to the borrower, collateral, lender, time, or other risk characteristics.

Model Comparison

It is a big challenge to compare credit (portfolio) risk measures for different portfolios over time. Most validation measures are subject to the risk characteristics of the time-varying underlying portfolio. Hence, the comparison of validation outcomes is very difficult, and financial institutions should not target minimum values for measures, as this may incentivize overfitting when these targets are not met. Good validation practice generally requires a balanced mix of a number of alternative measures, including out-of-sample and out-of-time validation techniques as well as qualitative robustness checks.

Model Risk

Various model validation measures suggest that parameter estimates and risk measures are subject to uncertainty. Following up on economic significance, credit risk analytics is still at an early stage when it comes to the understanding of the economics of the actual data-generating processes. The global financial crisis (GFC) has revealed that a large number of drivers have not been included in risk modeling in the past. Examples are credit product features, borrower behavior, collateral value changes, lending standards, and rating agency incentives. Model risk is typically multidimensional, and the confidence levels need to be tracked across the multiple dimensions; clustering should also be considered. It is often practical to address model risk using Monte Carlo simulations, as we have shown in our stress testing chapter.

Interaction with the Economy

Credit risk is cyclical and comoves with the macroeconomy. It is important to understand the degree of macroeconomic information that is included in models. Statistical models may underestimate the degree of macroeconomic variation, as many frailty/random effect studies show that unexplained systematic variation remains when controlling for idiosyncratic and systematic information. Risk measures based on market prices (e.g., share prices or CDS spreads) sometimes overestimate the systematic variation, as financial markets underprice risk in economic upturns and overprice risk in economic downturns; compare Borio and Drehmann (2009) and Cerruti et al. (2012) for critiques on market-based measures for financial system stability. As a result, correlations may be inaccurate, and consequently the tails of credit portfolio loss distributions and hence derived price and capital measures may be misestimated.

GUIDING PRINCIPLES FOR BUILDING GOOD CREDIT RISK MODELS

In order to build good credit risk models, special care should be taken in the data preprocessing, model estimation, model implementation, and model interpretation. The following list defines some guiding principles for building good risk models:

- Analyze the representation of historical data. Are past economic downturns representative for future economic states in terms of likelihood and magnitude?

- Check whether the data, model, and risk measures meet reasonable robustness checks, including prior expectations of the credit analyst and other stakeholders.

- Verify whether market-based risk measures and risk factors are subject to constraints and assumptions. Is there evidence for systematic underpricing or overpricing?

- Consider multiperiod outcomes in the risk models where appropriate. Many important risk aspects have multiperiod features. Examples are life cycle changes, loan amortization, rating migration, and the multiperiod funding constraints of borrowers and lenders during economic downturns (see Rösch and Scheule 2016b).

- Analyze the effect of the time value of money (interest rates and inflation rates) on the risk measures.

- Develop a proper understanding of financial instruments and financial innovations. Latest examples may include covered bonds, contingent convertible bonds, consumer credit lines, and reverse mortgages.

- Be aware that unexpected losses generally matter more for banks than do expected losses. Banks face regulatory constraints when the capital buffer (i.e., capital in excess of regulatory capital) is exhausted.

- Limit the maximum EAD through limit systems and exposure sharing.

- Understand that diversification is a very powerful risk mitigation instrument. Bank portfolios are often concentrated in terms of geography and asset classes by the operating business model. Risk diversification strategies are available, and some include securitization and derivatives.

- Analyze how credit risk interacts with other risk categories. One important example is liquidity risk. Liquidity risk is of equal importance for lenders and borrowers/counterparties. Lenders have to cover liquidity risk under Basel III (i.e., have to meet liquidity ratios). However, liquidity risk is often only partially included in risk models. Current models often focus on net asset value and income of borrowers but exclude liquidity constraints such as income shocks, repayment step-ups, margin calls, or product maturity.

■ Develop a deep understanding of the financial contract, the borrower behavior, and the interactions with the economy.

■ Be aware that the data-generating process remains to a large extent unknown. Hence, our current understanding of the realization of losses may change in the future. A periodic update of risk models is important.

REFERENCES

Basel Committee on Banking Supervision. 2013. "Regulatory Consistency Assessment Programme (RCAP)—Analysis of Risk-Weighted Assets for Credit Risk in the Banking Book." Basel Committee on Banking Supervision, July.

Borio, C., and M. Drehmann. 2009. "Towards an Operational Framework for Financial Stability: 'Fuzzy' Measurement and Its Consequences." BIS Working Paper 284.

Cerutti, E., S. Claessens, and P. McGuire. 2012. "Systemic Risks in Global Banking: What Can Available Data Tell Us and What More Data Are Needed?" BIS Working Paper.

Das, A., and R. M. Stein. 2011. "Differences in Tranching Methods: Some Results and Implications." In *Credit Securitizations and Derivatives: Challenges for the Global Markets,* 171–185.

European Banking Authority. 2015. "Discussion Paper—Future of the IRB Approach."

Institute of International Finance. 2015. IIF RWA Task Force Response letter to the EBA Discussion Paper "The Future of the IRB Approach."

Jobst, R., D. Rösch, H. Scheule, and M. Schmelzle. 2015. "A Simple Econometric Approach for Modelling Stress Event Intensities." *Journal of Futures Markets* 35 (4): 300–320.

Löhr, S., O. Mursajew, D. Rösch, and H. Scheule. 2013. "Dynamic Implied Correlation Modelling and Forecasting in Structured Finance." *Journal of Futures Markets* 33 (11): 994–1023.

Lützenkirchen, K., D. Rösch, and H. Scheule. 2013. "Ratings Based Capital Adequacy for Securitizations." *Journal of Banking & Finance* 37 (12): 5236–5247.

Rösch, D., and H. Scheule. 2005. "A Multi-Factor Approach for Systematic Default and Recovery Risk." *Journal of Fixed Income* 15 (2): 63–75.

Rösch, D., and H. Scheule. 2012. "Capital Incentives and Adequacy for Securitizations." *Journal of Banking & Finance* 36 (3): 733–748.

Rösch, D., and H. Scheule. 2016a. "Systematic Credit Risk and Pricing for Fixed Income Instruments." *Journal of Fixed Income,* 26 (1): 42–60.

Rösch, D., and H. Scheule. 2016b. "The Role of Loan Portfolio Losses and Bank Capital for Asian Financial System Resilience." *Pacific-Basin Finance Journal* (January).

Index

Page references followed by *e* indicate an illustrated figure.

Printed and bound by CPI Group (UK) Ltd, Croydon, CR0 4YY

24/04/2025

14661307-0001